Face,
Harmony,
and Social Structure

An Analysis of Organizational Behavior across Cultures

P. Christopher Earley

New York   Oxford
Oxford University Press
1997

Oxford University Press

Oxford   New York
Athens   Auckland   Bangkok   Bogota   Bombay   Buenos Aires
Calcutta   Cape Town   Dar es Salaam   Delhi   Florence   Hong Kong
Istanbul   Karachi   Kuala Lumpur   Madras   Madrid   Melbourne
Mexico City   Nairobi   Paris   Singapore   Taipei   Tokyo   Toronto   Warsaw

and associated companies in
Berlin   Ibadan

Published by Oxford University Press, Inc.
198 Madison Avenue, New York, New York 10016

Oxford is a registered trademark of Oxford University Press

Library of Congress Cataloging-in-Publication Data
Earley, P. Christopher.
Face, harmony, and social structure : an analysis of organizational behavior
across cultures / P. Christopher Earley.
    p.   cm.
Includes bibliographical references (p.   ) and index.
ISBN 0-19-511007-2
1. Organizational behavior—Cross-cultural studies.   2. Self-
perception—Cross-cultural studies.   I. Title.
HD58.7.E27   1997
302.3'5—dc21   97-6541

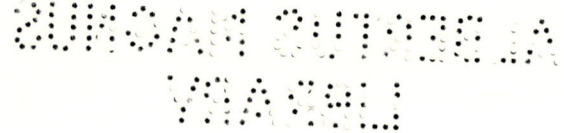

9 8 7 6 5 4 3 2 1

Printed in the United States of America
on acid-free paper

Face,
Harmony,
and Social Structure

To Elaine and "the guys,"
       who are firm believers in a life of continuous improvement,
and to my parents,
       who have stayed with me regardless of who I am not

Preface

As people interact with one another throughout their lives, a common thread is witnessed regardless of their culture, social context, organizational setting, participants involved, et cetera. This thread, face, reflects the struggle that people engage in for the purpose of self-definition and understanding. That is, a universal search for answering that age-old question of purpose and existence continues to haunt people's paths in life. At least one component, a central and critical one, of this endless search is a positioning of self relative to others in a social setting.

Face is at the heart of social behavior, and it provides a consistent linking mechanism to understand organizational behavior across cultures. In this book, I present a new conceptualization of face based on the existing literature pioneered by David Yau-Fai Ho, Hsien C. Hu, Erving Goffman, and Stella Ting-Toomey, among others. The approach I take diverges from the existing thinking on this construct in a number of ways that I describe in this book. For instance, I do not view face purely as a social construction or an exclusive product of social discourse. In placing a heavy emphasis on face as a purely social phenomenon, other researchers have confused the type of face with its source. In a critical way, face is an extension of self in a real or imagined social context.

The impetus for my approach to face and self is based on a number of influences. First, in my earlier work with Miriam Erez, we sought to define fundamental motives of the self that guide people's actions. In some regards, our model placed a great deal of emphasis on the self to the general neglect of the self-in-context. That is to say, people were examined as self-guided entities stripped of the general social setting in which they functioned. This is an exaggeration inasmuch as we attempted to link the self-concept (based on three base motives) to societal context defined by two primary cultural dimensions: power distance and individualism-collectivism.

Our purpose, however, was without question to examine cross-cultural, organizational behavior from an individual's personal viewpoint. To this end, we provided a starting point for the work contained within this volume. My purpose in this book has been to examine cross-cultural, organizational behavior in situ based on group, organizational, institutional, and societal contexts as well as self-perspectives. In my work with Erez, we provided a midrange model of behavior that might be used to guide very specific empirical research on the topic. In the present book, I am diverging from this approach in several ways. First, the model described in this book is a cross-level model along the lines described by people such as Robert J. House, Denise M. Rousseau, and Henry Tosi. Their approach and thinking were influential in shaping my desire to capture a cross-range phenomenon. Second, I attempt to provide a single, coherent force—face—as an engine driving the entire system. Of course, the downside to this approach is the inevitable oversimplification of the various forces operating in this system. However, my belief continues to be that only through such simplifications can conceptual work be linked to empirical observation, be it to support or to refute. Third, behavior is motivated socially in most instances (particularly behavior in an organizational setting), and this suggests the appropriateness of using a concept such as face as an engine for a general model.

I have chosen this path because much of the existing literature in the organizations area has failed to integrate the "micro" and the "macro" with cultural context. For example, much of the literature that addresses macro-oriented topics has been limited to comparative organization structure, political climates, et cetera. From a micro-oriented perspective, the literature abounds with a classification style of management practices across societies (applying typologies of values such as Geert Hofstede's work in formulating post hoc explanations of comparative differences in management practice effectiveness). There are, of course, some important exceptions to these limitations, such as some of the recent work by S. Ghoshal and C. Bartlett in describing behavior implications of strategic choices, Mark Peterson and Peter Smith's work on leadership across cultures, Christopher Brewster's comparative analysis of Human Resource Management practices used throughout the globe, Jeanne M. Brett and her colleagues and students' work, and my own work with Miriam Erez.

There is an even more pressing force underlying my writing of this book. Over the last decade, I have seen many researchers (including myself) struggle to integrate cultural context with organizational behavior in a meaningful fashion. The literature is plagued by reports using cultural values and dimensions in a post hoc, quasi-explanatory fashion as a way of dealing with empirical observations of differences in managerial behavior. Even the concept of culture continues to be a source of controversy. As I describe in Chapters 2 and 8, the debate concerning the construct of "culture" rages on. My own view is aligned with researchers, including Michael Bond and Mark Siegel, who suggest that debating the construct of culture is a scholarly exercise useful only for filling journal pages. Rather than sit on the sidelines and argue for one view or another, I provide a specific framework that has the strength (weakness) of empirical refutability. Simply stated, I argue that face (its essence as well as regulation) can be used to integrate various social and organizational mechanisms in predicting people's behavior.

Researchers in organizations have largely ignored many of the lessons of the past. We seem to misunderstand one another as we continue to pursue specific interests to the detriment of others' interests. We spend endless hours of debate arguing what the concept of culture is and is not, we accuse one another of underestimating the richness and complexity of social context, and we mock attempts by some to assess and test facets of society and human action.

Perhaps the strongest lesson we have learned is that to have a full understanding and appreciation of how and why people behave, and of the impact of such behavior on organizational functioning, we must have conceptual models that attempt to integrate lessons learned from various disciplines and not just the author's particular one.

Research has provided ample evidence that various work methods are effective in various, but not all, cultures, but we only can speculate why such differentiation occurs. It has been dishonest intellectually to rely on panacea explanations such as "we are just different" or "culture is too complex to understand it" as ways of dealing with these empirical observations. My approach using face lends itself to the rigor of controlled and systematic experimentation to tie specific, psychological manifestations of culture to work and social behavior. It is my belief that such an approach will clarify the understanding of how social context shapes individuals' reactions to management practices.

Many individuals contributed to the creation of this book. This theory is the accumulation of my research and experiences that have been shaped by a number of key individuals. I have had many productive conversations, discussions, and debates concerning face with a number of important people, including Michael Bond, Miriam Erez, Elaine Mosakowski, Nigel Nicholson, Harry C. Triandis, and Richard Whitley, to name just a few individuals. Despite such strong intellectual support and guidance, I take sole responsibility for the limitations of the thinking presented in this book and errors present.

I am grateful to the University of California, Irvine, my former dean, Dennis Aigner, and my colleagues for their continued support as I worked on this book. I would like to thank several people critical to my work on the concept of face, including my Ph.D. students (present and former) Cristina Gibson, Kristi Lewis, Amy Randel, and Katherine Xin. I also would like to thank C. J. Farrar for her invaluable assistance in many aspects of the preparation of this manuscript. Furthermore, my conceptualization of face and culture was greatly enhanced by comments that I received during presentations at the Hong Kong University of Science and Technology, IESE in Barcelona, London Business School, Manchester Business School, Nanyang Technological University of Singapore, Stanford University, and Washington University. Finally, I would like to thank the Hong Kong University of Science and Technology for its support during my visit in 1995.

I would like to thank the editorial staff at Oxford as well for their patience and help in shaping my treatise. Potential shortcomings of my thoughts marred by inadequate prose have been overcome due to the persistence and patience of the editorial staff. Particular thanks go to Herb Addison, who saw the promise in the topic of face in relation to organizations.

Finally, I would like to thank my international colleagues who have stimulated my thinking about international and intercultural issues. I continue to develop because my friends and colleagues continue to challenge the limitations of my thinking and conceptual development.

London, England   P. C. E.
January 1997

Contents

Face, Harmony, and Social Structure

I

Introduction and Overview

In a recent *Larry King Live* interview on CNN (June 24, 1996), a caller asked the night's guest, Ted Koeppel, host of ABC's *Nightline* news show, what Koeppel's most emotional reaction to a story happened to be during the more than 15 years that *Nightline* had been on the air. After a few moments of reflection, Koeppel said that a simple but poignant story illustrated his emotional moment. A number of years earlier, Koeppel had interviewed an 18-year-old, Eurasian woman who had recently come to the United States from her homeland of Thailand. The young woman was the child of an American father and a Thai mother. When asked what she enjoyed most about her visit to the United States, she replied simply that she liked being able to see the "sky." Koeppel asked her what she meant by this unusual comment, perhaps thinking that the pollution in Thailand marred a view of the sky or the extreme crowding of Bangkok blurred her perspective. She told him that in the United States she could look up and see the sky, but in Thailand she had to hold her head low in shame. Her story reflects a fundamental aspect of her self-definition in the context of social observers, or what is referred to as "face." Moreover, it reflects a marked difference in her self-definition as a function of changing cultural contexts.

With the increasing rate of internationalization of business, there has been an increasing desire to understand basic human activities. This changing emphasis and development of the "global village" is at the forefront of many people's minds. It is no longer possible to discuss organizational activities and employee actions without incorporating a contextual richness to such descriptions. Not only does such contextual richness include an immediate social context, but it also must deal with the international and cultural aspects of the social world as well. More than ever, understanding of employee action requires a knowledge of how action is related to the environment in which it is embedded. It is with this general focus that I examine a number of significant issues derived from the concepts of face, harmony, and social structure.

Everyone lives in a world of social interaction and discourse from which our most fundamental self-perceptions are derived. We gain a knowledge of ourselves and those with whom we interact based on many characteristics that become salient based on our cultural framework. To an American the car that one drives has symbolic significance, whereas to an Indian schooling is an important sign of position and status. It is through various types of social interactions that all people define themselves within their social community, and this self-definition lies at the very heart of human endeavor. This is a particularly important issue as we approach our move into the global village. People struggle with a desire for self-understanding and self-awareness in the face of the variety and ambiguity we encounter in a multicultural world. It is this struggle for self-definition in one's social system that is at the center of face.

In order to emphasize the importance of face and related constructs, I will use three popular examples of face-related actions from an international context. The first of these examples involves noted entrepreneur and financier Donald Trump:

> Who has done as much as I have? No one has done more in New York than me.

> My style of dealmaking is quite simple and straightforward. I just keep pushing and pushing and pushing to get what I'm after.

> I like thinking big. If you're going to be thinking anyway, you might as well think big.

> A little more moderation would be good. Of course, my life hasn't exactly been one of moderation.
>
> —Donald Trump, *Time,* November 20, 1989, p. 79

> He has yet to commission a really serious work of architecture. If he has a style, it is flashiness. It's a malady of the age. Trump just represents it the most.
>
> —*New York Times* architecture critic Paul Goldberger

Since the 1980s, Trump has made a number of significant acquisitions, including Trump Tower, a shiny and impressive collection of condominiums on Fifth Avenue with an 80-foot waterfall splashing down the pink marble walls of the atrium that cost $200 million to build in 1982; Trump Plaza, a 37-story castle that has housed many famous celebrities; and Trump Parc, a 37-story building overlooking Central Park. Trump owns an Atlantic City version of the Taj Majal as well as Eastern Air Shuttle, which he intended to rename the Trump Shuttle. The world's most opulent private yacht, the 282-foot *Trump Princess,* contains gold-plated bathroom fixtures, a rotating sun bed, and even a waterfall.

Trump was the son of a builder from Queens, New York, and learned the real estate business, and rules of negotiation, at a very young age. Trump was very young when he was brought into the building business by his father and was an aggressive and directed child. Sometimes Trump shows a genius for combining profits with publicity and altruism. For instance, New York City authorities closed down the Wollman ice-skating rink in Central Park in 1980 for refurbishing. City authorities were unable to complete their work within the budget, at which time Trump stepped in to help with the work. He completed the project, under budget, and now operates the rink at a profit, donating the money to charity. When authorities tried to honor him by planting a delicate Japanese pine in his name, though, Trump hesitated because he thought that the tree was not befitting his stature. He preferred a grander tree such as a sequoia. Trump's biggest personal expenditures have been on extravagantly luxurious residences. The builder of Trump Tower originally kept for himself a multi-million-dollar penthouse, but after finding out that yachtsman and billionaire Khashoggi (from whom Trump purchased his yacht) was buying a bigger unit, he wanted one just as big or bigger. So he went back to Trump Tower and took an adjoining triplex and then started tearing out walls. The resulting 50-room, $10 million conglomeration takes up all of the 68th and most of the 66th and 67th floors of the tower. Interestingly, the building actually has only 58 floors, but Trump felt that number wasn't sufficiently impressive, so he skipped some floor numbers to give his tenants a psychological boost. "There has never been anything like this built in 400 years," he stated, referring to his hand-carved marble columns and the walls lined in Italian gold onyx and the ceiling moldings of 23-karat gold.

The second example is that of Shintaro Ishihara, the successful Japanese politician and writer who came to the forefront of Japanese culture in the late 1980s by advocating that the Japanese take on their most challenging initiative, that of assuming a position in the world order. Ishihara first rose to prominence in 1955, when he published a popular anti-establishment novel, *Season of the Sun*. Elected to the Japanese Diet in 1968, he has since served as transport minister and head of Japan's environmental agency. In 1989, he voiced fiercely nationalistic views in his book *The Japan That Can Say No*. The book gained considerable attention in Japan and caused much dismay and disagreement in the United States. Coauthored with Sony chairman Akio Morita, the book was targeted at Japanese readers. Ishihara's most contentious chapters argued that Japan holds the technological balance of power in the world and that Japan must use its technological leverage to assume its rightful place in the world order. No longer must Japan walk in the footsteps of superpowers such as the United States. The following excerpts from an interview conducted by *Time* magazine (November 20) in 1989 illustrate his strong presence and focus:

I was in Washington two years ago, right after the U.S. Government slapped punitive tariffs on Japanese electronics goods over the semiconductor issue. The mood was hysterical. At a party an American politician told me that because the U.S. and the Soviet Union were moving closer together, the world power balance had shifted, and Japan was no longer very important. He had the nerve to tell me that the Americans and the Russians share the same identity because they are white. Well, that's fine. But if Moscow is looking to Washington for high technology, Japan is the country that has it. The Soviet Union is free to choose between Japan and the U.S. for high technology, just as we are free to choose between the U.S. and the Soviet Union. In fact, the U.S. can't make reliable one-megabit chips. Japan is the only country that can mass-produce high-performance semiconductors. When I said this at the party, the Americans turned pale. But let me remind you that I was only responding to American threats that Soviet-American détente left no room for Japan. . . .

If Americans who hold shares in Japanese companies demand American-style management at stockholders' meetings, we must clearly say no. That's what we did recently to T. Boone Pickens, a man with a disreputable reputation. America is in decline because of American managers who only care about their short-term gains so that they can boast about them at the next shareholders' meeting. Japanese managers use shareholders' meetings to explain their long-term plans and ask shareholders to bear with limited dividends. Japan has succeeded in rebuilding its economy because it has kept its idiosyncrasies, that is to say, management philosophy, labor-management relations and company-shareholders relations based on humane feelings. We don't have to change those characteristics just to please the Americans. . . .

Now the modern age has come to a close because of nuclear power and electronics. I think Japan will be one of the major players that will build a new world history. It can't be done by Japan alone. Active interaction with other countries will enhance technological developments. In this respect the U.S. will remain Japan's most important partner. There's no doubt the U.S.'s position as a global leader will continue. But from the Japanese viewpoint, the U.S.'s desire to keep Japan or other countries in the palm of its hand is annoying. The Americans should dispassionately put the present world in historical perspective. Their failure to do so will jeopardize not only their future but also that of the rest of the world.

We should remember that racial prejudice was a factor [in dropping the atomic bomb during World War II]. Ask Asians, Hispanics, Indians or blacks living in the U.S. whether whites are racially prejudiced or not. They would just laugh at the question. They would all answer yes. Whites are understandably proud that they undeniably have built the modern era. But the problem is that this historical pride has evolved into arrogance and racial prejudice against nonwhites. Now a nonwhite race, the Japanese, is catching up with the Americans and taking over the lead in advanced technology. The fact is not easy for Americans to swallow. I understand it's humiliating. But the time has come for Americans to give up foolish pride and racial prejudice. Japan overcame its humiliation (after World War II) to become what it is today. The Americans say the Japanese have become arrogant, but in my opinion, the racially prejudiced Americans are much more arrogant. Don't misunderstand me here. I personally like the Americans. I admire American society for its dynamism. . . .

The Americans are unique, and so are the Japanese. As for the question of whether the Japanese are a superior race or not, I think only our achievements can tell. The Japanese are excellent at connecting a new idea with merchandising. We may be unique in that respect. (81)

In a final example, I draw from a recent interview with the Muslim leader, Sheikh Omar Abdel-Rahman, who has come under increasing attention recently in connection with the World Trade Center bombing incident. Although Sheikh Omar has not lived in his native land since 1990, he is still of acute interest to Egyptian authorities. As many as several hundred thousand Egyptians recognize Omar as their spiritual leader, Al Jama'a al Islamiyya. During a difficult time for Egypt in which there is high unemployment, inflation, and scant housing for the nearly 60 million Egyptians, the sheikh's vision of an Islamic future appeals to many. He argues that the regime of President Hosni Mubarak spreads vice and immorality and that Mubarak is trying to stamp out the basic virtues and values espoused by Islam. An increasing number of young people in Egypt have come to embrace the ideology represented by Omar, and authorities now worry about the proliferation of small terrorist groups. "The danger," decries one Egyptian envoy, "is that fundamentalists may attain a level of faith that invites martyrdom." In discussing his views with *Time* columnist Jill Smolowe, Sheikh Omar commented as follows:

The regime in Egypt is a dictatorship. Mubarak rules by fire and iron; he rules in a police state; he rules by the emergency constitution and by harsh laws. I challenge Mubarak to survive one hour without his laws and emergency constitution. He is abusing human rights; there are so many injustices.

You have to leave him to his own fate, which is inevitable. One day the Egyptian people will have to overthrow him. You people of Egypt, you have to overthrow this unjust and arrogant ruler. . . .

Tourism is legal in Islam. But tourism is not gambling or dancing in nightclubs or drinking liquor. Tourists have to respect our public rules, our traditions and customs. They shouldn't abuse the dignity of the people or spread AIDS and fornication. We have to protect the rules of the land. . . .

I want to see that Egypt is ruled Islamically and that Mubarak's regime is overthrown and that every tyrant in the area is overthrown. . . .

[Q. How do you support yourself?]

A. Allah is the provider. (*Time*, November 18, 1994, 82)

I have chosen these three particular examples of behavior and values because they represent three fundamentally different manifestations of face, but with a universal emphasis on the concept of face itself. The description of American Donald Trump illustrates an emphasis on power, status, prestige, and the external trappings of wealth and accumulation. The anecdote of the tree is particularly symbolic of Trump's view of himself and his place in society. In rewarding him for his entrepreneurial work on behalf of charity, the city of New York wished to plant a special Japanese tree in his name as a token of thanks. His reaction was that the tree did not accurately represent who he was because it was a modest and somewhat uncomely tree. Instead, he thought that a more befitting symbol of his stature would be the redwood or sequoia, a grand and tall tree having great presence and appearance. His desire to maintain and exceed the accumulations of others (such as outdoing his yacht salesman, Khashoggi, in his apartment) illustrates Trump's orientation of face through material objects, position, and status. It is particularly interesting to note that much of what he credits for his visibility and stature in American (global) society is his unwillingness to lose a battle and insistence on fighting tenaciously in all matters.

Ishihara represents a very different form of face in that he emphasizes a nationalism for Japan and focuses on the relative gains that the Japanese people have made in industry and technology. For Ishihara, it is critical that Japan recognize its new position in the world order and that it is time for other groups (nations) to understand that their rule is nearly over. He pointedly discusses how white Americans' unwillingness to let loose of their subjective views of superiority cannot stand in the way of the Japanese people coming to greatness. It is not the personal accomplishments of Ishihara that are critical in his analysis, despite his obvious rise to power and influence in Japan. However, it is also not simply a nationalism or pride that drives his views as well. He views the Japanese people as having a moral imperative to take their rightful place in human society and move people forward: "The Americans should dispassionately put the present world in historical perspective. Their failure to do so will jeopardize not only their future but also that of the rest of the world." It is a general claim to greatness for the Japanese people as well as a view of the global order that seems at the heart of Ishihara's arguments.

Finally, Sheikh Omar Abdel-Rahman captures yet a different aspect of face. In the context of Islam and national rule in Egypt, Sheikh Omar emphasizes that there exists a very important moral order that has been violated. He argues that the Egyptian rulers since the time of Nasser have forsaken a holy perspective on ruling the Egyptian people and that through the tenets of Islam a kind and just role will be enacted by a leader. Sheikh Omar's view of himself, and other Muslims, focuses on religious values based on Islam and his personal significance is in maintaining a righteous life according to these principles. Another important facet comes from his presentation of self and face, namely, an emphasis on determinism and theological rule. This belief that God will provide and direct is reflected not only in Sheikh Omar's answer to how he will maintain his livelihood but also in his description of Mubarak, whose fate "is inevitable. One day the Egyptian people will have to overthrow him. You people of Egypt, you have to overthrow this unjust and arrogant ruler." According to the sheikh's cultural orientation, most of what happens (perhaps all) is determined by the will of God in response to people leading a holy and righteous life according to Islam.

These three perspectives on face illustrate the complexity of this construct across societal systems and cultures. As I will discuss more fully in Chapters 2, 3, 4, and 5, face lies at the very heart of how people define themselves and determines who they are within a given social system. For Trump, this self-definition is tied to accomplishments and accumulations, for Ishihara it involves the ego as a social entity, and for Omar it is based on religious action and lifestyle. These very different views of face have important implications for how people view themselves as well as how they define and interact with others. For example, Omar's description of Mubarak reflects a belief that Mubarak is not a righteous or religious man. Based on this, he clearly lacks what Omar would consider face, honor, or some spiritual essence. Ishihara views Americans as having little face because they fail to recognize their own position relative to that of the Japanese and, more important, the rightful position of the Japanese in the world order. Finally, Trump dismissed architecture critic Paul Goldberger's criticism on the basis that Goldberger wore a "cheap suit," so "what can you expect?" It is this divergence that presents the important and interesting challenge for understanding face in a global context.

Before I provide an overview of this book and my model, it is important that the reader be aware of the general approach that I take in my research and in the present discussion. In the next section, I examine the topic of levels of analysis because the examination of face in an international and cross-cultural context inevitably crosses levels of analysis. I follow this discussion with an examination of the underlying philosophy in my approach. I address these two topics because they are an important starting point for understanding why I have taken the particular approach that I have in this book and they raise important issues that the reader may wish to address in his or her examination of international and cross-cultural issues as well.

Levels of Analysis in Understanding Face and Culture

There is a particular irony to much of the research found in the fields of cross-cultural psychology and international management, namely, that the two literatures do little to inform one another concerning research. Perhaps this is because the two groups of researchers have so little in common that each does not think that the other has anything to offer. Of course, there are exceptions to this in international and cross-cultural research such as that of Hofstede (1980, 1991) and Schwartz (1992,

1993), who have bridged this gap, but this is the exception rather than the rule. Additional efforts have been made, including articles by Bond and his colleagues (e.g., Bond & Lee, 1981; Leung & Bond, 1989) as well as a special issue of *Academy of Management Journal* (Earley & Singh, 1995) and work by House and his colleagues concerning an international assessment of charismatic leadership. However, this style of research is still the exception and not as commonplace as would be expected. (I would note that in a recent survey of published studies discussed by House, Rousseau, and Thomas [1995], approximately 33 percent of the papers focused on what House et al. define as "meso" type research. This number may seem small, but it is unclear if they included international and cross-cultural studies in this group even though they are inherently meso types of studies to be conducted. Thus this figure may be somewhat understated, which would suggest that the trend for conducting meso style work is not an insignificant one.)

There are a number of reasons that the levels of analysis (implied by the "micro" orientation of psychologists and the "macro" orientation of international management researchers) have not been spanned. First, there is great comfort in staying within one's disciplinary boundaries and not having to confront fundamental assumptions of research ideology. Second, most training that is received teaches a researcher how to conduct work at a given level but not across levels. Personally, this book constitutes my first serious attempt at spanning the levels of individual to culture without ignoring the intermediate steps in the chain (such as organization, industry, etc.). Third, researchers are creatures of enacted environments, and training in a particular domain focuses individual effort on creating problems consistent with that training. Thus the physicist sees the world through laws of strong and weak nuclear forces, the linguist through the nature of grammar, and the international management scholar through businesses operating in diverse economies throughout the globe. Fourth, there exists very little cross-level theory with which to understand phenomena and make relevant predictions concerning organizational behavior. House et al. (1995) present a "meso theory" that is really a general set of relationships rather than a formally constructed theory. It is, however, a useful beginning along these lines. Additionally, the seminal work by Katz and Kahn (1978) concerning open systems theory is another approach that is meso in its basic nature, and Tosi (1992) presents a recent discussion of a model as well.

Cultural research in an organizational context cannot remain satisfied by such artificial segmentation and disciplinarian blinders. Effective research in this arena requires that a scholar capture the various linkages from a societal to an individual level while understanding the local phenomena as well as the linkages. This is, however, a Herculean labor.

The analysis of cross-level phenomena has received increasing attention in the organizational behavior literature. Calls for cross-level research, or so-called "meso" style (House, Rousseau, & Thomas, 1995; Klein, Dansereau, & Hall, 1994; Rousseau, 1985), are no longer infrequent or subtle. According to House et al. (1995), "Meso theory and research concerns the simultaneous study of at least two levels of analysis wherein a) one or more levels concern individual or group behavioral processes or variables, b) one or more levels concern organizational processes or variables, and c) the processes by which the levels of analysis are related are articulated in the form of bridging, or linking, propositions" (2). House et al. argue that meso research is critical for the understanding of organizational phenomena because an organizational context is a unique influence that is the interactive product of person and context. Similar conceptual arguments have been forwarded by Granovetter (1985) in his classic paper concerning embeddedness, Kanter (1989) in her work on innovation in organizations, and Schneider (1987, 1990) in his work on the Selection-Attraction-Attrition paradigm in organizations, among others.

There are a number of reasons why it is important to conduct meso style research in organizational phenomena. In their review of the organizations literature, Staw and Sutton (1992:26) state: "It is important to conduct research on the effects of aggregated beliefs (and emotions and behaviors) on organizational actions rather than to just assume that such effects will occur because they have been demonstrated in individuals or groups operating outside of the organizational context." They suggest that there are a number of influences from the micro to the macro levels in an organizational context such as powerful individuals who shape strategic thinking and decision making in an organization or the collective beliefs and values of individuals that make up the "climate" or "organizational culture." Likewise, macro organizational variables influence the nature of individuals' perceptions and values within those organizations. This is at the heart of Granovetter's (1985) concept of embeddedness, namely, that the assumption of a simple, rational actor in the economic paradigm is inadequate to capture the sophistication of an individual who works within an organizational (social) context.

These concerns hold true (especially) for international and cross-cultural research in organizations as well. I will focus on one particular problem that is critical in conducting international or cross-cultural research in organizations. This problem is one of a misspecified model underlying a set of constructs. In constructing a model, a researcher assumes that he or she is putting the key variables into a framework, and other variables left out are not important to the model. If there are, however, additional, unspecified variables that are correlated with the phenomenon of interest, then a misspecification occurs (James, Mulaik, & Brett, 1982) and erroneous conclusions may be drawn. For example, early in the development of organizational citizenship behavior, or OCB, it was thought that the consistent correlation between OCB and satisfaction represented a causal linkage: satisfaction causes OCB (Organ, 1987). However, more recent research found that a third, unspecified variable was driving both OCB and satisfaction, namely, organizational justice (Farh, Podsakoff, & Organ, 1990). By failing to include an important antecedent variable, an incorrect model was developed in this early literature. This dilemma is particularly relevant and salient to the international and cross-cultural researcher. Messick (1988) argued that one of the biggest dilemmas confronting cross-cultural psychology is that the inability to rule out alternative explanations of differences obtained in cross-cultural studies precludes firm conclusions concerning the importance of culture in an analysis of psychological phenomena. In conducting comparative or cross-cultural research, can a researcher adequately rule out competing hypotheses to those involving cultural differences? For instance, I recently witnessed a talk by a job candidate and new researcher who was looking at human resource practices in a number of different countries. Based on a general reading of Hofstede's (1991) typology, the researcher constructed a number of hypotheses concerning differences that would be observed between various regions (e.g., United States–Canada versus Pacific Asian Rim). Consistent with his predictions, there were differences in these regional groupings consistent with his hypotheses. Unfortunately, his "cultural" differences among these particular regions were perfectly confounded with other factors (e.g., religious orientation) related to but not synonymous with culture. Based on his design, it was impossible for him to conclude that similarities or differences were driven by culture or some other unspecified construct.

This dilemma is an inherent problem with cross-cultural research because "culture" is typically confounded with other attributes of a society, such as its various institutions, economic system, et cetera.

The related dilemma in meso style research, which seems to inevitably be the case in all organizationally related studies involving country or culture as an explanatory variable, concerns the problems induced by crossing levels of analysis. For instance, Hofstede (1980a) provides a nice discussion (see Klein et al., 1994, for a more recent and complete discussion of the topic) of the dilemma of aggregation using national data. In his study, Hofstede collected survey information from respondents from over 40 countries throughout the world. In analyzing his data, he pointed out a difficulty using the individual as the appropriate level of analysis. His argument was that the phenomenon of interest, culture, was best dealt with at a national level, and so aggregation was the only solution. By not doing so, he argued, a researcher would commit the "ecological fallacy" created by inappropriate comparisons across levels. For instance, imagine we have a cultural value that is correlated with some individual characteristic such as need for achievement motive. Further, assume that for the three cultures examined in our study the correlation within each culture of this value and need for achievement is $+.5$, but that the scatterplots for each relationship are structured such that Culture A is horizontally displaced from Culture B by one standard deviation and Culture C is horizontally displaced from Culture B by one standard deviation. If we examined the correlation of the cultural value to need for achievement in the entire sample (hence at a "global" level), the resulting correlation is very close to 0.0 even though the relationship within each culture is quite strong. At a global level, we conclude that the value and achievement are unrelated. More recently, Schwartz (1992, 1993) has approached this problem in his international assessment of values at the individual and societal levels of analysis. His conclusions are that the two levels show different patterns of values, but that there exists a great deal of overlap between the two. Other work along these lines includes that of Earley (1994), Leung and Bond (1989), Liska (1992), and Ostroff (1993), to name a few. Thus, although it is tempting to dismiss aggregation procedures as invalid and misleading, it is possible to yield useful comparisons across these levels.

Crossing levels of analysis presents a difficult conceptual task as well as an empirical one. In a recent debate of cross-cultural psychologists on the XCUL (Cross Cultural) Network (1994), the conceptual issues underlying levels of analysis for international work were brought forth in a discussion including Boehnke, Earley, Gabrenya, Kashima, Malpass, Marsella, and Schwartz. A number of interesting points were presented by participants in this discussion. For instance, the empirical mechanics of aggregating data imply that an aggregation procedure captures the relationship of one level to another. Is the mean of a group an appropriate representation of a culture? Might other characteristics of a distribution (e.g., skewness, variance) convey important meaning concerning "culture"? One example is the difference between a tight and loose culture (see Chapter 6 for a further discussion). It is reasonable that in a tight culture, one stressing conformity and adherence to social rules, the distribution of shared meanings, culture, would show less variance than in a loose culture. In this example, the nature of the culture itself shapes the distribution of some underlying value, and hence a simple, arithmetic mean may fail to capture adequately the complexity of the society.

How then can researchers define a culture and operationalize constructs appropriately? In the XCUL discussion, a point was raised concerning the way to define the boundaries of a group in order to understand "culture." One response was that researchers should not simply identify the group using general characteristics but should examine according to a degree of identification: "Perhaps it is better to group people according to their degree of ethnocultural identification. Thus you have an aggregate, but it is operationally defined. You don't study Japanese-Americans, you study the extent to which there are clusters of Japanese-Americans who embrace and endorse patterns of behavior that are associated with a life style or world view" (Marsella, 1994:172).

There is a nontrivial debate concerning cultural groups and the concept of culture that wages in many fields, including anthropology and organizational behavior. How should the construct of culture be dealt with conceptually? A number of researchers have commented on this topic in recent years, including Brett et al. (in press), Earley and Singh (1995), Geertz (1973), Leung and Bond (1989), Lytle et al. (1995), and Martin (1992), among others. Although there are a number of points on which this discussion has focused, a major issue discussed by the various parties concerns the nature of culture as an entity. While some view culture as a complex collage that is not properly understood from an elementalist perspective (Geertz, 1973), others argue that it can be understood using fundamental dimensions (Hofstede, 1991). Likewise, there is a debate whether or not culture is a real phenomenon existing outside the minds of various observers (Rohner, 1984). I turn to a more complete discussion of culture in Chapters 2 and 8.

Although the definition of a culture, society, group, individual, et cetera, is critical in a complete analysis of behavior in organizations, it is only a starting point. Once the key issues concerning analysis and aggregation are dealt with, the fundamental question remains, namely, what are the reasons that general, cultural influences may impact individual behavior and action in an organization? In other words, the aggregation procedure does not help us better understand the conceptual framework that underlies such aggregation. Quite the contrary, our aggregation procedures must be informed by our conceptual linkages.

It is in this spirit that I develop my conceptual framework in this book. I believe that the meso form of research is not only useful in conducting cross-cultural work in organizational behavior but also essential. Further, it is only through a meso type of analysis that a researcher really can understand and come to predict the potential role of society and culture in determining an individual's activities in an organizational context. The dilemma confronting the job candidate I discussed earlier, a problem highlighted by Messick (1988) in his pessimistic discussion concerning cross-cultural psychology, occurs because the new researcher had failed to specify the linkages through which culture impacts individual behavior in an organization. By specifying these linkages, it is possible for a researcher to understand *how* culture influences action, and not just *if* it does. This is where the concept of "face" becomes so very important in my analysis. As I will discuss in Chapters 2 and 3, face is a meso construct and it enables a researcher to link general aspects of a social system, culture, and society to an individual's behavior in an organization. It provides an explanatory mechanism for understanding how the same organizational context in two different nations can lead to very different individual-level activities and why the same individual-level actions can result in very different organizational contexts. Face is a very interesting construct for an additional reason, namely, that it is both meso as well as individual at the same time. There is an aspect of face that connects individuals to one another and individuals to groups within a social system. At the same time, there is an aspect of face that connects an individual to his or her unique identity. In this sense, the complexity and subtlety of face are well suited for a cross-level undertaking.

My approach has a number of specific assumptions that are not without cost or criticism. In order to make certain that these assumptions are explicit, I will now turn to a discussion of the values, assumptions, and beliefs that I hold concerning these issues, which constitute my research "culture."

General Philosophy

Although it is quite presumptuous for me to title this section "General Philosophy," what I mean to convey is the general conceptual stance that I take as I examine the topic of face in an organizational context. As Joanne Martin (1992) points out in her book on cultures within organizations, it is important that a researcher make clear his or her view of the world so that others can properly interpret the words that follow. As such, I present a general view of my thinking concerning this topic in Figure 1-1.

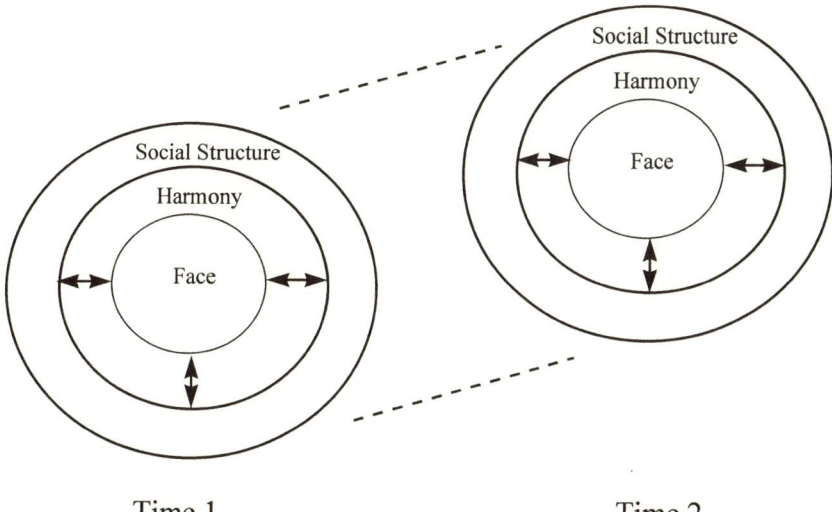

Time 1   Time 2

Figure 1-1. Embeddedness of Constructs

I have represented my general view of this approach using concentric circles that represent the various levels of analysis and contexts in which face operates. At a general level, the figure illustrates that face is a concept only properly addressed and understood within the context of a general social system in which various actors function and interact. It does not make sense to abstract face from the social milieu. Face is a concept that gains its significance only when examined from the perspective of the social system, and this is why previous empirical attempts at understanding this construct have fallen short. Three concentric circles represent social structure, harmony, and face, and these figures are repeated as a function of time sequence.

The concept of social structure is one that encompasses various aspects of a society, including culture and its related values, systems of institutions (e.g., political, economic, sociocultural), and the relationships among various actors within the system (e.g., organizations as actors within population communities, individuals as actors within particular organizations). Social structure in these terms refers to what Rohner (1984:131) calls the society, or the "largest unit of a territorially bounded, multigenerational population recruited largely through sexual reproduction, and organized around a common culture and a common social system." These last two characteristics, common culture and common social system, are particularly critical in my thinking about social structure since they capture the meanings shared within a society and its rules for conduct (culture) as well as the actual behaviors observed in that society (social system). As Rohner points out, the relationship of culture to social system can be thought of as analogous to that of language to speech. Culture allows us to understand the rules for action and activity, and a social system provides the specifics of what is actually observed or enacted. By my usage, social structure refers to the society because it encompasses both culture and social system properties. However, I am particularly interested in that aspect of society relevant to social exchange and interaction. In this sense, I view my approach as a midrange model intended to capture the various aspects of social system that are important for understanding the nature of face in organizations.

The innermost part of this figure refers to face, or the key construct in my approach to studying the cultural aspects of behavior. This concept was chosen because it is central to nearly all human activity, and it is a concept that has been mistakenly attributed to Asian cultures. Face refers to both internal and external presentations of oneself, and it is based on both morality defined in a social structure as well as a socially constructed representation by others. My basic argument is that although the way face manifests itself in various cultures may differ, everyone has a concept of face and this concept influences basic behavior and actions. It is the etic aspect of self that drives behavior along with other influences. I would not, however, argue that face is a sole determinant of peoples' actions, nor is it necessarily the most important one. However, face is an important and pervasive aspect of people's interactions.

Next, I have represented the concept of harmony as an intermediary between social structure and face with a number of two-ended arrows. Social structure and face represent content aspects of interaction, but harmony is not the same. I view harmony as the processes through which face is regulated in a given social structure. In this sense, harmony is not a "thing"; rather, it refers to a dynamic regulation of self within a given context. I would add that "harmony" is perhaps an awkward choice of terms because I do not mean to imply the common definition from a dictionary referring to harmony as an "inner peace" or "coordination with nature." By my usage, harmony refers to face regulatory processes such as Goffman's (1959) description of facework. However, I use this term rather than one such as "facework" because I do not want to limit my discussion to the dyadic exchange emphasized in Goffman's analysis. Harmony can capture face regulation within an individual's own psyche as well as with a large group of other people. It does not necessarily result in a balanced or equilibrium state, as the word might imply. In fact, it is more likely than not that harmony represents an imbalanced state for an individual because this process of regulation is both dynamic and somewhat chaotic.

The multiple sets of circles in this diagram represent another important aspect of how I approach this topic. More specifically, I concur with scholars such as Giddens (1984), who asserts that social structure is a misnomer and that we should really think of structuration rather than structure. That is to say, social structures are dynamic and evolving and understanding them from a static view means that we are not adequately understanding them. The representation that I provide depicting these concentric circles across various times is intended to emphasize that the regulation of face is temporally bound and that such a regulation will vary as a function of time. For example, at the turn of the century in the United States, a great deal of emphasis was placed on personal presentation and family origins. If your family had the right ancestry— that is, you had a true "blue" lineage—you were viewed as upper-class. Money alone was not sufficient for attaining a high status in the social world. However, as time has dragged on in the United States, this emphasis on lineage has declined a great deal, but the emphasis on monetary holdings and personal wealth has increased. Without question, Microsoft CEO Bill Gates is considered to have great status and power despite his rather modest upbringing. People do not question his prestige and status based on his ancestry. (Perhaps the exception to this transformation can be seen along the infamous Florida coast that houses such "old" families as the Kennedys.)

This diagram, then, captures my general view of the constructs in my model described in great detail in Chapter 2. I would emphasize that my approach is an eclectic one and I attempt to incorporate multiple levels of analysis in my discussions. However, it would not be academically honest if I did not, at the outset, remind the reader that I am viewing this framework from a psychological perspective, with the individual actor as the ultimate focus for understanding. My approach to this topic is somewhat similar to the style that Erez and I used in our earlier book, namely, that the individual is the starting point and ending point. Other aspects of this model are used in order to determine the best path to get from this start to the finish. However, in contrast to my earlier work, the emphasis here is on understanding individual action within a social context in which various aspects of the individual cannot be adequately understood without the context. As I will argue in Chapters 3–5, various aspects of face do not make sense if they are separated from the social circumstance in which they operate.

An additional caveat is in order at this point concerning the concept of culture, that I use. There are a variety of schools concerning the concept of culture, which can be crudely classified into the psychologist's two-by-two (Rohner, 1984), namely, behavioral versus ideational crossed with realist versus nominalist. Briefly, the behavioral versus ideational dimension posits culture as represented by behavior and material embodiments (behavioral) or by ideas, beliefs, values, preferences, and other symbols (ideational). The dimension of realist versus nominalist refers to the existential nature of culture, with the realist positing that culture exists outside of members of that culture and the nominalist arguing that culture has no form or existence separate from those who interpret and enact it. To the cultural nominalist, culture is a set of inferences made by an observer based on regularities or patterns of activity. In other words, it is a logical construct having no substance. My position and use of the term "culture" are best represented by the ideational realist, with some overlap with the nominalist position. I focus my analysis on shared meanings represented by values and beliefs of individuals, and I assert that culture has a significance quite separate from specific individuals within that culture. It is not merely a construct created through observation (epiphenomenal) or critical thought, and I agree that it is best thought of in terms of meanings and values. However, I would assert that much of what face means within a culture is based on the interactions and shared interpretations of individuals within that culture, as the nominalists assert.

I close this section by pointing out that it is not my purpose to pose a general model of society or social structure or even culture. It is my hope to provide additional understanding of how face influences various actions within an organization and how cultural and societal context shapes this process.

Organization of the Book

I organize the book into ten chapters along with a concluding section. Chapter 2 provides an overview of the specific model driving my thinking along with a brief description of the component parts. The basic model is captured by a cubic representation with the internal elements housed within a general, societal context. There are five basic elements to my model: face, harmony, social actor, organizational structure and context, and societal context. In this chapter, I discuss the overall framework along with how the various elements are interrelated.

Chapters 3–9 detail various aspects of the general model presented in Chapter 2. The progression of Chapters 3–9 takes a "micro" to "macro" perspective, beginning with an elaborate discussion of the key concept in this model: face. The concept of face is presented from a general perspective, along with a brief history of its presentation in the Eastern and Western literatures. Face consists of two primary forms, somewhat overlapping but distinct, which I will refer to using the pinyin translation of the Chinese terms posed by Hu (1944). These two types of face are lian and mianzi. Briefly, lian captures the moral character and morality of action whereas mianzi captures the interpersonal relation and personal prestige aspects of individuals. Chapter 6 presents a broader overview of a social actor as I use it in my model. Although I clearly believe face to be an important and universal construct, it is by no means the only force that directs an individual's behavior. In Chapter 6, I present a number of intrapersonal and interpersonal dynamics relevant to a social actor, such as role expectations (Katz & Kahn, 1978), personal values (Rokeach, 1973), self-concept (Markus & Kitayama, 1991), social identity (Tajfel & Turner, 1986), and normative constraints (Weber, 1947). These various influences on a social actor's behavior are integrated as well.

Chapter 7 captures a movement up in level of analysis from the individual to interindividual by focusing on social exchange notions that underlie harmony. In my usage, harmony refers to the rules and practices of social exchange derived from a particular societal and cultural context. In order to understand social exchange, I draw on work by Fiske (1991), who distinguishes among four types of social exchange relationships: market exchange, authority ranking, communal sharing, and equality matching. Market exchange is characterized by an emphasis on short-term and personal interests in which market rules for interaction dominate. Authority ranking reflects a hierarchical structure within an existing in-group. Communal sharing is a form of exchange attributed to egalitarian collectives such as Israeli kibbutzim, and equality matching is a specialized form of exchange in which resources of a like form and quantity are exchanged in a balanced fashion.

Chapters 8 and 9 capture a "macro" level of analysis by focusing on the organization's characteristics as well as the general features of the environment in which the organization functions, or the "organizational field." In Chapter 8, a discussion of six general cultural dimensions is presented. The cultural dimensions used in my model are: individualism-collectivism (Triandis, 1989b), tightness versus looseness (Witkin & Berry, 1975), relationship to nature (Kluckhohn & Strodtbeck, 1961), power differentials and masculinity/femininity (Hofstede, 1980a, 1991), and shame versus guilt (Mead, 1928). These specific cultural values are especially relevant to issues of face and social interaction. In addition, the nature of cultures in the context of my approach is discussed.

In Chapter 9, I present a number of key organizational features that are particularly relevant to the functioning of individuals within an organization. Much of this presentation is conceptually driven by institutional theory of organizations (Scott, 1994). Specific features of an organization that are discussed include technology, institutional roles, interorganizational dependencies, and communication. Needless to say, these features do not capture all aspects of organizations, but they are particularly useful for understanding face in an organizational context.

Chapter 10 provides a general integration of the model and an application of this framework for understanding face and behavior in four diverse cultural contexts: the Czech Republic, India, Sweden, and the United States. I apply the framework and discuss briefly the implications of face for management given the organizational and cultural contexts of these countries.

Finally, in Chapter 11 I present a brief overview of a research agenda for this work and the topic of face in organizations. I focus this discussion on a number of organizational examples, including reward allocation, negotiation, and feedback at the individual level and structure, governance, and interunit communication at the organizational level.

It is the purpose of this book to introduce the reader to these key concepts and to reinvigorate the research streams concerning face that were presented by such scholars as Goffman (1959), Hu (1944), and, more recently, Bond and Lee (1981), Deutsch (1973), Hwang (1987), Redding and Ng (1982), and Ting-Toomey (1994). I have received two rather interesting reactions to this proposed work in seminars and talks that I have presented. In the first instance, people who were somewhat unfamiliar with the concepts of face and harmony reacted by saying that it appears to be an important and interesting avenue for research. In the second instance, people who were familiar with these concepts, some of whom had conducted this type of research, reacted by saying that it appears to be an important and interesting topic that is virtually impossible to research. Specific comments ranged from "It is an Asian concept that we'll never understand in the West," to "It's interesting but too broad and encompassing to be captured in empirical work." Judging from people's reactions to the core concept of face, it seems that this universal construct is important but very elusive. It is the focus of this book to provide a framework for understanding and pursuing this elusive construct. After all, any construct that evokes as many visceral reactions from people across the globe as face does must be worthy of our study and critical thought.

2

General Framework and Model

Researchers have a great misunderstanding concerning the importance and relevance of culture in the study of organizational behavior. These debates include issues such as levels of analysis (e.g., Leung & Bond, 1989; Earley & Mosakowski, 1995; Hofstede, 1980a, b), conceptual scope of the culture construct (e.g., Earley & Singh, 1995; Hofstede, 1980a; Triandis, 1994), convergence versus divergence (e.g., Boyacigiller & Adler, 1991), culture divisibility or segmentation (e.g., Geertz, 1973; Martin, 1992), methodology (e.g., Lytle et al., 1995), and basic definitions (e.g., Jahoda, 1980; Rohner, 1984; Segall, 1986), among others. Add to these dilemmas the ongoing debate concerning the relationships of constructs across various levels of analysis in organizations (House & Rousseau, 1990; Rousseau, 1985), and it is clear that intercultural research in organizations faces a potential morass from which extrication is very difficult.

Despite this scholarly dilemma, the reality facing researchers is that organizations are increasingly diverse within single nations (Jackson et al., 1992), and they are globalizing at an exponentially increasing rate (Ghoshal & Bartlett, 1990; Newman, 1992). The various opportunities facing organizations pose nearly as many questions as potential gains. As Lytle et al. (1995) suggest,

> The opportunities of global markets present organizations with numerous challenges. How can companies best communicate with suppliers, distributors, and customers across cultures? What are the most effective ways to structure and manage cross-cultural joint ventures? How can managers best train and motivate employees across cultures? What are the most appropriate methods for organizations and their members to deal with intercultural conflicts? Each of these challenges calls into question the generalizability of theories in strategy, management, human resources, conflict, and organization behavior. (4)

While many opportunities for organizations exist, the practical reality is dampened by the lack of systematic empirical work and effective midrange theories that enable us to predict the most effective work systems and practices. The focus of this chapter is to provide a general conceptual overview of my model integrating concepts of face and harmony into a general social structure or social system. I hope that this midrange model will provide the direction for meaningful research concerning the role of interpersonal processes and self-concept in predicting cultural influences on organizational outcomes. As I will argue later, the concept of face is a central one to the functioning of all people in an organizational setting (as well as any social setting), and my model will attempt to clarify the relationships among face, organizations, and society.

While this model captures many facets of society and culture, I would emphasize that it is a midrange theory, meaning that I am attempting to specifically link an aspect of the individual (face) with specific aspects of his or her functioning in an organizational setting. The conceptual heritage of my approach comes from an individual differences focus using psychology, cultural values from anthropology, and institutional and structuration focus from sociology. An explicit disclaimer in presenting this model as a midrange theory is that it does not attempt to posit the origins of culture, nor does it attempt to explain all aspects of society or organizational functioning. I will argue, however, that the construct of face is a central one for many aspects of organizational life and that the pursuit and maintenance of face impact both individual-level behavior and organizational structure and content.

Before discussing the conceptual model for my book, I would pause for a moment and forward a number of definitions and terms that will be needed for the general discussion of my framework. After these clarifications, I will turn to a presentation of the general model, followed by a more specific discussion of the components of the model.

Basic Terminology

All people live in collectivities or groups in order to survive. People in a particular setting often share a number of characteristics, such as religion, political views, lifestyle patterns, and approaches to work. In developing my model, I will briefly discuss the idea of culture and its significance to my framework, although I will postpone a more complete discussion of component elements of culture until the chapter on societal context. At this point, I begin by examining several definitions and conceptualizations of culture and describe my use of the term. An important aspect of my use of "culture" lies in the idea that people vary in the ways they build their lives but that this variation is predictable within and across groups of people. This variability is the descriptive dimension of what is termed culture.

Needless to say, a broad and complete overview of "culture" is beyond the scope and aim of this book. I would add at this point that my approach to the incorporation of culture reflects a psychological orientation. The conceptual heritage for this perspective is presented in my earlier work with Erez (Erez & Earley, 1993), and it consists of an information-processing perspective of cognitive functioning. Using this type of approach, a researcher is enabled to make very specific predictions concerning how various facets of "culture" may potentially impact specific facets of an individual's interpersonal behavior. As I will point out, however, this style of conceptualization runs countercurrent to a number of existing definitions and frameworks employed in the study of culture. In order to clarify this point, I will explore an interesting discussion presented by Rohner in a special issue of the *Journal of Cross-Cultural Psychology* in 1984.

My individual-level analysis can be thought of as the local manifestation of cultural values and content on an individual. In other words, I view culture as a specific set of beliefs and values that are shared by individuals having a common geographic and resource base as represented by individual-level phenomena. While an individual's cognitions and values capture "culture," they capture individuals' unique experiences as well. Thus an assessment of cultural values through my individual level of analysis is contaminated by "culture" and "personality." While I discuss this point from a methodological view in another forum (Earley & Mosakowski, 1995), it is important to note that my representation of culture is at the individual level. It is this approach that I firmly believe will enable researchers to better understand (and detect) the true influence and significance of "culture" in organizational functioning.

My conceptualization is useful for several reasons. First, I can use the hierarchical structure of a cognitive representation of person-in-society as a way of describing affective response to culturally relevant situations (Lord & Kernan, 1987). A hierarchical structure aids us in understanding why merely altering specific expectations may not be sufficient in integrating culture and work practices. Second, this approach provides a consistent means of integrating cultural-level influences with individual-level actions. A reoccurring theme is that culture refers to shared knowledge and meaning systems (D'Andrade, 1984). Culture can be viewed as a hierarchical structure of beliefs and values, shared among individuals having a common background, that shape action.

Culture has been defined in a number of ways. A definition is proposed by Hofstede (1980a) who views culture to be the mental programs commonly held and used by people in a given society. Herskovits (1955:305) defined culture as the human-made part of the environment, whereas Triandis (1972) and Osgood (1974) define it as the subjective part of the human-made environment. The subjective aspects of culture include social events, beliefs, attitudes, norms and values, and shared roles. Definitions vary from very limited and focused, such as Shweder and Levine's (1984) view that culture is a set of shared meaning systems, to broad and all-encompassing, such as the view that it is the human-made aspect of the environment (e.g., Herskovits, 1955). Other definitions include Skinner's (1953) view that culture is a complex series of reinforcement contingencies moderated by particular schedules of reward and Schein's (1985) view that at the core of culture are the untested assumptions of how and why to behave. Hofstede (1980a) defines culture as a set of mental programs that control an individual's responses in a given context, and Parsons and Shils (1951) view culture as a shared characteristic of a high-level social system.

There are many influences of culture on the institutional and organizational levels of behavior. Culture shapes the type of organizations that evolve and the nature of social structures as they grow and adapt (Hofstede, 1980a). Societies shape their collectivities and social aggregates according to the rules implied by culture. Culture is sometimes viewed in terms of antecedents such as time, language, and locality variables as well as historical and ecological commonalties.

Another point is the embeddedness of culture. Culture refers to the core values and beliefs of individuals within a society that are formed in complex knowledge systems

(Lachman, 1983; Triandis and Bhawuk, in press). In addition, it refers to a pervasive set of values and beliefs that are encompassing but not immediately apparent to society members. Further, cultural beliefs and values can be understood at an individual level of analysis if we consider that individuals possess both cultural knowledge structures as well as individual, or specific, structures. Thus an individual's behavior within an organizational setting is a product of both culturally acquired and individually acquired (via unique life experiences) knowledge systems.

I will now turn to a brief discussion of their debate as a basis for my specific definition of culture in this book. This debate focuses on the degree to which culture is a societal-level versus individual-level construct. Rohner (1984:119) states: "I define culture as *the totality of equivalent and complementary learned meanings maintained by a human population, or by identifiable segments of a population, and transmitted from one generation to the next*" (emphasis in original). While Rohner states that the generation transmission of his definition may have exceptions, he concludes that the "equivalent and complementary learned meanings" are of critical importance. By this, he means that these meanings are not universally shared by an entire society, nor are they precisely shared. In other words, any two individuals from a given culture may hold slightly different meanings for the same event or construct, and these two individuals may have shared meanings with other parties in the society but not one another. As Rohner argues,

> It is probable that no single individual ever knows the totality of equivalent and complementary learned meanings that define the "culture" of a given population, and it is therefore unlikely that the person is able to activate, at any given moment, the full range of meanings that define the "culture" of his or her people. But complementary meanings free one from the necessity of having to know all of one's "culture." For example, most persons do not need to know how to behave as a physician or shaman if they are ill, only how to behave properly as a patient. (122)

He defines the concepts of social system and society as well. A social system refers to the behavioral interactions of multiple individuals who exist within a culturally organized population, whereas a society is defined as "the largest unit of a territorially bounded, multigenerational population recruited largely through sexual reproduction, and organized around a common culture and a common social system" (131). While I agree with many aspects of Rohner's presentation, there is an important flaw in his conclusion that the psychological assessment of culture is "untenable" and misguided. He has mistaken the view of culture from an individual-level perspective as being an extension of personality. Earlier I raised the point that culture is represented at the individual level through a person's beliefs, values, and norms (Wagner & Moch, 1986) as well as individual experience. Likewise, in Jahoda's (1984) response to Rohner's article, Jahoda points out that contrary to Rohner's assertion, culture (meaning systems) can be effective predictors of behavior.

What is useful from Rohner's definitions of society, social system, and culture is that it is possible to separate the various effects of these constructs on individuals' actions and behavior through the clarification of the concepts. For example, Rohner cites White's analogy of American football in describing the relationship of culture to social system. The point is that knowing the rules (culture) of football does not enable an observer to anticipate or predict the next play that will be made during a game (social system or resulting behaviors). Cultural knowledge allows the observer to judge the appropriateness or legitimacy of a given "play" but not to predict the content of the play. However, this distinction is not nearly so clear-cut as Rohner assumes. Again, I will draw upon the football metaphor in making my point. If I have an intimate knowledge of the rules and functioning of football, then knowledge of the given play in the context of the current game's status will enable me to predict (albeit with probabilistic accuracy) the next play to be run. If the score is tied at 20–20 and Team A has the ball on the defense's 30 yard line with 8 seconds left in the game, I can predict with high certainty that the next play for Team A will be a field goal attempt. If, however, the ball is on the defense's 40 yard line under the same conditions, I can predict that the play will be a long pass. Thus culture is not merely knowing the "rules" per se; it implies a knowledge of the interrelatedness of those rules along with "typical" or normative functioning of the rules. As a result, behavior of specific individuals and their personal beliefs and values can be predicted from culture.

Another important distinction is presented and evaluated in a recent book by Jo-anne Martin (1992). She presents a characterization of three general forms of organization culture: integration, differentiation, and fragmentation. Briefly, an integration view posits culture as shared meanings held in common. The differentiation view points out that subgroups exist within any given organization that likely differ in their shared meanings from one another. Finally, a fragmentation perspective suggests that culture is a differential network of meanings that are interrelated and reciprocally related but ill-defined and inconsistent. My interpretation of these perspectives is that they can be thought of using a factorial design that has two factors. The integration view is a main effects perspective, whereas the differentiation perspective is captured by an interaction term. Finally, the fragmentation view is best thought of as some form of within-cell variance or individual differences. Using this analogy, it becomes clearer that culture is not simply a monolithic construct capturing all of the minds within a given society. It is Rohner's idea of complementary but incompletely shared meaning systems.

So what, then, constitutes culture, social system, and society? In my usage, I define culture as the individual-level manifestations of shared meaning systems that are learned from other members of the society. This learning process can occur through a number of outlets including child-rearing practices, peer transmission, media, et cetera, and it is an ongoing occurrence, having decreasingly less impact as a function of maturation. A social system refers to those roles and positions existing in a society, including the pattern and nature of interactions. While resulting behavior is an important outcome from a social system, I differ from Rohner inasmuch as I view behavior as an outcome from a social system and not the system itself. A social system refers, then, to the connections and interrelationships among societal members, and these relationships are shaped and guided by culture. However, the distinction between culture and social system is not one of "rules of the game" versus "plays"; rather, it is the distinction of meaning and significance versus structured relations void of individual personality. In this sense, culture captures the meanings and personal significance of behavior for people, whereas the social system is the arena in which these meanings and significance are given direction and structure in which to manifest themselves. My metaphor is one of an artist having a certain concept he or she wishes to capture (culture) who then uses a particular medium (e.g., painting versus sculpture) with which to express the concept. What is important with this metaphor is that the concept is not independent of the medium; that is to say, the concept of romance expressed in oils is not identical to that of romance expressed in marble.

I follow Rohner's definition in describing a society as a territorially bounded and multigenerational group of people having a common culture or characteristic way of viewing the world. I find this conceptualization to be useful in that it provides a way of defining the boundaries for a society and predicting the limits under which we might expect to see a culture truly "shared." Perhaps the most important clarification is to emphasize Rohner's, as well as Martin's (1992), point that any given society consists of multiple subgroupings or social subsystems. This means that any two individuals coming from the same society may, in fact, possess a number of differences in values and beliefs. However, I would anticipate that they will still share many values and beliefs as well. In other words, the between-subgroup differences do not exceed the between-nation, or international,[1] differences.

With these definitions, I will now turn to a discussion of my general framework. I begin by reviewing the model, after which I present a brief description of the component parts of the model. Finally, I will describe the model as a general system.

General Model

My model brings together various culturally relevant constructs that span a number of levels of analysis. In fact, the levels of analysis presented in this model range from society to individual. Although such a grand leap makes for many difficulties, I will ultimately rely on the individual level as the discussion stage for various effects. My orientation (and bias) is one of individual psychology in which explanations are derived from human behavior within complex systems. Thus some of my discussion will address issues of a more macro, systems level and not just the individual level, but with ultimate reference to individuals behaving within those systems. I will describe the potential influence of cultural values on institutional practices within organizations, but with reference to how those practices impact individual employees or groups of employees. For example, consider the hypothesized relationship of uncertainty avoidance to institutionalization asserted by Hofstede. He suggested that countries high in uncertainty avoidance (his cultural dimension denoting the general level of tolerance for uncertainty in a given country) will often develop organizations that are more centralized and have many standardized rules and practices. These strong institutional norms provide a coping mechanism for employees working in these organizations. My discussion of this relationship would strongly echo this final comment, namely, that the institutional norms provide an individual-level coping mechanism. More strongly, I would posit that such mechanisms arise because of culture's influence on individual action and psyche. That is to say, employees and managers alike who are from a high uncertainty avoidance culture create institutions having a form in which standardized procedures for work, rules, et cetera, are present. It is certainly true that institutional practices impose themselves on employees' values and beliefs—for example, through socialization—and this reciprocal relationship is portrayed in the model. Perhaps it is not overly fruitful to debate the origins of these

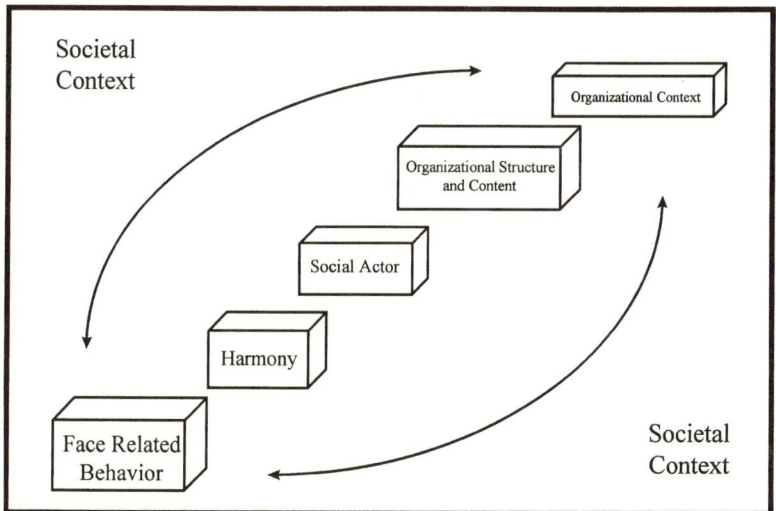

Figure 2-1. Organizational Face: A General Model

institutional practices; my framework depicts this relationship as a reciprocal one with the ultimate clarification presented at the employee level.

The general model that I employ is presented in Figure 2-1. The model consists of six basic parts: societal context, organizational context, organizational structure and content, social actor, harmony, and face-related behavior. Before turning to the specific components of the model, I would point out that the general framework of the model is consistent with the ideas put forward by Granovetter (1985), among others, concerning the embedded nature of relationships within society. In addition, I captured the general interrelations among the various component elements by placing them within the same three-dimensional space. This representation portrays Weick's (1985) notion of loose coupling applied to these various systems within the general frame. For example, the relationship between organizational context (e.g., industry type) and organizational structure and content (e.g., institutional practices employed in a given company) is not deterministic but probabilistic.

Another important aspect of this representation is that various components differ in their proximity to the front of the three-dimensional space. This metaphor represents the assertion that aspects such as harmony and face are more immediate and observable aspects in an organizational context. I observe people and their interactions with one another, and this is the focus of my model. The ordering presented in the model is not intended as an implied causal ordering; rather, I want to depict general influences and directionality in relation to the individual. The relative position in the dimensional space does, however, represent general salience of effects on consequent constructs. For example, the relationship of harmony on face is a very direct and immediate one, whereas the reciprocal influences of social actor and organizational structure and content are less direct.

A final, general observation of this model is that societal context is represented as an element somewhat different from the others. I have represented this construct as: (1) having no direct connections to any other element of the model; and (2) represented in the general, contextual space. As I will point out in the next subsection of the chapter, this differing representation occurs because of the embedded influences of societal context.

Societal Context

As I discussed earlier, society refers to the boundaries of a given group of people whose population is supported through multiple generations derived by internal growth. The boundaries are generally determined through national or international law, historical precedent, militaristic action, or international negotiation. Of course, this presents a number of difficulties, as presented in the ongoing affairs of Israel and the Palestinian Liberation Organization, Chechnya and the Russians, and the former Yugoslavian Republic. Geographic boundaries often are in dispute, particularly if natural resources or military advantage is at stake. Therefore, even this general definition of society can be difficult to operationalize. However, it is not the nation-state that is the focus of my model. I am using the construct of societal context to describe the culture of a group of people. Of course, culture is not the only relevant characteristic of societal context, and I will discuss more completely other general systems in the chapter on society, but the focus of my model is on the relevance of societal context as largely influenced and appropriately characterized by culture, or shared meaning. I refrain from simply using the term "cultural context" instead of "societal context" for the reason that society represents more than just culture, and I believe it is important to clarify this distinction. From a methodological viewpoint, this is the point raised by Earley and Mosakowski (1995), Leung and Bond (1989), and Lytle et al. (1995), among others, in describing cultural hypotheses using societal variables.

In describing societal context, I refer to the most relevant aspect of society for my particular thesis, namely, the cultural values and beliefs shared among individuals. Again, I would emphasize that this is not the only aspect of society, and I will discuss other aspects later in the book. For example, the economic system employed within a given nation will have direct and indirect effects on employees within organizations. During my visits to the People's Republic of China in the mid-1980s, the incentives and values of markets were met with strong skepticism. In 1990, I noticed a large banner at a silk-dyeing factory, and I asked my interpreter what the Chinese characters meant. He replied, "To be rich is good." Quite a shift in political and economic ideology in a very short period! (Of course, the conversion to a market way of thinking is not quite so clear-cut as this simple example would make it appear. The praise concerning becoming wealthy is emphasized as an important method through which the entire country can grow and prosper. Rather than being viewed as greedy or selfish, making money is viewed as helpful to one's in-group, community, or danwei [work unit].)

In discussing the societal context, I want to emphasize the depiction of this construct in the model as unattached to any other single construct. In fact, the three-dimensional representation is intended to emphasize the pervasive influence of societal context on all aspects of individuals and their organizations. It is not just through the shaping of institutions that societal influences impact employees' actions. The way we view ourselves, the significance of our actions and behavior, et cetera, take shape based on our membership within a given society. Therefore, this aspect of the model is represented by the entire dimensional space rather than some more direct, causal effect. Likewise, the figure depicts that societal context is the "dimensional soup" in which the various constructs "float" and these constructs flavor the soup. Not only are the way people behave and the types of organizations that exist shaped by societal context, but they shape society as well.

My specific operationalization of societal context in this book is through various aspects of culture, or shared meaning. More specifically, I examine societal context through six basic cultural dimensions. I have chosen these particular dimensions because they are conceptually relevant to the social processes underlying face. They do not, however, represent all aspects of culture (just as they don't represent all aspects of society). These six were chosen because of their relationship to face and not because they represent or depict all aspects of cultures. Therefore, I will present these dimensions as a starting point for further discussion and not as the final solution with regard to aspects of culture relevant to face. What these dimensions share in common is a relevance for interpersonal interaction and morality, which are key in understanding face.

The six dimensions that I have chosen to focus on are individualism and collectivism, tightness versus looseness (sometimes referred to as field dependence versus independence, respectively), relationship to nature, power distance, guilt versus shame, and masculinity and femininity. While the reader familiar with Hofstede's (1980a, 1991) famous typology of values might recognize several of these dimensions,[2] the others are somewhat less popular in the organizations literature. I will briefly describe each of these dimensions, and I will give a more complete description of each in Chapter 8.

Individualism and collectivism refers to a wide range of values and beliefs. They have their origins in Emile Durkheim's discussion of collectives and have received a great deal of conceptual amplification from Triandis and his colleagues (e.g., Triandis, 1989a; Triandis et al., 1986) as well as empirical clarification from Wagner and Moch (1986). Parsons and Shils (1951) discuss individualism and collectivism as the tendency of an actor to pursue self-interests versus those of his or her collective. Their emphasis on goals and interests constituted a limited role of individualism and collectivism. Hofstede posits that individualism is a conglomeration of values concerning the relation of a person to his or her collective or group. An individualistic society is one in which the self-concept is defined in an individual whereas a collectivistic society is one in which an individual is defined with reference to an in-group context.

Tightness versus looseness refers to the extent to which rules and norms are present and enforced within a given society (Witkin & Berry, 1975). In a tight culture, characterized by many rules governing individuals' actions (Glenn & Glenn, 1981; Triandis, 1989a), individuals are expected to conform with existing practices and deviation from those rules is discouraged or condemned. The recent "deviations" of several Americans in Singapore illustrate the consequences of violating expectations for behavior in a tight culture. This cultural dimension is particularly interesting because it has a strong individual-level manifestation that has received much research attention, namely, what is termed psychological differentiation (e.g., Witkin & Goodenough, 1977; Witkin, Goodenough, & Oltman, 1979). At an individual level, tightness versus looseness is manifest as an individual's capacity to distinguish between an object and its frame or context. Individuals from a loose culture can readily separate object from field, whereas individuals from a tight culture cannot do so. In an organizational context, this suggests that employees from a tight culture are contextually sensitive and use contextual information in order to make sense of particular occurrences. For example, an employee from a tight culture will likely rely on the setting in which job feedback is provided as a way of interpreting it. If the feedback is provided in a public forum, its meaning will be determined, in part, by the reactions of observers to the interaction of employee with his or her superior.

The third cultural dimension is relationship to nature (Kluckhohn & Strodtbeck, 1961). This dimension refers to the beliefs and values concerning the relationship of a person to nature. Kluckhohn and Strodtbeck argued that there are three general aspects of this dimension: person against nature, person in harmony with nature, and person subjugated to nature.[3] Mastery over nature is typical of Western countries in which people believe that through expertise, technology, and effort nature can be harnessed and controlled. A society characterized by harmony with nature, typical of Pacific Rim countries, is one in which people seek a balance and coexistence with nature. In the third form, subjugation to nature, life is viewed as predetermined or preordained by chance or God. In such a society, it is believed that a person can do little to affect nature per se; rather, a person's role in life is to fulfill what he or she was destined to do. Such a view is characteristic of Muslim-based cultures found in the Middle East (Lane & DiStephano, 1992).

The fourth dimension is power distance (Hofstede, 1980a, b, 1991). Power distance refers to the relative distribution of power and degree of inequality in a particular culture. More than simply a stratification issue, power distance captures the degree of acceptability of power differentials in a given culture. For example, in a high power distance culture such as Malaysia, individuals who have a great deal of power are viewed as different from individuals who lack power. More important, the perceived legitimacy of these powerful people to influence the actions of those who are less powerful is high. In other words, not only do these powerful people have more power, but they and those who are less powerful perceive that they exert power to influence the actions of those who are less powerful. In a low power distance culture, people are thought to be equal, and so it is not considered appropriate or acceptable for someone to influence the actions of another person.

The fifth dimension is Hofstede's concept of masculinity versus femininity. Although this label has been somewhat troublesome, the underlying cultural construct is a useful one. Masculine cultures are those in which an emphasis on competition and activity exists, whereas more feminine cultures emphasize cooperation and personal development. As Hofstede (1980a) argues, people in masculine cultures emphasize work over their leisure, whereas people in feminine cultures emphasize leisure over their work. The hard-driving, work-oriented nature of the Japanese (masculine culture) can be contrasted with the dominant emphasis of the Swedes, who seek to improve life conditions for their citizens as well as transform work into a livable condition.

Finally, there is the dimension of shame versus guilt that was nicely characterized by Mead (1928) in her work on various primitive cultures. This dimension captures the nature of people's relationship to their own moral principles as well as to those of other people. I would posit that this dimension is highly related to individualism and collectivism, but I will address it separately in order to emphasize its particular contribution to understanding the impact of face violations with moral overtones. In a guilt-based culture individuals emphasize personal responsibility in determining their reactions to inadequate responses to a given situation, whereas in a shame-based culture individuals may experience negative consequences (internally as well as externally imposed) of responses or situations not under their control. For example, a person from a shame-based culture who is physically limited (e.g., vision-impaired) may feel shame even though such a limitation is completely out of his or her control. A person coming from a guilt-based culture who has the same limitation does not experience the same negative consequence or personal blame.

Organizational Context

The organizational context in this model refers to the general situation in which organizations operate within a given society. There are a variety of influences on the nature of industrial organization within a given society, including synergy attributable to collections of organizations of a common type, or what is referred to as the organizational field (Giddens, 1989; Kanter, 1972); political influences on structure (Clegg, 1977; Piven & Cloward, 1971); economic system and rules for exchange and governance (Nelson & Winter, 1982; Williamson, 1975, 1981); ecological forces (Wholey & Brittain, 1989; Freeman, 1982; Hannan & Freeman, 1977); and institutional practices (DiMaggio & Powell, 1983; Meyer & Rowan, 1977).

All organizations operate in a general context influenced and shaped by a number of characteristics derived from other organizations. I will adopt the general perspective of institutional theory in describing many of these effects and influences. According to Scott (1994), the effects of institutional arrangements is strongest at the level between society and an individual organization.

The central aspect of the organizational context for my model is that of the organizational field. By an organizational field, I am referring to an aggregate of organizations that collectively constitute an institutional influence on particular organizations (Scott, 1994). As stated by DiMaggio and Powell (1983:148), organizational fields are represented as "those organizations that, in the aggregate, constitute a recognized area of institutional life: key suppliers, resource and product consumers, regulatory agencies, and other organizations that produce similar services or products." These fields are critical for understanding the nature of organizations because they shape the practices and activities considered adaptive and acceptable for members within the field. For example, Coser, Kadushin, and Powell (1982) describe the nature of the American publishing industry. Through various institutional forces, the college textbook industry has moved from a relatively diverse one to a dichotomous one in which publishers are either large bureaucratic entities or small special-interest ones. Another example of these pressures concerns the development of training programs for expatriates (e.g., Black & Mendenhall, 1990; Black, Mendenhall, & Oddou,

1991). During the 1980s, there has been a proliferation of expatriate training programs in the United States, in large part a response to the relatively high failure rates of expatriate work assignments. These programs are developing an increasingly strong similarity of components and attributes, likely attributable to the dissemination of information through common external consultants, in a general atmosphere of training ambiguity. The forces within organizational fields through professionals or what is labeled "normative institutionalization" (DiMaggio & Powell, 1983:152) impel organizations to adopt many of the same practices because of the common training of the organizations' managers.

From my perspective, the significance and importance of these institutional effects in organizational fields cannot be ignored. Many of the reward and recognition systems so integral to a focus on face issues may have their roots in the practices that are isomorphically transferred throughout a given organizational field. In many ways, the institutional practices discussed are cultural transmission practices as well. This suggests that to understand the relative impact of organizational practices on an individual's actions requires the mapping of cultural influences not entirely dissimilar to institutional influences. Further, institutional influences that become the dominant influence and pattern for an organizational field may spread to regional economies (see Galaskiewicz & Wasserman, 1989), which suggests that there has been a reciprocal impact on society at large. Thus the institutional forces that shape an organization within a given field will not only impact the social actor within this organization but also eventually shape the general society in which the organizational field is housed. Of course, an organizational field's two-way influence (from field to society as well as field to individual) changes both society and social actor, and, as a result, the field itself is reshaped.

As I mentioned earlier, there are a number of other influences emerging from the organization context, including economic and political factors. For my purposes, I will focus on how these types of influences operate using an institutional framework because it is through such a system that the impact (and reciprocal influence) on the social actor may be most directly ascertained. This is not to say that the economic and political influences of the organization context operate solely through institutional effects, but I will narrow my scope and focus primarily on this path.

Organizational Structure and Content

The most salient and direct influences on a social actor, and those most directly affecting harmony, are the aspects of an organization defined by its structure and content. Whereas in the last section I focused on the field in which a given organization is embedded, organization structure and content refer quite specifically to those influences inside an organization that are thought to influence a social actor and social regulation of face. Of course, a large number of organizational characteristics can be included in a discussion of social behavior and face within a company, but I will focus on five primary facets: technology, institutional roles and rules, intraorganizational dependencies, communication systems, and governance structures. Prior to discussing these specific facets of organizations, it is important to note that I have selected aspects that bear the most direct relevance on a social actor within a given organization. The impact of each facet on an employee's actions may be direct, such as having a communication system requiring face-to-face contact, or indirect, such as having a highly decentralized structure with loose interdepartmental dependencies. In the first example, a heavy reliance on face-to-face encounters increases the likelihood that face regulation will be highly salient to employees because threats to face are immediate and undeniable. In the second example, a loose structure may make the likelihood of face threats between departmental managers somewhat lower because actions of one department will not immediately and directly impact the outcomes of another department.

The influence of technology on social behavior and face regulation comes through a variety of avenues. A basic premise is that technology does not change the importance of face per se, but it moderates the impact of one person's actions or the organization's actions on another interacting partner. This moderating influence can be made a beneficial one by removing the salience of face-to-face encounters and thereby reducing direct threat (Soon, et al., 1993). It can also be made detrimental by isolating an employee from others with whom he or she wishes to interact. This is particularly important in its implications for face. If face is largely the product of a socially constructed process, then removing the social component of the interaction may be problematic for people attempting to maintain and regulate their face. While much of the research on computer-mediated feedback and interaction has focused on removing the potential for threat, less attention has been directed toward the potential detrimental impact of computer-based interaction on self-definition in an organization. At the extreme, it leads to speculation of a completely alienated employee who has no sense of personal status or position but interacts for task-related reasons alone.

A second facet of an organization's content concerns the institutionalized roles and rules that dictate action. This aspect is related to the previous section involving organizational fields and institutional practices. The normative isomorphism described by DiMaggio and Powell (1983) focuses on the importance of professionalism in shaping organizational practices. Needless to say, these rules and roles will greatly affect interpersonal functioning. For example, a colleague in the area of finance commented that it is standard practice for finance faculty to brutally attack one another during a job talk or lecture presentation. They consider such actions a useful means for developing better understanding and rigor. This practice is quite difficult to contend with, however, in a specialty area not so accustomed to it. As a result, these actions were interpreted by people in other specialties—for example, organizational behavior—as rudeness and an attack on the person presenting research. The loss of face for the candidate also implies a loss of face for the hosts in this example to the extent that external reputations of schools become prevalent to the detriment of the institution.

Intraorganizational dependencies will influence face and social regulation in a company as well. A simple example is that of a company having a very strong set of interdependent departments. In this case, the actions of one department will strongly affect another department. To the extent that the departments' managers have their face (and various outcomes) tied to their departments, this suggests that action will result in reaction. In a highly decentralized and loosely coupled type of organization, such relationships are probabilistic and less likely to stimulate face threats.

The types of communication media used (e.g., technology or computer-based) will impact the type of actions that a person engages in, as will the communication patterns that exist in a company. Additionally, the nature of communication itself with its inherent characteristics (e.g., limitations due to individuals' personal attributes and cognitive capabilities) will influence face. For example, communication through a formal network will increase the stake that communicators have in their self-presentations. This suggests that they will be increasingly concerned with what is said, how it is said, and what it might imply about them personally. Information conveyed about oneself (background, attributes, capabilities, etc.) will be guarded and sparse because the formal chain increases the likelihood that this information will be widely available to a range of powerful organizational members.

Finally, the governance structure within an organization will influence the way people perceive themselves, the types of information about themselves that they will communicate to others, and the types of incentives and sanctions that potentially can build or tear down face. In a company with a strong emphasis on central authority and punishment of incorrect behavior, many of the actions undertaken by an employee will be of an avoidance form. Further, employees will utilize the weaknesses and failures of others to enhance their own face (relative comparison). This is because it is not in their personal interest to take chances and risk punishment, so their face will depend on the mistakes of others to give them a relative gain. Organizations with a strong participatory emphasis will stimulate face behavior having to do with individual inputs, and this may have the side effect of increasing the frequency of face threats through inadvertent slips.

While the emphasis I have used so far is a downward one (organization's impact on the social actor), there is an important upward influence as well. In fact, I will argue in a subsequent chapter that much of the nature of an organization is structured by individuals' desires to maintain and regulate face. People engage in actions that will benefit themselves and actively shape their environment to increase opportunities to gain face while minimizing threats. This is not merely a socially constructed reality or sense making (Pfeffer & Salancik, 1978); it refers to an active shaping of an organization's content to ensure that key opportunities for face regulation are not lost.

Social Actor

"Social actor" refers not only to the psychological makeup of a person within a society but also to the various immediate constraints acting on that individual that define how he or she interacts and behaves. With regard to the psychological aspects of the actor, I should point out that I take an information-processing approach consistent with my work with Miriam Erez (Erez & Earley, 1993). Briefly, models of information processing explain how information from the environment is selectively recognized, evaluated, and interpreted in terms of its meaning for the individual and how it affects behavior. Central to this idea is a person's sense or knowledge about the self, as the self is an interpreter of organizational content and structure as well as cultural influences. The self is a composite view formed through direct experience and evaluations adopted from significant others (Bandura, 1986; Markus & Kitayama, 1991). When these important figures in our life collectively share similar values, this is one way in which culture impacts individual action. This suggests that the self is an important unit of analysis for understanding differences in employees' subjective experiences of organizational phenomena. As Erez and I have argued, the self has the capacity for self-evaluation and generates needs for self-enhancement and for the preservation of positive self-esteem. These needs are shaped partially by culture and partially by individual experiences. This means that the psychological profile of the social actor provides an important link between culture and action. The psychological profile of the social actor is a dynamic structure interpreting the social patterns around us. The psychological aspect of the social actor is a person's mental representation of his or her personality, identity, and social roles (Kihlstrom & Cantor, 1984). The functioning of the self-concept depends on both the motives being served and the social setting in which action occurs.

However, viewing the social actor as independent from the social milieu from which he or she acts is an inadequate representation; there is no meaningful way to speak about people abstracted from their community (Sampson, 1989). Long-term attachments and commitments to the social environment help define who people are (Sandel, 1982). For example, Bandura (1986) proposed that the self-concept is a composite view of oneself that is formed through direct experience and evaluations adopted from significant others. Other researchers argue that the social actor is uniquely defined through the shared understanding of what humanity means in a given culture. Therefore, viewing the psychological aspect of a social actor yields an incomplete picture in need of contextualization and embeddedness.

A group's norms become the internalized standards against which individuals judge themselves. In a structural sense, a social actor can be thought to contain a collection of schemas, prototypes, goals, or images that are arranged in a space (Sherman, Judd, & Park, 1989). This view of the self contains descriptive information about traits, roles, and behavior, as well as rules and procedures for making inferences and evaluation (Erez & Earley, 1993; Kihlstrom & Cantor, 1984). The social actor is multifaceted, consisting of multiple roles (Gecas, 1982; Katz & Kahn, 1978). Individuals are known to be more committed to their central roles because they are more consequential to their conduct of behavior (Stryker, 1980).

But what of the exogenous (to the actor) influences that shape behavior? A number of different elements influence a social actor. As I mentioned, the roles that a person enacts are critical in understanding his or her behavior. Within an organizational setting, a person is required to enact a variety of roles that are often in conflict or ambiguous (Katz & Kahn, 1978). These roles are an important means through which new employees are socialized (Van Maanen & Schein, 1977) and provide valuable assistance to the organization in helping facilitate interactions. People enact a variety of roles that may be mutually contradictory or incompatible as well. In such a case, the resulting role conflict or role ambiguity may have significant dysfunctional consequences. Regardless, roles are an important exogenous influence on an employee's behavior within an organizational setting.

Other important influences on the social actor are the group memberships he or she has as well as the potential interdependencies among these various groups. A particular employee may belong to a union, be a member of a bowling team, and regularly attend a particular synagogue, and each of these groups will impose particular constraints as a consequence of membership. These constraints are not the same as the roles enacted by the employee but they may provide the rules for how to enact a role within each group. If two of these groups have a strong interdependence (e.g., through common memberships), this would influence the extent to which those constraints may become internalized by the actor or, at least, how firmly the actor holds true to the constraint. While these constraints may seem inhibiting, they may be liberating inasmuch as the employee does not need to justify particular actions (e.g., wearing a funny-looking pair of shoes for bowling).

These two aspects of the social actor, psychological and external, jointly influence the actor's behavior in a given organizational setting. However, it must be remembered that a social actor has the potential to shape his or her organizational setting as well. An important part of my framework is the assumption that the actor does not merely respond to particular contextual cues or influences. Quite the contrary, the actor actively shapes the nature of his or her organizational setting in order to facilitate personal and collective motives and desires. What this suggests, then, is that in order to understand the formation and shaping of a given organization, a researcher must understand the impact of a social actor on the formation processes. Further, understanding an actor's motives and style of interacting will help a researcher better understand this shaping process.

A social actor is best thought of as an intentional and reciprocal determinant of an organization's content and structure as well as a social setting's patterns of interaction. The underlying determinant of a social actor's motives and intentions is face as it manifests itself in an organizational context. Through a better knowledge of face, it is possible to understand how a social actor's behavior will be directed at his or her social system and organization.

Harmony

The concept of harmony may be the most immediately troublesome in my model simply because of a labeling issue. Perhaps the term "social exchange" or "social regulation" or "social discourse" would be as appropriate, but it is my desire to bring the connotative meaning of harmony to the forefront. To me, "harmony" refers to the nature of interpersonal interaction and actions engaged in by social actors within a given organizational content and structure. In this context, harmony refers to the systems-level dynamic processes through which face and other behaviors are regulated. It is best viewed as a dynamic process of regulation, as opposed to a static or stable outcome.

Throughout this book, the idea of harmony will be that of social regulation, that is to say, the regulatory aspects of interpersonal interactions. This includes such things as exchange principles and practices, communication (literal and symbolic), expectations concerning others' intentions and actions, and social and personal reactions to action. Harmony denotes more than just a balance point or an equilibrium node within a given social system. It represents the activity of social actors who are engaged in active discourse in order to facilitate the display, development, and manipulation of face. In other words, balance does not simply mean that a system will achieve equilibrium in some physical sense. It suggests that a social system operates with actors who behave intentionally in order to achieve a particular balance among themselves.

A number of forces and styles of exchange direct the nature of harmony in any given social system. From an individual level, the influence of social actors' desire to regulate face propels harmony. From a societal level, cultural values and norms concerning social regulation impact harmony. From an organizational level, institutional practices and organization structure influence harmony.

Harmony is thus conceptualized as a process rather than an outcome or static construct. It is the process through which actors' face is regulated and maintained in a given societal and organizational context. Cross-cultural researchers have identified four general types of ties among social actors that I will draw upon in discussing harmony. These ties come from the resource theory proposed by Fiske (1991), and they have been integrated into a concept of cultural values in recent work by Chen, Meindl, and Hunt (1996) and Triandis (1994). Social ties refer to the forms of interdependence that occur in relationships in a sense, and they dictate the expectations and rules that operate during exchange for people. These four ties are market pricing, authority ranking, communal sharing, and equality matching, and they form a continuum based on the longevity of the relationship, expectations shared among the interacting parties, and the rules of exchange that operate as the parties interact and exchange resources. For now, I will characterize these ties as follows. Market exchange is characterized by an emphasis on short-term and personal interests in which market rules for interaction dominate. Authority ranking reflects a hierarchical structure within an existing in-group. Communal sharing is a form of exchange attributed to egalitarian collectives such as Israeli kibbutzim, and equality matching is a specialized form of exchange in which resources of a like form and quantity are exchanged in a balanced fashion. It is these four forms of ties that vary as a function of societal context (cultural values) and are differentially employed by social actors in order to regulate face.

Using these various ties, I will examine three topics of regulation: patterns of interaction, expectations of intent, and social and personal reactions to action. By patterns of interaction, I am referring to the nature of the social ties that bind individuals and how this impacts their willingness and quality of exchange. Not only is the type of exchange rule practiced in these ties different, but so is the willingness of the parties to endure hardships on behalf of the exchange. For instance, an employee who has a primarily market relationship with his or her company views mutual exploitation as a natural course of events. The employee's focus is on maximizing his or her outcomes, with an assumption that the organization is doing the same thing. If there is a difficult time ahead (e.g., economic strife for the company), the employee will likely exit the company and severe his or her ties if he or she has an opportunity to do so. Thus not only is the pattern of how the employee interacts with his or her organization shaped by self-interests, but it is also influenced by a short view of the relationship characterized by an unwillingness to take on the company's burdens. In Chinese, it is said of some people, "Ren zou, cha liang," or, "Person leaves, tea is cold," in which the tea symbolizes friendship and loyalty. This is the type of interaction underlying a market exchange.

Another aspect of regulating interpersonal behavior is that of the expectations of others' intentions for action. By this I mean that an important aspect of harmony is based on the assumptions a person makes concerning others' intentions and anticipated actions. Many of the face-related actions that we engage in are anticipatory of others' willingness or unwillingness to facilitate the display of face. Goffman refers to this aspect of facework as a central component of people's concern over their own face as well as the face of others. In a somewhat individualistic context, it might be argued that the anticipation of others' willingness to facilitate face maintenance is due to personal desire to gain face in return. However, this maintenance and regulation process may be more group-oriented in the case of a collectivist (Chang & Holt, 1994).

Finally, the social and personal reactions that people have to actions in an organizational context are guided by the desire to regulate face. Reactions to various reward schemes, negotiations, job enhancements, and technological innovation are all tied to the regulatory aspects of face. For example, the job changes implied by an enrichment or enhancement program (Hackman & Oldham, 1980) suggest that employees will be provided additional autonomy, job challenge, et cetera. All of these characteristics are presumably a positive benefit for the employee and the organization. Why, then, are such innovations often met with resistance? A traditional answer focuses on employee resistance to change, a finding dating back to the time of Lewin (1951) or Coch and French's (1948) study of participatory management in the Harwood Pajama Factory. The idea is that with change comes uncertainty and threat through the inherent risk of ambiguity. Another hypothesis is that employees react to a change in self-definition by resisting change because it forces them to rethink who they are in a given social system. Erez and Earley (1993) refer to such a resistance using the psychological motive of self-consistency or a desire to maintain continuity in one's life and work setting. This is related to face as well inasmuch as these changes can imply that an employee's self-view is now altered by the change in the work context. An employee who has always been a welder does not want to change into a painter because such a shift will question who he or she is in a fundamental way.

Face

This construct is at the heart of my model and framework because it is face that is the outcome of various interactional processes. "Face" refers to a person's self-identity as well as social identity. It has a variety of aspects that I will describe in more detail in the next chapter. In short, face refers to those aspects of the self that an individual chooses, or attempts to choose, for him- or herself. Face has been generally defined as the positive aspects of self that are claimed (Goffman, 1959), but this is a bit misleading because it can have significant negative aspects that are not easily abandoned or ignored.

The conceptualization of face has roots in the early 1900s, with most of the early work conducted by Asian scholars who viewed face as a predominantly Chinese/ Asian concept. "Face" refers to a universal aspect of interaction concerning how we present ourselves as well as a basis for self-evaluation. It is a form of exchange and type of interaction among two or more parties within a defined social context. There are generally two categories of face, lian and mianzi, which I will discuss in the next chapter. The first aspect of face, lian, concerns the rules underlying moral character and basic ethics of a person in a given society. Although these rules have culture-specific (emic) manifestations, people operate in all cultures relying on certain universal (etic) morals (Wilson, 1993). For example, Wilson argues that there are four universal morals shared by all people: sympathy, fairness, self-control, and duty. Others have argued for various listings of values or morals, including Etzioni (1973), Kluckhohn and Strodtbeck (1961), Parsons and Shils (1951), and Schwartz (1992), to name a few.

The second aspect of face, mianzi, reflects the interactional aspect of face. That is to say, mianzi captures the aspect of face that reflects a person's interactions with others in his or her society. The metaphor of a tree and its bark is one that recurs in many Chinese sayings about face (e.g., "Ren yao mian, shu yao pi," or "People have face, tree has bark"; Yan, 1995). This metaphor is useful because it suggests that face is the outside that protects the inside (as bark protects the inside of the tree) and that an important aspect of bark aids in the definition of a given tree. Further, the bark provides the environment in which other creatures in the ecological system can live and flourish, just as face provides the setting needed for social systems to operate effectively.

Casual observers often seem to attribute the construct of face to Eastern cultures, whereas I argue that it is a universal construct that regulates many organizational activities involving people. The negotiator who takes an entrenched position as a result of having been insulted by a negotiating partner may harm himself to spite the other (Tjosvold, 1974). This reaction is clearly one of face—in this case, it is the negotiator's attempt to regain face by appearing strong and invincible. Likewise, an employee who rejects performance feedback and discounts its source may be engaging in face-saving behavior. As Goffman (1959) points out, many of our responses (in the West) are influenced by our desire to enhance and protect face. We engage in activities that we predict will add to our face, and we avoid those that may detract from it.

As I will argue in the next chapter, face is a universal construct, but its component elements differ in significance according to culture and societal context. For instance, mianzi is relied on by individualists in order to secure outcomes and/or rewards that others may possess. Self-worth is strongly related to those material, prestige, positional, and power-related resources an individual has acquired, and others recognize such an accumulation. A collectivist is concerned with the lian of in-group members, because the in-group assures satisfaction of material needs and in-group relations are an important outcome of group functioning. A group member who shows a flawed character threatens the very existence of the in-group by disrupting group harmony, failing to contribute to the group's welfare, or taking a disproportionate share of the group's resources. For instance, a soldier who falls asleep at his or her post threatens the existence of the unit and, therefore, shows that he or she places his or her own comfort over the lives of others. In a collectivistic culture, such an act is very threatening because group membership is long-term and the action reflects a priority of individual interests over those of the in-group.

The significance of face and its regulation is captured by the idea of "facework" as described by Goffman (1959:1–5). By facework it is meant the methods through which people who interact with one another regulate each other's face. For instance, if I interact with a student and my student comments on a mistake that I made in a published paper, I will lose face. However, Goffman argues that a natural tendency in this circumstance is for the student to offer a means through which I can regain my face. For example, this student might point out that the mistake was likely a typographical error not under my direct control and that the mistake might also be characteristic of other highly productive researchers who cannot waste time checking every little detail. Finally, the student might suggest that my willingness to admit the error reflects my real position as a scholar since someone less influential would deny any imperfection. Regardless of the "offering," there is a critical point at which I must be willing to accept or reject this offering. If I choose to accept it, then face-work is completed and my face is restored. However, I might choose to reject the student's comment by denigrating the student's own position ("Perhaps the reason that you think my article is in error is because you haven't developed a mature view of research in your program!"). A variety of possible sequences and actions might be taken. The key point, however, is that people have some "face" and its regulation is important in daily functioning between oneself and others.

But what underlies the importance of face? While a number of authors have argued that face is an important variable for understanding interpersonal interactions, it is somewhat less clear what function face provides in a social system. It is my assertion that the motive underlying face is a primary one for every person, namely, the motive of self-definition. All people seek to understand who they are in their social system, culture, and society. A desire for self-definition leads us to use both internal as well as external cues in order to assess our actions in relation to others. Face is so central to what I do because it is through face that I understand who I am. Much like the act of looking in the mirror, our interactions with others, as well as our own introspection concerning our personal actions, signal to us who we are in a given social system and how we should act and behave. Without this critical information, people become confused and pathological. It is this experience of facelessness that is closest to Merton's (1968) idea of anomie experienced by members of society.

A final point that I raise in this section refers back to the relative balance or importance of lian and mianzi across various cultures. While there are general main effects for each type of face in various cultures, there are important subtleties for each form of face that I will describe in more detail in the next chapter. For example, a Hong Kong colleague asked me whether someone in Hong Kong who purchases an expensive automobile such as a Mercedes-Benz is focused on mianzi and not lian. My response was that it would not negate the importance of lian over mianzi, but that even thinking about just mianzi may be somewhat misleading. In an individualist culture such as the United States, I would interpret such a purchase as a status symbol intended to convey the message that the person is important and wealthy. In Hong Kong, such an action may signal that one's family and friends are important and wealthy. Although this might seem to be splitting hairs, I think that it reflects the complex nature of mianzi. The construct itself is universal, but its manifestations are likely to have a number of emic aspects.

Connections among Elements of the Model

I have discussed a number of the general connections among parts of the model. The most fundamental assumption I make in this model is that the social actor is the ending and beginning of the various influences observed in the model and that face (its regulation, maintenance, and development) is the impetus for activity in this model. By this I mean that I will examine these various constructs from the perspective of the social actor who is building a world around him- or herself in order to maintain and regulate face. It is an active and purposive process, but it is not one in which the actor is omniscient or fully rational. There is a great deal of reconstruction and sense making in this world, and many subtle motives and drives underlie the actor's actions shaped by group, organizational, and societal influences. The actor is unaware of many of these influences and, at the same time, is a causal agent in their change and evolution. Just as Hofstede refers to culture as "mental programming" and Granovetter (1985) discusses the nature of embeddedness for organizations within markets, the social actor controls and is controlled by the social system in which he or she operates through his or her desire to regulate face.

Why is face so central? As I will argue in the next chapter, face is a fundamental question and issue for all organizational members (and all humans). It is through face that we maintain a sense of who we are and of our personal significance in a social system. As with the metaphor of being faceless, people who lack face are alien creatures within their social context.

This leaves us with the perspective that the model is a bottom-up influence, which is not strictly true. In this model, a social actor is guided by face regulation as well as his or her roles enacted, organization, and culture. But it is face that is at the forefront of a person's interactions in an organization, and it is face that is the most directly assessed and analyzed in trying to understand the subtle influences of culture on employee behavior. While the underlying reasons for face-related actions may be terribly complex, these actions are readily observed, and thus they provide us with important leverage for researching differences in organizational behaviors across societies.

A final point to be made is that in addition to the embeddedness and subtlety of culture, a number of competing influences on face are derived from sources that differ in immediacy to the social actor. For instance, the organizational structure of a company may be such that tight control systems imply a fundamental distrust of employees. The impact of these control systems on employees is that they regulate face through more instrumental relationships with the organization. However, the immediate work group of this social actor may be a long-term and close-knit community that leads the nature of exchange to be of an expressive form. What, then, is the resulting pattern of interaction in such a contradictory situation? The more immediate influence will have the most profound impact on face regulation. In this example, the expressive forms of exchange and interaction will dominate as long as the work group is present and/or involved in the interaction.

Social distances between the social actor and others are not the only factors influencing social exchange. Another important factor is the nature of change and habituation of action relative to a social actor. If a social actor engages in a strongly habituated behavior, it is unlikely to be changed or manipulated unless there is a significant change in the actor's work context. It is through change that habituation may be identified and acted on by a social actor, and this change may be initiated at quite distal sources, such as the organizational field or general context.

Summary

In this chapter, I have presented the general conceptual framework and model that will be used throughout this book. In addition, I have provided some definitional clarity for a number of concepts that I will explore throughout the book, including society, social system, and culture, using discussions from Rohner (1984), Jahoda (1980, 1984), and Martin (1992), among others.

The model that I present is a psychologically based analysis of how culture and society impact organizations and their functioning and how organizations and employees reciprocally influence one another. Societal context is operationalized through one of its most central aspects: culture. Further, culture is conceptualized in this framework as a complex pattern of divisible values and beliefs shared among a group of people, which can be depicted at the individual level (albeit with some conceptual and methodological difficulties). The impact of societal context on various aspects of the model is through a subtle, indirect influence often referred to as an embeddedness or loose coupling (Granovetter, 1985; Weick, 1985). By this it is meant that the influence of culture is not a direct one on employee behavior. However, as Erez and I argue (Erez & Earley, 1993) elsewhere, the individual is ultimately the conduit through which culture influences workplace activities and behavior. It is through the individual's processing of information and experiences that we capture the important influence of societal context on organizations.

Although I have presented my overview of the model from a "top-down" perspective, I now reverse this presentation in order to discuss the details and significance of each part of the framework. I begin my detailed discussion in the next chapter, which is on face. This chapter will contain the most complete discussion of the various elements of the model because face is the basic building block of the entire framework. It is the regulation and maintenance of face that drives all of the various aspects of the model that involve employee behavior within an organizational context. More important, it is the concept of face and its relative balance on lian versus mianzi that enables me to incorporate and predict the impact of various aspects of a culture on employee behavior. My emphasis, then, is not simply on discussing face as an emic construct with a multitude of unique manifestations that are not generalizable. My purpose is to describe the universal aspects of face and how its regulation is influenced by general cultural factors as well as organization-specific characteristics and functioning.

Notes

1. Throughout the book I will use the terms "international" and "intercultural" as well as "cross-national" and "cross-cultural" interchangeably. Some fields (e.g., communications, negotiation) have given these terms different meanings. In the case of the "inter" prefix, it is used to denote comparisons when two or more nations (cultures) meet and interact. The prefix "cross" denotes a comparison among two or more nations (cultures) in which each system is studied as an independent group.

Although this distinction makes some sense at a national level, it is difficult to use in a pure form in an individual-level analysis of culture, such as the one I pose in this book. For instance, within a given society there may be many overlapping subgroupings that make such a distinction problematic. For example, is a comparison of the relevance of participative management among Mexican-Americans versus Anglo-Americans in Southern California cross-cultural? Clearly, these two groups represent differentiated cultures (Martin, 1992), but they also interact with one another in a variety of contexts. If a Japanese company has dealt with American consumers, suppliers, and importers, is an examination of employees of this company intercultural and not cross-cultural? The intercultural distinction seems to make the most sense at the initial contact stage of two or more cultures, but it seems to me to be much less clear-cut at anything except the national level for early contact. Therefore, I will use the terms "intercultural" and "international" as the superordinate terms that include cross-cultural (and comparative national) comparisons.

I will concede, however, that if the specific example under examination is that of two non-overlapping distributions of individuals on some cultural characteristic(s), then the distinction makes more sense. However, this situation is unlikely given my operationalization of culture as beliefs and values of individuals. This implies that there are distributions within any society on particular cultural dimensions and that these distributions are likely to have substantial variability. If one is to concoct two groups of individuals who represent the polar extremes on a given cultural dimension, then this seems to capture more fully the essence of the intercultural distinction. In most organizations, however, it seems that this is a very unlikely state of affairs.

2. These dimensions are individualism, power distance, and masculinity versus femininity. I would note, however, that although many people attribute these dimensions to Hofstede, this is not completely accurate. Hofstede himself points out the historical origin of several of his dimensions. For example, the construct of individualism was first introduced to modern organizational theory by Parsons and Shils (1951). Power distance or differentials have long been the focus of international political theory and Marxism (Clegg, 1977). Hofstede's categorization scheme as a totality, however, is a unique contribution that has given rise to many organizational studies of national culture.

I would also note that my exclusion of Hofstede's uncertainty avoidance and Confucian dynamism dimensions is due to two primary reasons: first, these two dimensions are not as immediately applicable to an etic analysis of interpersonal process and face; and, second, they appear to be emic constructs and so they are inappropriate for my etic framework. However, it is important to note that the nature of Confucian relationships is captured in both the notion of face and the power differentials that exist in a society.

3. Kluckhohn and Strodtbeck (1961) use the word "man" instead of "person." I have updated the term with no substantive change of meaning.

3

Face and Social Context

Although a great deal of research and theory has been directed toward the understanding of social interaction, self-presentation, and related concepts, the nature of how people present themselves in a social dynamic is not well understood from a cultural perspective. A fundamental aspect of action is that we interact in a given social context for a variety of purposes, and a critical aspect of this interaction is the way we present ourselves and are judged in the presence of others. Self-worth, from the view of self and others, as well as the perceived image of others, is at the very heart of a concept of face (Goffman, 1959, 1967; Ho, 1994; Hu, 1944; Redding & Ng, 1982; Ting-Toomey & Cocroft, 1994). Face refers to a universal aspect of interaction concerning how we present ourselves as well as a basis for self-evaluation (Ho, 1994). Within an organizational framework, it is our face that regulates exchange and action, and face is responsive to both individual motives and needs as well as cultural variations in values and symbolic meanings.

I begin with an overview of the face concept using Eastern and Western perspectives. After this introduction, I provide a general framework for understanding face followed by a depiction of face regulation derived from Goffman's (1967) notion of facework, Brown and Levinson's (1978) model of politeness, and Ho's (1994) face dynamics.

Definition of Face

A commonly cited definition of face is "the positive social value a person effectively claims for himself by the line others assume he has taken during a particular contact. Face is an image of self delineated in terms of approved social attributes" (Goffman, 1967:5). A person's face has both internal and external components, which are often observable in social settings. The internal component refers to an inner voice or reflection, much like the invisible observer of Adam Smith's (1759/1976) moral sentiments, and the external component refers to an attributed aspect of a person's self-presentation. For example, an employee who steals company supplies answers to both his or her conscience and potential observers. From Goffman's perspective, a critical external aspect of face is the symbolic nature of a person's actions within a given social context. Thus an employee who steals may lose face in a company having high moral standards of conduct, but he or she may not lose face in a company in which such actions are ignored or reinforced by peers. Face, then, captures those aspects of self externally presented to one's peers and community as well as internal standards of actions as shaped by important referent others. In this sense, I define face as *the evaluation of self based on internal and external (to the individual) judgments concerning a person's adherence to moral rules of conduct and position within a given social structure.* This definition captures two general facets of self, namely, moral conduct and position in a social setting. Further, it posits that these facets are based on judgments of self and others in combination. Thus, face is not simply a product of self-perceptions, nor is it a result of external evaluators' perceptions alone.

The significance of face in a society is captured by Ho's (1976) description:

> Face is the respectability and/or deference which a person can claim for himself from others, by virtue of the relative position he occupies in his social network and the degree to which he is judged to have functioned adequately in that position as well as acceptably in his general conduct; the face extended to a person by others is a function of the degree of congruence between judgments of his total condition in life, including his actions as well as those of people closely associated with him, and the social expectations the others have placed upon him. (883)

This characterization of face is at the heart of the concept, namely, that face is not a unilaterally possessed attribute of an individual. "Face" refers to a form of exchange and type of interaction among two or more parties within a defined social context. In one of the first thorough discussions of the face concept, Lin (1939:199–200) in his book *My Country and My People* states:

> Face is psychological and not physiological. Interesting as the Chinese physiological face is, the psychological face makes a still more fascinating study. It is not a face that can be washed or shaved, but a face that can be "granted" and "lost" and "fought for" and "presented as a gift." . . . Abstract and intangible, it is yet the most delicate standard by which Chinese social intercourse is regulated. . . . Face cannot be translated or defined. It is like honor and is not honor. It cannot be purchased with money, and gives a man or a woman a material pride. It is hollow and yet is what men fight for and what many women die for. It is invisible and yet by definition exists by being shown to the public. It exists in the ether and yet cannot be heard, and sounds eminently respectable and solid. It is amenable, not to reason but to social convention. (quoted in Chang & Holt, 1994:99)

Yang (1945) discusses face similarly, arguing that it is not some physical manifestation of a person but that it represents the prestige and status a person has attained as well as the moral character of an individual (Chang & Holt, 1994). This is captured by Yang's argument that "when we say that a man wants a face, we mean that he wants to be given honor, prestige, praise, flattery, or concession, whether or not these are merited. Face is really a personal psychological satisfaction, a social esteem accorded by others" (1945:167). In a related vein, King (1989, cited in Chang & Holt, 1994) posits that face has both an external, social aspect as well as a moral element, "which impels a person to work hard and to achieve higher moral standards" (99).

Likewise, Lim (1994:210) suggests that face has three overriding characteristics: it is public and not private; it is a projected image and it may or may not be veridical with others' estimations; and it is those aspects of the self that are perceived by the self as being positive.

Lim's argument is that face is a public phenomenon not easily abstracted from a given social context. In other words, face is the image of oneself in the eyes of others, and so it is not sufficient for a person to consider his or her self-referents alone in evaluating face (e.g., "I am a famous person whom others respect") because these self-assessments may not be veridical or consistent with reality. Lim goes further, asserting that face is different from other constructs such as self-esteem or pride because face cannot be lost or changed through private acts. For example, if a person heroically stops a fire from starting in an abandoned building without any witnesses, his or her face has not been strengthened. For a number of reasons that I will turn to later, I disagree with Lim's position that face is purely a product of others' estimations and perceptions. To the contrary, I argue that at least the source of face, that having to do with an internal referent, is a personal characteristic drawn upon wherever a person may venture. This is the "scarlet letter," as well as "badge of courage," that must be worn and experienced through cultural attributes of shame and guilt (Mead, 1928). Nevertheless, a dominant view espoused by scholars is that face is thoroughly understood only in a social context, a position to which I ascribe as well.

In a related vein, many of the Western conceptualizations of face rely on the role of social interaction as a defining criterion for face. As Goffman (1959:1–2) asserts, "The person's face is clearly something that is not lodged in or on his body, but rather something that is diffusely located in the flow of events." Brown and Levinson (1978), in their classic model of politeness, argue that face is a product of social etiquette in a given situation. Further, Penman (1994) posits face to be an active aspect of social interaction in the courtroom context with her model of legal action. Again, face and facework are posited as emerging from the interactions of multiple, interacting parties.

To Asian scholars addressing this issue, the separation of person from context and hence the detachment of face from person is mixed. In Hu's classic work (1944), a major characteristic of face, lian (discussed further in Chapter 5), involves a person's endorsement and enactment of the rules of moral conduct guiding individuals' actions in a society.[1] As I will argue subsequently, this aspect of face is regulated by the values and norms of one's culture and is, at times, a person's personal property or characteristic. This point is reaffirmed by Ho (1976:874), who states that "face is attached to persons" and not just a characteristic of office held, position, lineage, et cetera.

An additional dimension of face, mianzi (see Chapter 5), operates in a predominantly "public" fashion. Mianzi is not solely a personality characteristic or personal attribute according to Ho's (1994) recent work—it is a product of a social context. In a general sense, mianzi reflects that aspect of face primarily derived from the social perceptions of others. Chang and Holt (1994) further assert the interdependence of mianzi[2] and social relations when they state:

A full understanding of *mien-tzu* as a specifically Chinese cultural concept necessitates considering the complex connections among relations *(kuan-hsi),* human emotion *(ren-ching),* and face *(mien-tzu).* If the interactants' *mien-tzu* is not properly taken care of, the relationship may be damaged even if there is no conflict over substantive issues. One might conclude that, given the importance of *mien-tzu* for the Chinese, showing respect for each other's *mien-tzu* in any interactional situation constitutes, in itself, a "substantive" issue. On the other hand, *mien-tzu* also contributes to effective interpersonal relating, given the fact that it encompasses both emotional and pragmatic elements. One may have sincere emotional concern for the other, and consequently show respect for the other's *mien-tzu;* conversely, respect for another's *mien-tzu,* as one part of the interactants' relational responsibilities, can be utilized to help one to function within Chinese society. One sees the mutual permeation of the emotional and the utilitarian in personal, business, and political interactions, all conducted under the name of *mien-tzu.* (123)

The second point raised by Lim is whether face is a projected versus actual image held by others. He argues that an important aspect of face is what others are willing to say about you rather than what they may believe. Essentially, a person's face is based on what others are willing to verbalize and act upon. Although it is clear that individuals must rely on the actions of their colleagues, underlying beliefs and opinions held by these colleagues are also important and may eventually "spill out." Likewise, a position put forth by Chang and Holt (1994) argues that face, mianzi, is best captured by the social relationships among interacting parties, including their ties and statuses. It is not sufficient, then, to talk about pretending that someone has face because that face may be derived solely from the legitimated authority structure in which the parties are embedded. For example, a supervisor who has legitimate authority and power has a degree of mianzi vis-à-vis his or her subordinates. If, however, this supervisor is perceived to be professionally incompetent (perhaps having achieved the position through contacts or job tenure), his or her mianzi is weak relative to that of another person in a similar position who is perceived as competent. People's expectations concerning an individual's competence will indirectly impact their subsequent performance (e.g., see Eden, 1984, and the Pygmalion effect) and hence their mianzi.

Finally, Lim suggests that face is focused on the positive social values representing the self. That is to say, a person's face represents those positive and desirable aspects of actions and self rather than the negative ones. This is consistent with a large body of work referencing self-concept, including Erez and Earley (1993), Markus and Kitayama (1991), and Triandis (1989b), among others, and of course Goffman's original definition of face. As Lim correctly points out, however, there are a multitude of values that might be considered "positive" depending on the cultural system in question. For example, in U.S. business, a general bluntness in communication is sometimes seen as lacking tact and sensitivity. Although American businesspeople are known for being "direct" and "to the point," there is a general level of politeness described in doing business with Americans (Harris & Moran, 1986). In contrast, Katriel (1986) discusses the Israeli Sabra community, in which a frank discussion of ideas is favored. In such a community, the use of *dugri* speech, or speaking to the point, is viewed as a positive and face-affirming aspect of social discourse (Erez & Earley, 1993; Ting-Toomey & Cocroft, 1994:313). Having worked with an Israeli colleague for many years, I can echo that many Israelis see a blunt form of feedback as highly desirable, and they are somewhat baffled by Americans' desire to carefully "couch" criticism in lengthy rhetoric of praise.

However, face is not solely determined by a person's self-perceptions or impression management tactics. As a result, the correspondence of the image projected by a person to others' perceptions may be quite disjointed (Michael Bond, personal conversation). That is to say, the veridicality of self and other perceptions may be quite low at times, and so face must be considered as a product of both self and other referent perceptions and attributions.

Thus a general overview of face suggests that it has several defining characteristics. First, it generally represents the evaluated aspects of self, as defined by society and internalized by an individual, self perceived and projected toward others. Second, it has both internal and external bases. Thus it does not merely reflect the positive aspects of a person. Face captures the positive and negative aspects of self with the assumption that a person's self-perceptions are dominated by positive characteristics that may only correspond weakly with others' perceptions of characteristics. Third, face represents rules of moral conduct and righteousness as well as status or position in a social structure. I now turn to the Eastern and Western origins of the face concept.

Eastern Origins of Face

Seminal work on face, from an Asian perspective, is presented in a paper by Hu (1944) titled "The Chinese Concepts of 'Face.' " In this paper, Hu distinguished between the two general forms of face, lian and mianzi. Briefly, Hu argued that a Chinese context provides for two forms of face, one concerned with moral character (lian) and one concerned with reputation and status (mianzi) through "getting on in life" (45). Both forms of face have numerous variations, which Hu discussed, such as individuals having no character ("bu yao lian," or not wanting lian) or giving others face ("gei mianzi"). Lian represents the relationship of a person's actions and character to the confidence of society in the person's integrity and moral character; the loss of lian represents a loss of societal confidence in a person's ability to function within the community. According to Hu, lian refers to both a social sanction for the enforcement of moral standards within the community as well as an internalized representation of such sanctions. An important point is that lian has both an internal and external aspect, with the determinants for both being the values that are dominant in society and, as I will argue shortly, the values that are universal or etic.

Mianzi refers to the prestige or status that is held by individuals by virtue of their actions, networks, position, et cetera. Hu uses the interesting example of the extreme desire to maintain mianzi in describing this construct:

> One day a Manchu visited a tea-house. He was hungry, but had only just enough money to buy one small piece of pastry covered with sesame-seeds. As his grumbling stomach could not be pacified by such a small piece, he looked longingly at the seeds dropped on the table. He desired very much to pick them up, but feared to lose prestige in front of all the people. A bright idea hit him: using his finger as a brush and saliva as ink he wrote on the table, thus picking up the seeds and conveying them to his mouth. Some seeds had

fallen into a crack and he had to use ingenuity to get at those. So he pretended to become angry and banged his fist on the table, jerking the seeds out of the crack. Then he started writing again and picked up the seeds. This story is told to ridicule the exaggerated desire for *mien-tzu* among Manchus, a weakness they share with poor aristocrats in many parts of the world. (58)

This story illustrates the nature of mianzi as an external endorsement of one's position and stature within a social system. There are overlaps between mianzi and lian according to Hu as well. For instance, someone who becomes obsessed with mianzi ("yao mianzi" or to want face) may be viewed as unconcerned with lian. Such a person is thought to be pretentious and desirous of living beyond his or her station in life at the sacrifice of character. Another traditional view of face includes Lin's discussion of face as a critical aspect of Chinese social interaction (1935).

More recently, Ho (1976) has followed the Hu tradition by providing a discussion of lian and mianzi in relation to other aspects of self-concept, such as standards for behavior, personality variables, honor, dignity, and prestige. He argues that face needs to be distinguished from many other constructs. For example, he states that face is not a standard of behavior; rather, it is gained or lost based on assessments of an individual vis-à-vis standards of behavior. Likewise, face is not a personality variable because it arises in the context of social evaluation and not private evaluation. Although I would agree with Ho's point that face is not simply a personality characteristic, I would contend that it is not merely a social evaluation. This is particularly true for the concept of lian, which is, as I argue later, largely determined by the cultural themes internalized by an individual. If one's conscience is categorized as a social evaluation (given impetus and direction through society's teachings), then it is reasonable to say that lian is, in part, a product of an internal evaluation. An employee who is given an opportunity to steal from his or her company may not do so (we hope!) even if there are no external observers to witness the event. In such a case, we say that the employee's conscience was his or her "guide"; clearly, this employee is choosing whether or not to engage in a given action based on what referent others might think as well as avoiding the internal conflict arising when such actions conflict with a person's sense of self (Erez & Earley, 1993). Ho also argues that face is not equivalent to status, dignity, or honor. He poses that status defines a person's position in a social system quite independent of the occupant's personal characteristic. This assertion is somewhat at odds with his assertion that Stover's (1962) position is correct, namely, that face is reflective of one's position in a social system and not a personal attribute. This would make status and mianzi very difficult to disentangle. Probably a more useful position is that face encompasses specific characteristics such as status, dignity, and honor, as well as a variety of other constructs reflective of functioning within a given social system. Finally, Ho separates the concept of prestige from face, arguing that prestige is somewhat more of a characteristic of the individual rather than the individual's social role enacted and hence more similar to a personality characteristic than is face.

Hwang (1987) provides a discussion of face, renqing (favors and emotion), and guanxi (social obligations and relationships) in proposing a model of social ties (relationships) and social tactics. He argues that face and its maintenance will differentially influence the type of tie used by a person (e.g., expressive versus instrumental versus mixed) and, therefore, the exchange practices among interacting parties. His focus is on the importance of face in maintaining status and position. In his model, he is most concerned with the nature of facework as a technique for impression management. Drawing heavily from Goffman's dramaturgical theory, Hwang argues that one's mianzi determines the position occupied as well as the privileges experienced. Thus a great deal of emphasis is placed on the cultivating and safeguarding of mianzi.

Some empirical research on the nature of face has been conducted by Bond and his colleagues (e.g., Bond & Lee, 1981; Bond, Leung, & Wan, 1982; Bond & Venus, 1991). In a study of face-related behaviors, Bond and Lee (1981) reported that their Chinese participants were empathetic to people (fellow students) who had conducted themselves inadequately in a mock presentation, and the participants attempted to help these speakers to retain face. In a more recent study, Bond and Venus (1991) examined the impact of personal and in-group insults to the reactions of experiment participants. Among other findings, they discovered that participants who were insulted publicly were less likely to attempt some form (direct or indirect) of rebuttal or retaliation than participants who were insulted privately. Bond and Venus conclude that this may be, in part, attributable to the Chinese tendency to avoid conflict in order to regulate face. Interestingly, their data suggest a main effect for personal versus in-group insult such that rebuttal and retaliation were greater for an in-group insult than for a personal insult. As Bond and Lee comment, this finding is consistent with an explanation that might be derived from the cultural dimension of individualism versus collectivism.

In one of the empirical assessments of face in an organizational context, Redding and Ng (1982) surveyed 102 Chinese middle-level executives in commercial, trading, and engineering companies in Hong Kong. In addition, they interviewed 73 executives and asked them to relate an incident involving face from their personal experience, yielding a total of 91 separate incidents. These interviews were content-analyzed, and the survey data were analyzed. They found that 100 percent of their sample reported that face-related behaviors were a very important aspect of doing business in Hong Kong, and 97 percent of their respondents stated that not having face inhibited business-related activities. The researchers also found that not only was the positive inducement of face important (e.g., respect for recipient's achievements and accomplishments), but people avoided conflict when possible. This is consistent with the view that face is socially based; to avoid conflict suggests maintaining face. As an example, Hu (1944) describes an elderly gentleman who intervened in an argument between two young men. The older man asked them to cease their conflict on behalf of his mianzi ("kan wode mianzi," or "look at my mianzi"). Conflict is seen as a failure of reason, and it only yields a winner who is strong and not necessarily right. Face is used to ensure that a social system does not break down as a result of the argument or quarrel.

Ting-Toomey (1988) presents a general model of communication and negotiation in which face is seen as a core element. Her model borrows from the dual concerns approach to negotiation and conflict management in that she overlays a notion of positive and negative face (derived from Brown & Levinson, 1978) onto a concern for self-face versus a concern for other-face. (This latter dimension is derived from Pruitt's dual concerns model of conflict management, which separates these two dimensions in conceptualizing conflict management handling strategies.) Her model entails a contrasting of positive versus negative face with self-face versus other-face concerns. In addition, she contrasts her two-by-two design with two cultural values, individualism/collectivism and high/low context cultures, in order to make a series of predictions concerning face and conflict management/negotiation styles. According to her model, collectivists are very concerned with the preservation of harmony and maintaining positive self-evaluations. If an in-group member is threatened, the response to such a threat is not due to an individual face response; rather, it is due to the desire to avoid conflict within the in-group context.

In a recent collection of papers edited by Ting-Toomey (1994), a number of Asian scholars have posed models concerning face and its regulation. In one paper, Ho updates his earlier work concerning face and facework (the regulation of face). Although most of his work is similar to his earlier work, there is a new emphasis on the dynamic aspect of face and its regulation. To this end, Ho introduces the idea of "face dynamics" in order to capture the idea that face is a socially derived and dynamic characteristic. In another paper Lim introduces a tripartite scheme for face, including autonomy-face, or a person's image that is under direct, volitional control; fellowship-face, or an image that a person is a worthy group member; and competence-face, or the image derived from personal ability. He argues that these categories of face are universal motives for people and that each has a corresponding form of facework associated with it. For example, fellowship-face is supported by a solidarity form of facework. By solidarity, Lim suggests that face is regulated to the extent that one accepts others as part of the in-group. This means that actions that create or enhance membership in an in-group are a solidarity strategy (e.g., using jargon to create a barrier between in-group and out-group).

Although these papers update the concept of face and its regulation through facework, there seems to be a marked shift away from the concept of lian toward that of mianzi. Although some authors argue that the two terms are heavily overlapping (e.g., Chang & Holt, 1994; Ho, 1994; King, 1989), there seems to be a strong emphasis on mianzi and an ignoring of lian. We can only speculate why this shift has occurred. It may reflect a preference that several Asian scholars have posited in their writings (e.g., Ho, 1976) toward contextualizing the concept of face in a social system. In fact, Ho (1976:882) chastises Western scholars, stating: "Now the Western mentality, deeply ingrained with the values of individualism, is not one which is favorably disposed to the idea of face. For face is never a purely individual thing. It does not make sense to speak of the face of an individual as something lodged within his person; it is meaningful only when his face is considered in relation to that of others in the social network." Perhaps another reason is that individual-based disciplines such as psychology have underemphasized face because of its social component. Regardless, there seems to be a marked shift from conceptualizing face as a moral and individual construct to seeing it as a contextually derived evaluation of self by others.

Western Origins of Face

In the West, the greatest attention to social exchange relevant to face and self-presentation is evidenced in the work of Erving Goffman (1959, 1967). As Goffman (1959:5) wrote,

> Every person lives in a world of social encounters, involving him either in face-to-face or mediated contact with other participants. In each of these contacts, he tends to act out what is sometimes called a line—that is, a pattern of verbal and nonverbal acts by which he expresses his view of the situation and through this his evaluation of the participants, especially himself. Regardless of whether a person intends to take a line, he will find that he has done so in effect. The other participants will assume that he has more or less willfully taken a stand, so that if he is to deal with their response to him he must take into consideration the impression they have possibly formed of him.
>
> The term face may be defined as the positive social value a person effectively claims for himself. . . . Face is an image of self delineated in terms of approved social attributes—albeit an image that others may share. (5)

To Goffman, face is both a characteristic of the person and a characteristic derived from the social system. Although many authors cite Goffman's assertion that face is "something that is not lodged in or on his body, but rather something that is diffusely located in the flow of events in the encounter and becomes manifest only when these events are read and interpreted for the appraisals expressed in them" (7), he also points out that "although his social face can be his most personal possession and the center of his security and pleasure, it is only on loan to him from society; it will be withdrawn unless he conducts himself in a way that is worthy of it. Approved attributes and their relation to face make of every man his own jailer" (10). Thus the concept of face is both a socially derived evaluation and an individual possession.

A key concept in Goffman's early work was the idea of "line," or the pattern of verbal and nonverbal actions engaged in by a person. Face is the resulting evaluation of a person by others dependent on the line he or she has chosen. If a person's line is consistent with his or her internal image of self, then that person is said to have or be able to maintain face. Goffman's model focuses on the regulation of face through social interactions. He suggests that there are two primary ways to regulate face or conduct facework, namely, avoidance and corrective. Avoidance facework refers to a class of actions such as directly avoiding contact with another person, verbally avoiding "sensitive" topics or ones that might be inconsistent with the line he or she has chosen, avoiding providing potentially embarrassing comments, providing the recognition merited by another person's status, tactful blindness or ignoring of potential faux pas, or trying to cover up a slip in line (e.g., a strong male figure who claims that the tear in his eye is due to an irritating eyelash rather than a tender moment during a movie).

Corrective facework refers to a class of actions used after a threat to face has occurred. Goffman referred to the sequence of face threat to facework to equilibrium reestablished as "interchange." The purpose of corrective facework was to help the social unit maintain equilibrium through the process of interchange. For example, if I notice that someone else's stomach is growling and comment on it, this may make the person feel self-conscious or embarrassed. At this point, our social unit is in a disequilibrium state. I might attempt to correct this situation by commenting, "I know how you feel; I skipped breakfast this morning and my stomach is churning." This would be a self-initiated challenge to the original offense. Alternatively, the offended party might choose to challenge me by pointing out my lack of discretion or his or her embarrassment. My action does not, however, ensure that equilibrium will be restored since my interacting partner may choose to ignore this "peace offering" or choose to escalate the disequilibrium by attacking my position (e.g., "I was always told that noticing someone's stomach growling is rude and boorish"). A critical aspect of Goffman's corrective process is that the attempt to regain equilibrium may be instigated by any party (including the party whose face was threatened), and the movement back toward equilibrium depends on various participants' reactions. Finally, if the offer is accepted by the offended party, then it is anticipated that the offer is reciprocated with a symbolic thank-you. Thus the general form of Goffman's corrective process is: challenge to offering to acceptance to thanks.

Facework may be used in an aggressive fashion as well. Goffman points to a number of strategies through which individuals can influence others. For example, a colleague of mine seems to have no pretense of social skills, and he readily offends people. He is able to do so because the norm for social interaction in my organization and culture dictates a benevolent overlooking of such social atrocities. He is able to use his boorish manner in order to offend without retaliation. In addition, a person may use personal modesty as a means of leveraging compliments from others, thereby enhancing face, or might even maneuver others to insult him or her in order to utilize their guilt as a means of subsequent control.

With the risk of oversimplifying Goffman's (1974) more recent theorizing, his basic metaphor is that of the actor in the theater of life. As a daily drama unfolds, Goffman argued, people participate in social interactions or performances, relying on self-presentation and impression manipulation in order to regulate their self-image. In his dramaturgical theory, he classified social behavior into two categories—front-stage and back-stage (Goffman, 1967, 1974). Front-stage behavior is those aspects of self that others view, and back-stage behavior is inner and intimate aspects of self that are private and ego-threatening.

A number of points derived from Goffman's analysis are important for my thesis. First, the dynamic aspects of face, face threats and facework, are crucial in understanding the concept of harmony that I will discuss in more detail in a subsequent chapter. As Ho (1994) emphasizes with his invention of the term "face dynamics," it is best to think about face using a dynamic rather than static model. Through various actions, people constantly change their face, as well as the face of others, by accident or on purpose. For example, if I ask a job candidate about some aspect of his or her research paper, not only a factual component but also a strong face component is involved. I may inadvertently challenge the applicant's face if he or she is unable to field my question. Similar to Penman's (1994) analysis of courtroom behavior, many aspects of inquiry are not directly related to the acquisition of factual knowledge. Although Goffman's analogy of the stage is useful in understanding those aspects of self that are revealed to others, Penman's utilization of the courtroom may be the missing and complementary metaphor concerning an external agent's approach to the self. Much of what we say and do with regard to others involves such posturing. In fact, quite a bit of it involves posturing vis-à-vis the other person. People interact for purposes of determining and reaffirming others' status, and, thereby, their own. Thus if I ask a job candidate about a particular topic, I am not only obtaining factual information but also finding out about his or her personal status as a researcher and the corresponding face, as well as reasserting to my colleagues that I am a prominent and noteworthy researcher myself. Is it any wonder that the "butterflies" experienced when a question is asked during a job interview may be nearly as severe for the inquisitor as they are for the recipient?

A second important point of Goffman's analysis is that facework operates according to the type and circumstances of the infraction. Pointing out a minor indiscretion such as having mustard on one's mustache is more easily handled than an accusation of plagiarism. As I will point out in the final section of this chapter, indiscretions concerning lian are of a more serious and potentially irreparable nature than those involving mianzi—particularly in cultures for which lian is central. I would suggest, then, that an important distinguishing feature concerning the process of facework is the nature of the infraction relative to the culture in which the infraction occurs.

Finally, Goffman places a great deal of emphasis in his later work on the role of face in reasserting position within a given social system. I think that this point is very important to an understanding of why face may seem to be more critical in some cultures than in others. It is particularly related to those cultures in which relative position is highly differentiated. In more egalitarian cultures, I would anticipate relatively less emphasis on face, at least in terms of mianzi. So, for example, although face seems integral to members of many Asian cultures, it seems to be less critical to members of more egalitarian cultures. An important modification of this point is that the specific type of face emphasized, lian or mianzi, differs as well as a general emphasis on face. Although Swedish managers may be very concerned with the moral character of their employees, Chinese managers may emphasize the material aspects of work in their company. However, I would again emphasize that I am talking about relative trade-offs and not dichotomous choices. A person merely has to travel the streets of Stockholm to see that brand names and materialism have taken hold to a certain degree in Sweden, a country whose culture generally emphasizes lian.

In their work on politeness and social discourse, Brown and Levinson (1978) utilize Goffman's approach to face. Their purpose was to develop a general model for understanding the nature of face-to-face communication through the use of a simple model of interaction. Their approach begins with the assumption of an individual who is the speaker of a given language and who is rational and has face. In terms of face, their "model person (MP)" has two basic desires: first, MP wants his or her actions to be unimpeded; and, second, MP wants his or her goals to be desirable from others' views. The researchers view face as the public self-image a person wishes to claim for him- or herself. These two aspects of face, negative (e.g., basic claim to territories and preserves reflecting a desire to act unimpeded by others) and positive (e.g., consistent self-images maintained in order to be socially desirable to others), operate rationally in predicting actions and behavior. They involve a number of face-threatening acts (FTAs), including pressuring someone to act in a certain fashion and reminders, threats, or dares (negative face), as well as expression of disapproval or criticism of others, disagreements or challenges, and out-of-control behavior (positive face). With regard to politeness, Brown and Levinson argue that people minimize their engagement in FTAs with "redressive action" (i.e., they attempt to counteract the potential face damage of the FTA by doing it in such a way as to provide an "out") if they must commit an FTA.

A large literature on the topic of impression management (e.g., Jones, 1964; Jones & Pittman, 1980; Richardson & Cialdini, 1981; Tedeschi, 1981; Tedeschi & Riess, 1981) has emerged in the West that is related to face. Although the emphasis of this literature is generally on mianzi and not lian (particularly given that impression management refers to an active manipulation in order to shape others' view of oneself), it is useful to note that many of the strategies and tactics used in managing impressions have application to face and facework. For instance, Tedeschi and Riess (1981) discuss several reasons why people engage in impression management, such as social role-playing in symbolic interaction, avoiding blame and gaining credit, maintaining self-esteem, controlling power and social influence, and creating a connotative impression (e.g., evaluation and potency) for instrumental value. Throughout this literature, impression management and self-presentation are discussed as ways for a person to maintain and manipulate a positive self-image power similar to the outcome of acquiring mianzi.

Another topic in which face plays an important role is that of negotiation and conflict management. Numerous authors discuss the relevance of self-presentation and face as elements of the negotiation process (e.g., Neale & Bazerman, 1991; Pye, 1982; Ting-Toomey, 1988). Although this literature is too voluminous to review thoroughly here, I will discuss a few of the examples of Western research concerning face in a negotiation and/or conflict management context. The first example is the model proposed by Ting-Toomey (1988), in which conflict management is viewed from the perspective of self-face versus other-face crossed with positive face and negative face. Although one of the initial empirical tests of Ting-Toomey's model (Ting-Toomey et al., 1991) was conducted using mainly Asian samples, I include this framework in the "Western" section because it is based largely on three Western models (Goffman's facework, Brown and Levinson's politeness model, and Pruitt's dual concerns model). Their primary findings were that individualism-collectivism was related to the face dimension of concern for self-face versus concern for other-face and that particular aspects of self-face versus other-face were differentially related to conflict management styles used in their samples.

In a different stream of work, Tjosvold and his colleagues (e.g., Tjosvold, 1973, 1983; Tjosvold & Huston, 1978) conducted a series of studies using a framework proposed by Deutsch called social face theory (Deutsch, 1961, 1973). Deutsch's approach was derived from the Goffman framework and emphasizes that people will act in order to project a positive image in a variety of social settings. It differs from impression management, which is focused on the active manipulation of self in accordance with what perceived others consider valuable rather than internal views of self (Tjosvold, 1983). Tjosvold suggests that people act on face in order to disconfirm views suggesting that they are weak or incompetent through a variety of strategies, including aggression toward the accuser, threats, control strategies, and claims of superiority. In this literature, individuals have been found to pursue strategies that reverse a disconfirmation (threat to face or negotiator competency) even if such strategies result in reduced payoffs. In fact, such threats to face often result in intransigence such that the offended party will refuse further bargaining (Tjosvold, 1974).

Another interesting finding from this literature concerns the role of "conditional climates," or the social setting, in which actions occur. Although Brown and Garland (1976) found that friends were more concerned with face than were strangers,

Blanchard, Weigel, and Cook (1975) showed that people were less concerned with face in cooperative relationships than in competitive relationships. These two findings suggest that an important consideration in understanding the relevance of face to social relationships is the maturity of the relationship. If one extrapolates from these two studies, it appears that there is some curvilinear relationship of face concerns to relationship such that concern for face is at some moderate level in the relationship. If the relationship is new or very well established (presumably highly cooperative), then concerns over face are somewhat attenuated. If, however, the relationship is forming but not fully developed, face becomes of greater concern. A significant cultural effect may be operating as well. For example, I argue in Chapter 8 that particular dimensions of culture may operate to moderate the relevance of the two forms of face. For example, in a collectivistic culture, concerns for lian may weigh heavily in the balance because people are long-term members of a limited number of collectives. More simply, in-group members from a collectivistic culture do not choose one another—that is to say, they are often born into or assigned such memberships based on societal guidance, and they remain members of the in-group on a relatively long-term basis. For example, up until recently workers in mainland China were assigned to their work units *(danwei)* by the Communist Party. These employees had little opportunity to leave their companies or work units. In such a situation, trust in the character of in-group members is crucial because whom you associate with is fixed. Thus lian becomes critical to the well-being of the in-group. The findings described by Brown and Garland (1976) and Blanchard et al. (1975) reflect an individualistic perspective such that mianzi is important in a loosely coupled in-group because it signals who has significant power and status.

A related topic is that of feedback-seeking behavior developed by Ashford and her colleagues (e.g., Ashford & Cummings, 1983; Ashford & Tsui, 1991). According to this view, people are information receivers in an environment capable of providing a variety of information from various sources (Greller & Herold, 1975). Further, people's use of performance cues is active, not passive (e.g., Ashford & Cummings, 1983; Ashford & Tsui, 1991). People seek out information, consciously and unconsciously, about their actions in order to structure and interpret their worlds, and information that helps to maintain one's self-concept receives central attention.

Triandis (1995) offers a "sampling-probability" explanation of culture and behavior. According to this theory, individuals' cultural backgrounds guide the type of information they attend to and the frequency with which it is sampled. Triandis argues further that individualists and collectivists look to or sample from three types of selves (public, private, collective) with different propensities. The public self is a generalized "other" person such as a prototypical stranger, the private self is oneself, and the collective self is one's in-group. The "self" a person samples from most heavily will be influenced by cultural values, but these values are not limited to individualism-collectivism and include many other factors such as face.

Much of the work on feedback seeking reflects the assumptions offered by Goffman that people desire to put forth (front-stage) a positive self-image for others to view and engage one another in order to maintain or bolster this image. Much of what accounts for people's actions is derived from this desire to convey a positive self-image, although feedback-seeking research does not provide a great deal of detail concerning regulatory mechanisms underlying tarnished images or the potential connection of images related to interdependent groups of employees.

A final area that I address is that of embarrassment. Research in this area has been conducted by Edelmann and his colleagues (Edelmann, 1990; Edelmann & Hampson, 1979) as well as Schlenkar (1980, 1982). Edelmann classifies face-saving techniques into five general categories: apologies, accounts (e.g., excuses), avoidance (e.g., escape), humor (e.g., laughter), and aggression. In a review of international studies concerning embarrassment, Edelmann found that the majority of his respondents reported using a "no verbal response" way of dealing with embarrassment. (However, this study presents a difficulty inasmuch as the majority of the respondents did not specify any response whatsoever, which suggests that there may have been some reporting error biasing the results of the survey.) Although this study suggests that the styles used by people for verbally dealing with embarrassment do not vary substantially across countries, more research is clearly needed on this topic.

Toward a Conceptualization of Face

So what, then, constitutes face? As I stated earlier in this chapter, my use of face consists of two general parts. First, there is a distinction between face tied to rules of conduct versus face as a position in a social hierarchy. Second, there is a distinction between the source of these perceptions, namely, internal versus external reference. In addition, there is a distinction among qualitatively different forms of face.

I present a two-way categorization of face in Figure 3-1, and I provide some examples in Table 3-1. According to this typology, two dimensions and two referent

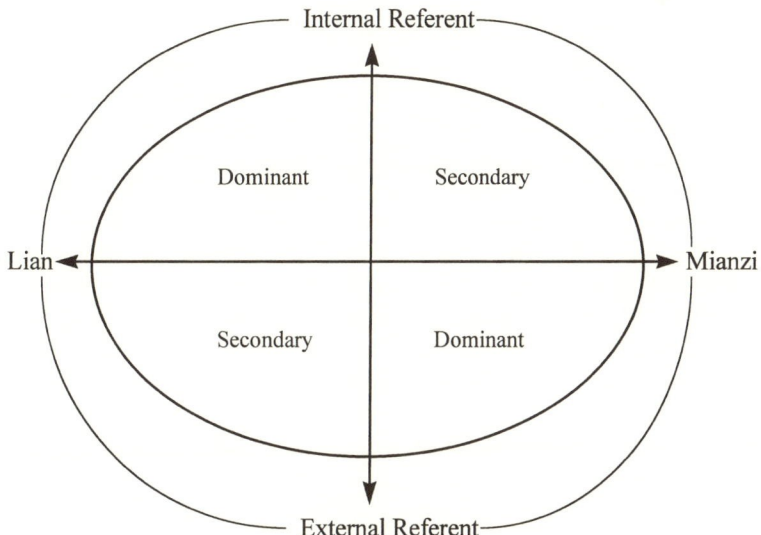

Figure 3-1. An Overview of Face

Table 3-1. Taxonomy and Examples of Face in Organizations

Source of Face	Lian	Mianzi
Internally enacted	Self-evaluation based on adherence to moral standard of behavior internally referenced. Example: feeling of personal guilt because of a failure such as inability to achieve a self-set work goal.	Personal view of one's accomplishments. Example: personal status for working at a major research university.
Externally enacted	Social evaluation of the morality/ goodness of a person's actions. Example: recognition of a person's integrity and honor for engaging in extra-role work behavior.	Social recognition of a person's position vis-à-vis other social actors. Example: recognition of a person's position in a company based on office location, expense account, parking space, et cetera.

sources of face can be combined to form four general groups of face characteristics. The first dimension involves the type of face under discussion, namely, lian versus mianzi. (In Chapters 4 and 5, I discuss each of these forms of face in further detail.) The basic logic of this distinction stems from the linguistic guidance provided by Hu (1944), among others, but my use of these constructs differs from the existing literature. Whereas the existing discussions of lian and mianzi treat the constructs as either an internal/external judgment of self (e.g., Hu, 1944) or overlapping versions of self as derived from a social interaction (e.g., Ho, 1994), I define lian as a set of rules for moral conduct and mianzi as a person's position within a social structure. In this general sense, lian reflects the enactment of "correct" behavior (and values/beliefs/ norms underlying those behaviors), whereas mianzi reflects an outcome state of social interaction.

Briefly, lian is a person's adherence to moral or evaluative rules of conduct based on universal, societal, organization, and community standards for accepted behavior. Lian reflects a legitimization of an individual within a given society. A person lacking regard for lian is viewed as a sociopath or outsider. For example, killing is a universal violation of ethical principles, with the only systematic exceptions due to events such as wars or classifications of "other groups" as nonhuman (e.g., Nazi German views of Jews). (Even in these extreme cases, such actions are often deemed as unethical and immoral by external referents or even the cultures themselves after the fact.) In an organizational context, lian refers to the adherence and maintenance of work norms and principles that are endorsed by an organization as desirable, such as voluntarily working late, helping new employees with their work, et cetera. The general topic of organizational citizenship behavior pioneered by Organ and his colleagues (e.g., Organ, 1987) and addressed more recently by Farh, Dobbins, and Cheng (1991) and Farh, Earley, and Lin (in press) from a cross-cultural perspective suggests that several etic dimensions of citizenship behavior are engaged in by employees. For instance, conscientiousness (e.g., discretionary behaviors on the part of an employee that go well beyond the minimum role requirements of the organization in the areas of attendance, obeying rules and regulations, taking breaks, working hard, and so forth) and altruism (e.g., discretionary behavior that has the effect of helping others around him or her [mostly peers, clients, supervisors] with an organizationally relevant task or problem) are etically endorsed aspects of work performance that reflect a person's lian or adherence to moral conduct.

Mianzi is a characteristic of a person that reflects his or her standing in a social hierarchy, such as position, status, role, et cetera. A CEO of a large multinational corporation (MNC) has much mianzi, whereas an administrative clerk has relatively little. Likewise, an employee who is relied on by others as the "local expert" for computer networking information has mianzi attributable to his or her knowledge. Power and mianzi, however, should not be confused. Whereas power is the capacity to influence the actions of others (Pfeffer, 1992), mianzi involves the evaluations of a person's position in a hierarchy relative to others. Is it possible to have mianzi but not power? It might be argued that this is the dilemma faced in Britain with the monarchy. Prince Charles has mianzi (although recent scandals might challenge this assertion) as a monarch, but he has little formal authority and power. Such assertions have been made about the U.S. vice presidency as well, namely, that it is a status position having little real power. These are, however, exceptions, and people who have a great deal of mianzi typically have social power. Mianzi is derived from a number of different characteristics, as I will describe in Chapter 4.

The second dimension concerning face involves the locus from which it is derived. Face is derived from both internal and external (to the person) sources. That is to say, face reflects an interaction of self and others' perceptions and attributions. There are at least two useful ways to address the nature of person perception as it relates to face. First, the content of person perception can be discussed from a cross-cultural viewpoint. What characteristic(s) appear to be used by people as a basis for their personal and other social perceptions? Just as some researchers have sought to define the general nature of values and beliefs that underlie societal culture (e.g., Kluckhohn & Strodtbeck, 1961), others have focused on the constituent elements of person schema and perception (e.g., Bond & Forgas, 1984). Second, the source of these perceptions constitutes an additional element of social perception of face. I employ a basic dichotomy in characterizing the referent source, namely, internal versus external sources. However, it is useful to further delineate the external category into additional subcategories.

The linkage of a person's social context and culture to person perception is not well understood by scholars (Bond & Forgas, 1984; Smith & Bond, 1996). The importance of this connection to face is that it represents the link of context to face inasmuch as face reflects self and other perceptions. Although the research on person perception is at a developmental stage in the literature from a content perspective (Bond, 1996, personal communication), a potential connection can be made through an examination of the personality traits underlying person perception. In other words, if we understand the mapping of fundamental personality traits onto judgments concerning face, it becomes possible to understand the potential relationship of cultural context on face as well. In one of the first studies of its type, Bond and Forgas (1984) examined the nature of personality traits (the so-called "Big Five" traits, namely, introversion/extroversion, emotional stability, conscientiousness, openness, and agreeableness, identified by McCrae and Costa [1987]) in understanding social perception for samples of Australians and Hong Kong Chinese. They found that the general structure of these traits held up across the cultural boundaries but that there was significant variation in relative importance of particular dimensions related to the cultural variation observed in their samples. In other words, they provided some of the earliest evidence for the etic nature of the Big Five while demonstrating relative importance variation substantively related to cultural orientation. In subsequent work, Smith and Bond (1994) argue that the relationship of personality traits used in social perception to cultural values can be illustrated using Hofstede's classification scheme. For example, they suggest that masculine cultures are associated with the personality traits of conscientiousness and low agreeableness. Individualism is associated with extroversion, as might be expected, and Confucian dynamism is associated with emotional stability, according to their thinking.

The reasoning presented in Bond's work with Forgas and Smith points to a very important linkage of cultural context to personality traits. Implicit in their arguments is that certain cultural contexts can be characterized by certain cultural value orientations. These contexts give rise to particular institutions, lifestyle patterns, environmental settings, et cetera, and these entities influence cultural members' personality structures. If this trickle-down linkage holds true, what then might it imply about face? The key question is whether it is possible to map the general types of face, lian and mianzi, to particular clusters of personality traits used in person perception.[3] For example, it is possible to make a prima facie case for lian being related to the traits of agreeableness, conscientiousness, and emotional stability, whereas mianzi would be related to extroversion and openness.

Thus it may be possible to link social context to lian and mianzi through these mediators of social perception. This linkage may span several types of gaps, such as societal context to face or organizational context to face. Although this mapping points to a potentially interesting content component of face, it does not describe the process aspect of social perception related to face. I now turn to a discussion of two general sources of these social perceptions, namely, internal versus external referents. It is important, however, to keep in mind that the reliance on particular referents will be influenced by societal, organizational, and social context. This suggests that different referents will tend to be relied on more by people from varying cultural backgrounds—a conceptual position posited by Triandis's sampling-probability hypothesis (1995) as well as Markus and Kitayama (1991) and supported by empirical work of Earley, Gibson, and Chen (1996). For example, someone who is from a high power distance culture is more likely to sample from an interdependent (external) referent than someone who is from a low power distance culture because it is important for the former person to maintain a delicate balance of position within a given social hierarchy.

An internal referent reflects a person's own intrinsic system for evaluating face. For instance, an employee working for a prestigious company may derive mianzi from knowing that he or she works for a famous company. This form of mianzi is not dependent on others' social constructions concerning the company even though it can be influenced by it. (A person's own view of his or her mianzi will likely affect others' view as well. An employee certain of his or her personal stature will influence fellow employees' views of him- or herself by his or her actions and attitudes [Bandura, 1986].) Lian also can be derived internally. A person who commits an immoral act (loses lian) does not need an external referent to witness the deed in order to experience guilt. A great deal of social behavior in a collectivist society such as

China relies on such internalized regulation of moral behavior (Redding, 1992). In fact, citizenship behavior is generally predicated on the assumption that behavior is voluntary and not contingent upon reward and is regulated internally. Likewise, theories of motivation such as goal setting (e.g., Locke & Latham, 1990) posit that employee performance is enhanced by goals, in part, because they pose a challenge. Setting and attaining challenging goals is an internally regulated activity, and a person's experience of satisfaction for achieving a goal is due to a face-related effect, namely, enhancing perceived competence and ability (Erez & Earley, 1993).

Lian is most directly tied to internal referents. A person's perceptions of his or her adherence to society's rules of conduct is often a very personal and internal aspect of social behavior. For example, an employee who engages in citizenship behavior displays lian to the extent that he or she views his or her actions as intentional and without anticipated reward and that relevant others attribute his or her actions to similar conditions. I point out the potential influence of others' attributions because they will influence a person's internal states indirectly through their impact on the social milieu. Eden's (e.g., 1988) work on self-fulfilling prophecies in organizations demonstrates the impact of others' perceptions on a person's internal perceptions of self. Mianzi is derived from internal standards as well, as I describe subsequently in this section.

Face is a product of externally anchored perceptions as well. Mianzi is most obviously tied to the actions and reactions of others. An employee who gets a promotion, a company car, a key to the executive washroom, et cetera, has gained mianzi in front of his or her peers. The respect that a senior executive receives from his or her junior managers signals a bolstering of mianzi. Behavior in an organizational context reflects the giving and exchanging of mianzi in a dynamic fashion. During important negotiations over a joint venture, who attends the negotiations, where the negotiations are held, and who sets the agenda all reflect the relative status of the parties. Americans are often surprised to discover in negotiating with the Japanese that key decisions and commitments cannot be made by the Japanese representatives. At least one explanation for this is that key Japanese decision makers have sufficient mianzi that they are represented by others in conducting the details of a venture. They would lose mianzi if they were to get bogged down directly in the details of a negotiation—particularly at the early stages of negotiation. From an organizational viewpoint, such distancing provides the Japanese with leverage over their negotiating partner because they cannot be inadvertently "dragged into an agreement."

Lian can be derived from external sources as well. If a male employee continually engages in sexual misconduct (e.g., harassment of women coworkers), he will be labeled as lewd, perverted, and/or immoral in most work contexts. A moral judgment has been made concerning his conduct by others, and his lian reflects such conclusions. Work colleagues will treat him with suspicion or disdain, and his subsequent actions will be influenced by their reactions.

A debate emerging in the face literature concerns face as a personal attribute versus face as an emergent characteristic of social discourse. Ho (1994:271) typifies a situational approach: "Face is a field concept: it takes full recognition of the individual's embeddedness in the social network." I would caution that there are aspects of face that are, in fact, the singular possession of the holder. Ho argues that face is a public phenomenon alone. Using the metaphor of a musician, he argues that a solo musical virtuoso relies on the audience existing in his or her mind; the musician imagines him- or herself to be in the presence of an entire orchestra and audience even when practicing alone. However, I disagree with this characterization; a soloist in the presence of an audience and orchestra may, in fact, only be aware of his or her own music and actions. Especially for actions that have strong implications for morality and ethics such as obeying societal laws, it is not the audience that defines face in any immediate way—it is the actor. Thus face is not merely the by-product, or perception and attribution, of observers, as is argued by several of the researchers in the communications field (e.g., Ho, 1994; Ting-Toomey & Cocroft, 1994); it is both personal possession and interactional property. Indeed, it is the interactional aspect that gives rise to an individual's self conception of face. I view the sources of face as reciprocally interdependent. Just as a person's self-perceptions of face will influence his or her actions in the midst of others, a social context will impact on his or her self-perceptions (Eden, 1984).

I might add one final example to further illustrate my point. A common example of a person having much face is that of the affluent manager. Does this manager require an audience to have face? Does face "go away" when the manager is alone? Does this manager only attain face by "imagining" or "realizing" interactions with subordinates? Clearly, face associated with status and position is quite separate from observers, although it may have been shaped by them at an earlier point in time, and this face can be lost or gained by an individual who occupies that position, much like Weber's (1947) idea of legitimate authority or French and Raven's (1959) concept of legitimate power. To the institutionalist (e.g., Scott, 1994), this face is derived from the institutional rules surrounding a particular role occupied by the person. For example, Scott (1994) argues that institutions shape behavior in a number of ways, including representational rules (shared ways of understanding the world), constitutive rules (identities that are linked to specific behaviors and action routines), normative rules (expectations for "correct" behavior that are internalized by actors and reinforced by the beliefs and actions of others), and enforcement mechanisms imposed by society. The constitutive rules are especially relevant to the nature of face derived from the role an individual occupies. It is the constitutive rules that determine the nature of an actor's authority and power within a given institutional structure; such authority is independent of the other actors' observations. Strictly speaking, this is not a personality characteristic or attribute; it is independent of direct observation of others and does not require the position holder to mentally construct an audience in order to have face.

Although I will discuss this in more detail in subsequent chapters, a similar argument can be made concerning the interdependence of lian and mianzi. My position is that these are not the same construct, but they are interdependent through process interactions. For example, a subordinate who gives his or her superior proper respect (mianzi) at a business meeting with new clients will receive both mianzi and lian. He or she reaffirms his or her lian by adhering to the social expectations of paying respect to his or her superior, and this enhances the superior's mianzi in front of the new clients. At the same time, the subordinate receives status from the respected superior, who acknowledges the respectful act, and gains mianzi. Did the subordinate show respect simply to get mianzi in return? If so, then this is not an act that reinforces external assessments of lian since it was not done for sake of enacting moral rules of conduct. Because it is possible (by examining intentions) to separate the impact of an action on lian or mianzi, the concepts are clearly different, but it is just as clear that they are interdependent.

As I suggested, if one was to posit the primary versus secondary sources of face, the general origins of each will depend largely on the societal context in which face is operating. I will return to this point in more detail in the chapter on societal context, but, ceteris paribus, lian is most directly derived through internal sources, whereas mianzi is derived from external sources. Why is this? Lian reflects the rules of conduct for behavior that are taught through early socialization experiences during childhood, school, et cetera. It forms the basis for normal interaction within society, and it is ingrained into each person at a very early age. These rules are relatively fundamental to functioning in a society (e.g., thou shalt not commit adultery), and they guide behavior in a general fashion. These are general rules for behavior that generalize across settings and time. Just as we are taught as children not to steal from our parents, we endorse rules that punish those who steal as adults from their company. These rules of conduct reflect deeply embedded values of a society that do not easily change within a single generation (Hofstede, 1980a).

Mianzi, in contrast, is transient in many ways. Not only does a person's mianzi increase or decrease with various social encounters, but what constitutes a basis for mianzi changes as well. For example, prior to the 1970s an expatriate assignment often reflected poorly on an employee, suggesting that he or she would "never be heard from again" and had been sidetracked by his or her company. More recently, such assignments have become highly desirable in American MNCs, reflecting the grooming process whereby a manager is prepared for executive levels in a company. Clearly, the mianzi gained or lost attributable to an expatriate work assignment has changed in the last 20 years. Actions and outcomes associated with mianzi can be highly transient as well. For instance, the proper style of dress, car to drive, bars to frequent, et cetera, denote who is "in" or "out" each season in some social circles.

This discussion reflects a difference between lian and mianzi that I will discuss further in subsequent chapters. Lian reflects an evaluation by self and others concerning a person's adherence to *rules of conduct* within a social structure, whereas mianzi reflects an evaluation by self and others concerning a person's possession of resources that *position him- or herself* within that structure. Both types of face are derived from an interaction of self and other perceptions and social behavior.

Face Regulation and Face Dynamics

In the previous sections, I addressed a few aspects of face regulation and face dynamics. In this section, I will clarify the regulation of face in both forms. Like Goffman (1959), I assume that people view face as an important characteristic of functioning in a social system, and therefore, they operate so as to maintain and/or enhance face as a normal part of social interaction. The important question becomes, how do people enhance and/or maintain face during their interactions with others?

The two forms of face are regulated in somewhat different fashions during interactions. Whereas lian is largely dependent on internal sources of review, mianzi is largely dependent on the social system and interaction. A basic regulatory system somewhat similar to a homeostatic, or control, cycle is not satisfactory to capture face dynamics. Such a metaphor fails to capture the symbolic nature of face, and it presumes tight control between face and an individual's actions. However, the interactional nature of face precludes such a tightly coupled system of regulation. Take, for example, the case of mianzi loss. Two professors meet at a scholarly conference for the first time. In meeting his junior colleague, Professor X comments, "It is a great pleasure to meet you; I have read your work and enjoy it greatly," to which Assistant Professor Y responds, "Thank you. I am pleased to meet you. What do you do research on?" As it turns out, Professor X conducts his work in the same area as Assistant Professor Y, so Professor X loses mianzi because of Y's seeming snub of X. Now enters Associate Professor Z, who works in this research area as well and who comments, "Professor X, good to meet you—I enjoy your work. Would you introduce me to your colleague? How do you do, Assistant Professor Y; are you interested in this research as well?" Although this exchange implies that X and Y both have lost mianzi, there are a number of interactive effects as well. It is not simply that Assistant Professor Y has snubbed Professor X or that Associate Professor Z has snubbed Assistant Professor Y while complimenting Professor X. In this example, X may discount Y's snub because of Z's snub of Y or perhaps because of Z's compliment to X. The two effects will influence X's resulting mianzi as well because Y's snub of Professor X is discounted as a result of Z's actions. Z's actions are particularly challenging to Y because of the status difference between Z and Y, and Y's compliment to X accentuates the status difference between X and Y. Thus Y's mianzi is reduced as a function of having been shown publicly (by Y's comment) to be ignorant of X's research stream as well as Z's apparent ignorance of Y's research. Y's mianzi is reduced by these external influences as well as an experience of embarrassment (internal state) based on knowing that Y snubbed a famous professor, reflecting a naiveté concerning the profession. A tightly coupled control model is unable to capture the complexity and symbolic nature of this interaction.

What model can be used to capture these dynamics of face? I think that Goffman's process of exchange is a useful starting point, namely, that people engage in various behaviors that sometimes enhance or derogate others' face. Much of his emphasis is on face loss and the social rules of conduct in order to cope with the loss, but additional emphasis needs to be placed on individual motives for face maintenance and gain. In other words, people do not simply interact based on and responding to face loss or avoiding "face threatening acts" (Brown & Levinson, 1978); people interact for the purposes of reasserting and defining their position in a social system and hierarchy. They do so based on a number of motives, including status, power, and affiliation motives. Therefore, a proper model of face dynamics must incorporate the idea that people are interacting for the purpose of companionship and affiliation as well as self-definition in a social system. Social indiscretions, or faux pas, occur by accident or design during the process of social discourse. If someone derogates another person's face, it may have been intentional or accidental, but it is for the purpose of interaction rather than face regulation per se. That is not to say that we always interact for social gain, but that the style of interaction is typically regulated by varying degrees of an affiliation motive and a desire for self-definition.

Why would someone purposefully seek to detract from another person's face if affiliation is an important motive? Quite simply, such actions may be viewed as a means for further cementing a relationship with desired others (showing off to the boss by tearing down a coworker). Although our actions may be generally guided by an affiliation motive, the point is that affiliation helps us to define our own position and functioning (and meaning) within a given social system. It is not just a desire to befriend others; nor is it an impulse to reduce uncertainty or ambiguity. It is a search for who we are in our social context.

Face dynamics, then, result in self-definition based on one's personal interactions with a very limited group, interactions with extended families and friends, work units or organizations, or interactions within a general social system. Although a complete discussion of self-concept is beyond the scope of this book, others have addressed this topic elsewhere (e.g., Erez & Earley, 1993; Markus & Kitayama, 1991). My point is that face regulation revolves around a desire for self-definition and affiliation. People may give mianzi and, consequently, help others achieve desired goals, but they do so because it enables them to better define who they are in their social milieu and reaffirm social relationships among people.

The idea of face dynamics in my framework is that a desire for self-definition and affiliation motivates people to engage others in a practical as well as symbolic fashion. An employee who chooses to ask a superior a question about a project is not only trying to make a good impression (Ashford & Tsui 1991) but also trying to understand his or her position within the organization and its social environment. It is this latter point that suggests face research can help researchers better understand interpersonal dynamics in organizations. Much of the research on impression management, as well as feedback seeking, has been based on the assumption that people interact to gain social credit, in some form, for themselves. Although this may well provide a partial explanation, people also interact in order to understand their relative place in a social system and to clarify their relationships with others. Thus an employee who asks a supervisor how to use a database may not simply be trying to "look good" or improve work performance. Rather, this employee may be trying to understand who he or she is in the organization as well as how to interact with others.

The cognitive-processing limitations that I mentioned earlier result from the natural limitations facing people in their capacity to process information as well as accurately perceive the environment. It goes without saying that people have inherent limitations in their capabilities to process information (e.g., Kahneman & Tversky, 1984; March & Simon, 1958; Wyer & Srull, 1980). In terms of face, there is a dual difficulty because people need to reconcile and incorporate environmental and interpersonal cues with their existing self-perceptions and are acting on information that is symbolically conveyed by others in their social system. An employee who asks a supervisor how to use a database has to figure out the boss's reaction to the request and what it implies about the boss's impression of the subordinate. Further, this information must be integrated into the employee's existing face as derived from the employee him- or herself and the face derived from the social context (e.g., coworkers). Thus face is "reshaped" as a result of the interaction with the boss, perhaps in a desired direction, having important spillover effects for face.

An additional complication is that a supervisor's reactions to and interactions with a subordinate have additional implications for others in the organization. As another employee observes an inquiring subordinate interact with the boss, he or she may form a particular reaction/impression concerning the activities (e.g., he or she thinks that the new employee is attempting some form of ingratiation), which may have ripple effects on face derived from the general organization. The inquirer may not become immediately aware of this spillover effect, and the resulting impact on the employee's face may not surface immediately. In fact, the inquirer's actions may operate on the social system and change the subsequent evaluations of various observers. For example, if a respected senior-level manager engages in a given action such as taking home company property, this may redefine the dominant values in an organization, which, in turn, implies different evaluations for employee theft. Consider an employee who has not heard about this shifting practice and observes a friend taking home a company typing table. This person may not choose to say anything directly to his or her friend, but the friend's lian has been lost from the other person's viewpoint. In the future, his or her perception of this friend's lian will influence how he or she works with the friend. Even if the person later observes that such "acquisitions" are overlooked by the company, his or her friend's action will have been processed as a dishonest act, which will be difficult to recode as acceptable. Evidence from social cognition shows that the initial coding conditions of information or events have a strong influence on subsequent processing and retrieval (Wyer & Srull, 1980).

The importance of social context is evident because a person's face varies as a function of a particular setting. In some instances, an employee has much face, whereas in other circumstances he or she has little face. However, this variability is primarily in reference to mianzi rather than lian. As described earlier, lian is primarily an internally derived aspect of face, and so it is much less malleable due to the social setting. Returning to the employee theft example, the extent to which honesty is an internalized aspect of a person's value system will determine the impact of such an action on lian. In other words, the impact of theft on a person's lian occurs even if fellow employees endorse such an action. What suffers from the theft, as a social phenomenon, is mianzi. An employee not only loses personal status but also may weaken the bond between him- or herself and others. However, if the employee has not internalized a strong value of honesty or has encoded that employee theft is not a dishonest practice, then he or she will not lose lian. This is tempered somewhat by the external aspect of lian. Recall that lian has an interpersonal aspect as well as the internalized referent. In this case, the employee's lian may be reduced through subsequent feedback that he or she receives from important social others (friends).

This last example raises a final complication of face dynamics, namely, that lian and mianzi are differentially impacted by the social system. As argued earlier, these two aspects of face are derived from internal and external sources, but to differing degrees. The status of being a CEO of a large organization represents mianzi that is not solely dependent on a social system. The CEO carries within him- or herself knowledge of such mianzi, and this will impact how he or she interacts with others. Such "attitude" impacts the perceptions of others and, in turn, influences their attributions concerning the CEO even if they are not cognizant of his or her position. Through interpersonal style, communication patterns, and nonverbal cues, his or her mianzi is conveyed. It is in this sense that I argue that mianzi is not simply a characteristic conveyed during a social interaction. It is part of the CEO's self-definition.

In parallel, lian has a secondary external component that does not rely solely on internal reference. Of course, lian is ultimately tied to the social system in which a person operates because it is through such life exposures that a person's values are internalized. Additionally, it should be noted that certain classes of values are etic in nature, or universally shared, as discussed in a subsequent chapter. Although cultures differ in the relative emphases placed on these values, as well as their position on a continuum underlying the values, they are universally present in all cultures and form a basis for lian.

Summary

There are several important distinctions between lian and mianzi. Although mianzi is conceptualized as a currency of self-status, to be lost or gained, lian results from an adherence to rules of conduct endorsed in a given society. The newborn child has lian as a birthright; only the experienced child may earn mianzi from his or her family and peers. A second and perhaps more important distinction is that lian, as ascribed, can either be maintained (through engagement of moral acts) or be lost, but *it cannot be recovered easily after it is lost.* For instance, an employee who steals will be forever branded as someone with a moral weakness and thus must be monitored by the organization. In this sense, one's actions forever forge moral character through a potential fall from grace. Michael Milken's infamous legacy of junk bond deals and Nick Leeson's debacle with Barings Bank in Singapore have led to their loss of lian. Although in recent times Milken has attempted to restore his reputation (e.g., through a controversial lecture program at UCLA and benevolence demonstrated through donations to a cancer research program), many people fundamentally question his underlying values and motives. Given that lian is a birthright whereas mianzi can be earned, the Milken case illustrates that someone can lose lian while maintaining mianzi. In Milken's case, he maintains a great deal of wealth and power despite questions concerning his moral character. How can lian be restored once it is lost? This is best addressed by examining theological practices in many cultures. In Christianity and Judaism, a person can eventually gain pureness of character after death, even if he or she led an immoral life, through a final forgiveness (Hick, 1967). Although an immoral person can regain redemption during he or her lifetime in unusual cases (e.g., saints who have overcome their inherent limitations), such redemption usually occurs at the point of confession and death (Hick, 1967). In Buddhism, moral purity and enlightenment cannot be regained during a single lifetime (with a few obvious exceptions, such as Siddhartha); only through successive rebirths, ethical actions, and proper meditative thinking can a person achieve spiritual purity (Smart, 1967). Thus lian is lost or maintained during any single lifetime, but it is not easily regained. In this sense, lian refers to a predominantly internal characteristic of a person, whereas mianzi captures the outcomes of one's actions in a social context.

I have described in this chapter a framework for understanding the nature of face dynamics or regulation. Although this approach bears some commonality with that of Goffman, there are several notable differences. First, Goffman's approach focused on the nature of face loss over that of face gain or general interaction. In his system, a driving force is the actions people take in order to maintain and promote face as well as shield themselves from the loss of face through their symbolic interactions. In my model, people engage in face-related behavior in order to satisfy desires for affiliation and self-definition within a given social system. Thus it is not so much of an aversion-avoidance system as is characteristic of Goffman (1959, 1967) and Brown and Levinson (1978). Second, there is an important difference between the two forms of face and how they are impacted through social interaction. While mianzi is contextually sensitive (through a complicated set of interpersonal iterations), lian is more internally than contextually sensitive. Third, I have not made a large distinction between "front-stage" and "back-stage" because I do not see them as nearly so distinct as posited by Goffman. Although it is true that individuals consciously reveal particular aspects of themselves according to the setting, it is not evident that their presentations are as rational as suggested by Goffman. Rather, I would suggest that people reveal aspects of themselves in accordance with their determining their self-definition and position in a social system. The purpose of face-related behavior is not simply to reassert and gain face.

A model of face posits that individuals vary on two aspects of self-presentation, namely, an emphasis on values and moral character (lian) and an accumulation of status and prestige (mianzi). In the case of lian, it is a fundamental birthright and a characteristic that may be maintained or lost but not gained. A fall from grace is a relatively permanent one. With regard to mianzi, it is a social exchange currency that can be gained or lost with each and every social interaction.

The literature reviewed so far suggests that there are two general forms of face: lian and mianzi. Although each appear to be relevant to all countries, there seems to be a generally strong concern with mianzi among Western scholars and an increasing emphasis on mianzi among Asian scholars. In the next chapter, I specifically address the construct of mianzi along with its significance in my general framework. In Chapter 5, I turn my attention to a discussion of lian, including an examination of why this somewhat ignored aspect of face is critically important for understanding the operations of organizations across cultures.

Notes

1. In the context of this book, I adopt the pinyin version of the Chinese terms "lian" and "mianzi" in discussing a model of face. Although both terms have linguistic denotative meanings referring to one's physical face, "lian" has the connotative meaning of shame and value, whereas "mianzi" refers more directly to the "outside" or external reputation of an individual. A more specific definition and operationalization will be provided in this chapter.

2. Hu used the Giles system of translation, and so his terms differ somewhat from the pinyin I use. Thus the term "lian" is equivalent to his term "lien" and the term "mianzi" is equivalent to his term "mien-tzu."

3. I wish to thank Michael Bond for his inspiration concerning this point, including a number of lengthy conversations concerning the potential contribution of personality traits and person perception in understanding culture's impact on face.

4

Mianzi as a Form of Face

The linguistic origins of face stem from ancient Chinese, with the term "mianzi" predating "lian." "Mian" is a term dating back to 4 B.C., and it had a connotative meaning of ego as it relates to society (Hu, 1944). The significance of mianzi takes many forms, which focus on a person's sense of self in relation to others and the general society. "Lian" is a more modern term, relatively, dating back to the Yuan Dynasty (1277–1367), and it seems to be more dominant in northern and eastern China. To a much lesser degree, lian has penetrated the south of China, including the Guangdong Province, where the term "mianzi" is more widely used.

The ascribed versus achieved aspect of face is very important. Although mianzi functions much like a social exchange currency, with fortunes potentially acquired or lost as a result of key encounters, lian is an inherent aspect of a person's existence. Mianzi is a concept that cannot be separated from social context. In this sense, it is not merely the prestige or position that a person has in a company. Nor is mianzi merely the wealth possessed or the beauty held. Mianzi is a product of an individual's character within a particular social system. It does not make a great deal of sense to talk of someone's mianzi without reference to a social context. In this way, mianzi is best conceived as an embedded aspect of an individual's relations within a social system (Granovetter, 1985). This idea is understood by looking at the historical nature of the concept in Confucian-based societies. According to the basic tenets of Confucianism, a person's life revolves around five basic relationships: emperor-subject (or righteousness), father-son (or closeness), husband-wife (or distinction), elder-youth (or order), and friendships (or faithfulness). The idea of mianzi is the proper regulation of a person's life according to these five relationships. An additional key characteristic concerns the importance of emotion and propriety (li) as they are involved in these relationships (Li, 1975). Briefly, individuals follow particular rules or norms of interaction regulating mianzi in order to maintain a balance, or harmony, in their relationships. They are not simply a normative imposition of society; rather, they reflect an internal desire to maintain the proper balance in these five forms of relationships. This is perhaps the greatest difference between the regulation of mianzi in a Confucian-based and in a Judeo-Christian-based culture; namely, mianzi functions as a means of regulating relationships in a Confucian culture and as a means of defining position and functioning within the relationship in a Judeo-Christian culture. Although the result of both philosophical systems implies an outcome of establishing position within a given social system, it is for very different reasons. This suggests that for a Western executive, a large office and ample fringe benefits symbolically assert his or her position in the organization (and social system), but for a Chinese executive, such perks establish the connections among his or her cohorts. (I present this as an argument with a dichotomous outcome, but it should not be viewed in this fashion since there will always be elements of both characteristics among both groups.) Thus it is important to realize that an emphasis on mianzi across two very different cultures does not necessarily mean that members of both cultures wish to act the same way. There are many facets of mianzi and many associated outcomes.

In this chapter, I begin by discussing the various factors underlying the construct of mianzi. I describe a number of contextual factors that contribute to the gain, loss, or maintenance of mianzi in most cultures. In this regard, I posit that mianzi can be thought of as the interactional combination of personal and external referents' social judgments of an individual. I then discuss these judgments as based on social perceptions and conceptualized in terms of basic facets of personality structure.[1] Finally, I examine the dynamics underlying changes in face in a social and personal context.

Contextual and Personal Factors Underlying Mianzi

Mianzi can be thought of as related to a number of different contextual and personal factors. To better understand these, it is important to revisit the basic definition of mianzi; namely, it refers to the interactive combination of personal and external referents' social judgments concerning a target person. That is to say, it reflects how I view myself as well as how others view me. In this section, I break down the factors contributing to mianzi into two general categories, self as independent versus self as interdependent, following the work of Markus and Kitayama (1991) and Triandis (1995), among others.

Self as Independent

In this section, I discuss the factors of mianzi that are most directly attributed to a person as a characteristic of self. There are a number of these characteristics, and some of the ones that I discuss might be cross-classified as well. I begin with a discussion of personal attributes as they relate to face.

People who possess culturally endorsed physical attributes have mianzi. For example, in American society (as in other cultures as well), physical beauty is an important attribute, as exemplified by the health club craze that has swept the country. Physical characteristics, personal mannerisms, accents, and clothing all constitute personal characteristics that can convey mianzi. A person who is physically beautiful has mianzi, as does a person speaking with an "intriguing" accent. Likewise, the clothes worn by a person convey important information about his or her status, and, ironically, the information conveyed may be symbolic and not literal (e.g., someone wearing "grunge" styles conveyed the height of fashion awareness).

More subtle attributes of a person convey and signal mianzi as well. For instance, in some cultures the place you received your education (the "Oxbridge" education in the United Kingdom) plays a significant role in determining mianzi. Other less obvious attributes of a person that signal mianzi include such characteristics as style of speech (work usage and choice, intonation, etc.), intellectual style, humor and wit, knowledge of current events, and cosmopolitan perspective. These various characteristics constitute the personal attributes of a person.

Additional characteristics, such as a person's position in a company, the type of company he or she works for, profession, vocational choice, are what Katz and Kahn (1978) call ascribed roles, or those aspects of a role attached to the role itself. In other words, a person receiving a promotion to an executive position in his or her company receives the accolades of position regardless of his or her characteristics. These are the legitimate sources of authority that come with the given position. A person's choice of profession also sends an important message concerning mianzi. In Western cultures, the choice of a profession such as medicine is seen as prestigious and having mianzi. In Chinese culture, a university professor has much mianzi—a refreshing change for this American professor when he travels to China for teaching and research purposes! Association with particular institutions provides mianzi as well. Certainly the Stanford professor has mianzi not afforded the state university professor. In this sense, mianzi can be acquired by a person simply due to his or her associations with objects or institutions that have mianzi or status.

Self as Interdependent

An important and interesting feature of mianzi that makes it distinct from related constructs such as self-esteem, honor, and reputation is that it can be given or taken by people other than the target. In this section of the chapter, I discuss a number of ways that mianzi can be characterized as a resource transferred or conveyed by others. Mianzi reflects a person's status in a social structure as perceived by self and others. If a person with a great deal of mianzi praises someone with less mianzi, the first person's mianzi is conveyed to the recipient. Likewise, by associating with people who have much mianzi, a person receives mianzi. These examples illustrate that mianzi is a characteristic that can be derived from associations with others in a social context. Interestingly, these associations do not have to be overly explicit or intentional. Thus if I hang around the "right" people long enough, their mianzi is transferred to me even if it is not their explicit intention to do so.

The interdependence aspect of mianzi reflects other types of interpersonal connections. Individuals who have many social connections reflect strong mianzi. I often counsel my former Ph.D. students to organize symposia for professional meetings because it provides them with an opportunity to expand their social networks. An extensive social and professional network provides junior faculty with an opportunity to acquire mianzi.

Social and Personal Regulation of Mianzi

Mianzi can be acquired through a variety of means and practices. The general classes of actions related to mianzi and its regulation can be categorized into several dimensions: mianzi claimed by an individual and defined by social interaction (Chang & Holt, 1994), gain versus loss of mianzi, and self-directed versus externally directed mianzi. Before discussing these specifics, a general note concerning the regulation of mianzi is appropriate.[2]

A useful way of conceptualizing the general process of mianzi regulation is through an analogy borrowed from Herzberg's two-factor theory (1966). According to Herzberg's view, employee performance is the product of two different motivational processes, namely, those driven by hygiene and those driven by motivator factors. Hygiene factors include a domain of rewards that are predominantly material, such as pay, bonuses, company car, et cetera. In contrast, motivator factors include a domain of rewards that are intangible, such as recognition for superior work, praise, et cetera. Herzberg argued that hygiene factors are useful only in maintaining job performance and satisfaction at a baseline level; motivator factors are needed to raise performance and satisfaction beyond this level. From this distinction arose the distinction between extrinsic and intrinsic forms of reward. Despite the subsequent questioning of Herzberg's studies and conclusions, the analogy is useful in describing some of the dynamics of face gain and loss. I would posit that the regulation of mianzi is not symmetrical. Face loss is analogous to the hygiene component of Herzberg's model in that it centers at some equilibrium point from which it may drop as a function of social and personal interactions. This loss of face can be overcome through directed action toward the face threat (e.g., discrediting the source of face loss) or through bolstering related face components. I would suggest that mianzi subject to this influence changes across time for any given person but that it reflects a type of face that is threatened. In contrast, gaining face is analogous to Herzberg's motivator factors, suggesting that face can increase as a monotonic function of a person receiving mianzi from self and others. I have illustrated these processes in Figure 4-1. For example, if Microsoft releases a product that CEO Bill Gates endorses as "revolutionary" (e.g., Windows 95) and it fails to meet expectations, his status as a guru of the software industry suffers (see Point A in Figure 4-1). If he follows this up with the introduction of a different but highly innovative product, then he can bring his general reputation back up to some equilibrium point (Point C). Gaining face, however, is reflected in an additive model such that events represented by Points B and D have cumulative effects on Gates's reputation. Thus his recently built large mansion as well as his personal fortune detailed in international rankings of the wealthy add to his mianzi.

From this description, it is important to note that face gain and loss are not symmetrical. People are often concerned more with the avoidance of losing face than with gaining it, and a loss of face has a stronger impact on people's perceptions of a person. The lack of success of the Apple Newton hurt John Scully's reputation in the computer industry in a way that was difficult to overcome despite the success of numerous other projects. In this sense, the loss of mianzi mirrors the loss of lian. However, several caveats are in order. First, loss and gain of mianzi reflect categories of factors. In the case of Scully's Newton project, he lost mianzi related to his role

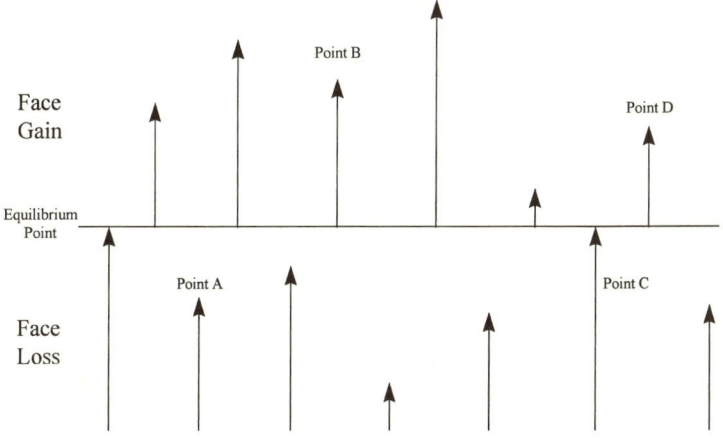

Various Influences on Mianzi

Figure 4-1. Regulation of Mianzi

in the computer industry. However, this is not to say that this effect washed over into other areas of his work or life. To gain back this category of mianzi, Scully needs to prove his expertise in the industry. From a more general perspective, Scully has mianzi attributable to various other facets of his life (e.g., personal wealth, record as key executive in other companies). Thus Scully can gain mianzi in other facets of his life even if one aspect is threatened. With this said, however, I would argue that the various categories (as I discussed in the last section) are interdependent to varying degrees depending on the culture. In some cultures (e.g., the United States), a person's work role is strongly tied to his or her mianzi in other aspects of his or her life. Thus loss of face in one category may wash over into other categories. Second, face loss is moderated by the centrality of the factor to a person's self-concept (Erez & Earley, 1993). If face loss is based on a concept central to a person's self-view and social circumstance (e.g., Scully's computer fiasco), then it is relatively more difficult to bring that facet of face back to some equilibrium point. If loss is tied to a tangential aspect of self, then the loss can be more easily overcome. Face gain, however, reflects a more consistent effect, with various forms of gain adding onto one another. The relative valence of a particular gain is tied to its centrality to the self. Finally, the equilibrium point illustrated in Figure 4-1 is important in understanding the relative contribution of face loss and gain to a person's overall face. The equilibrium point reflects a general point of face reflecting self and other evaluations at a given point in time. This point is dynamic and is expected to shift over time. However, in the short run, it reflects a target for regulating face loss, and it is only when this equilibrium point is maintained that face gain has a strong presence. In other words, if a person's central concept of self is threatened, face gain will have little effect until an equilibrium point is reestablished.

As suggested earlier, mianzi is not merely a personality trait; it is a product of personal and social evaluation. It is, however, a personal characteristic inasmuch as certain individuals place relatively more emphasis on the status attributable to mianzi. For example, in Chinese culture a person who wants mianzi ("yao mianzi") is someone who is obsessed with gaining face to a point of distraction. Such a person may appear to be more concerned with having or gaining face than with conforming to social values and judgments. Additionally, a person who wishes to be honored or revered by others is concerned with having mianzi.

Although mianzi as claimed by an individual is not insignificant, mianzi is most directly a product of social interaction (in contrast to lian, which is primarily a characteristic of an individual). As a product of social interaction, mianzi can both facilitate and hinder social relationships for a number of reasons. For example, a person can use his or her mianzi to "take care of one's mianzi" (Chang & Holt, 1994; Hu, 1944) by making certain that the other person's mianzi is reinforced or bolstered. For example, an advertising executive who wishes to enhance the mianzi of his or her employee may offer him or her an opportunity to work on a prestigious advertising campaign. This honor signals to the employee's work colleagues that he or she is viewed as a "rising star" in the ad agency. Additionally, mianzi reaffirms a person's position within a given social system and network. Executives have more mianzi than shop floor workers. (This seems true in most cultures but is less prevalent in more egalitarian societies than in more power-stratified ones.)

The second dimension of mianzi concerns its gain and loss. Unlike lian, mianzi is a type of "commodity" that a person can gain or lose through daily interactions with others as well as personal actions. Mianzi is a type of social recognition unit that can be shared, exchanged, and lost. In terms of interaction with others, we can lose our mianzi through our ineptness only to regain it after reaffirming our capability. Employees may gain or lose mianzi differentially, depending on a variety of contextual conditions. For example, a new employee has a great deal more latitude in making mistakes without losing mianzi than does a seasoned veteran. Likewise, a highly trusted employee may be permitted more mistakes that are attributed to "eccentricity" than a moderately experienced employee. A curvilinear relationship of job tenure to mianzi loss is expected, although the most senior and trusted employees are the ones with the most mianzi to venture and retain. Interestingly, this point is related to Holland's (1973) idiosyncratic credit theory of leadership, which argues that with increased expertise, accomplishment, and seniority comes the latitude for idiosyncratic behavior. Why does our CEO insist on having meetings in rooms with round tables and green tablecloths? It is this quirkiness that subordinates attribute to accomplishment and brilliance. How, then, is mianzi gained and lost?

First, mianzi is gained as a result of a person's role enacted in an organization. Although a janitor has little mianzi derived from his or her role, a senior executive has a great deal. Status of position in an organizational hierarchy provides face directly through the prestige of a job title as well as indirectly through organizational "perks" such as a company car or an expense account. Second, mianzi is gained through physical attributes and characteristics. An attractive, model-like man or woman has mianzi attributable to physical appearance. Often a physically attractive person is considered more capable than a less attractive one in a variety of cultures (with the standards of beauty differing, of course). Likewise, the "dress for success" or "power dressing" phenomenon is not without basis in a society (e.g., the United

States) in which physical appearance plays an important role. The clothes we wear, the cars we drive, and our personal appearance contribute to mianzi. Third, a person can gain mianzi by acting "beautifully." Someone who shows him- or herself to be generous gains mianzi through "beautiful" actions. For instance, someone might help out a homeless person or contribute to a charity and enhance mianzi.

These three factors enhance mianzi through an individual's personal actions, but mianzi is an exchangeable social currency as well. For instance, a graduate student gains mianzi when a visiting scholar praises his or her question at a talk, and an employee gains mianzi by receiving company recognition for an innovative suggestion. A person gains mianzi through instrumental relationships with others, such as a famous relative (e.g., Billy Carter, who gained instant notoriety, much to the chagrin of his presidential brother) or an important friend. Excelling at neighborhood competitions (e.g., putting up the largest holiday display in one's front yard or giving the biggest dinner party in the community) can increase one's mianzi. Likewise, mianzi can be increased by putting on a public display showing personal success in order that the community recognize personal achievements. Goffman (1967) argued that such an activity is an important signaling of one's position within a social structure.

The previous examples have focused on the personal and situational aspects of accumulating mianzi. In many respects, the loss of mianzi is more important than the gains one might achieve simply because of an innate desire to safeguard one's accomplishments. A person might lose mianzi in a number of ways. First, direct criticism, particularly from powerful others, has a consequence of siphoning off a person's mianzi. Second, the exposure of a person's mistakes or weaknesses in public will dilute mianzi. Third, penurious individuals, such as Dickens's character Ebenezer Scrooge, may lose mianzi. Interestingly, someone who has less mianzi may have the power to adversely affect the mianzi of a more powerful individual. For instance, a low-level employee can dilute the mianzi of a powerful leader by claiming that the leader had acted inappropriately, in a way not becoming to the leader's status, toward the employee. By not affording the employee reasonable respect, the leader loses his or her respect (mianzi) from others. Mianzi can be lost through poor investment decisions, economic troubles, et cetera. The recent U.S. film *Falling Down* depicts a newly unemployed aerospace engineer who cracks under the strain of losing his job, wife, and self-respect. For approximately a month after having lost his job, the once-respected engineer continues to maintain the facade that he is gainfully employed among his relevant reference group (i.e., his mother, with whom he lives). Thus just as fortunes are made and lost, so is mianzi.

The final dimension underlying mianzi is the distinction of self-directed versus externally directed actions. By this, I mean that behavior related to mianzi may be focused either on acquiring or maintaining one's own mianzi or on influencing the mianzi of others. Not only is mianzi an obligation between two or more people, but it creates its own obligations as well. For example, if I ask someone to use his or her mianzi in order to get my son into Berkeley, I have created an obligation to that person if he or she chooses to help me. The person may not help, however, because he or she does not want this obligation and the implicit relationship to me. Some people refuse to help others not because they begrudge helping but because they do not wish to accept the implied relationship/obligation. By doing a favor, however, I gain not only the other person's obligation, which is a form of mianzi, but additional mianzi for having helped the person. Therefore, this externally directed mianzi has two sides.

Self-directed mianzi refers to the general class of actions that a person engages in to maintain or increase his or her mianzi through a direct means. For example, if a manager throws a big party to show his or her position and importance, this is a self-directed form of mianzi. Self-deprecation, as described by Goffman (1959), that is intended to solicit compliments or reassurances from others would be an additional example of self-directed mianzi. As I mentioned earlier, actions that convey to others a person's personal importance are self-directed forms of mianzi.

Externally directed mianzi may have the result of enhancing a person's own mianzi (as in the example I gave above), but it does not have this outcome as its focus. If I help someone obtain an interview at a local company through my contacts, this is externally directed mianzi. Although it conveys to others my relative position and status, it does so indirectly by enhancing someone else's mianzi. As professors use their reputations in order to secure job interviews for their graduate students at prestigious universities, their mianzi is externally directed. If the students receive such interviews (or job offers), the professors' personal mianzi is enhanced as well. The point is that both self- and externally directed forms of mianzi may result in personal development of mianzi, but self-directed mianzi is a direct process.

A Structural View of Mianzi

In this section, I approach the discussion of mianzi from a personality and person perception perspective. There has been a great deal of research in the field of personality psychology based on the so-called Big Five traits of personality. This model posits that five basic traits underlie personality structure in terms of fundamental content: extroversion, neuroticism, agreeableness, openness, and conscientiousness (McCrae & Costa, 1985).

The origin of the five-factor model is most often attributed to the work of Tupes and Christal (1961) on personality assessment in the U.S. Air Force. In subsequent work, Norman (1963) realized the potential of this categorization scheme and refined it further into the traits of extroversion, agreeableness, conscientiousness, neuroticism, and culture. Interestingly, much of this work is based on a "natural language" approach, meaning that researchers based their measures (and subsequent factor models) on the adjectives naturally occurring in a language system. Indeed, such an approach has demonstrated surprising consistency for a five-factor model across very different cultural settings based on instruments developed indigenously. More recently, many studies have elaborated on the original model (e.g., McCrae & Costa, 1987), posing a five-factor model based on an adjectival approach.

The five factors underlying personality reflect the basis of personal and social evaluations of a target individual. Extroversion reflects characteristics such as being sociable, fun-loving, affectionate, friendly, and talkative. It corresponds to more traditional concepts such as talkativeness and liveliness. The key factors accounting for the extroversion factor appear to be sociability, cheerfulness, and assertiveness, being active, and seeking sensations. Neuroticism reflects a dimension that is widely accepted in personality and clinical psychology. It is reflected by characteristics such as worrying, insecurity, self-consciousness, and uneasy temperament. People who score high on neuroticism may adopt irrational beliefs like self-blame, possess disturbed thoughts, and experience emotional distress (McCrae & Costa, 1987). The third factor, agreeableness, reflects a broad dimension capturing agreeableness versus antagonism. People who score low on agreeableness (high on antagonism) seem to set themselves against others and are mistrustful and skeptical, uncooperative, stubborn, and rude. Their sense of attachment to others is weak, and in extreme cases such individuals resemble sociopaths.

The fourth personality trait is conscientiousness, and it is opposed by undirectedness. Conscientiousness is reflected by adjectives including "hardworking," "ambitious," "scrupulous," "energetic," and "persevering." A person who scores high on conscientiousness is purposeful and guided by goals and plans, whereas a person who scores high on undirectedness is lazy, unguided, and disorganized. Finally, the fifth personality trait was originally referred to as culture (Norman, 1963), reflecting such traits as intelligence, sophistication, and intellectual curiosity. More recently, McCrae and Costa (1985, 1987) provided evidence and further analyses supporting a modification of this trait to be more accurately labeled openness. Openness to experience means that an individual is original and imaginative, has broad interests, and is daring and interested in new experiences. Openness is associated with intelligence, but it should not be confused with intelligence. Although people who score high in openness are often intelligent, there is not necessarily a high correlation between the two constructs, and they load on separate factors in analytic models (McCrae & Costa, 1987).

The usefulness of a personality structure approach to face can be traced to two basic relationships. First, people's social and personal perceptions are related to interpersonal behavior. For example, a number of studies conducted by Eden and his colleagues (e.g., Eden, 1984; Eden & Ravid, 1982) on the Pygmalion effect (based on Rosenthal's original work with the construct) have demonstrated the potential impact of social perceptions on an individual's subsequent behavior. Eden's work has demonstrated on numerous occasions that the expectations, for example, of a supervisor shape the social world of a subordinate, resulting in substantive differences in the quality of performance. This finding is consistent with those of the symbolic interactionist school as well as more recent work in organizational studies on the topic of sense making in organizations.

The basic logic of such an influence is that the social context in which a person functions provides a number of direct and indirect cues concerning expectations and feedback about behavior. This information flow can be subtle and indirect as well as quite direct and obvious. The result of this information flow is that a person's actions are shaped accordingly. This effect is particularly strong if the sources of information are valued by the target person such as in the case of strong work group norms, charismatic leadership, et cetera.

The flow of information is more complicated than this discussion has revealed so far. Although the social milieu has an important impact on people's actions (and their interpretation of the world around them), people have an impact on their environment as well. People do not passively accept the social evaluations of others inasmuch as they often engage in feedback seeking, impression management, et cetera (Ashford &

Cummings, 1983). This suggests a more complex interdependence governing personal and social perceptions. For example, an employee who has a high degree of personal efficacy will engage more actively in his or her work than someone who is lacking efficacy (Bandura, 1986; Wood & Bandura, 1989). The result of this engagement is that the first employee will be more successful, other things being equal, than the low-efficacy colleague, and this will impact on others' perceptions and judgments concerning his or her capability. Further, these expectations of others will influence their style of engagement with the employee—for example, a supervisor will provide the employee with increasingly challenging work assignments. As the worker continues to complete these assignments, his or her efficacy continues to build, which, in turn, cycles back through to his or her external referents. These performance-expectation-context cycles can be highly beneficial if they are oriented in a positive direction, but they can be detrimental as well if their direction moves an employee into a low-performance cycle.

The key point in this discussion is that the nature of an employee's personal judgments, as well as those of external referents, actively shapes work behavior. The role of personality structure in this development is that the content of people's perceptions concerning mianzi can be thought of in terms of the five-factor model of personality. In other words, a person's mianzi can be reflected in his or her personality profile. For example, a person who is high on extroversion, openness, agreeableness, and conscientiousness and low on neuroticism has more mianzi than someone lacking these personality traits. Why is this? I am not arguing that these traits determine mianzi or social status in some existing hierarchy. Rather, I am positing that these traits can be used to operationalize a person's mianzi. That is to say, a person who has mianzi will be perceived by him- or herself and others according to these personality traits.

Of course, a central question is the directionality of these traits, as well as their universality. First, I have suggested that extroversion, openness, agreeableness, and conscientiousness are positively related to mianzi, whereas neuroticism is negatively related. This assertion clearly reflects an American framework, and it seems likely that the socially desired direction of these traits will differ as a function of cultural context. For example, in a tight (strong, social norms) culture (Witkin & Berry, 1975), high extroversion may be associated with ignoring social norms and rules, a trait considered to be undesirable. Likewise, agreeableness might be viewed as reflecting a lack of commitment and energy for a highly masculine (Hofstede, 1980a) culture with its emphasis on a fast-paced and aggressive approach to life. My point is that although the five personality traits appear to occur in a wide variety of cultures (many of them radically different from one another), this does not mean that using the five-factor model to capture the content and hence the magnitude of mianzi requires emic calibration. Similarly, the relative contribution of each factor to the social perception process is likely to vary as a function of culture (Smith & Bond, 1994). For instance, a culture stressing individualism is likely to place a high value on an openness dimension, since "doing your own thing" (Triandis, 1995) is predicated on an assumption of openness to experience. In an authoritarian and hierarchical culture (e.g., high power distance), conscientiousness and dedication to one's role in society are likely to be highly valued characteristics.

A second consideration is that there are likely to be a number of emic, or indigenous, personality traits in any given culture not encompassed by a five-factor model. For example, Bond (1996, personal conversation) has commented that Hong Kong Chinese typically generate an eight-factor model that subsumes a five-factor approach. That is to say, in Hong Kong Chinese society, a number of additional personality traits arise (such as modesty, social conformity, and group dedication) that are not contained in a five-factor model. However, the evidence appears to support the view that cultures exhibit at least five factors (with very similar content to those from the American research stream), suggesting that these five factors are etics. If this is so, the use of trait ratings may provide a common metric for understanding and assessing mianzi across cultural boundaries. The key, of course, is to determine the directionality and relative weighting of each of the traits in order to form a global judgment of mianzi.

A final, and related, problem concerns the way one might combine personal and social judgments of mianzi using this approach. As I defined it in Chapter 3, mianzi captures both an individual's self-assessment and the assessment of others in a social context. Certainly personality traits can be solicited from self and others, as has been the focus of work by a number of researchers (e.g., McCrae & Costa, 1987). In general, the results from American researchers suggest that an adjectival approach to assessing the Big Five by self and peers provides a high degree of similarity. For example, McCrae and Costa (1987) used two data sources, self and peer, to assess personality traits in an analysis of 275 respondents (with a corresponding 738 peers). Their findings showed correlations ranging from .39 to .45 of peer-to-self ratings of the individual traits. As might be expected, the traits showing the lowest correspondence were those with the fewest behavioral anchors (e.g., conscientiousness), but the overall results are surprisingly strong and consistent. These results suggest that a simple additive model might be used to capture a person's mianzi. In an organizational context, a 360-degree feedback scheme might be used to assess self, peer, subordinate, and superior estimations of mianzi. This approach would provide a number of different social contexts that might help people understand how mianzi relates to work behavior across tasks.

There may be a potential concern with this approach to assessment. In some recent work by Bond (1996, personal conversation), he examined the structure of the Big Five (as well as several additional indigenous Chinese traits) and found a remarkably low correspondence between self and peer ratings of traits. In his study, Bond had groups of college students work as a team on a number of projects during the course of a semester class. The team projects determined a significant portion of each student's course grade, and the assessments of the personality traits were made after the students had worked together approximately three months. Using an overall composite of the Big Five, Bond found that the correlations between self and peer ratings were not significant although both constructs independently predicted an individual's self-rated life satisfaction. He suggests that the low correspondence between the two assessment sources may reflect a strong norm of restraint in Chinese society and a desire to withhold explicit displays of judgments and attitudes toward others. The "closed" nature of Chinese culture may act as a moderator in this case such that cues concerning one's personality are not readily displayed (e.g., someone low on agreeableness suppresses his or her anger and disregard for others given cultural norms of modesty and restraint). As a result, the cues observed by Americans leading to strong correlations between peer and self ratings are perhaps absent for the Chinese. My point is that the combinatorial method for using self and other ratings of personality may be problematic from a cultural viewpoint. There may be an additional difficulty as well across cultures. The general awareness of others (perceptiveness in a social context) may be tied to cultural context. For instance, people from a tight culture are often highly aware of others around them, whereas people from a loose culture are not. This suggests that the relationship of self to other ratings vary as a function of cultural characteristics for a variety of reasons.

Although there are a number of clear limitations to using a personality traits approach to understanding mianzi across cultures, there are a number of potential benefits as well. The richness of factors influencing the mianzi a person has is both a benefit and detriment. This richness provides many interesting opportunities for linking independent judgments concerning personality to mianzi, and it provides an opportunity for a common metric (the Big Five) of comparison across very different cultural settings. Clearly this approach has potential worth extensive exploration.

Summary

The focus of this chapter has been to present some specific aspects of mianzi. In contrast to lian, mianzi reflects face after an initial attachment or legitimization occurs. Mianzi reflects the various personal and situational aspects of an individual that provide information concerning position relative to others in a social setting. This information can be acquired through a variety of means ranging from personal characteristics to interpersonal processes. It reflects a characteristic that is best thought of as a social exchange currency that can be gained, lost, given, or taken through a variety of interpersonal processes.

A number of processes underlie the exchange and maintenance of mianzi. I have proposed that the gain and loss of mianzi does not reflect a symmetric process. A person who loses face in a given category cannot compensate for that loss except in the same or a similar category, and mianzi for any given factor has a set point relative to gains and losses. In the case of gaining mianzi, the process reflects a cumulative effect, with various forms of mianzi contributing to a person's overall mianzi. Given the general nature of a person's self-concept (Erez & Earley, 1993), mianzi loss is a larger concern for a person than is mianzi gain. Ironically, the typical performance feedback provided to subordinates by their superiors is negative, suggesting at least the potential for a loss of mianzi. This suggests that performance appraisals have great but largely unrealized potential to benefit face.

Finally, I discussed a specific method through which mianzi might be assessed, namely, an application of personality theory to face. Through an integration of personal and peer judgments of a person's personality, it is possible to assess the content of face across a variety of cultural settings. Although this approach has much potential, there are a number of potential drawbacks, including differential capacity of people displaying the behavioral cues associated with personality assessment, differences in individual perceptiveness to behavioral cues, et cetera.

Notes

1. I would like to thank Michael Bond for his insights concerning this conceptualization of mianzi. This approach was developed during a short visit to the Technion–Israel Institute of Technology, and I would also like to thank the faculty of industrial management and engineering for their helpful comments as well.

2. I would like to thank Albert Goldberg and Gadi Harel for their suggestions concerning the regulation of mianzi.

5

Lian as a Form of Face

Hu described lian as "the respect of the group for a man with a good moral character, the loss of which makes it impossible for him to function properly within the community. *Lien* is both a social sanction for enforcing moral standards and an internalized sanction" (1944:45) Further, he referred to mianzi as "the kind of prestige that is emphasized in this country; a reputation achieved through getting on in life, through success and ostentation. This is prestige that is accumulated by means of personal effort or clever maneuvering" (5).

The two general forms of face, mianzi and lian, differ in a number of ways even though some scholars argue that they are heavily overlapping (e.g., see Chang & Holt, 1994; Ho, 1976; and King, 1989). In terms of simple definitions, lian involves moral character, social obligations, and ethicality, whereas mianzi involves the prestige, status, and social recognition that a person receives or possesses. In my formulation, I assert that lian reflects *an evaluation based on the extent to which a person adheres to and endorses the rules of moral conduct in a given society.* Lian captures the initial legitimization of an individual as a member of society. That is to say, lian establishes that a person wishes to be a fruitful and productive contributor to a given society. In this sense, lian reflects a person's birthright (Hu, 1944). This argument is consistent with some writers such as Ho (1976:870), who states that lian is "something to which everyone is entitled by virtue of his membership in society and can be lost only through unacceptable conduct. As Hu stated, 'All persons growing up in any community have the same claim to *lien,* an honest, decent "face." ' " However, not all scholars who address the concept of lian accept that it is an ascribed characteristic. Even in his recent work Ho (1994) calls into question his earlier assumption about the nature of lian when he states:

> We are tempted to claim that the entitlement to a basic face is universal. Tragically, we cannot. I was wrong when I stated: *"Lien* is something to which everyone is entitled by virtue of his membership in society and can be lost only through unacceptable conduct" (Ho, 1976, p. 870). History is replete with instances where some members of a society

are by definition excluded from the entitlement of *lien:* invalids, slaves, and members of an "inferior race" or a lowly caste (e.g., the untouchables in traditional India). Such exclusion is an expression of prejudice in its deepest form: the negation of *humanhood* (a newly coined term). An individual is judged and treated solely on the basis of group membership—given a number, but nameless, as in a concentration camp. There is no individuality and no individual self. Individual identity is reduced, and becomes identical, to collective identity—defective unclean, even subhuman. (279)

Although I fully agree with his statement that some members or groups of people in a given society may not be extended full representation or participation, this is not to say that they are not afforded lian by their cultural group. The point is that there may be substantial differences among cultural groups in the determination of who can be considered to be human or possess what Ho calls "humanhood." For example, a tribe of Brazilian Indians refer to themselves (as is the case for a number of peoples) as "the humans." Although this tribe does not express anger or aggression toward other groups, they nevertheless view themselves as human and others (including the encroaching Brazilian farmers and construction workers) as less than human.

Certainly some people would argue that many of the atrocities committed during World War II were attributable to one cultural group refusing to acknowledge the humanity of other groups. However, this does not mean that people are born without lian in a given cultural group or even within the context of all humans. On the one hand, lian may be thought of as an ascribed characteristic acknowledged by a specific cultural group. For instance, in some cultural groups lineage is an important characteristic (e.g., the British aristocracy). In other groups, racial or ethnic origin is a key factor. On the other hand, it is possible to think that lian is a universal aspect of being, as I will discuss in another chapter. Using this reasoning, one might ask why any cultural group would view another cultural group as "inferior."

It may be possible that through a variety of circumstances and history a cultural group may lose its lian as well. Dictatorial leaders who themselves have little or no lian may lead a group of people in such a way that they lose their lian or morality. Such may be the case for groups within general cultures, such as the Gestapo troops loyal to Hitler. This subgroup of Nazis was largely responsible for the tragedies that occurred during World War II. My argument, then, is not that groups within a culture are not afforded lian; rather, a particular subgroup or subculture may engage in acts that deem them as lacking lian. Although "untouchables" in India are members of a low caste (Sinha, 1990), this does not mean that they are viewed as evil or lacking morality.

The two concepts of lian and mianzi may have substantial overlap depending on the specific cultural context in which the constructs are discussed. For example, an Indian colleague described the potential interdependence of lian and mianzi. After thinking about these concepts, he commented that in his community, the Bengali region of India, there is a trade-off between the two forms of face. Those individuals who seek mianzi are viewed as having given up their lian to do so. In other words, the pursuit of recognition and status must have come at the expense of personal morality. In American companies, employees who are obsessed with the pursuit of power and position are often viewed with suspicion by work colleagues. Thus the cultural frame in which face is discussed plays a significant role in understanding the potential overlap that may exist between lian and mianzi.

Conceptual Overview of Lian

Lian refers to an interesting aspect of face. Lian captures the basic moral character of a person that is acquired as a birthright (Hu, 1944), and it involves a person's respect derived from a society based on his or her adherence to the rules of moral conduct in a society. In this sense, everyone is born with lian and it is through moral acts that each person reaffirms it. However, lian is not some latent genetic characteristic. It refers to the social perceptions of self and others concerning a person's behavior and intentions. Through a variety of socialization experiences, children acquire the rules for appropriate (moral) behavior in their society just as adults learn the expectations concerning moral behavior in an organization. My argument is that lian is not just a social perception held by external referents concerning a target individual. For example, Hu cites the example of a Chinese college student who became intimate with a fellow student. After getting his girlfriend pregnant, the young man reneged on his promise to marry her, and in a fit of depression she hung herself in the young man's dormitory. As a result, the young man was arrested and sentenced to 10 years in jail. The public sentiment was that the young man's character was flawed, and he lost lian (i.e., was said to have no moral character). His ill-fated lover had lost lian as well and took her own life (in private) as a result. This story illustrates that lian has both public (the young man being sentenced to a jail term) and private (the young woman overcome by shame hanging herself) judgments involved in its determination. Of course, moral actions need not correspond with law. For example, the fall 1995 bombing of an Israeli bus by the Palestinian group Hamas resulted in the deaths of more than 20 Israelis. To the Israelis, this was a wanton act of terrorism and the members of Hamas have no lian; to some Palestinians, the members of Hamas are freedom fighters justified in their armed resistance.

In defining moral goodness or character, a number of scholars have argued for etic standards or universal values. As early as Adam Smith's essay *The Theory of Moral Sentiments,* published in 1759, the idea that people's personal pursuits are tempered by their natural sentiments, such as pity and compassion, was posited. Smith proposed that people have compassion in observing the plights of others, and this basic, moral principle guides our pursuits. Similarly, Durkheim (1933) argued that the enforcement of social contracts requires a willingness of people to pursue those contracts and legitimate them. The moral value of duty drives an adherence to social laws and contracts.

Values-Based Approach to Lian

A number of scholars have developed typologies of values.[1] For instance, an early view of values was presented in Parsons and Shils's (1951) extension of Parsons's *The Structure of Social Action.* Their model posited that social or individual action occurs within the constellations of three interdependent systems—social, personality, and cultural systems. A social system has three parts: it involves an interaction between two or more actors; the situation toward which the actors are oriented includes others who are the object of cathexis; and actors behave in concert as a function of a collective goal orientation. The personality system has several characteristics: first, the system consists of interconnections of actions for a given actor; second, actions are organized according to a structure of need-dispositions; and third, the goals and actions of the individual are not random, but they operate according to a specified structure. Finally, a cultural system has several characteristics. First, the system is guided by the organization of values, norms, and symbols that guide the choices made by actors and direct their interactions. Second, a cultural system is more abstract than either the individual or social system, but these elements can be transmitted to the other systems. Third, a pattern of regulatory norms is not random, but pieces within it are coordinated. Finally, a cultural system represents a pattern of interrelated parts that form value systems, belief systems, and systems of expressive symbols.

The most relevant aspect of their model for an assessment of values and morality is the value-orientation component of the actor's orientation and commitment to particular norms, standards, and criteria of behavior. Specifically, Parsons and Shils (1951) argued:

> Whenever an actor is forced to choose among various means objects, whenever he is forced to choose which need-disposition he will gratify, or how much he will gratify a need-disposition—whenever he is forced to make any choice whatever—his *value-orientations* may commit him to certain norms that will guide him in his choices. . . . On a cultural level we view the organized set of rules or standards as such, abstracted, so to speak, from the actor who is committed to them by his own value-orientations and in whom they exist as need-dispositions to observe these rules. Thus a culture includes a set of *standards*. An individual's value-orientation is his commitment to these standards. (59–60)

Five primary value orientations were used to define and categorize various cultures. These value orientations, or pattern variables, are affective versus affective neutrality, self-orientation versus collectivity orientation, universalism versus particularism, ascription versus achievement, and specificity versus diffuseness. Parsons and Shils refer to these five dichotomies as "pattern variables" and the specific resultant combinations of all five variables as "value orientations." Affective versus affective neutrality is the acceptability of individuals to experiencing immediate gratification. In an affective culture, individuals are permitted to indulge in immediate gratification, whereas in an affectively neutral culture individuals restrain themselves from such excesses. Self-orientation versus collectivity orientation is discussed at greater length in the chapter on societal context, but, in brief, it involves the relation of an individual's pursuit of self-interests versus collective interests. According to self-oriented values, individuals pursue their own interests and "do their own thing," whereas individuals who have strong collectively oriented values view their acts in terms of their impact on important others. Universalism versus particularism concerns the role of general rules in guiding action. Universalistic values reflect a broad set of rules and policies that guide all individuals' actions, and conformity to these standards is expected, whereas particularistic values suggest that people's actions are guided by the unique aspects of the situation and its relevance to specific aspects of the actor. Ascription versus achievement involves how an individual is judged in a society. In an ascriptive culture individuals are judged by attributes they possess (e.g., social group membership and possessions), whereas in an achievement culture individuals are judged by their actions and performance (e.g., skills, work habits). Finally, specificity versus diffuseness concerns the extent to which relations among actors and objects are limited. Diffuse values suggest that the relation of the actor to the social object can be quite indirect, whereas in a specific culture this relation is quite narrow and limited (Erez & Earley, 1993).

With regard to lian, these pattern variables can be thought of as etic standards for moral conduct in a given social system and society. In other words, the morality of action is defined uniquely by examining the pattern variables in their aggregate form. These pattern variables are often presented as the five "dimensions" (e.g., see Hofstede, 1984:36) of culture, but this is somewhat misleading because Parsons and Shils emphasized that the pattern variables together constitute a system. Their argument is that these variables represent five general choices that an individual must make to give a situation specific defined meaning. To be a pattern variable, a given set of alternatives must derive directly from the problem of which mode of orientation will be dominant. Thus people's judgments of their own lian, as well as the lian of others, are based on a congruence of actions relative to these patterned choices.

Another perspective on the assessment of values was developed and presented by Rokeach (1973). He developed a general model of values and the self that has been used by a number of researchers in describing variations in values (Hofstede, 1980a; Rokeach, 1973). Rokeach compared samples of people from various ethnic and social origins within the United States as well as samples of students from a number of different countries. The relation of values to an individual's belief system and definition of the self is central to Rokeach's model. A value is "an enduring belief that a specific mode of conduct or end-state of existence is personally or socially preferable to an opposite or converse mode of conduct or end-state of existence. A *value system* is an enduring organization of beliefs concerning preferable modes of conduct or end-states of existence along a continuum of relative importance" (Rokeach, 1973:5). Two kinds of values, instrumental (moral and competence) and terminal (personal and social), have a relationship to a person's value orientation. Moral instrumental values involve modes of conduct (e.g., behaving honestly) and do not necessarily correspond to particular end-states. Competence instrumental values concern personal accomplishment and self-actualization. The personal and social terminal values involve a self-centered versus a society-centered focus on valued end-states. In a collectivistic culture, individuals focus on their social terminal values, although this does not imply that they disregard personal ones—it merely argues a prioritization of desired end-states. Values also imply a preference pattern and a conception of preferability. They emphasize the desirable rather than simply something that is desired. A value is a conception of something that is personally or socially preferable to an individual.

The personal, social, and cultural experiences of an individual shape a value system that is the basis of lian. What is relevant for one person is not necessarily imposed on others. For example, a person may value honesty and, as a consequence, not steal anything (even pencils or paper clips) from his or her employer. However, this person may not expect his or her work colleague to adhere to this strict standard in order for him or her to be viewed as "honest." Values are organized into systems that have a number of implications for an individual. After an individual learns a particular value, it becomes integrated into an organized system of interrelated values in a hierarchical structure. Just as with values, value systems are relatively stable but not permanent.

Lian is based on the values acquired by a person. Values are standards that lead people to take positions over issues, predispose people to favor particular ideologies, guide self-presentations, make it possible for people to evaluate and judge themselves and others, act as a basis for morality and competence comparisons with others, guide people concerning what ideas of others should be challenged, and tell them how to rationalize beliefs and actions that would otherwise be unacceptable so as to preserve face (Rokeach, 1973:13). Value systems act as general plans for conflict resolution and decision making as well and motivate our actions in daily situations. According to Rokeach (1973), values serve to motivate in several ways:

> If we behave in all the ways prescribed by our instrumental values, we will be rewarded with all the end-states specified by our terminal values. Terminal values are motivating because they represent the super goals beyond immediate, biologically urgent goals. Unlike the more immediate goals, these super goals do not seem to be periodic in nature; neither do they seem to satiate—we seem to be forever doomed to strive for these ultimate goals without quite ever reaching them.
>
> But there is another reason why values can be said to be motivating. They are in the final analysis the conceptual tools and weapons that we all employ in order to maintain and enhance self-esteem. They are in the service of what McDougall (1926) has called the master sentiment—the sentiment of self-regard. (14)

Values exert a powerful motivational influence in three ways: they are instrumental to attain desired end-states, they are desired end-states, and they help to define and reinforce a sense of self. More important for my discussion, Rokeach argues that these values play an important role in determining a person's motive to maintain face, or the "master sentiment." Thus Rokeach's framework proposes the relevance of certain forms of values (instrumental) that are utilized in maintaining face as well as particular end-states (terminal) that form the basis of an etic notion of values.

How does the master sentiment shape a person's lian? This overarching framework of values is depicted in a general model of belief systems. Rokeach organizes an individual's belief system into ten subsystems that can be visualized as a series of concentric circles. At the innermost circle are a person's cognitions about the self, or self-image. The next layers that follow (in sequence moving away from the self) are terminal value system, instrumental value system, attitude system, attitude, cognitions about own behavior, cognitions about significant others' attitudes, cognitions about significant others' values or needs, cognitions about significant others' behavior, and cognitions about behavior of nonsocial objects. Value systems play a central role in an individual's belief system. The ultimate purpose of the total belief system including value systems is to maintain and enhance an individual's self-image, or face. In addition, contradictions among subsystems will usually result in a change in the subordinate system. So if an individual's attitude is changed through some organizational intervention (e.g., an empowerment lecture given by a consultant) that is in conflict with an existing value (e.g., following the boss's orders without question), the attitude change will be temporary and the attitude will likely return to a more consistent position. Although values can be easier to change than attitudes, a value that conflicts with an individual's face will likely change, whereas an attitude that conflicts with behavior is less likely to change. The impetus for change according to Rokeach's value model emphasizes self-dissatisfaction arising from contradictions among subsystems. Greater contradictions exert a stronger influence on an individual's face, so change is more likely to occur. Rokeach argues that affective experiences of self-dissatisfaction, and not cognitive contradictions, are what give rise to changes. Negative affect gives rise to self-dissatisfaction, and change occurs as a result. An attitude and a value that are contradictory will likely be resolved by a change of attitude unless the attitude is more consistent with a person's face. In this case, an individual will be most likely to change the conflicting value in order to maintain the attitude that is consistent with face.

Kluckhohn and Strodtbeck (1961) argued that there are five basic value orientations underlying cultures and thus guiding lian. These orientations are human nature (good versus mixed versus evil crossed with the mutability of the goodness), man–nature (subjugation to nature, harmony with nature, mastery over nature), time (past, present, future), activity (being, being-in-becoming, doing), and relational (lineality, collaterality, individualism). "Human nature" refers to the innate goodness of people. A counterexample of this comes from the idea that people are evil, as evidenced in traditional Puritan thought. Emphasis was placed on controlling and regulating behavior to prevent evil from spreading. The man–nature aspect involves the relation of the individual to nature. For instance, many Asian cultures stress the view that man must be seen as a harmonious part of nature, whereas the orientation of most Anglo Westerners is that of man over nature—that is, dominance of nature through technological means. The time orientation refers to the time frame salient to a group. For example, Chinese culture places a great deal of emphasis on ancestral obligations and rites (related to the Confucian principles of relationships and the five moral principles; see Chang & Holt, 1994). Such a past orientation is contrasted with the future orientation of Westerners, who are often discontent with their current setting and seek change for the better. An activity orientation concerns self-expression in activity. In a being society, emphasis is placed on immediate gratification and spontaneous action, much like Morris's Dionysian dimension. A being-in-becoming society focuses on action and accomplishment—measurable achievements. Finally, the relational orientation involves an individual's relation to his or her collective, similar to Parsons and Shils's self-orientation versus collectivity orientation. The addition of the lineality component is interesting because it adds a temporal dimension to the value-orientation concept.

Perhaps the most widely cited work on values developed for the study of organizations is that of Geert Hofstede (1980a, 1980b, 1983, 1984, 1991). Although Hofstede's values perspective was developed at the nation-state level, the categorization scheme has been applied to employee values as well. Hofstede developed a four-dimension typology of cultural values (later augmented by a fifth dimension discovered in his work with Michael Bond at the Chinese University of Hong Kong, labeled Confucian dynamism). According to Hofstede (1984:21), culture is, "the collective programming of the mind which distinguishes the members of one human group from another." These mental programs are prescribed ways of doing things or acting, and they vary according to levels of uniqueness. At the lowest level there are universally shared mental programs (e.g., biological systems including flight-or-fight responses and emotional displays). Collective programming is shared among individuals who have a common time, place, and language. Finally, the individual level of programming involves those aspects of an individual that determine unique personalities. These mental programs, particularly at the individual level, guide a worker's actions.

According to Hofstede's empirical work, the value dimensions on which cultures vary are power distance, uncertainty avoidance, individualism, masculinity/femininity, and Confucian dynamism. Power distance refers to the extent to which members of a culture accept inequality and large differentials between those with power (e.g., superiors) and those with little power (e.g., subordinates). In low power distance cultures (e.g., Sweden) less emphasis is placed on obedience of children, whereas in a high power distance culture (e.g., Singapore) parents strongly emphasize obedience of children. Uncertainty avoidance reflects the emphasis on ritual behavior, rules, and labor mobility within a culture. High uncertainty avoidance is found in countries that report high levels of stress, such as Japan and Belgium. Individualism reflects the extent to which individuals emphasize their goals over those of their clan or group. Individualistic cultures are characterized by members who strive to achieve their own goals, who have narrow family structures, and whose movement among groups is a function of self-interest, whereas collectivistic cultures are characterized by members who emphasize the needs of the group over self-interests and live in extended family structures. Masculinity/femininity refers to societies that differentiate on the basis of activity and gender. For instance, a masculine culture emphasizes differences between genders, whereas in a feminine culture gender differentiation is minimal. The centrality of work in a person's life is greater in a masculine than in a feminine culture, and quality of life is emphasized over work in a feminine culture. The feminine culture is characterized by individuals who "work to live" rather than "live to work" (Hofstede, 1980b). Finally, Confucian dynamism refers to a time and causal orientation. People from one extreme of Confucian dynamism focus on linearity of time and place an emphasis on the future, such as the British and Americans. Other people emphasize a connection to the past and place an emphasis on reciprocal causation of events, such as the Chinese and Japanese.

From a lian perspective, Hofstede's variations in culture have individual-level manifestations as well. As an example, Triandis (1995) refers to the individual-level aspects of individualism-collectivism as idiocentrism-allocentrism. Cultural values have an individual-level representation that forms the basis of lian. Of course, membership within a given social system and culture does not guarantee that every member will share a cultural value (Martin, 1992; Triandis, 1995). However, these cultural values will contribute, along with personal experience, to a person's underlying definition of lian. Thus, in a highly masculine culture, for example, I would anticipate a relatively strong orientation toward those aspects of lian that relate to activity, accumulation of wealth, et cetera (as well as an increased emphasis on mianzi over lian).

A number of other value systems have been described in the literature. With regard to lian, it should be noted that many of these cultural values have important individual-level counterparts. In other words, cultural values are mapped onto individual values that form the basis of social perceptions concerning lian. For example, Morris (1956) looked at philosophical orientations across cultures through a series of studies he conducted. His empirical work was a logical extension of his philosophical work, and he developed a values scale using this background. He used a tripartite framework to develop a set of ways that people live as indicators of their values. The basic values reflected in the various lifestyles were Dionysian (characterized by indulgence of desires and overt expression of enjoyment), Promethean (characterized by the tendency to actively shape the world and adapt it to human's interests), and Buddhistic (characterized by self-regulation and control as well as temperance of our desires). Morris applied his lifestyle scenarios to student samples from the United States, India, Japan, China, and Norway, and he found that American students were activist and self-indulgent and less subject to social restraint and self-control, whereas Japanese students had a general orientation toward people and society. The Chinese students showed a strong tendency toward enjoyment and activity as well as self-sufficiency.

Other studies of values include work by Ronen and his colleagues (Ronen, 1978, 1982, 1986; Kraut & Ronen, 1975; Ronen & Shenkar, 1985), which focuses on cluster and small space analysis of various countries using a number of basic values. A highly regarded study that still serves as a basis for many current studies was the classic work of Haire, Ghiselli, and Porter (1966) on managerial values. In this study, Haire et al. surveyed managers from 14 countries concerning their attitudes and values toward work relationships, organizations, leadership, and work goals, among others. Whitely and England (1980) analyzed the responses of managers from the United States, Japan, Korea, India, and Australia to England's Values Questionnaire. Maehr and Braskamp (1986) developed a personal incentives model to describe the responses of 575 American and 467 Japanese managers. They found that Americans emphasized affiliation, recognition, and social concern more than the Japanese, who emphasized financial incentives, tasks, and excellence.

Several studies of values, norms, and beliefs address component aspects of culture, such as the work of Bond and his colleagues (e.g., Bond, 1988a; Leung & Bond, 1984), which focuses on equity and equality norms/values held in Asian versus Western cultures. Bond (1988) developed a Chinese values survey that consists of 40 items, and his study of 20 cultures demonstrated several clusters of values: Confucianism (emphasis placed on filial piety, moderation, humbleness, and sense of shame), Oriental tradition (emphasis placed on industry, kindness, loyalty to superiors, and courtesy), and relationship orientation (emphasis placed on tolerance of others, harmony with others, solidarity, patience, and courtesy). Bond correlated his factor scores with those of Hofstede and found a significant relation only between his dimensions and Hofstede's power distance and individualism.

Finally, recent work by Schwartz and his colleagues (e.g., Schwartz, 1992; Schwartz & Bilsky, 1987) concerns Schwartz's model of a universal structure of values. Schwartz and Bilsky developed a theory of values by viewing values as cognitive representations of three universal requirements: biological needs, interactional requirements for interpersonal coordination, and societal demands for group welfare and survival. The core of this approach is the interaction among goals, interests, and motivational domain. Goals are the instrumental versus terminal aspects of values, and interests involve an individualist versus a collectivist versus a "both" orientation. Motivational domain consists of eight aspects: enjoyment, achievement, self-direction, maturity, security, sociability, restrictive conformity, and social power. Schwartz and Bilsky (1987:553) combine these facets of values through the use of a mapping sentence and define a value as "an individual's concept of a transituational goal that expresses interests concerned with a motivational domain and evaluated on a range of importance from range [sic] as a guiding principle in his/her life." The unique combinations of levels of the three facets can be used to characterize individuals from particular cultures. For example, an ambitious person is likely to have an instrumental goal, individualistic orientation, and achievement motivational domain. Schwartz and Bilsky used small space analysis to analyze value data from 455 Israeli schoolteachers and 331 German students, and their results provide support for their model. Schwartz (1993) has examined the structure of values at both the societal (national) and the individual level. Although he has observed some differences, it is interesting note that there is a very strong similarity between the two structures. Again, this suggests that cultural values play a highly significant role in determining the values that underlie lian.

Wilson (1993) has argued for four universal morals, namely, sympathy, fairness, self-control, and duty. He argues that these four sentiments constitute a moral sense in all peoples and that there are discernible social and biological imperatives underlying these sentiments. Sympathy is the capacity for being affected by the experiences of others. For example, Wilson discusses the case of a hospital benefactor who gives a generous gift and receives public recognition in return. Although the benefactor may have provided the gift for public recognition, Wilson queries why observers would recognize the act if they suspected that the deed was not purely altruistic. He concludes this is because people wish to encourage in one another the sentiment of sympathy, even in a potentially jaded act. In fairness, Wilson suggests that there are outcome and procedural standards by which actions are judged as fair or just, a finding well supported in an organizational context (e.g., Baron & Cook, 1992; Bazerman, Loewenstein, & White, 1992; Greenberg & Folger, 1983; Lind & Tyler, 1988; see Rawls, 1971, and Thibaut & Walker, 1975, for a more general discussion of justice). For example, individuals provided with an opportunity to express their reactions to an evaluation system ("voice") experience stronger feelings of procedural and outcome fairness and perform better than individuals not afforded such an opportunity even if "voice" occurs without concomitant decision control (Earley & Lind, 1987). Studies conducted in Hong Kong and elsewhere verify a cross-national similarity of procedural justice effects (Leung, & Park, 1986). Self-control is an individual's restraint in the present on behalf of the future. For example, a student pursuing doctoral studies may live as a pauper for a number of years in order to obtain the skills, knowledge, and credentials needed to obtain a prestigious faculty position. Likewise, an organization that channels its extra profits into research and development rather than issuing extra dividends will ensure a more profitable future for itself (and its shareholders). Finally, Wilson's concept of duty represents an individual's willingness to be faithful to obligations derived from society, family, and important referent others. For instance, Huston, Geis, and Wright (1976) studied the actions of a number of "good samaritans" (people who intervened on behalf of others during a crisis). They found that many acted because it appeared to be the "right thing to do" rather than out of sympathy for the victims per se. Through these four sentiments, Wilson argues, people function and behave within a society.

General Framework of Values and Beliefs for Lian

This discussion suggests that there are universal standards or values that constitute the rules underlying a person's lian. Although some people may emphasize duty over sympathy or self-control over fairness, these standards exist throughout the world. From the perspective of face, people's actions are judged in terms of their impact on and reflection of these moral sentiments. Thus, if we encounter someone who displays the Hobbesian tact of self-absorption and sociopathology, we judge this brute as lacking honor, merit, and conscience.

Based on the existing literature, there are at least eight general values that cut across cultures. I have listed these values in Table 5-1 along with a brief description of each. I have classified them into two general groups, namely, social relatedness and moral imperatives. By social relatedness, I mean those values that are relevant to the proper functioning in a social system. These values manifest themselves in the social system rather than within an individual. For example, affiliation is a value reflected in all cultures and is a type of social relatedness value. Rebuffing such a value is viewed as sociopathology or neuroticism, and people who reject affiliation reject societal membership as well. Moral imperatives are universal dispositions of the person toward justice or goodness. Wilson's construct of self-control is a moral imperative as well, even though its consequences may have important ramifications for the social system to which a member belongs.

As described in Table 5-1, there are three types of social relatedness values. First, there is the value of affiliation, which refers to the importance of social ties and interaction. People seek out contact with others. Second, sympathy refers to Wilson's characteristic of being affected by the actions and situation of others. When we see someone else who is in need, we react affectively to this person. Although a person might argue that this occurs for selfish reasons ("Imagine if I was in that position"), it may be, as Wilson argues, that people encourage sympathetic reactions in others to benefit others. Third, family origins are the connections that a person has to his or

Table 5-1. Overview of Values in Societies

General Value	Specific Value	Description
Social relatedness	Affiliation	Desire to interact socially and form ties with others
	Sympathy	Affective relation to others in terms of their needs and personal circumstance
	Family origins	Importance of family unit for purposes of biological survival and perpetuation
Moral imperatives	Self-awareness	Importance of self-definition and determining one's place in a social system
	Duty	Willingness to forego individual goals/outcomes in order to pursue goals/outcomes that are necessary for the survival of the social system
	Good versus evil	Correctness or acceptability of action
	Spirituality	Emphasis on uniqueness of being human
	Justice	Emphasis on distribution and process aspects of reward/ punishment allocations in society

her family. This value is best traced back to biological necessity, through which reproduction is a needed component of a social system.

There are five types of moral imperatives as values. First, there is the value of self-awareness, according to which that all individuals seek to determine their position and purpose in the world. Self-awareness involves the fundamental question of who we are in our social system. Self-definition is the single most critical value, and it underlies many of our actions. Second, duty represents a person's relationship to his or her social system as well as collectives or in-groups. People invest their self-definition in their collective, and this results in a willingness of the individual to subordinate self-interests to the interests of the collective if required. It also captures the Parsonian characteristic of affectivity. Third, there is the value of goodness. In all cultures, certain behaviors are considered counterproductive to the culture and "evil." For example, all social systems condemn the murder of societal members for personal gain. Likewise, most cultures condemn pedophiles and familial inbreeding. These taboos have likely arisen because of biological needs, although there are several notable exceptions typically attributable to a lack of appropriate social partners. Fourth, the value of spirituality exists in all cultures. That is not to say that all cultures have a sense of a singular godlike entity, but they believe that humans possess some characteristic unique to them. It is this point that relates to the idea of harmony or balance found in many cultures. Finally, the value of justice exists in all societies. This value has two important components: distribution and process. Although some people emphasize additional forms of justice, I would broadly define distribution justice as related to all aspects of outcomes (reward or punishment), with process referring to all procedures through which outcomes are distributed or allocated. Thus these two forms would encompass more specific forms that are discussed in the justice literature (e.g., Brockner et al., 1993; Greenberg & Folger, 1983; Greenberg, 1982; Lind & Tyler, 1988). (Although both types of values constitute lian, there are differences in the form emphasized in particular cultures. Again, I would emphasize that these are values concerning individuals within social systems and not the cultural values to which they are related.)

Connecting Values to Lian: Social Perception

As I suggested in Chapter 3, the linkage of societal values to face can be mapped through their influence on personal values, personality structure, and social perception. The linkages that I am describing are multitiered. First, societal values and norms influence individuals' values through a number of mechanisms (see Chapters 8 and 9), including organizations, educational institutions, political systems, et cetera. These various institutions are structured such that the reward systems reinforce the endorsement of particular values over others. For example, there has been a "teaming" of American business and business schools. As a result, an increasing endorsement of such management techniques as empowerment, participation, employee involvement, et cetera, has occurred in the American workplace. A quick perusal of trade books offered by American authors reveals a plethora of such techniques. Thus clusters of societal values are associated with corresponding clusters of personal values (Schwartz, 1993).

The second linkage occurs between personal values and social judgments concerning lian. One possible linkage is explained by the relationship of personal values to individuals' beliefs and cognitions, as suggested by Rokeach (1973) and Schwartz and Bilsky (1987). Another possibility, suggested by Bond and Forgas (1984) and Smith and Bond (1994), is that cultural values influence social judgments of others through their impact on personality traits. In other words, cultural and personal values potentially influence judgments of lian based on the personality profiles of societal members. So, for instance, in a culture stressing agreeableness, such as Japan, people's judgments concerning lian will be linked to rules of conduct related to helping behavior, conflict avoidance, harmony, et cetera. That is to say, personality traits will co-vary as a function of societal culture, and these traits form the basis of social perceptions of lian (and mianzi). I reemphasize, however, that these perceptions are not simply judgments of others; rather, they represent a combination of self and other perceptions. A manager's lian is a function of his or her introspection of self, perceptions of others' views, and the others' views as they influence the social milieu.

As I suggest, the relationship of these societal and personal values to lian varies across particular cultures. Although my basic assertion is that lian is a birthright and that it is something that may be lost but not easily regained, there are some important subtleties to this argument. First, how are the social perceptions based on these values or judgments concerning character related to societal and personal values? I agree with Hu's (1944) assertion that people born into a given society assume that all individuals are potentially endowed with these qualities. That is to say, people may all develop a sense of justice, affiliation, goodness, et cetera, and these values are necessary for the proper functioning of social systems. For example, what organization can function without a just reward system? Although short-term success may exist, such an organization will not be viable in the long run if its systems of rewards are viewed by employees as unjust and unfair. (Again, I would note that the specific definition of fairness may differ across companies in various cultures. The point I am making is that all companies in all cultures have some rules to define justice.) What about religious groups that advocate that people are evil or inherently sinful? According to Calvinist doctrine, people are assumed to be impure, in some form; otherwise they would appear godlike. Although someone may not necessarily be born good or pure, it is asserted that through righteous acts he or she may become good or pure—and, more important, anyone can achieve this purity through the right lifestyle or choices. Few religions, for example, postulate that only a select few are allowed access to a "heaven" or plane of spiritual awareness, and it is generally assumed that everyone can achieve such awareness through various processes. Although everyone may not be assumed to be "good" in a given culture, everyone is possessed with the capability to achieve some spiritual awareness or purity. If one chooses to abandon such a pursuit, then lian is lost (or abandoned).

From the proximal perspective of organizational functioning, this discussion implies that organizational members have a basic claim to certain values and that this claim must be honored in order for someone to maintain his or her lian. The act of joining an organization signals an implicit agreement between company and employee that the employee will receive compensation in return for services provided. An employee who fails to honor commitments is rejected as unfaithful or untrustworthy, and an organization that arbitrarily promotes or rewards people is viewed as biased or unjust.

Another characteristic of lian concerns its degree of interchangeability. I said earlier that not all of the values underlying lian are comparable in terms of their relationship to lian. What I mean by this is that some of the values are more central to lian, depending on the culture (Smith & Bond, 1994). Although these values exist in all cultures (etic), they may vary in relative salience across cultures. For example, in the United States the value of justice is very important, whereas it may be of less importance in mainland China. Cultures will vary in what they consider to be the most salient aspects of lian, or moral character. This suggests that the astute researcher must examine these values within a given social system to understand which ones will be the most potent or relevant. If justice is highly salient in a culture and a manager is deemed unjust, then his or her lian is lost and may not be regained. However, if this manager is deemed as impersonal and detached from his or her subordinates and an affiliation value is less salient, then he or she may not lose lian.

What if lian is lost? Earlier I asserted that lian is best thought of as something ascribed to societal membership and that it can be lost but not easily regained. Again, this statement must be modified to reflect that some aspects of lian are more critical than others, depending on the culture. Certainly the loss of lian is neither irreversible nor binary. Individuals may lose small amounts of lian and still function within a social context. For example, U.S. president Richard Nixon lost lian as a result of the cover-up and subterfuge concerning Watergate. Despite this situation and his near impeachment, Nixon continued to be adored by many people. He lost lian with regard to his actions on Watergate, but he still retained some lian (perhaps with regard to his foreign policy initiatives). However, it would be difficult to view people such as Charles Manson or Adolf Hitler as anything but reviled criminals. They lost lian completely because they so strongly violated values of goodness, justice, et cetera. In such an instance, their lian cannot be regained. Certain violations of values (e.g., murder) are so fundamental to all societies that lian is lost and not regained.

A difficulty that this point raises concerns the philosophy of redemption and rehabilitation for one's actions. Again, I would return to the example of a religious group that assumes people are born impure. The point is that if a person commits a crime, he or she can receive redemption according to many religions (e.g., by accepting God). As I described earlier, lian is carried with someone and cannot be hidden to oneself. Although Michael Milken was convicted of criminal acts and he sought to redeem himself through various benevolent acts, he lost lian and it cannot be recovered quickly or easily. However, in religions prescribing forgiveness lian may be reaffirmed. Applying this to an organization suggests that in the cultures of particular companies moral violations can be overcome through subsequent citizenship behavior or contribution.

How is lian regulated and balanced? For example, a colleague from the Bengali region of India commented that in his culture if someone gains great wealth it is assumed by others that it must have been at the cost of goodness of character. Lian is gained through a trade-off with mianzi—particularly the material aspects of mianzi. Certainly this view is expressed in the West through such phrases as "selling your soul to the devil" and "giving your right arm" for material gain. Many religious orders require their members to give up a significant part of their wealth, or all of it, in order to develop proper spirituality. Implicit in such actions is that lian competes with mianzi in a zero-sum game. Still, in some cultures, a person acquires both lian and mianzi through personal actions. For example, in the 1700s, Catholic priests led a relatively affluent lifestyle and were viewed as having both lian and mianzi.

Does lian exist separate from social evaluation? Although most of the thinking of Goffman and others has focused on the social setting as the critical factor in determining face and facework, I assert that lian is not something that entirely depends on the immediate social context. As presented in Figure 3-1, there are internal and external referents for lian, and the internal referent is dominant. Although it may take an audience (class of students or colleagues) for me to establish my mianzi as a professor (external referent), lian is carried within as well as evaluated from the outside. If an unjust person has lost lian, then it does not matter if he or she goes to a new town/city. The loss of lian reflects a fundamental aspect of his or her character regardless of the "publicness" of such an act. Whereas mianzi depends largely on a social structure and judgments of referent others, lian is housed primarily within the domain of the individual, even though it may manifest itself in the public domain through interpersonal exchange.

This last point is related to Mead's (1928) notion of guilt versus shame as well. Mead used this categorization approach to understanding various cultures. In a guilt-oriented society, a greater emphasis is placed on individual action as a cause of guilt. It is through one's volition that one commits immoral acts, and so one experiences guilt. Shame is based more in one's general, social context, and it may be attributable to circumstances outside one's control (Ho, 1976). For example, an employee feels guilty for stealing a computer program from his or her company whereas he or she feels shame for wearing thick glasses. People in cultures emphasizing shame over guilt will often take on personal burdens of change even if they are not immediately responsible for a given outcome. For example, the Japanese growth in savings has been attributed to the general sense of shame that the Japanese experienced after World War II (Chang & Holt, 1994) as a societal means of atoning for their actions. This suggests that for the Japanese lian is more closely aligned with shame. Mianzi is more in the domain of volition; guilt may be a motive that gives rise to a person's attempt to acquire more mianzi.

In the next chapter, I turn to the topic of the social actor. Although face remains an important focus of my discussion, many of the dynamics underlying the nature of face and social interaction are better understood in a more general discussion of the social actor. My focus will view the social actor as a self-aware and purposive individual who enacts various roles in his or her social environment.

Note

1. Although a number of people have advocated that moral standards and values are relative to and within any given culture (e.g., Benedict, 1934; Martin, 1992; Resaldo, 1989), my position is that universal aspects of moral action differ in the relative level of activation in a given culture. Thus, although a moral value such as fairness is universal, the specific manifestations of fairness found across societies vary. For instance, U.S. managers endorse the distribution of resources based on an equity principle, whereas Indian managers endorse the distribution of resources based on need (Sinha, 1990). In both societies, there exists a fairness norm; what particular rule is employed (equity versus equality) varies by cultural setting.

6

The Social Actor

The focus of my discussion in the last two chapters was on very specific aspects of a social actor—mianzi and lian. However, such a view understates the importance of contextual aspects of a person's environment and general facets of a person's personality and idea structure while it overstates particular internal facets. I do not mean to imply that a social actor responds to and influences his or her social context simply to regulate face. By focusing on the concept of face, I think that researchers can gain new insights into the social processes that we observe in organizations (and elsewhere), but I do not mean to imply that face is the only relevant motive underlying a person's actions. The social actor in my model is a complex character who responds to external and internal stimuli (Scott, 1994), actively engages the environment (Ashford & Tsui, 1992; Ashford & Northcraft, 1992), enacts aspects of his or her social milieu (Weick, 1969), and engages in sense making in order to interpret observed patterns.

If a social actor is viewed as a dynamic and inquisitive character in an organization, what are the key aspects of an actor that make it possible to understand organizational behavior? I present five basic categories of social life that are directly relevant to how an actor operates and behaves in an organization. First, the personal values held by individuals are of central importance for understanding face. As I discussed in Chapters 3–5, a number of fundamental values drive lian and mianzi, and I will discuss these briefly in the context of a social arena in which an actor operates. Second, a person's self-concept is at the very heart of a social actor. Using work from Markus and her colleagues (e.g., Markus & Kitayama, 1991) and my earlier work with Erez (Erez & Earley, 1993), I will describe a model of self-concept in which face plays a central role. Third, an individual's self-identity based in various social groupings will be explored in work by Tajfel, Turner, and their colleagues (e.g., Tajfel & Turner, 1982; Turner, 1986). Fourth, role expectations are clearly an important aspect governing employees' concepts of duty, choices of action, et cetera (Katz & Kahn, 1978). A great deal of research attention has been focused on the nature of roles that employees enact as well as the relationship of those roles to expectations of employee behavior. Finally, I will discuss the normative constraints facing a social actor in terms of socialization processes (e.g., Van Maanen & Schein, 1977) as well as normative influence (e.g., Asch, 1951; Katz & Kahn, 1978).

Personal Norms and Values

As I discussed in Chapter 3, values play a fundamental role in any conceptualization of face and a social actor. Values are the foundation from which both facade and social definition are constructed, and they guide, albeit indirectly, most volitional action as well as habituated behavior. So voluminous is the topic of values that any attempt to describe them will inevitably fall short. However, I will draw upon some of the major theorists who have discussed the significance of values (in addition to my prior discussion of Parsons, Kluckhohn, Rokeach, and others in Chapter 5), including Kohlberg (1969), Rokeach (1973), and Smith (1991), among others.

In a general sense, values involve both the aspects of the world to which we orient ourselves and the features of people themselves (Smith, 1991:5). A widely accepted definition of value is from Kluckhohn, who said: "A value is a conception, explicit or implicit, distinctive of an individual or characteristic of a group, of the desirable which influences the selection from available modes, means, and ends of action" (1951:395). The significance of this definition lies in three aspects: First, value is a construct that lies within an individual or a group, and there are predictable patterns of groups based on their individual memberships. This is a very important aspect of my approach to culture because it is at the individual level that I observe the manifestations of cultural influence, that is to say, at the individual values level. This is not to say that culture can be simply reduced to an individual differences analysis of values, but I argue that these local representations of values (local to the individual level) are important in order to tie cultural effects to individual actions. Second, a value directs the actions and strategies for action that are pursued by an individual. This is an important characteristic in order to link macro-level cultural values to individual actions and reactions such as those related to face. Third, values capture the desirable rather than the desired (Smith, 1991:5). This means that values capture general orientations rather than impulsive wants or preferences.

A number of specific models and frameworks have been proposed in order to understand values and morals in society. For example, Kohlberg (1969) refined and expanded on Piaget's analysis of moral judgment and produced a six-stage model for moral reasoning. The six stages fall into three broad categories: a premoral level concerning the pain-pleasure principle; conventional morality, having to do with what is lawful, right, and proper as defined by a society; and a postconventional aspect characterized by reasoning in terms of social contracts and general, universal principles. In a related vein, ethicist Girvetz (1973) in his book *Beyond Right and Wrong: A Study in Moral Theory* describes a useful analysis or morals and values. He distinguishes among three categories of morals. First, there are the aesthetic and prudent uses of good, right, and ought. What is good is an immediate and preferred state such as Kohlberg's premorality. The emphasis on the immediate outcome is consistent with our dominant pattern of preferences. Second, Girvetz distinguishes between good and right in moral terms such that certain conduct is good because it is judged as lawful or acceptable given dominant standards of conduct. In this sense, behavior or conduct is good because it is right, not simply because of given consequences or outcomes. Finally, there is the truly ethical situation, which is evidenced only when a person must act in an ethically ambiguous situation. In such a setting, only the highest level of ethical development leads an individual to attain a moral pattern of action that supersedes his or her individual set of interests or preferences.

Thus far, this discussion of values suggests that they are critical in guiding action and are dynamic facets of a social actor subject to their own growth and development. Additional facets to values guide action and provide a conduit through which cultural effects are evidenced. Rokeach (1973) compared the relation of values to an individual's belief system and definition of the self. To Rokeach, values imply a preference pattern and a conception of preferability. They emphasize the desirable rather than simply something that is desired. A value is a conception of something personally or socially preferable for an individual that is organized into systems that have a number of implications for an individual. After an individual learns a particular value, it becomes integrated into an organized system of interrelated values in some hierarchical structure. Just as with values, value systems are relatively stable but not permanent. Values are standards that lead people to take positions on issues, favor particular ideologies, evaluate others, et cetera. More important, values enable a social actor to engage his or her world and reconcile various contradictory experiences and information, as I described earlier.

A number of aspects of values are important to a social actor. Whereas Rokeach (1973) argues that values are, in some fashion, shared prescriptions of beliefs within a given social system, it is possible to think of values as somewhat independent of social enactment. Indeed, we will not have standards for the desirable without some experience in social action (e.g., approval of extra-role behavior from respected superiors in a company), but a number of aspects of an individual's values are uniquely developed and not truly shared with others. Consistent with my distinction of individual representations of cultural values (Earley, 1994), the argument is that there are aspects of an individual's values that reflect individual eccentricities as well as shared influence from society. Additionally, values impact the collective perceptions (subjective experience) of people in a social system that, in turn, influence the transmitted aspects of shared values. In other words, values for the individual are both cause and effect of individual and shared experiences.

How do values relate to face and a social actor? Most basically, people engage in face-related behaviors as a way of defining their position in a social system that is *of their own making*. A social actor operates in a structure that does not exist independently of the participants with whom he or she is interdependent, and understanding the actor's position requires that he or she work in an enacted environment based on behaviors guided by values. I do not wish to get into a "chicken-egg" debate concerning the causal sequencing of events; however, I would emphasize that values guide our actions and that these actions constitute the interdependencies making up our social system, which shapes our values. For example, an employee who engages in organizational citizenship behavior (OCB) by working late hours for no pay is rewarded by his or her supervisor through formal recognition in his or her work unit.

The employee engages in these actions because he or she has a value of dedication and commitment to the company. What is the consequence of this minidrama? Not only does this reinforce the employee's positive attitude toward OCB (assuming that the employee "values" such recognition), but it also signals to other employees the significance of OCB in these forms. Recognizing and desiring such outcomes, other employees engage in similar actions. Eventually, the result is that a general values shift is observed in the social system (company), which further legitimates OCB in employees' eyes. For our original target employee, these changes have reinforced commitment and loyalty as significant values along with the associated behaviors (e.g., helping coworkers, working late), and they have now become more salient than other existing ones. Now that OCB has become an institutionalized practice, it is no longer viewed as extra-role behavior by our employee, who will seek additional outlets of behavior for this value of OCB (i.e., dedication and loyalty or commitment to his or her company). However, the specific aspects of OCB previously engaged in have become institutionalized actions, which are expected of all employees. In this example, the early OCB actions of the employee (given life through his or her values) have caused a change in the social system, which has, in turn, changed the employee's perception of his or her own work responsibilities. In addition, the cycle has resulted in a shift in value prioritization that will eventually cause the system to continue its evolution.

A desire to define oneself in a social system is a universal motive. Face-related actions are a way in which a social actor enacts a reality to understand him- or herself relative to others. Values guide the specific actions that he or she engages in and reflect his or her socially learned beliefs, and personality traits (shaped by cultural and personal values) shape his or her perceptions of self and others. A social actor, then, is best conceptualized as a product and producer of values and judgments through shared and unique human experiences. The "line" (Goffman, 1959) that is engaged in by an individual reflects these values, and values guide the type of information sought in order to establish and maintain face.

Self-Concept

Many of the models in international research seem to push the personal concept of self out into the periphery. In this section, I will focus on the self-concept and its role in understanding organizational behavior in an international context. The primary sources of my discussion are Markus and Kitayama (1991), Triandis (1995), and Erez and Earley (1993). In addition, I will draw from other research concerning self-concept, including that of Cushman (1990) and Sampson (1981).

Information-processing models used in social cognition rely on the processing capacity of an individual to explain how environmental cues are selectively recognized, evaluated, and interpreted in terms of their meaning for the individual and how they affect behavior. A useful starting point in describing these effects is the storage bin model proposed by Wyer and Srull (1980). In this model, individuals are thought to have several broad types of memory, short-term versus long-term, and a number of processing aspects to memory, recall, and interpretation. In the long-term memory of a person, there are "storage bins" that are collections of schema, traits, characteristics, et cetera, based on a common theme (person, place, event, etc.). As demands posed by the immediate environment make salient particular aspects, a controlling function (executor) coordinates the retrieval of relevant information from long-term memory to be processed with new information within the short-term memory. Although the specific dynamics of the Wyer and Srull model are not germane to my discussion, what is useful is the analogy that a social actor relies on internal information and cues stored in a long-term memory as well as cues and information generated from a social context. What this suggests is that a construct such as a cultural value can influence a person's judgments through a direct impact (e.g., reactions to witnessing a specific cultural ritual such as a marriage ceremony) as well as an indirect impact (e.g., affective and cognitive reactions to a marriage ceremony based on internalized views of marriage). These various processes underlie each person's self-concept. Regardless of cultural or societal origin, all people have a self-concept. What varies, however, is the nature of what the "self" means across societies (Markus & Kitayama, 1991; Miller, 1990; Triandis, 1995). What I would anticipate is that some form of information processing occurs for all people, but the specific nature of the processing is an emic phenomenon. Likewise, self-concept is a universal, and an important function of face-related behavior is helping the social actor define his or her position within a given social system.

Self-concept is a link between culture and work behavior (Erez & Earley, 1993). It is shaped by culture and the social environment, and it directs and focuses the social actor toward behavior that can satisfy its underlying motives. Culture consists of generally shared values and norms of a society (Rohner, 1984), and these values and norms are transmitted from one generation to another through socialization, learning, and direct reinforcement (Bandura, 1986; Rohner, 1984; Jahoda, 1984). A person's self-concept is dynamic, and it actively interprets the world around us. It influences a number of psychological processes such as information processing and affect as well as interpersonal processes such as attribution, interpersonal interaction, group memberships, et cetera (Markus & Kitayama, 1991). Thus the self is a person's mental representation of his or her personality, identity, and social roles, and its operation depends on a person's motives and needs and the nature of the social context in which a person operates.

It is this last aspect, the importance of the social context in which a person operates, that has directed new research streams in cross-cultural organizational behavior. Humans are social creatures, and their self-understanding is derived from a social context (Etzioni, 1973; Sampson, 1989). It is our relationships to others and our relative position in a social system that provide for self-definition. Without such definition, a person is likely to suffer from anomie (Merton, 1968) and alienation (Sampson, 1989). Bandura (1986) proposed that the self is a composite view formed through direct experiences as well as through the external evaluations of others. Likewise, Gecas (1982) describes the general movement within sociology in which a person is defined through his or her membership in a social system, as reflected by the responses and perceptions of other members in the system. A reference group's norms become the internalized standards against which people are judged (Smith & Bond, 1994). The significance of a social system for understanding the self-concept is highlighted in recent work on institutional theory by Scott (e.g., Scott & Meyers, 1994). He argues that a person's actions are best characterized by a dynamic view in which the concerns for self-interest, effectiveness, strategic behavior, and rational calculation and innovation are components of a modern view of institutional influences. This point is also central to Giddens's (1984, 1989) view of structuration in society (see Chapter 6 for a further discussion). By structuration, Giddens refers to the reciprocal effects of actors and social structures within social systems. While structure has traditionally been viewed as static, Giddens argues that it is best thought of as a dynamic factor that houses and influences social actors as well as being a by-product of their subjective interpretation and reconstruction. Thus the social actor is both cause and effect of the social system in which he or she operates.

The conceptual framework often employed in understanding how information relevant to self-concept is stored and organized is derived from social cognition. According to this approach, self-concept is viewed as a person's representation of his or her own personality, experiences, and values, formed through experience and thought and encoded in memory along with other representations (Kihlstrom, et al., 1988). Using the Wyer and Srull (1980) approach, self-concept can be thought of as a set of schemas or generalizations about the self derived from social experiences and internal evaluations. These schema have both content and process in that they contain information about a person's characteristics as well as procedures and processes through which these characteristics are realized. For example, an employee might have a self schema focused on honesty. This implies that he or she not only would describe him- or herself as honest, trustworthy, and reputable, but his or her self schema will have implied action sequences such as returning a lost wallet unopened, reporting unethical work behaviors of others, et cetera. The content of self-conceptions forms the structure, and it anchors the self in the social system. Self-evaluation deals with the dynamic dimension of the self. At a structural level, each schema is a generalization about what the self is and contains descriptive information about traits, roles, and behavior, as well as procedural knowledge of rules and procedures for making inferences and evaluation for its own functioning and development (Kihlstrom & Cantor, 1984).

So what, then, is a self-concept? The self is multidimensional, consisting of many role identities (Gecas, 1982; Hoelter, 1985), traits, and characteristics (Markus & Wurf, 1987). People differ in the specific makeup of the parts constituting a self schema, as well as the relative importance of these individual parts. However, the metastructure of self-concept is based on a hierarchy with the most general aspects of the self at the top, followed by more specific attributes (Cantor & Kihlstrom, 1987; Marsh, 1986). In addition, a schema is constructed in which certain aspects are more central than others, with the central traits more substantial for the self-concept. Individuals are known to be more committed to their central roles because those roles are more consequential to their behavior (Etzioni, 1973).

Information included in self-schema is great and varied, including information concerning our past, present, and future. However, not all information is accessible all the time. In information-processing terms, self represents declarative knowledge consisting of abstract and concrete factual attributes and features. The aspects of personality brought to our attention at any particular time are determined by contextual factors (Kihlstrom et al., 1988). That part of the self that is active at any moment is called the "working self" or the "self-concept of the moment" (Markus & Kunda, 1986; Markus & Wurf, 1987). The working self deals directly with the social environment. Compared to the deeper levels of the self-concept, it is more accessible and malleable, and it is quite strongly connected with the current situation in which a person operates. The configuration of the immediate social environment determines which aspect of the self is accessed and processed.

In addition to its structure, self-concept is actively regulated through a number of psychological processes (Erez & Earley, 1993). These processes include goal setting for behavior relevant to self-concept, strategy selection and development to attain these goals, self-monitoring in order to determine distance from goals, judgments concerning the worth of various goals, and self-reinforcement in the attainment of the goals (Locke & Latham, 1990). While some theories emphasize self-reinforcement as critical for self-regulation (Bandura, 1986; Kanfer, 1980), others emphasize information rather than rewards as the critical determinant of attempted changes (Carver & Scheier, 1981, 1990).

A significant view of self-concept from a cultural perspective is presented in Markus and Kitayama's (1991) theory. They provide the initial discussion of how culture and self can be integrated. According to their approach, a person's self-concept is represented by a collection of associations of memberships and activities. Using the metaphor of Venn diagrams, these associations vary in size, degree of inclusiveness, and degree of overlap with other associations. For example, an individualist might have a relatively small degree of inclusiveness (e.g., small family membership) but a large degree of overlap with other groupings (e.g., membership in friendship, work, or social activity groups). Based on Triandis's (1995) discussion of individualism and collectivism, it would be expected that a collectivist would have a relatively high degree of immediate association (high inclusiveness) but a high degree of distinctiveness (little overlap with other associations). Interestingly, Holt and Chang (1994) argue that mianzi may create the opportunities for a dynamic rebalancing of these associations, as I discussed in Chapters 3 and 4. More specifically, they argue that by extending mianzi to members of a certain group, a person can "connect" two distinct (and separate) in-groups. If person A is a member of in-group X and has mianzi relevant to in-group Y, then he or she can create a connection between groups X and Y through his or her mianzi. Seen from this perspective, the role of face may extend from simply regulating in-group activity to securing desired relationships and resources with various important out-groups.

According to Erez and Earley's (1993) cultural self-representation model, people have the capacity for self-evaluation, and this capacity generates a need for the preservation of a positive self-esteem. Self-regulatory processes work to ensure that a person maintains a positive view of him- or herself in a variety of operating environments. A person's self-concept, then, is partly of its own origins (Gecas, 1982). Erez and Earley (1993) argue that three basic motives guide a person's self-concept: enhancement, efficacy, and consistency.

Self-enhancement is a person's desire to feel positively about him- or herself. It is affected by environmental influences and by psychological processes of sampling, assessing, and interpreting the environment. Research on self-enhancement demonstrates the existence of self-serving bias in information processing (Gecas, 1982). For example, numerous studies have demonstrated that people attend more to self-referent information than to information that is directed toward others (Kihlstrom et al., 1988). In a study by Rogers, Kuiper, and Kirker (1977), subjects were asked to recall information about a list of personal traits. In one condition they focused on the attributes of the trait, and in another condition they were asked to judge whether or not certain traits were self-relevant. In the latter condition, subjects recalled more items than in the former condition. Researchers suggest that this type of self-serving bias occurs because of the relative accessibility of certain memories over others. Accessibility of a memory is a function of the degree to which the stimulus information makes contact with existing knowledge during encoding (Kihlstrom et al., 1988). Self-referent information is more highly recalled than any other type of information because it is more central to our thinking. Self-relevant information is recalled better than irrelevant information, and it is recognized more readily (Erez & Earley, 1993; Markus & Wurf, 1987).

One of the manifestations of a self-enhancement motive is the general tendency of people to distort reality in order to selectively maintain a positive self-image (Gecas, 1982). For example, people choose to judge others on dimensions that are personally relevant and not on other dimensions. They prefer and seek out positive information about themselves, and they selectively sample, interpret, and remember events that support positive self-concept.

A need for maintaining a positive self-image is, of course, a key aspect of understanding why face concerns are so critical to organizational behavior. Self-image needs are shaped partially by culture and partially by the unique individual difference characteristics of the person (Markus & Kitayama, 1991). For example, Triandis (1995) gives the example of a boy from a collectivistic culture whose goal is to excel in school in order that his parents be proud of him as his contributions positively reflect on his family. Pride of this child is based on a positive contribution to the family and not simply to himself. However, in an individualistic culture, the child's focus is on personal accomplishment for individual recognition. Thus different influences on the self emerge in different cultures, and consequently, different managerial approaches will be effective in satisfying needs for self-enhancement.

The second motive of Erez and Earley's model is self-efficacy—Bandura's (1986) motivation concept. Perceived self-efficacy is "a judgment of one's capability to accomplish a certain level of performance" (Bandura, 1986:391). People generally avoid tasks and situations they believe exceed their capabilities. Efficacy judgments promote the choice of situations and tasks with high likelihood of success and eliminate the choice of tasks that exceed one's capabilities. According to Bandura (1986), four sources modify a person's self-efficacy, namely, enactive attainment based on mastery experiences, vicarious experiences, verbal persuasion such as "pep talks," and physiological states that generally degrade efficacy (e.g., symptoms of fatigue, stress, and anxiety indicate that a person is not at his or her best and, therefore, has lower efficacy).

Efficacy has been mainly developed with respect to the individual (Bandura, 1986). However, a perceived collective efficacy is crucial for what people choose to do as a group, how much effort they put into it, and how persistent they are when facing failures (Gibson, 1995). The strength of groups, organizations, and nations lies partly in people's sense of collective efficacy (Bandura, 1986; Earley, 1993). It is not clear how, exactly, collective efficacy is shaped by the social environment and whether it is more likely to develop in certain cultures than in others. Collective efficacy is likely shaped by the history of group successes and failures as well as a group's interpretation of an immediate work context. The relative salience of individual versus collective efficacy is shaped by culture (Earley, 1993; Earley, Gibson, & Chen, 1996). In collectivistic cultures an emphasis on teamwork and collective action exists, so it is likely that many employees have had many of their successes in a group context. This suggests that their efficacy will be highest if they are working in a group context. In contrast, people from individualistic cultures experience less teamwork, and so their sense of collective efficacy may be lower than that of members of successful teams in collectivistic cultures.

However, recent empirical evidence suggests that the relationship of cultural background to individual and collective efficacy may not be so clear-cut. Earley, Gibson, and Chen (1996) examined the potential trade-offs of feedback source on individualists' and collectivists' self- and collective efficacy. Drawing from Triandis's notion of sampling and culture, we hypothesized that culture and feedback source would interact. More specifically, we hypothesized that individualists who were provided with high-performance individual feedback would have a stronger sense of self-efficacy than those who were provided with low-performance individual feedback, regardless of group performance feedback they might have received. In contrast, collectivists would attend to and sample from group performance feedback and not individual performance feedback. Using samples of full-time managers from the Czech Republic, mainland China, and the United States, we found that individualistic managers who were provided feedback indicating that they were performing well did not experience increased self-efficacy unless this feedback was accompanied by group feedback showing that their group performed more poorly than they did themselves (contrasting feedback). However, for the collectivistic managers, only when high-performance self-feedback was accompanied by high-performance group feedback did their efficacy (individual and collective) improve. This study suggests that the efficacy-building process at the individual and collective levels is not merely the product of a direct congruence idea.

The final motive of the self from Erez and Earley is that of self-consistency. A sense of consistency enables people to connect current events with prior experiences in order to maintain a coherent self-concept. Such coherence is necessary for operating effectively in the world (Epstein, 1973). Self-consistency has two effects on people's psychological processing of events: it leads to the active construction of memories and selective perceptions in line with previous events, and it directs people to behave according to their values and norms.

Self-consistency is illustrated in a number of ways. For instance, people tend to see themselves as similar across time even if they have undergone serious life experiences such as divorce or death in the family. People also construct worldviews that are consistent with their self images. Finally, people often ignore or discount information that is incongruent with their self-perceptions (not just negative information, but positive information as well). The desire for consistency affects the perceived legitimacy of organizational phenomena such that activities consistent with an employee's values and beliefs are more likely to be accepted than ones that are more alien.

In understanding the significance of the social actor from a self-concept perspective, it is important not only to consider the underlying motives of the self, as Erez and Earley argue, but also to understand the source of an individual's judgments of the self. Breckler and Greenwald (1986) proposed that self-worth is determined by three possible sources. First, self-worth is a product of the public evaluation gained from others. Second, it is a self-evaluation determined by personal standards. Third, it is based on the contribution one makes to the collective to which one belongs.

These three sources, public versus self versus collective, form the basis of Triandis's (1995) sampling approach to self-concept. He uses these three sources as a way of describing how cultural values may influence the formation, development, and modification of a person's self-concept. The public self represents cognitions concerning generalized others' view of the self (Robbins, 1973; Triandis, 1989). It is sensitive to the evaluations of significant others and seeks to gain their approval. The private self represents cognitions that involve traits or actions of the person, and it focuses on internalized standards of behavior. The private self represents a person's view of what makes him or her unique and unlike others. Finally, the collective self is guided by collective action, that is, achieving the goals of and fulfilling one's role in a reference group. The collective self corresponds to Tajfel's (1978:63) notion of social identity as "the part of the individual's self-concept which derives from his/her knowledge of his/her membership in a social group, together with the values and the emotional significance attached to this membership."

Triandis argues that the formation of the three selves is modified by culture. He sees the self as an active agent promoting differential sampling, processing, and evaluation of environmental stimuli. It is the sharing of similar forms of information processing by people who live in the same social environment that shapes their subjective culture. Further, he argues that people sample these selves with different probabilities in different cultures. The development of the private self is enhanced in individualistic cultures, which emphasize self-reliance, independence, and self-actualization. In this setting, people pay attention to their distinct characteristics compared with others and look for opportunities for expressing their individuality. The collective self is most directly tied to collectivistic cultures, which emphasize conformity, obedience, and reliability. They tend to be homogenous and view the world in terms of in-groups and out-groups. People in collectivistic cultures are most attentive to similarities with other group members that strengthen their group identity. Empirical findings demonstrate that people from the Pacific Rim countries sample their collective self more frequently than do Europeans or North Americans (Bond & Cheung, 1983; Trafimow et al., 1991). However, as I discussed earlier, this interaction effect is not as straightforward as once thought (Earley et al., 1996).

Therefore, a person's self-concept is an important link between individual action, social context, and cultural setting. By understanding the aspects of the social environment that shapes self-concept, it is possible to better understand the nature of face in my general model.

Self-Identity

The nature of sources of self-concept drives the way in which people define themselves with regard to others. According to Breckler and Greenwald (1986), these three sources—public, private, and collective—can be thought of as ranging in a continuum of social development. The first developmental stage is reflected in a reliance on the public aspect of self, with an emphasis placed on conformity to social rules and on demonstrating that one is socially acceptable. The second stage refers to the development of the private self, which is a product of the internalization of values and standards from salient others. This stage is one of ego development and the formation of a personal consciousness involving standards of behavior, goals for achievement, and a sense of responsibility for personal and family outcomes. The final stage is that of the collective self for which in-group goals become internalized and a person focuses on how he or she might best contribute to in-group welfare. The collective stage is related to self-identity since identity is formed through reciprocal relationships in a particular social environment (Abrams & Hogg, 1990:5–7; Gecas, 1982). People are more committed to role identities that are essential for their social relationships (Hinkle & Brown, 1990; Stryker, 1980).

There exists, however, debate concerning the role of these sources of self-concept as a developmental sequence. Some psychologists argue that these sources are a continuum, as depicted above, and that the dilemmas of anomie (Merton, 1968) and alienation (Cushman, 1990) are explained by societies in which members fail to move from the private to the collective forms of self-concept. The "empty self" described by Cushman (1990) depicts individuals who have failed to develop a sufficiently strong ego identification with society, which results in their detachment from others. Increasingly, researchers warn that the individualistic focus of Western society is inhibiting people from developing a more social approach to their personal identities, and, therefore, they are alienated from society.

The relationship of a person to the social environment is an important aspect of the social actor in my model. While the self-concept aspect focuses on how individuals define themselves vis-à-vis external and internal cues, it does not explain the significance, nor the occurrence, of social memberships. A social identity is a key component for understanding the social actor. Although a voluminous literature has addressed the concept of social identity in psychology, sociology, anthropology, and political science, I will limit my discussion to the contributions of Brewer, Tajfel, Turner, and their colleagues.

A fundamental question facing social psychologists is why people form in-groups and why those in-groups are preferred over other groups (so-called out-groups). An interesting finding that stimulated much research on this topic was presented by Henri Tajfel (1972) and Tajfel, Flament, Billig, and Bundy (1971). In his early work, Tajfel demonstrated the now famous intergroup bias effect, namely, that individuals placed in groups (even completely contrived or random ones) will discriminate in favor of their fellow group members over out-group members. This finding led to Tajfel's (1972) social identity theory (SIT). Tajfel (1978) distinguished between three levels of abstraction of self-categorization: superordinate level of the self, based on one's identity with the common features one shares with other human beings; intermediate level of in-group–out-group categorizations based on social similarities and differences between human beings that define one as a member of certain social groups; and subordinate level of personal self-categorizations based on differentiations between oneself as a unique individual and other in-group members. The salience of any level of self-categorization varies with the frame of reference. There is an inverse relationship between the salience of the personal and social levels of self-categorization. The former emphasizes the unique and distinguishable characteristics, whereas the latter emphasizes the similarities and commonalties with other group members.

An implication of SIT is that an individual's self-image will be enhanced as a result of intergroup comparisons. Oakes and Turner (1980) examined this proposition and found support for the self-image enhancement effects of out-group discrimination. However, Vanbeselaere (1987) found that SIT offered a limited explanation concerning a cross-categorization situation with a cross-categorization reducing intergroup bias and discrimination. Vanbeselaere's findings may be reconciled with SIT if we consider that the salience of personal and group identities may interact with degree of categorization and internalization of group norms.

A related aspect of SIT concerns the process explanation concerning why individuals demonstrate an in-group favoritism as demonstrated by Tajfel and others. This desire to explain the underlying process of intragroup behavior gave rise to self-categorization theory (SCT) (Turner, 1985). According to Turner (1985:78), SCT "is concerned with the antecedents, nature and consequences of psychological group formation: how does some collection of individuals come to define and feel themselves to be a social group and how does shared group membership influence their behaviour?" This theory is focused on the underlying cognitive aspects of why social identity comes to pass. SCT proposes that: (1) self-concept is the fundamental component of a cognitive system; (2) an individual's self-concept has many interrelated facets; (3) particular facets of the self are activated by specific settings; (4) cognitive representations of the self take the form of self-categorizations; (5) these self-categorizations exist as part of a hierarchical system; (6) self-categorization occurs at a minimum of three abstraction levels, namely, human versus nonhuman, in-group versus out-group, and personal self-categorizations that define and differentiate individual group members from one another; (7) self-categorizations at any level tend to form and become salient through comparisons of stimuli defined as members of the next higher level of self-category; (8) the salience of self-categorization leads to an accentuation of intraclass similarities and interclass differences; and (9) there is a functional antagonism between the salience of one level of self-categorization and other levels such that the salience produces perceived intraclass similarities and interclass differences at other levels as well. Further, Turner et al. (1987) argue that individuals are motivated to maintain a positive self-evaluation of self-categories through a comparison of self and other member characteristics with prototypes of the next higher level of categorization.

SCT has several interesting features that can be used to describe cultural influences (Erez & Earley, 1993). Turner et al. (1987) argue that group formation occurs for several reasons. First, groups can form as a result of spontaneous or emergent social categorizations from the immediate situation. Second, they occur as a result of some preformed, internalized categorization scheme available from cultural sources such as work class, gender, race, et cetera. Although SCT does not predict the importance of particular cultural bases with regard to group formation, Erez and Earley suggest that such a categorization proves to be very important in understanding group behavior in culturally heterogeneous groups. The basic premise that individuals use preformed categories in forming in-groups, as well as in making judgments about out-groups, is important for understanding group processes in various cultures. For example, Bontempo, Lobel, and Triandis (1989) looked at the relation of in-group identification and internalization of goals among a Brazilian sample and an American sample. They asked individuals how likely and how desirable it would be for them to perform some costly act for an in-group member (e.g., visit a sick friend in the hospital) using both a public and a confidential forum. They found that individualists publicly said that they would take on the burden but confidentially stated that they were unlikely to do so and that even if they did perform the action, they would not enjoy doing so. Collectivists did not differ between the public and the confidential forum; they reported that they would undertake the costly action and that they would likely enjoy doing so. The nature of group membership (categorization) implies different responses in terms of cultural characteristics. This suggests that the nature of group membership, or the norms that emerge for member behavior, varies across cultures, and thus the features defining self-categorization are also likely to vary culturally.

Another limitation of traditional SCT and SIT approaches to understanding social identity is that group memberships appear to be largely based on psychological processes of individual attachments to others, as if group membership is entirely volitional. Such an individualistic view may not accurately capture group memberships in more collectivistic cultures. The nature of in-group membership is largely dictated by cultural norms in collectivistic societies (Erez & Earley, 1993; Smith & Bond, 1994; Triandis, 1989). These memberships are both preformed and stable, so the group formation process described by SCT may be, in part, moot. The nature and precision (salience) of categorization may vary as well. To the individualist, in-group membership is variable and so categorizations may be quite "fuzzy" or ill-defined. An individualist who is asked whether a friend constitutes "family" may be uncertain and judge the friend in terms of many characteristics before deciding. A collectivist who is asked a similar question may respond with an immediate affirmation because his or her categorization of in-group is more restrictive and well defined.

At this point, it is important to consider what SCT and SIT imply about the social actor and face. Taken together, SCT and SIT provide an important balance between an individualistic focus common in Western psychology (Gabrenya, 1988; Jahoda, 1988) and the social relativism implied by the interpretivists in anthropology (Geertz, 1973). From the perspective of my model, both theories play an important role in understanding an individual's position within a social system, as well as how that individual relates to others within the system. As I argued earlier, one of the primary reasons that face (in its multiple manifestations) is a critical variable is that a primary motive of people is that of self-definition within a social system. This is not meant to reflect an individualistic bias suggesting that all people focus on the self as a fundamental unit of analysis. Clearly, this is not the case for many cultures. For example, Geertz (1974) discusses the relationship of the Balinese to self and society:

> There is in Bali a persistent and systematic attempt to stylize all aspects of personal expression to the point where anything idiosyncratic, anything characteristic of the individual merely because he is who he is physically, psychologically, or biographically, is muted in favor of his assigned place in the continuing and, so it is thought, never-changing pageant that is Balinese life. It is dramatic personae, not actors, that endure; indeed it is dramatic personae, not actors, that in the proper sense really exist. (288)

In this cultural context, self is abstracted to the identity and role a person assumes within Balinese society rather than a singular sense of "who I am" per se. Self-identity reflects the demands placed on the individual (and eagerly assumed) by society such that the definition of self that I described in the last section becomes an emergent property of this societal identity. In my work with Erez, we argued that the self is the ultimate conduit through which culture influences work behavior; to this I would amend the proviso that self is a multidirectional conduit in which culture influences behavior reciprocally and that a social system shapes an individual's conception of self.

SCT and SIT contribute to an understanding of identity for the social actor in that SIT promotes the idea that only through understanding group memberships can we understand an individual's notion of identity, while SCT helps us better understand the specific reasons for such an attachment to our various identities. What is still lacking, however, is an adequate sense of how our identities shape our notions of categorization (as I suggest above) and how these identities are derived from the structure of a general social system. Clearly, group structure in society is not a random occurrence, and it is this structure that reflects cultural influence. In some societies, skin color becomes a highly salient characteristic of group membership, whereas in others it is relatively inconsequential. Likewise, certain cultures emphasize religious background as a key determinant of group membership. Size of groups, interdependence among groups, et cetera, vary across cultures (Triandis, 1995), and these factors have important implications for self-identity.

In this sense, the social actor becomes an important factor for understanding how extraindividual characteristics (e.g., organization, society, culture) influence interindividual (e.g., group) as well as intraindividual (e.g., self-concept, identity) characteristics. Self-identity, then, becomes a question of a person's position within a given group structure as well as the relationship of a particular group to others within a social system. It does not make sense to isolate such intergroup structures from an individual's identity, since such an identity is likely (inevitably) to be the product of multiple group memberships with overlapping features.

This discussion suggests that self-identity plays an important role in determining face for a social actor by defining appropriate face-related actions and expectations as well as delimiting the targets for whom the actions are relevant. For example, an employee who chooses to question a superior in a public context has multiple identities operating—as a subordinate in a hierarchy, work group member, organizational member, et cetera. Cultural norms will influence an employee's willingness to "talk back," but it is the specific identities and their corresponding roles that will heavily determine the employee's specific actions. Thus we may well see employee behavior that appears to be inconsistent with cultural norms or values but is consistent with specific identities. An inconsistency with general cultural norms for one group membership (e.g., subordinate in a hierarchy) may be consistent with other memberships (e.g., work group member). As people regulate face, they do so as members within a complex social system that has multiple group memberships and loyalties.

Role Expectations

While a discussion of values, self-concept, and identity is a useful basis for understanding the social actor, this approach suggests a very strong individual level of analysis. From a more macro perspective, a number of significant influences are exerted on an employee by his or her organizational membership. The very nature of face suggests that some aspects of self-presentation and interaction are placed on an actor as if they were a mask to be worn. It is these expectations that are essential to social interaction and structure. In a more formal sense, these expectations are the various roles that we play within an organization or other social system. As Katz and Kahn (1978:186) argue, "To the extent that choice of concepts can contribute to so complex a synthesis, the concept of role is singularly promising. It is the summation of the requirements with which the system confronts the individual member; it is the example most frequently given when one asks for a concept uniquely social-psychological and, for a concept in the vocabulary of a young science, it has a long history." In this section, I will discuss the basic nature of roles and their influence on face and the social actor.

The role episode as described by Katz and Kahn (1978) provides an interesting and useful starting point for discussing roles and a social actor. A role episode, in its simplest form, consists of two actors, a role sender and a role receiver. A role sender conveys to the focal, or target, person a particular set of expectations concerning a role to be enacted, and the recipient chooses to ignore or attend to various aspects of the role conveyed. It is through the focal person's role behavior that a role sender can interpret the nature of what was received, processed, and chosen to be acted on, although the specific actions or events operating can be highly ambiguous. Additionally, exogenous (to this dyad) influences may change the nature of roles sent, received, and acted on by the participants. Katz and Kahn pose three such additional influences: interpersonal factors, attributes of the person, and organizational factors.

With regard to specific actions or role-related behaviors, recurring actions engaged in by an employee are coordinated with and related to actions of others in a predictable fashion (Katz & Kahn, 1978:189). It is this collection of interdependent actions and behaviors that constitutes a social system in their framework. There are a number of potential difficulties with an individual's role because of these various interdependencies. The focus on a "role set," or collection of these interdependencies, suggests that understanding a social actor can only be fully accomplished through an assessment of the net or web of interdependencies entangling an actor's role(s). For example, a shop steward answers to a number of constituencies. The steward must balance his or her workmates' interests with the concerns of his or her superiors. Additionally, individuals may span the boundaries between multiple organizations or enact what Adams (1976) refers to as the "boundary role position."

Other difficulties confront a social actor with regard to roles. For example, roles may be ambiguous or in conflict, such as when an individual is assigned competing and conflicting roles by powerful others. Role conflict may cause significant problems, such as stress and health problems. Likewise, role ambiguity may result in a number of dysfunctional consequences for an organization, including increased turnover (Katz & Kahn, 1978) and reduced performance (Locke & Latham, 1990). To some extent, a highly useful aspect of a motivational technique such as goal setting is that it clarifies expectations concerning performance and employee behavior (Locke & Latham, 1990).

In the case of role conflict, difficulty arises when competing demands put a social actor into a quandary concerning how to resolve those demands. In certain cases, such as when independent, multiple demands are placed on an employee (such as having two sets of work orders and projects to complete), this conflict may be resolvable in the short run by reallocating additional effort or time toward the completion of each task. However, if the role demands are new or unfamiliar, it may not be possible for a job incumbent to reallocate sufficient attention to complete the multiple demands with which he or she is faced (Kanfer & Ackerman, 1989). However, role conflict may be inescapable if the demands originate from outside and inside the actor simultaneously. Take, for example, an employee who is asked to work increasingly long hours, to the detriment of his or her family life. If the employee has a strong sense of face originating from his or her role as a family member, then this demand may not be easily reconciled with the competing demand of having to work extra hours. An employee whose face is based on mianzi derived from job success may view these competing role demands quite differently. As Goffman (1959) suggested, a role incumbent may choose to distance him- or herself from the constraints of a role, resulting in an unwillingness to enact the role's demands. In this case, the role set (interdependent roles constituting a social system) must compensate for the lacking actions in some fashion, such as reallocating another person's role to cover the missing parts. This form of substitution and evolution is quite natural, and it is witnessed in many single-parent American families where children assume some of the responsibilities of the missing parent (e.g., older children help care for younger children while the single parent is at work). Such adaptations, however, suggest a comparable adaptation of face in order to reconcile a person's self-definition in the new role set. This is one example of how the changing nature of a role set, and the corresponding expectations and demands placed on role members, can influence a social actor's face. In the recent press, Marsha Clarke, the female prosecuting attorney in the trial of O. J. Simpson, was accused by her ex-husband of neglecting her children. He argued that her time devoted to the case was to the detriment of her children. A number of commentators argued that this was a potentially critical case for working mothers because it sent the message that a single mother must be not only an excellent career person but also a readily available mother for her children despite the constraints of time. This role conflict has important implications for face because the relative emphasis that the district attorney placed on these demands based on her own beliefs, as well as the emphasis thrust upon her by her role set and broader society, will influence her interpretation of self.

Role difficulties can arise from ambiguity as well. It is the case of role ambiguity that often leads to deficits in motivation and strategic direction for a social actor. If I am told that my job is to create an innovative environment for my employees and thereby make my division profitable, it is unclear where my specific actions may lead me. Is my focus on innovation, and if so, what exactly does it mean to "create an innovative environment"? Should I instead attempt to make my division profitable, and does profit mean *any* profit? Should I attempt to link these two directives by developing an innovative environment that results in profitability? These various outcomes are quite ambiguous, and the way to achieve them is vague as well. How prevalent are such ambiguities in work organizations? Graen (1976) reported that 80 percent of the people recruited for administrative posts at a public university reported not knowing what their supervisors wanted even after having been on the job for more than nine months. Many managers reported setting explicit goals for their employees, but when questioned about what constitutes an "explicit" goal they offered such replies as "do a top-notch job" or "make the most of the situation that you can."

A particular difficulty for a social actor who is in an ambiguous role environment is that face-related behaviors are often misdirected based on erroneous assumptions of who determines the role set. An assistant professor new to a business school is quickly told that teaching is "important" to achieve tenure. What "important" means is often ill-defined, and the result is often an over- or underemphasis on teaching duties to the detriment of the assistant professor's tenure chances. What should this assistant professor emphasize in dealing with others? Is face derived from personal status as a teacher or as a researcher? Should the assistant professor utilize his or her resources to become an effective teacher and present such a view to others? At my own institution, new professors are often labeled as researchers versus teachers as a function of limited interaction during which they present their "face" concerning their priorities. Of course, for a university emphasizing research output and contribution, a teaching label is not an obvious benefit.

Thus far, I have not made explicit the contribution of roles and role sets to a social actor's face. There are two general ways in which roles influence face, namely, by externally imposed expectations (to the actor), which make salient certain aspects of face over others, and by internally generated expectations, which act as a filter through which face is constructed in a social context. In the first case, a number of expectations are transmitted to a social actor concerning how he or she should act and behave based on general rules of society, organization-specific demands, and individual differences of other members in the role set. These expectations are particularly salient under several conditions. For instance, new job incumbents are highly susceptible to the demands imposed from the external role set because of the general ambiguity they face and their inherent desire to reduce this ambiguity (Van Maanen & Schein, 1977). If there is a large status differential within a given role set and the culture is one that strongly emphasizes subordination to powerful others—a high power distance culture in Hofstede's (1980a) terms—then external role demands will have a strong influence. External role demands will have a strong influence if the work environment is highly turbulent and unpredictable as well. In this case, an employee will adopt the reference point of other role incumbents in order to reduce uncertainty. In these examples, the impact of an external influence results in an increased emphasis on mianzi regulated through an acquisition from others. In other words, an employee will attempt to regulate face (mianzi) by satisfying or exceeding role demands imposed by powerful other agents in the role set. Face is lost to the extent that such attempts to satisfy these powerful agents fail. Thus, for example, a new employee seeks to please the boss through the employee's ability to meet deadlines because such recognition enhances his or her mianzi.

These external agents shape the employee's sense of face as well. The most obvious example of this is that external agents in the role set provide the rewards that shape face. Another important influence is not through the specific, volitional actions of the agents but through the emergent property of role differentiation as a function of organization size and structure. For instance, several researchers have found that organizational variables such as size are positively related to role differentiation in organizations (e.g., Barker & Gump, 1964; Blau & Schoenherr, 1971). Larger organizations result in more differentiated role structures, and, therefore, role sets are more complex and interdependent. This suggests that potential role ambiguity and conflict will increase as organization size increases, and, therefore, the impact on face as externally defined will increase. In the extreme, such as at research universities, a social actor's (e.g., a professor's) face is largely anchored in the social perceptions of others in his or her role set. It is no coincidence that many promotions or salary negotiations hinge on external offers for a faculty member. Although some would argue that this is merely the marketplace in action, an alternative explanation is that the ambiguity surrounding a given professor's stature creates a difficulty for his or her immediate role set (e.g., dean and colleagues at his or her university), and the larger research community, or at least another competing university, is relied upon to provide an analysis of face. A social actor is largely a socially constructed occupant of a specific role in his or her role set. I would argue, however, that unlike Katz and Kahn's more general idea of role behavior the specific role cannot be completely divorced from the individual who occupies that role because the role incumbent shapes the role from within as well.

The influence of a role on a social actor comes from within the incumbent as well as from external sources in the role set. Take, for example, an employee who is asked by his or her company to engage in what he or she considers to be disreputable actions, such as bribing foreign officials in order to secure drilling rights in a developing nation. This employee may have a strong sense of face derived from his or her lian that opposes bribery as a means of getting things done. In this case, at least three competing pressures confront the employee. First, there are the demands imposed by the company to secure foreign drilling rights through whatever means necessary, including bribing officials. Second, there is the internal demand of engaging in morally correct behavior (sidestepping for now the debate concerning the true meaning and significance of bribery in other social systems) that seems to be at odds with the first set of demands. Third, there are other internal demands for someone highly focused on lian, such as wanting to demonstrate loyalty and duty to one's company. In this example, there are multiple demands from internal sources. If the employee is truly focused on lian, then it is most likely that these internal demands will play the greatest role in predicting the actual behavior of the employee.

To complicate matters further, the line between external and internal demands can be quite fuzzy at times. Take our employee facing the demands of bribing foreign officials. What if the "external" demand is imposed by someone who has referent power (French & Raven, 1959) or charismatic authority (Weber, 1947) over the employee? In this case, it is conceivable that the external demand will be interpreted by the employee as an internal demand, assuming that he or she internalizes the act as having legitimacy given its source. In other words, if my respected boss advocates bribery, then perhaps it is not an illegitimate action after all. The reconciliation of prior beliefs with these newly conveyed ones will depend on the hierarchical relationship of the various beliefs and sources, as I described in the section on value influences using Rokeach's (1973) model.

There is an additional interactive relationship of a social actor to face involving the roles he or she enacts. To a certain extent, the role set that exists is constructed by the members who interact with one another. In this sense, a role set is an enacted and emergent property of a social system. It is only through the sense making of individuals within the social system that various roles emerge. Furthermore, these roles can be highly transient as a function of interactions among role incumbents as well as influences from outside of the role set. An interesting example of this formation is presented in Martin's (1992) case discussion of OZCO from a fragmentation perspective. In her analysis, she points out that what happens in this company is as much an emergent property of the disagreements and inconsistencies observed as it is the result of any calculative, orderly plan or system. Thus role incumbents are shaped as much by the inconsistencies in a role set as by the rational consistencies.

Normative Influences

A great deal of research in social psychology and sociology has focused on the topic of norms and normative influences. As a starting point, I examine the concepts of legitimacy and authority because they are critical for understanding the significance of normative influences on social actors.

Legitimacy and authority are fundamental concepts in Weber's (1947) analysis of organization. He argued that there are several different forms of authority, including traditional, or an established belief in the sanctity of immemorial tradition; rational-legal, or a belief in the legality of rules; and charismatic, or a transitory characteristic that emerged as a revolutionary force to reorient a system toward a new social order. The concept of traditional authority is consistent with a monarchy in that people follow rules not because a person performs a given role or position per se but because that person has rightfully inherited the position. It is a legitimacy derived from a multigenerational form of transference.

The rational-legal form represents to a system in which individuals follow rules and laws rather than the dictates of specific individuals. It is this form of authority that Weber envisioned as the most useful for organizations in order to enhance efficiencies and provide a just environment for employees. In Weber's bureaucratic structure, a system of roles is provided in which unnecessary overlaps and potentials for conflict are avoided, maximum flexibility exists given that specific role incumbents are irrelevant (the role itself is what is critical), and role ambiguity is eliminated. Legitimacy is derived through the depersonalization of roles, and rules apply to roles rather than to specific individuals.

Weber argued that charismatic authority is not actually a stable trait of an individual; rather, it involves faith in a leader's exemplary character, which is inherently unstable. He argued that charismatic authority would inevitably lead to a change, or revolution, with a shift toward formal rules and traditions. The role of the charismatic authority is to create and institutionalize new orders of rules, traditions, and procedures that eventually supplant the charismatic leader. Weber suggested that charismatic authority was control derived from position within a social structure tied to qualities of the position holder. Eisenstadt (1954) further described charismatic authority:

> In contrast to any kind of bureaucratic organization of offices, the charismatic structure knows nothing of a form or an ordered procedure of appointment or dismissal. It knows no regulated "career," "advancement," "salary," or regulated and expert training of the holder of charisma and his aides. It knows no agency of control or appeal, or local baili-

wicks or exclusive functional jurisdictions; nor does it embrace permanent institutions like our bureaucratic "departments" which are independent of persons and purely personal charisma. (20)

Thus charismatic authority is an aspect of social structure in which a particular leader (position holder, emergent or elected) influences the actions of followers.

From a normative influence perspective, authority structures legitimate behavior expectations for a social actor. According to Weber (1947), legitimacy exists at three levels: formal law, legal norms, and societal and moral justification. Formal law constitutes specific rules and statutes enacted by governmental bodies or executives. Legal norms are the more generalized codes or principles upon which more specific laws are shaped (e.g., constitutional rights in the United States). Finally, societal norms are more general principles that are held by a given society concerning the moralistic aspects of action and consequences. Of course, societal norms are, at times, at odds with the specific demands from formal law or legal norms. For example, Antigone's dilemma concerning burying her brother is an example of societal norms at odds with state demands.

Why do individuals comply with these various forms of influence? This is a basic question of societal membership. Philosophers, sociologists, and psychologists argue that an inevitable tension is created when an individual succumbs to membership in a social system. Rousseau's social contract and Freud's conflicts between civilization and the id reflect such inherent tensions for a social actor within society. To be a member of a social system implies control and subjugation of individual interests in favor of those critical to the collective. A social actor complies with imposed norms because without such compliance, the system will cease to function. It is this legitimacy of membership in a social system that provides significance for face, without which an actor would not care about social acts and the consequences of those actions. As I mentioned in Chapter 3, the Chinese phrase "bu yao lian" (does not want face) refers to the misanthrope who does not desire full membership within a particular social system.

How, then, do normative influences shape a social actor and face? A number of factors lead to compliance within organizations (Katz & Kahn, 1978:307), including early socialization (e.g., childhood experiences) and deference to rules as valued in a society; legitimated and appropriate symbols of authority (e.g., a supervisor accepted in the United States as a source of work-related orders but not family guidance); clarity of legal norms (e.g., clarity of what a rule is and how it originates); use of specific penalties and presentation of enforcement potential (e.g., maintaining a police force to monitor driving speeds on a freeway); and expulsion of violators (e.g., imprisonment). The importance of these influences on compliance is that a social actor desires to secure and understand his or her position in a social system through face, and compliance with organizational and societal rules enables face regulation through action. Through early socialization, a child comes to understand the significance of evaluation from self and others and desire a positive evaluation. This evaluation not only provides the rewards of personal reaffirmation but also defines who the person is. While authors such as Freud (1930), Katz and Kahn (1978), and Weber (1947, 1958) view normative influence as a strongly coercive or negative-avoidance process, maintaining face is a rewarding aspect of compliance as well. In societies stressing strong interpersonal dependence (e.g., tight societies), compliance is rewarded through enhanced face. This comes from external sources (e.g., being admired by one's peers) as well as internal ones (e.g., feeling that one's duty to society has been fulfilled). In this case, even an external source (e.g., peer admiration) may be relevant to a person's internalized values or moral correctness. Peer admiration is desired because it reaffirms an actor's legitimacy in a given social system. For an employee who works hard and puts in long hours, it may reflect a desire to show one's work-mates that he or she won't let the group down. In contrast, in individualistic cultures (Triandis, 1995) compliance with norms enables an individual to acquire face from others or from external sources (e.g., acquiring financial wealth). Compliance is an implicit rule underlying the principles of exchange in instrumental relationships. As long as these exchange rules are adhered to, orderly and systematic exchanges may occur. If, however, a party in the exchange ignores the rules or attempts to violate them, then the transaction is threatened and opportunity to bolster face is lost. Compliance is a necessary component of effective transactions and exchanges among societal members.

Integrating the Influences on a Social Actor

In this section, I will attempt to connect the dots that constitute a social actor. Of course, any such attempt is bound to be incomplete, but I will try to deal with the complexity and murkiness of this topic by focusing on the topic at hand, namely, face and face-related behaviors. As I have described each of these aspects of a social actor, it should be clear that I cannot categorize them as simply internal versus external influences on a social actor. For example, in the values section I emphasized that values are both causes and effects of individual action and a social system's structure. Many aspects of a person's view of him- or herself are based on a constructed analysis of the environment (Triandis 1972). I will now turn to a discussion of these interactive and cross-level influences on a social actor.

For the sake of illustration, I will use the example of employees who are working in two different social systems (two different countries in this case) based on work I conducted a number of years ago (Earley, 1986) among American and British assembly-line workers who manufacture automobile tires. Each worker receives a bare rubber inner tube, to which several layers are adhered using a special adhesive and a pressure device that solidifies the bond of treads to the tube. Next, the tire is transferred to a vulcanizing machine, which completes the construction and transformation process. Work conditions are dirty, noisy, and uninviting in many respects. A motivational intervention was introduced to increase productivity through goal setting (Locke & Latham, 1990). In one instance, the motivational scheme of goal assignment (stressing a specific and challenging, but attainable, goal) was introduced by a shop floor supervisor. In another instance, the scheme was introduced by a shop steward, or union representative. (Additional variables introduced in the study that are not germane to the present discussion are omitted here.) The result was that in the United States, the goal program achieved general success regardless of who introduced it to the target employee. However, substantial differences were observed in the British setting, with a clear superiority of the scheme when introduced by a shop steward. In this work, I assessed several general cultural values, including individualism-collectivism and power distance, and I found power distance to be significantly related to the moderating effect of country of origin. At the time, I concluded that the source of a goal program was tied to the class differences found in British work settings.

How might the various facets of a social actor interact to produce such a differential effect of goal program source? The relatively large power differentials observed between British managers and shop floor workers reflect a long history of industrialization and class structure (Earley, 1986). Employees have a general set of values concerning the legitimacy of their superiors as sources of influence in Britain that differs in magnitude (but not in direction based on most observations) from that in the United States. They view many organizational interventions with suspicion, and interventions that have not passed through their duly elected stewards are even more suspect. This reflects a strong difference in self-concept between workers and managers, a difference that is reflected in general society for class-based systems. Employees in the United States, however, do not view this dichotomy as quite so inflexible, and many employees view management opportunities as real and attainable. These value and belief differences suggest that the British worker will reject influence attempts from a manager, at least in part, because his or her identity is based on other shop floor workers as an in-group or reference group. For a British worker, face is maintained through reaffirmation of group membership as a shop floor worker and a rejection of management's influence attempts; for an American worker, face is maintained through group membership as well, but it can be further enhanced by promotion to floor supervisor and beyond. A British worker reinforces membership within his or her social class by focusing on the differences between self and management, and action is directed at keeping these differences clear-cut. The analysis must go one step further to suggest that the rejection of management's influence attempt legitimates the social system of differences that are prevalent in traditional, manufacturing sectors of British work. However, this relationship would be problematic in the United States to some degree, since movement occurs somewhat more fluidly between levels of blue- and white-collar positions. In order to maintain a stable self-concept, American employees accept a different relationship of management to the shop floor that stresses the potential for cooperation. This argument is modestly supported by the changing nature of industrial policy in the United States, including the ever-decreasing size and scope of union representation.

What this suggests, then, is that British shop workers regulate their face according to rules of class membership, work group identity, and a self-concept based on these categorizations of in-group and out-group. For the American worker, identity in each group is somewhat fuzzier and there is an expectation that face can be enhanced through the attainment of promotions to higher positions in a company.

However, these various relationships evolve with time. Certainly the work atmosphere when I conducted these studies was quite different from the current work atmosphere in Britain. There has been a legitimization of British management by employees as a way of dealing with long periods of economic difficulty. Such is the case in the United States as well, reflected by a strong Republican representation in recent elections. Basic uncertainty and concern over their welfare have created ambiguity concerning people's basic view of who they are in society, and the shift in political orientation is an effort to reestablish this definition (and reduce uncertainty of life). I would be surprised if my earlier results were nearly as pronounced now given these shifts in roles and expectations concerning who has the best interests at heart in society.

What I am arguing is that these various aspects of a social actor are dynamic and highly interdependent. A complete understanding of the face-related actions that are engaged in by individuals depends on their self-concept, salient values, and roles enacted, as well as normative influences from referent others.

Summary

In this chapter, I have explored and discussed the significance of a social actor to my general model. A number of important issues arise from this discussion. First, a social actor operates in a complex environment driven from outside as well as from within. The importance of various internal aspects of an actor such as personal values, self-concept, and identity has been contrasted with that of additional aspects of role expectations and normative influences. Second, a social actor is both cause and consequence of a social system. A social actor is a symbolic construct defined by subjective experience (Smith, 1991:44) as well as a causal agent of his or her own making. Frank (1973:27) describes the self-concept and our subjective reality as "highly structured, complex, interacting set of values, expectations, and images of oneself and others, which guide and in turn are guided by a person's perceptions and behavior and which are closely related to his emotional states and his feelings of well-being."

Third, values are critical inasmuch as they guide our courses of action given a variety of social circumstances, as well as our judgments of social behavior. Although I have argued that there are fundamental values that are universal (Chapter 3), it is important to reemphasize that the local, or emic, manifestations of these values provide for the symbolic construction that I refer to above. When an employee is confronted with choices for action in an organization, the general direction or impetus underlying activity is derived from the values held by the employee, even though these values may not take specific form in outcomes. However, even though the situation may overwhelm any single value held by an individual (Mischel, 1973), this does not mean that values are unimportant or inconsequential. Only through understanding values do we gain insight into roles enacted, effects of normative influence, et cetera.

Fourth, normative influences and identity shape values and cognition as well as our self-concept. In trying to understand a person's self-concept, it does not make sense to remove a social context. Without a social context, some people's conception of selfhood does not even make sense. For example, Geertz (1973) describes his experiences in studying the Balinese notion of self-concept:

> The most striking thing about the culture patterns in which Balinese notions of personal identity are embodied is the degree to which they depict virtually everyone—friends, relatives, neighbors, and strangers; elders and youth; superiors and inferiors; chiefs, kings, priests, and gods; even the dead and unborn—as stereotyped contemporaries, abstract and anonymous fellowmen. Each of the symbolic orders of person-definition, from concealed names to flaunted titles, acts to strengthen the standardization, idealization, and general-

ization implicit in the relation between individuals whose main connection consists in the accident of their being alive at the same time. . . . The illuminating paradox of Balinese formulations of personhood is that they are—in our terms anyway—depersonalizing. (389–390)

For the Balinese, self-concept is entirely based on social relationships and connections. Thus face-related actions gain their significance in terms of these interdependencies and not the individualistic perspective often presented in Western literature (Sampson, 1977).

Thus far, I have emphasized the micro-level aspects of the model while arguing for the importance of macro-level influences. In the next chapter, I will turn to the nature of how social actors interrelate. It is the pattern of interactions and their relative equilibriums that I refer to as harmony. The various styles of interaction are influenced by face as well as cultural views concerning the nature of transactions within a given society.

7

Harmony and Face

What is the relative significance of each form of face to social interaction within a cultural context? This is a question best addressed by examining the nature of the interdependence of a person with his or her social context. This chapter focuses on developing a dynamic view of interpersonal exchange as influenced by face. Although such an attempt is by no means original, it is crucial that face be thought of in terms of regulation and evolution if we are to connect it with the dynamics of the systems in which it is embedded and operates. Previous work on face has been largely descriptive in terms of its component elements (e.g., Hu, 1944; Ho, 1994), and such presentations using a theoretical perspective have largely ignored the dynamic aspects of its regulation. The most significant work on face from a dynamic perspective is undoubtedly Goffman's analyses concerning face and facework, as discussed in Chapter 3 at great length. Few authors have explicitly recognized and emphasized the relevance of a changing and dynamic social environment to understanding face and its various manifestations.

In this chapter, I begin with a general discussion of the term "harmony" and its relationship in my usage to concepts such as balance and equilibrium. I view harmony as capturing the regulatory processes through which face is exchanged, adapted, and built upon via various social interactions. In this sense, harmony is viewed as an exchange concept and not some socially desirable outcome in which various states of nature are congruent with human desires or actions. I use the concept of harmony rather than equilibrium because it reflects that there is a socially desired balance point in the presentation and regulation of face (defined by the social community) and that this balance point is constantly moving and changing. However, it would not be unreasonable for the reader to think of my use of "harmony" as comparable to an economist's use of the term "equilibrium" or a physicist's use of the term "steady state." After reviewing briefly the general concept of harmony as a form of social equilibrium, I turn to the nature of those processes underlying its regulation, namely, social exchange practices. Finally, I discuss the relation of face regulation through harmony to people's expectations of others and reactions to various social interactions within an organization.

Harmony, Balance, and Equilibrium

In its simplest form, harmony represents a state of affairs in which there is a balance achieved among various potentially opposing forces. These forces do not need to be mutually exclusive of other forces, nor must they directly conflict with one another, but their relationship to a given entity is such that their influence will tend to overcome the natural state of inertia acting on the entity. In an organization, a number of forces act on an employee, including orders from his or her superior, expectations of colleagues, demands of attention from subordinates, and personal expectations for action (Katz & Kahn, 1978; Lewin, 1951; Tsui & Ashford, 1991). A very common manifestation of such tensions is interpersonal, arising from competing expectations and demands of organizational members (Neale & Bazerman, 1991). Other common manifestations of such tensions are role conflict, personal alienation (Merton, 1968), intergroup or interunit tensions (Kramer, 1991), et cetera.

For my purposes, I define harmony as a dynamic equilibrium resulting from a set of exchange processes through which face is regulated in a social context. It refers to the type of social exchange, expectations concerning oneself and others' behavior, and social perceptions in a given social context. It is not simply a balance point or equilibrium, but it does represent a general movement toward such a point and incorporates the social rules that are used in such movement. For example, harmony within a group of collectivists may reflect the sharing and exchanging of personal resources among members in order to attain an equal distribution of resources. In a high power distance culture, harmony may reflect an employee's willingness to accept directives from a powerful organizational member. I note, however, that harmony is not a "state" or equilibrium point, a topic I will discuss in more detail shortly. It refers to *the processes operating as people in a social system regulate face in order to develop and maintain their sense of position and identity in the system.* Although some disciplines use the concept of equilibrium to capture a static state, there is a growing recognition that many equilibriums are dynamic and not static, and this implies that the processes underlying behavior of such dynamic systems are critical. Thus I use "harmony" not to represent some "ideal" congruence of individuals' actions with nature or their organizations but to capture the rules that underlie employees' behaviors in organizational settings across the world.

Fields have dealt with the concept of harmony in a variety of ways, and its balance and equilibrium have counterparts in many disciplines. Before I describe my view of the concept, it would be useful to overview several of these conceptualizations.

Equilibriums, or steady states, are fundamental to physical laws of nature. For example, a chemist defines a chemical reaction as in a steady state, or equilibrium, if the energy exchange is balanced with the transformation of atoms and molecules in a given system. Equilibrium is the state in which chemical reactions have come to completion or complementarity such that they cancel one another. To a physicist, a physical system is in equilibrium if the behavior of objects within the system is regular. Using Newton's first law, an object at rest will stay at rest unless acted upon by additional forces; a simple conceptualization of equilibrium is a state in which there are no forces acting on an object or the summated influence of forces acting on an object is equal to zero. Although the concept of equilibrium has long implied a steady state, or balance, more recent thinking and research (over the last three or four decades) have stimulated a great deal of interest in dynamic equilibriums and chaotic systems (Gleick, 1987). In such systems, an equilibrium is not a static or predicted state but an observed, regular pattern that is not predicted from a determined relationship; it is highly influenced by initial starting conditions. In such systems, initial starting conditions have a profound effect on the eventual behavior of the system. So, for instance, the flapping of a butterfly's wings in Beijing may cause a tornado in the United States as the effects of the butterfly's movements are exaggerated and mutated through successive iterations of the system (Gleick, 1987). The concept of a dynamic equilibrium is simply illustrated in chemistry by a chemical reaction (e.g., the addition of acetic acid to water) in which multiple chemical reactions continue in such a manner that they offset one another. Although there is the potential for further reactions, a tenuous balance is achieved unless further changes are introduced into the system (e.g., addition of more acetic acid).

To an economist, the concept of an equilibrium is central to most theories. Equilibrium is thought of as follows: "Although the market price may be independent of any one agent's actions in a competitive market, it is the actions of all the agents together that determine the market price. The equilibrium price of a good is that price where the supply of the good equals the demand" (Varian, 1993:282). In a simple example of housing in Hong Kong, the scarcity of available units makes certain that the demand for inexpensive housing is never fully satisfied. The result is that housing costs continue to increase until the point at which the market (renters) can no longer afford housing. Of course, this example understates the complexity of additional factors, including demographic shifts, wage fluctuations, business cycles, government intervention, et cetera, but the basic point remains that there exists some point above which renters will not pay for housing. In this simple example, the forces acting on the market are twofold: the supply of housing and the demand by renters. If one plots the intersection of these two curves, supply versus demand, an equilibrium point is reached.

The concept of equilibrium is used in economics for nearly all forms of exchange among people. For example, the Cournot equilibrium describes the balance point for multiple firms producing a given good. At the equilibrium point, each firm is maximizing its profits based on its beliefs about the other firm's output decisions. In the Cournot equilibrium, neither firm will find it profitable to change its output once it discovers the choice actually made by another firm, and each firm optimally chooses to produce the amount of output that the other firm expects it to produce (Varian, 1993:458). In a discussion of Keynes's general theory, Torr (1988:19) describes equilibrium as a "state of rest," which may or may not be brought about by supply and demand forces. In Schumpeter's analysis (1935), a notion of equilibrium is established through creative evolution and destruction. New policies and practices destroy existing ones as a result of entrepreneurial creation. Schumpeter suggested that this creative innovation on the part of entrepreneurs occurs as a result of a relatively stable (i.e., state of equilibrium) environment in which the entrepreneur can generate new practices based on the observations of a well-coordinated and predictable pattern of economic activities (Loasby, 1991:17).

Of course, many economists have called into question assumptions of equilibrium and rationality in forming a new view of economic theory (Loasby, 1991). For example, Hahn (1984:59) presents a somewhat unorthodox view of equilibrium when he states: "An economy is in equilibrium when it generates messages which do not cause agents to change the theories which they hold or the policies which they pursue." Each agent uses relevant theory to interpret each message from the economy and thereby generates a given forecast. Based on each forecast, a given agent's policy generates particular actions (appropriate to the policy), and these actions influence and change the system. What is important is not only that new information stimulates the development of new policies but also that the system stays in equilibrium as long as the subsequent information from the economy does not require the agent to continue adapting or changing his or her policy. In other words, a change in the economy is a necessary, but not sufficient, condition for disequilibrium to occur. In his treatise on the basis for economic behavior, Von Mises (1949) makes a similar point in that he asserts that information exchange and psychological interpretations of market conditions underlie equilibriums.

From both an economic and psychological viewpoint, Hahn's analysis is very intriguing. In an economic view, equilibrium can be maintained even though prices and demand may shift, providing that these shifts do not alter the agents' policies and knowledge. This argument is consistent with Schumpeter's analysis as well, since disequilibrium is brought about through the effects of new knowledge on existing routines and practices. From a psychological perspective, the role of an individual actor within an economic system is significant and meaningful, since the identification of an agent concerning poor policies seems to imply an impact on the economic system given the lack of intermediate structures (Loasby, 1991). In other words, there isn't sufficient development of the relationship of an individual agent to the general system to buffer his or her impact even though it is clear that agents have differential influences on general systems.

From a psychological perspective, Kahn's and Schumpeter's approaches are useful because they highlight the relative impact of knowledge and information as sources of change for a system. This suggests that shifts away from equilibriums may be directly attributable to information that is gained or shared within a system, such as the signaling information conveyed in face. Many problems arise, however, from this information-driven approach. For example, Mosakowski (in press) uses notions of primary and secondary causal ambiguity as a means of describing the difficulties firms have in adjusting to innovations within their industry. By primary ambiguity, she means changes that are not at all predictable but merely reflect random fluctuations. Secondary ambiguity means patterns that firms attempt to understand but are largely influenced by complex factors not easily predicted. As a result, firms may attempt to model secondary ambiguity and use it on their behalf, even though such actions are futile.

Another dilemma facing an economic equilibrium is that even if one assumes that it is stable and attainable, an equilibrium such as a Pareto efficiency is not necessarily a socially desirable one. In other words, a Pareto-efficient equilibrium does not necessarily imply normative assessments of desirable distribution of income, wealth, et cetera. As Varian (1993:299) points out, efficiency is not the only goal of economic policy.

Equilibrium and balance have been dealt with in other ways by organizational sociologists. For example, Giddens's (1984) notion of structuration points to a dynamic view of social systems. An equilibrium point is a constraining concept in his view because it creates an illusion of stability where none really exists. Giddens suggests that social systems be viewed in terms of several constructs, including structure, or the rules and resources organized as properties of a system; system, or reproduced relations between actors and collectivities that are organized as regular social practices; and structuration, or the conditions governing the continuity or transformation of structures and, therefore, the reproduction of the systems themselves. He uses the concept of structuration in order to capture the dynamic nature of social systems in stating:

> The concept of structuration involves that of the *duality of structure,* which relates to the *fundamentally recursive character of social life, and expresses the mutual dependence of structure and agency.* By the duality of structure I mean that the structural properties of social systems are both the medium and the outcome of the practices that constitute those systems. . . . The identification of structure with constraint is also rejected: structure is both enabling and constraining, and it is one of the specific tasks of social theory to study the conditions in the organisation of social systems that govern the interconnections between the two. (1984:69–70)

Thus, for Giddens, an equilibrium is not viewed as static; rather, he focuses on a given pattern of interaction that changes as a function of time. The impetus for this change over time comes from various influences on a social system, including the actors, resources available, environmental shifts, et cetera.

The notion of equilibrium plays a somewhat different role in conceptions used by organizational ecologists and evolutionists (e.g., Hannan & Freeman, 1977; McKelvey, 1982; Baum & Singh, 1993). In this conceptualization, drawn from the field of biological evolution and ecology, equilibrium and balance are based on the relationship of actors within niches in their adaptation to the demands of the environment. Such a balance is never long-term because random fluctuations in the environment (e.g., changes or depletion of key resources) throw the system into a state of disequilibrium. In McKelvey's (1981) treatise on organizational evolution and dynamics, he suggests that a variety of forces, including individual mutations and adaptations, can influence the balance within a given ecosystem. For instance, the random occurrence of a chance discovery, such as 3M Corporation's stumbling across the Post-it note, can have a significant impact on a company's success within its competitive niche. Likewise, random or unpredictable events, such as the discovery of oil reserves, can have a profound impact on the nature of social structures and practices within a culture, such as shifts attributable to the discovery of oil in Saudi Arabia, Kuwait, and other Middle Eastern countries.

To the institutional theorist, equilibrium reflects a general process of imitation and transmittal. Institutional theory presumes that the practices engaged in by usually powerful and influential organizations become the adopted standard for other, similar organizations (Scott, 1994). In fact, institutional theory is sometimes criticized (e.g., Giddens, 1984) because according to its views the forces of institutionalization should grind innovation and change to a halt. In other words, the forces of mimetic, coercive, and normative isomorphism (DiMaggio & Powell, 1983) should lead to similar institutional structures and practices within a given industry, a finding that has mixed empirical support (see Scott & Meyer, 1983; Zucker, 1987). Thus equilibrium is a state of isomorphism in which the relevant actors within a system are copies of one another in process and structure.

A traditional but still useful description of such tensions and processes in a social psychological framework is that of Lewinian field theory (1951). In Lewin's classic model, there exists a general domain of influence in which a person (P) operates and functions—the environment (E). Within E there exist a number of forces, F1 to Fn, each moving P toward some desired goal (G). (It is assumed that the goal is desired by those parties propelling P in such a direction.) It is assumed that these forces act on P in such a fashion that the resulting movement (change) of P can be estimated through vector addition (presuming that the forces have magnitude and direction that are measurable and constant). In this sense, harmony represents the point at which these forces are reconciled and P is no longer in a state of movement or motion (the vector sums become equal to 0). In Lewin's terms, the nature of harmony reflects a balance of forces acting on P in E such that their summated influences are equal to 0.

To the social psychologist or organizational behaviorist, the concept of equilibrium may involve an individual's participation within a given social setting. For example, in group dynamics much attention has been devoted to the concept of the free rider (Olson, 1965) or social loafer (Latane et al., 1979). People are assumed to be maximizers or optimizers of their subjective expected utility by many psychological theories (e.g., expectancy theory à la Vroom [1964]). Such a constraint poses a problem for collective action, as is suggested in Olson's *Logic of Collective Action* (1965). Olson argued that participation in large groups, or collectives, is not likely because an individual may be better suited to pursue individual gain through defection. For instance, Olson (1965:11) argued: "A lobbying organization, or indeed a labor union or any other organization, working in the interest of a large group of firms or workers in some industry, would get no assistance from the rational, self-interested individuals in that industry." The dilemma, then, is that it is rational for an individual participating in a collectivity to pursue self-interests over those of the collectivity while assuming that the collectivity will ensure the attainment of a desire good.

In a similar vein, Latane et al. (1979) documented the "social loafing" phenomenon. In brief, social loafing is the tendency of an individual participating in a group performance activity to withhold effort if his or her personal contribution is anonymous. With accountability, however, the incentive for an individual to loaf is removed. More recent work (see Harkins & Petty, 1983, for a review) suggests that the impetus to "defect" or loaf can be influenced by a variety of characteristics, including cultural factors (Earley, 1989), anonymity (Harkins & Petty, 1983), "sucker" effects (Kerr, 1985), and cognitive demand (Weldon & Gargano, 1985).

With both the collective action and social-loafing paradigms, a sense of equilibrium is established by examining the concept of exchange. If individuals maintain their actions according to expectations for returns, then an equilibrium exists. In other words, a balance is struck as a consequence of the expectations a person has in contrast to his or her efforts to pursue alternatives. A somewhat different perspective is held by Gersick in her work with temporal activities for task-performing work groups (e.g., Gersick, 1988; Gersick & Hackman, 1990). Gersick describes the role of time as an equilibrium notion and points to a number of significant deficiencies in the existing group literature that emphasizes a standardized process approach to group development (so-called stages of development including forming, storming, norming, etc.). She suggests that for task-performing groups, there is a critical "middle point" of temporal progression (not necessarily the chronological midpoint) that activates a group's progression. Additionally, she argues that group development is best thought of using a punctuated equilibrium notion that is often used in the physical sciences. A punctuated equilibrium suggests that certain groups will not continue to develop over their history; rather, they will reach a particular point and stabilize unless some critical event takes place. For instance, a work team may form and develop norms for behavior but remain at this stage. Only with some dramatic event (e.g., a key member of the team leaving to take a job elsewhere) will the team continue its movement and development. Thus Gersick points out that equilibriums might best be thought of as temporary stable points subject to shifts caused by significant environmental changes.

Based on this discussion of equilibrium and balance in various fields, it is possible to extend my original conceptualization of harmony in relationship with face and social structures. Harmony captures the rules and patterns through which face is regulated. Such regulation is the product of the types of exchanges that occur in a given society based on shared principles. For example, Goffman's (1959) concept of face-work presumes that a general norm of equity and politeness operates in a society. If I violate someone else's face concept (e.g., comment that a fashion-conscious colleague's clothes are inappropriately tailored), our social system is forced into disequilibrium or disharmony. That is to say, the processes through which face is regulated and maintained have been violated. In this system, I am motivated to engage in facework or provide my colleague an "out" (e.g., follow this faux pas with the comment that this idiosyncratic tailoring is consistent with Lagerfeld's new line for Chanel), and it is likely that my colleague will accept my "offering" in order to bring the system back to a steady state. Of course, the actual behavior of a person depends on his or her personal predispositions (e.g., social grace, empathy) as well as cultural rules (e.g., Israeli dugri, or candid, speech) for such engagements. My point is that harmony captures the nature of the exchange, the elements utilized, and the manner in which participants conduct themselves.

Unlike the physicist's or economist's concept of equilibrium, harmony is not a purely etic construct. In Hahn's approach to economic equilibriums, a key influence in disrupting equilibrium is a change in agents' knowledge as a function of an intervention or disturbance to the system. The nature of the disturbance or its source does not matter; what is crucial is that the occurrence changes agents' knowledge and policies for action. My use of harmony differs in that it is socially constructed or embedded. In other words, influences acting on agents in a system also provide these agents with new, or changed, knowledge. As such, harmony is an emic concept tied to the specifics of a given cultural context. However, it has etic qualities inasmuch as there are four general exchange processes underlying harmony, as I describe in the remainder of this chapter.

Harmony thus involves the nature of engagement, rules of exchange, and expectations of parties. It is not simply a balance point or congruence between interacting parties' behaviors and expectations. In the next section, I elaborate on the first of three components of harmony: patterns and nature of exchange.

Patterns of Interaction and Exchange

How, then, do exchanges take place in a society, and how do these exchanges influence and reflect the concept of balance or harmony? I will begin this section by reviewing a number of prominent views concerning social exchange along with the approach presented by Fiske (1991) in his resource view of exchange. My focus is not on the content of exchange per se (as Foa and Foa, 1974, emphasize) but on the nature of the relationships among parties who exchange face as a resource not fully captured in existing approaches.

Classic work on exchange relationships can be traced to Homans (e.g., Homans, 1958, 1961) and his initial conceptualization of exchange and distributive justice. In brief, Homans viewed social exchange from an operant conditioning perspective using principles of economic exchange (profit as a function of rewards minus costs). He suggested that

> social behavior is an exchange of goods, material goods but also non-material ones, such as the symbols of approval or prestige. Persons that give much to others try to get much from them, and persons that get much from others are under pressure to give much to them. This process of influence tends to work out at equilibrium to a balance in the exchanges. For a person engaged in exchange, what he gives may be a cost to him, just as what he gets may be a reward, and his behavior changes less as profit, that is, reward less cost, tends to a maximum. Not only does he seek a maximum for himself, but he tries to see to it that no one in his group makes more profit than he does. The cost and the value of what he gives and of what he gets vary with the quantity of what he gives and gets. It is surprising how familiar these propositions are; it is surprising, too, how propositions about the dynamics of exchange can begin to generate the static thing we call "group structure" and, in so doing, generate also some of the propositions about group structure that students of real-life groups have stated. (1958:606)

For Homans, social exchange involves social interactions in which some form of resource is given to or taken from others. It is important to note that his formulation does not simply capture an economic exchange in which expectations of repayment are explicit and in-kind but involves intangibles such as vague types of resources to be exchanged that have indeterminate repayment schedules (Blau, 1989). It is also quite significant that Homans viewed the structure of an exchange as an important determinant of the content and nature of the exchange.

Homans cited Blau's (1955) analysis of sixteen agents in a federal law enforcement agency as evidence of the importance of structure on exchange. In this example, Homans suggested that the willingness of low-status individuals to interact with high-status individuals to acquire information/expertise they needed in order to complete their work was dependent on status differentials. His argument was that low-status individuals (newer people who lacked specific expertise) asking high-status individuals for job aid was an approach-avoidance conflict of exchange. On the one hand, approaching these individuals enabled the low-status employees to get their work done. On the other hand, by soliciting advice from others an employee signals that he or she is inferior to the provider of aid, and such help creates an implicit obligation for reciprocation or dependence. According to Homans, it was this dual tension that led low-status employees to query their close (in terms of status) colleagues more frequently than high-status employees. Highly competent employees tended to enter into exchanges with many others, but these exchanges were moderated in frequency because less competent employees tended to pair off with one another. The resulting pattern was one in which a limited number of high-status employees exchanged help for prestige with less-competent employees, and less-competent employees tended to exchange help and liking with others of equal status. What appears to be lacking in Homans's analysis of interaction is the differential nature of these relationships and what this implies about the willingness of parties to exchange particular types of resources. For example, Homans's restrictive view of exchange valuation (overdetermined by an operant and economic perspective) fails to capture the importance of relationship quality in determining the nature of the exchange. In other words, the quality of the relationship will often dictate the type of exchange expected, even if a bi-directional exchange must take place (Ashford & Cummings, 1983).

Another significant view of social exchange was proposed by Emerson (1962) in his classic article, "Power-Dependence Relations." To Emerson, social exchange was conceptualized in terms of power differentials and dependencies among various people in social groups. He argued that social relations typically entail mutual dependencies. For example, an employee who depends on his or her supervisor for job-relevant information is in a weaker power position since the supervisor is capable of withholding such information. However, this relationship is typically bidirectional in that a supervisor is ultimately judged by his or her ability to get an employee to perform his or her work effectively. Unbalanced power relationships do not always lead to an equalization of power. Emerson illustrates this point with the example of an unpopular, puritanical woman who is dating a popular man. If the man comes to realize his advantage over the woman, he may try to take advantage of the relationship by soliciting sexual favors contrary to the woman's morals. What might be the result? According to Emerson, the unbalanced power situation might become balanced (e.g., the woman may decide that dating is not useful and devote herself to her career, thus removing the popular man's advantage) or remain unbalanced (e.g., the woman may decide to change her morals and succumb to the advances, thus maintaining the man's advantage). In his more recent work, Emerson shifted to an elaboration concerning the exchange relationship from a social actor's perspective in an attempt to clarify the nature of values and how they relate to social exchange. He argued that exchange needs to be thought of as related to value domains (general categories of valued outcomes). Emerson sought to achieve two general aims (Cook, 1987), namely, to specify what is meant by cardinal utility or subjective value and to provide a guide for theory and research concerning the determinants of value in exchange.

Of course, Emerson's approach has much in common with the social exchange work of Thibaut and Kelley (1959; Kelley & Thibaut, 1978). In their approach, Thibaut and Kelley viewed dyadic exchange from the perspective of relative power and dependence. They developed an extensive and elaborate framework for understanding social exchange and dependencies in their research. An interesting and important point that they raise in their model concerns the paradox of integration within a group context. The paradox is that the very basis for the social attraction of one person to another person (or a group) creates a social dependence that is to be avoided. In other words, a person who establishes links with members of a group shows that he or she has interests in common with them and shares the values they endorse. In order to establish and strengthen his or her participation in the group, this person demonstrates that he or she values what the group has to offer and endorse. However, doing so demonstrates a dependence on the group as a source of reward and legitimization. The very qualities that attracted the person to become a member of the group repel him or her because the fact that the group has reward power over him or her implies that at some future point the group may demand repayment of rewards. The potential obligation for reward repayment keeps the person somewhat at a distance. It is this paradox of social exchange that I will return to shortly from a cross-cultural perspective.

Another important perspective on social exchange was presented by Blau (e.g., 1989) in his work on social structure. Although the perspectives I have presented so far are distinctly micro (psychological) in their emphasis, Blau's work has a strong macro sociological flavor to it. Blau suggests that social exchange is best thought of as a product of structured social relationships in which dependencies are based on these structures. According to Blau, exchange can be viewed in Homans's (1961:13) terms, namely, "as an exchange of activity, tangible or intangible, and more or less rewarding or costly, between at least two persons." Blau suggests that two basic principles underlie social exchange: an individual who receives a reward from another person is obligated to that person, and to discharge this obligation, a person must furnish benefits to the person who provided the reward. Blau further distinguishes social exchange from other forms of exchange, including economic exchange (based on an explicit recognition of repayment), involuntary exchange (e.g., giving a wallet to a mugger in "exchange" for not being hurt), and a purely altruistic form of exchange (e.g., giving to a charity with no expectation or recognition or repayment). It is this last form of exchange that Von Mises (1949:196) referred to as an "autistic exchange," meaning a one-sided exchange without the aim of being rewarded by the recipient or other parties.

In discussing social exchange, Blau (1989) uses the interesting example of a person who uses exchange as an opportunity to gain great power. He suggests:

> The ability to distribute valuable possessions becomes a socially defined mark of superiority. The extreme illustration of this process is found in the institution of the potlatch among the Kwakiutl and other Indian tribes. These ceremonies are, to quote Mauss, "above all a struggle among nobles to determine their position in the hierarchy to the ultimate benefit, if they are successful, of their own clans." For this purpose, feasts are given in which the host not only distributes but actually destroys huge quantities of valuable possessions in order to shame others who cannot match his extravagance into submission. (109)

In this sense, high status is acquired through the great expenditure of wealth, or as Mauss (1954:35, as cited by Blau, 1989:186) points out, "The rich man who shows his wealth by spending recklessly is the man who wins prestige." It is interesting to note that this attitude of expenditure is not entirely inconsistent with the attitudes of Donald Trump that I presented in Chapter 1.

Although exchange theorists such as Homans and Blau suggest that the roots of social solidarity are found in the relationships that bind actors, a structural view suggests that it is not the relationships per se but their structure that is critical (Gillmore, 1983). Gillmore builds on this idea in her presentation of empirical evidence of structure and its impact on social exchange. She draws on Levi-Strauss's (1969) and Ekeh's (1974) perspectives on social exchange in discussing the role of structure. These authors posited that structures characterized by a restricted form of exchange—in which every transaction from person A to person B is reciprocated in kind with a transaction from person B to person A—produce social relationships that are instrumental and lack solidarity (Durkheim, 1933; Ekeh, 1974; Gillmore, 1983). These restricted forms of exchange are based on an expectation of reciprocity that fosters a general sense of literal indebtedness counterproductive to the development of trust and a common welfare. This type of exchange relationship eventually leads to a fragile relationship that creates intensely self-interested parties who are often in conflict concerning their "fair share" in an exchange. Gillmore contrasts this form of relationship with the "generalized exchange relation" in which a given party does not reciprocate an exchange directly with the giver of the resource. In other words, employee A receives a resource from employee B, but employee A does not reciprocate to employee B. Instead, employee A gives to employee C, who is also a member of their in-group. An individual in such an in-group feels obligated to give back to other members of the in-group but not to the original provider. This idea of giving is consistent with the Chinese principle that if you receive a favor from someone, you are obligated to grant favors to 10 others. In an empirical test of the impact of social structure on exchange relationships, Cook and Gillmore (1984) found that a restricted exchange relationship does not foster solidarity, but a generalized exchange relationship does.

I now turn to a discussion of the resource exchange model proposed by Foa and Foa (1974). Their model can be used to categorize and structure a wide array of resources as well as to describe their pattern of exchanges, including functional relationships among interacting parties. According to their model, a resource is defined as anything that can be transmitted from one party to another. They define and categorize six major types of resources: love, or an expression of affectionate regard, warmth, or comfort; status, or an evaluative judgment conveying high or low prestige, regard, or esteem; information, or any advice, opinions, or instructions; money, or any coin or token that has some standard of exchange value; goods, or any products or objects; and services, or any activities enacted for a person (Donnenwerth & Foa, 1974:786).

To understand the relative contribution of these six resources to exchange, Foa and Foa hypothesized that two general cultural dimensions underlie resource exchange. The first dimension, universalism versus particularism (Parsons & Shils, 1951), indicates the extent to which the value of a given resource is influenced by the people involved in the transaction. For example, money is a universal resource, meaning that it has value to the recipient no matter who provides it or, in the case of finding a $20 bill on the floor, even if no one provides it. In contrast, love is a highly particularistic resource whose source is extremely important to its value. If I am provided with love by someone whom I don't know, it has much less significance to me than if it is provided by my spouse. In this case, love represents a resource that is particular to the person providing it (and, arguably, the circumstances under which it is given).

Second, Foa and Foa use the dimension of concreteness versus abstractness to describe the tangibility of the resource. Services and goods involve the exchange of some overtly tangible activities or products. In contrast, status and information represent abstract or symbolic resources because they are typically conveyed using verbal or paralinguistic behaviors.

The resource exchange model is graphically depicted using an X–Y grid (with universalism-particularism on the Y-axis and concreteness-abstractness on the X-axis, each axis moving toward particularism or abstractness, respectively) in which the six resources are represented as a circle. The resources appear at the 12 o'clock (love), 2 o'clock (services), 4 o'clock (goods), 6 o'clock (money), 8 o'clock (information), and 10 o'clock (status) positions, respectively. All of the classes of resource are represented as points but are best thought of as ranges since each has elements more or less related to adjacent resources (Foa, et al., 1987). For example, an expression of love such as the verbal statement "I love you" has much in common with the adjacent element of status and information (i.e., it is more symbolic) whereas an expression of love such as a hug or kiss is related to goods and services (i.e., it is more concrete). Finally, the ordering of the resources indicates their relative similarity. For example, Foa et al., (1987) suggest that love is closest to status and services, whereas it is furthest from money. Information is proximate to status and money but distant from services. (This represents a troublesome aspect of the model since it seems difficult to view love as a form of service or information as distant from a service.)

An important aspect of the Foa and Foa model is that it is one of the few exchange models that has been tested in a cross-cultural and international context. While the other models I have described (e.g., that of Blau or Homans) have received extensive attention in the Western literature, the extent to which they are culture-bound in their assumptions is unclear. For example, much of Homans's work (and work derived from his principles) has been based on an equity assumption of distributive justice. However, ample empirical evidence (see Leung, in press, for a nice review) from the cross-cultural literature demonstrates that such an assumption is culture-bound and that other allocation rules are used in various societies. Foa and Foa's model has been assessed in a number of different countries, including Israel, the Philippines, and Sweden, and among Spanish-speaking Mexican-Americans (Foa et al., 1987). Their results provide empirical support for the etic nature of the resource exchange model, including similar rank ordering of resources and small differences in mean rank position of adjacent resources across their various samples. Interestingly, they seem to discount the single consistent anomaly in their data, namely, that the information resource is inconsistent and contradictory across their sampled countries. That is to say, the relative position (rank order) of information as a resource is inconsistent across samples and in the context of their framework. It is not at all clear why this anomaly occurs; however, it is conceivable that information plays a different role in relationships across cultures. In a high power distance culture, information (represented by expertise) is emphasized as a symbol of power and status; this may not be the case in a low power distance culture (Hofstede, 1980a). Hofstede argues that, or example, teachers are respected as an important source of knowledge in high power distance cultures but not in low power distance cultures. As a result, information seems to play a varying role in social exchange depending on the culture in question.

As I suggested earlier, harmony involves the processes through which face is regulated in a social context. As can be seen in these models, face can be viewed as a powerful form of social resource. In particular, mianzi is clearly tied to various types of resources depicted by Foa and Foa, including status, love, and services. If a powerful person gives his or her personal endorsement to a less powerful person, the less powerful person has gained mianzi. The powerful person has said, "This person is worthy of X." This form of exchange is a transference of status to the recipient, who then has an enhanced social standing. However, this "gift" is not without debt, as these models of exchange illustrate. In order to balance, or maintain harmony, an implicit debt is owed to the face provider. Indeed, the purpose behind the provision of face may be to create a debt in the recipient that will be called upon in the future. Thus gaining mianzi through another person's actions creates a bond of indebtedness. However, the discussion presented by Blau and others concerning the paradox of interaction (the approach-avoidance dilemma I described earlier) misses the significance of exchange in various cultures. In the case of Western culture, a form of indebtedness occurs that cannot be reciprocated immediately lest the relationship degrade into Gillmore's "restricted" form (i.e., a low-trust, highly instrumental relationship). As Blau (1989) argues, reciprocating too quickly signals to the giver that the recipient is unwilling to form a relationship symbolized by the indebtedness. For example, an employee who insists on repaying a loan of some money for lunch immediately upon returning to the office signals to his or her lunch companion that he or she is unwilling to owe the companion anything—he or she does not wish to be in a long-term relationship with that person. This suggests that giving mianzi cannot be rejected unless the intent is to create hostility in the provider. This conclusion is limited culturally because it presumes that the relationship is the by-product of the exchange and not the reverse! In collectivistic cultures, group membership may be determined primarily by family relationships (Triandis, 1995) and not specific exchanges. In studying the importance of exchanges, the nature of the parties' underlying relationship needs to be understood. This relationship is not the product of the exchange, as is argued by sociologists (e.g., Blau, 1987; Turner, 1987); it is determined by cultural context and setting.

Lian is connected to such resources as love and information in the Foa and Foa model. Most directly, lian signals to self and others information concerning a person's moral character. It is an information resource that establishes underlying motives and purpose in conducting one's activities. For instance, the "autistic" exchange depicted by Von Mises (1949) signals a form of altruism that people respond to and acknowledge (Wilson, 1993). Wilson's argument is that people respond to this form of exchange not because they believe inherently that the giver is sincere, but because they want to think that people are capable of such actions. In this case, the signal (information) contained in lian is that *others* are capable of altruistic actions in society. Lian can be thought of as a form of love as well. Upholding the dominant and basic human values such as respect for others signals a caring and love for society. By maintaining lian, a person demonstrates love for other people in an abstract sense.

An important aspect of Foa and Foa's research is that resources are generally expected to be repaid in-kind. That is to say, if someone gives us love, we are expected to reciprocate with love and not another, more distant, resource (e.g., money). Studies by Turner, Foa, and Foa (1971) demonstrate that if unlike resources are used to reciprocate in an exchange (e.g., giving money in return for love), repayment requires a disproportionate return, and the exchange may still be viewed as unsatisfactory for the parties. This suggests that the natural balance point, or harmony, will reflect norms of reciprocity and similarity. By norms of reciprocity, I mean that in some cultures an exchange is expected to be two-way, but in others such an outcome violates expectations (i.e., it insults the giver). By norms of similarity, I mean that some resources may be interchangeable in certain cultures but not in others (e.g., Foa encountered difficulty in handling the resource of information). Thus the nature of harmony within an interacting group depends on the type of relationship employed in a given culture. It is this type of relationship, or social tie, that I now describe in relation to face and harmony.

Social Ties and Harmony

The various exchange and equilibrium models discussed to this point share the general position that exchange processes are based on universal and consistent patterns. Even in the Foa and Foa work, with its origins in social exchange across cultures, there is an implicit assumption that exchange is based on a consistent principle of equity across cultures even though the specific resources to be exchanged vary. I now turn to a discussion of an exchange framework that provides an opportunity for linking societal and organizational levels to individual ones.

A recent model proposed by Fiske in his book, *Structures of Social Life* (1991), examines an interesting perspective on exchange in social interaction. Fiske argues that four basic forms of social behavior are the universal aspects of social exchange. The first form, *communal sharing,* is the behavior observed in a family context. Resources in such a circumstance are shared according to need, and people monitor their own consumption of community resources. The second form, *authority ranking,* involves resource allocations based on status differentials. For example, in traditional Chinese society the eldest son gains control over the family's resources after the death of his father. In nearly all organizations the CEO receives more attention and respect than a shop-floor employee. The third form, *equality matching,* is the distribution of resources based on an equality principle. In other words, each person (by virtue of his or her humanity) is equally deserving of a comparable share of resources in a community. This form of exchange emphasizes reciprocity and fairness and is characteristic of Western Systems of justice. Finally, the fourth form, *market pricing,* involves an equity-based distribution of resources using general market principles. In this case, if someone works twice as long as others in a company, he or she should receive twice as much as others receive in terms of reward.

According to Fiske, social behavior is based on these four universal resource exchange principles, but the specific form generally endorsed varies within and across societies. As a result, a common institution such as marriage occurs as an etic, but its underlying impetus may differ. For example, in certain cultures people may marry for love (i.e., communal sharing), but in other cultures they may marry for position and status (i.e., authority ranking) (Triandis & Bhawuk, in press). An important aspect of Fiske's argument is that all four principles exist within each society, but they vary in relative magnitude of importance, as well as specific manifestation. So market pricing may be very important in the United States but less so in Sweden. Further, it may manifest itself in the United States as individual achievement over others in a business context (e.g., the corporate "rat race") but in Sweden as a social achievement (e.g., individual achievement in an environmental cause). However, it is present in both countries. (A difficulty with Fiske's argument is that although he endorses a fragmented view of culture [Geertz, 1973; Martin, 1992], he argues that motivated action can be viewed as a general property of a given culture [1991:386–389]. This suggests that these resource allocation principles are motivated at a cultural level but not well represented as shared meaning systems—an apparent internal contradiction of his model as he crosses from an individual to a macro level of analysis.) A useful aspect of Fiske's analysis and model is that these four exchange principles are acting in a quasi-independent fashion within any given culture. This suggests that social relationships may be governed by principles that are, at times, complementary, independent, or even conflicting. In terms of an equilibrium perspective, Fiske suggests that social equilibriums are tenuous and fluid because of the complexity of interaction among the four resource principles.

I adopt the four forms of social exchange described by Fiske. In Figure 7-1, I present the four exchange forms in relation to two general cultural dimensions—individualism and power distance—along with their hypothesized relation to lian and mianzi. Although I present just two cultural dimensions in this figure, I discuss a main effects approach to each cultural dimension later in the chapter, and the logic of my analysis for Figure 7-1 can be applied to other clusters of cultural dimensions. Before I discuss the specifics of the figure, some clarification of my nomenclature is

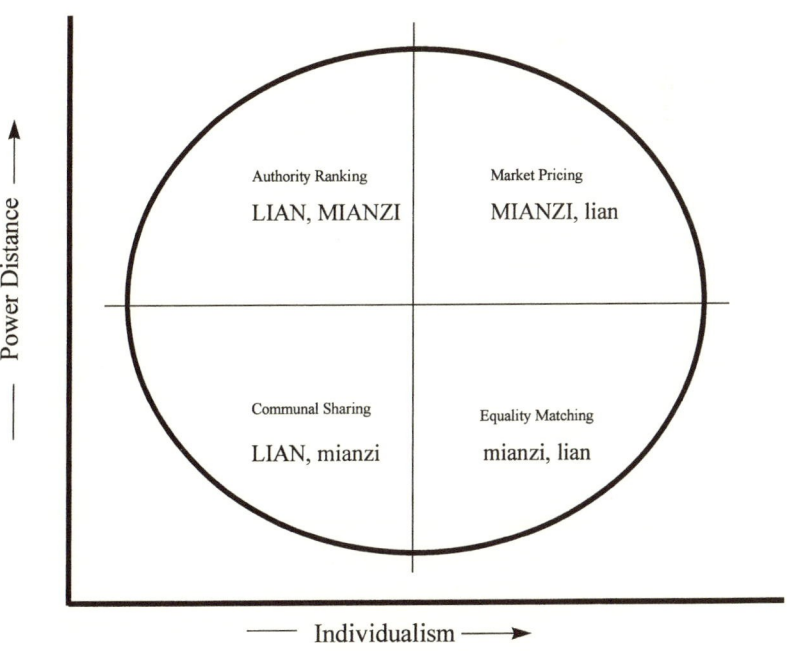

Figure 7-1. Cultural Values and Social Exchange Principles

in order. Specifically, I adopt two conventions in representing the relative strength of lian and mianzi in a given quadrant. First, face represented by uppercase letters denotes relative importance in a given society. For instance, in the upper right quadrant, mianzi is represented as "MIANZI," meaning that it is salient in this quadrant, and lian is represented as "lian," meaning that it is relatively less salient. Second, the types of face are presented in relative order of importance. For instance, in the lower right quadrant, mianzi is listed before lian, suggesting its relative importance. Note, however, that in this quadrant both constructs are represented by lowercase letters, suggesting that they are relatively less salient than for a society in the upper left quadrant. Although I propose relative differences in salience, this does not suggest that face exists in a given quadrant. Additionally, a society with lian in uppercase letters versus one with lian in lowercase letters does not imply that the former is higher in moral character than the latter. It simply suggests that lian is relatively more salient to people within that culture.

The significance of these forms of social ties/interdependencies to face lies in the nature of how face is maintained, gained, or lost. In the final section of this chapter I briefly discuss these relationships as a function of the five cultural dimensions described in Chapter 8. Before I discuss these dimensions in relation to harmony, several caveats are in order. First, I would concur with scholars such as Geertz (1973) and Fiske (1991) who suggest that there are multiple, and sometimes conflicting, exchange patterns within any given culture. Although I present and discuss the role of social exchange and cultural values to face in "pure" forms, these representations are necessarily oversimplified. In every culture, we can expect to find all forms of social exchange. However, I agree with Fiske's point that there are dominant forms that are characteristic of specific cultures, and it is the dominant pattern that I have attempted to represent in my discussion. Second, the specific content of these exchanges and relationships varies as a function of cultural context. Thus, in the United States having an expensive imported automobile may represent mianzi as a general category (e.g., a tribute to personal status), but in Hong Kong owning such a vehicle may represent a different manifestation of mianzi (e.g., a tribute to the success of one's family or company).

Before I point to the specific and dominant trends within each form of cultural context, some general discussion of social exchange and forms of face is in order. Mianzi can be traded or exchanged in a manner analogous to a physical product in a variety of interdependence structures. Although mianzi can be exchanged in any of the four models, it is most heavily emphasized in an authority-ranking or market-pricing context because it can provide individuals with desired material or status gains. For example, a person might ingratiate him- or herself by complimenting the boss on his or her golf game in order to gain a promotion or a raise. While a market-pricing exchange is characterized by a strong norm of reciprocity and equity (Ikeh, 1974; Hwang, 1987), communal and equality matching arrangements are characterized by an increasing emphasis on the relationship itself as an important outcome. In these exchanges, mianzi may be exchanged as a means of further strengthening the relationship for future interactions rather than simply obtaining an immediate outcome or reward. As Gillmore (1983) points out, an immediacy of exchange characterizes a restricted form that tends to foster a market-pricing relationship. For instance, a subordinate might ingratiate him- or herself to facilitate a relationship with his or her boss as well as to obtain a raise. In this circumstance, a good relationship (i.e., friendship) becomes an important outcome. Thus a subordinate may give mianzi to his or her superior in order to foster a stronger social relationship with the superior.

Lian is most likely the relevant domain of authority ranking and communal exchanges. Why is this? In brief, in exchanges among strangers the only rules that need to be endorsed are those that impact and regulate exchange. Questions of moral character are minimized through an emphasis and dependence on rules of exchange (e.g., equity or reciprocity), and the market becomes a surrogate for moral character (Fiske, 1991; Homans, 1961; Williamson, 1975; Wilson, 1993). In such a case, the rules of exchange are the defining characteristics of social goodness, and lian becomes less critical to successful exchange (except for those instances in which people who do not have lian are not trusted to follow the market rules). However, given the relative stability of authority-ranking and communal exchanges, the question of lian becomes of tantamount importance. There are at least two reasons for this. First, people in these exchanges are concerned with maintaining and promoting this relationship as an end rather than for personal gain. For instance, Hwang (1987) describes three characteristics that integrate a typical Chinese family into a cohesive financial unit: (1) every member gives his or her personal income over to the family; (2) the family is responsible for every member's daily expenses; and (3) the family's surplus is shared equally. Thus the need to regulate financial exchanges in authority ranking in order to secure personal gain is inapplicable. Second, individuals in authority-ranking and communal exchanges are highly concerned with the moral character of their compatriots because a violation of moral principles threatens the existence and stability of the collective. While market forces may govern a market-pricing arrangement, an authority-ranking and communal form is regulated through personal integrity and devotion to the good of the relationship. The success of the family depends on maintenance of the relationship itself.

It is important to note, however, that face is not inevitably tied to a given type of exchange practice. That is to say, a communal exchange is not always characteristic of an emphasis on lian, nor is a market-pricing exchange always characteristic of an emphasis on mianzi. As I will discuss in the next section of the chapter, there are instances in which a dominant form of social tie is associated with a secondary form of face.

As I discussed in Chapter 2, the importance of social exchange practices in my face theory is that they provide a critical linkage of societal and organizational context to individual behavior and face. In other words, people's cultures shape the nature of social exchange practices, and these practices guide the form(s) of face valued in a given society. Thus a person from a high power distance and collective culture endorses a general form of social exchange based on an authority-ranking model. In this context, it is important that people maintain the rules needed for sustaining the viability of their collective (lian) as well as reinforcing the relative statuses of members within the collective (mianzi). Group welfare requires an important balance of trust and endorsement of group structure through lian along with a concomitant exchange of mianzi to reinforce relative position within the collective.

This general logic can be applied to the remaining three forms of exchange. Fiske (1991) describes communal sharing as a relationship of equivalence in which people are merged (for the purposes at hand) so that the boundaries of individual selves are indistinct. It is characterized by the fact that people attend to group membership and have a sense of common identity, while the individuality of separate persons is not marked. Members of the group are undifferentiated with respect to the dimensions to which people are attending. . . . People have a sense of solidarity, unity, and belonging, and identify with the collectivity: they think of themselves as being all the same in some significant respect, not as individuals but as "we." (13)

While I agree with the general sentiment of Fiske's notion, a communal exchange does not necessarily presume that people in a relationship develop a "we" mentality (e.g., as in Triandis's concept of the horizontal individualist found in Sweden or Australia). A person from an individualistic culture such as the United States is perfectly capable of forming quasi-communal relationships while maintaining a strong sense of the individual. The heavy emphasis in American management on empowerment programs, teamwork, participation, et cetera, points to communal-like work relationships. In terms of the market-pricing form, individuals "interact with others when they decide that it is rational to do so in terms of these [market] values." This type of exchange is best characterized as operating through a heavy emphasis on lian and less emphasis on mianzi. After all, the emphasis in this quadrant is on a communal/collective arrangement in which members share power equally. As a result, there is little interest in acquiring mianzi since it inevitably enables in-group members to differentiate among themselves. The Israeli kibbutz represents an extreme in these terms inasmuch as new members devote their possessions and wealth to the kibbutz and personal ownership of goods is minimized (Erez & Earley, 1993). Further, differential role statuses are minimized in kibbutzim although some differentials occur (Tannenbaum et al., 1974). Lian is a critical factor in this context because the security of a collective depends on its group members' adherence to rules for group survival. Social dynamics including loafing, free riding, and exploitation are avoided through the endorsement of moral rules of conduct (Earley, 1989).

In a market-pricing relationship "people denominate value in a single universal metric, typically price (or "utility"), by which they can compare any two persons or associated commodities, qualitatively alike or unalike" (Fiske, 1991:15). In a market relationship, individuals seek to influence others through various means, and although some trust and mutual support exist, individuals do not view the relationship itself as an end. People share common characteristics (e.g., coming from the same town or region) and some common goals, but each person views him- or herself as the central point of an interaction. While an authority-ranking exchange is relatively stable and long-lived, a market-pricing exchange can be quite short-lived, such as the single exchange between a shopkeeper and an out-of-town visitor in need of supplies. However, market arrangements need not be terribly short-lived; as long as interacting parties find their exchanges to be mutually satisfactory, market-pricing relationships can be quite long-term. (At first glance, someone might suggest that if market pricing becomes long-term, it is likely to become an authority-ranking or communal form. In other words, as people interact over time, they come to trust one another and form an implicit in-group. However, this need not be the case because a single defection by one party ["unjust" action] will disrupt the relationship.) In a market-pricing model, mianzi is very important and serves as the foundation of the relationship.

People enter into transactions in order to gain relative advantage over one another as they exchange resources. Lian is important inasmuch as people adhere to basic rules of exchange, but these rules can be quite simple and straightforward.

Finally, an equality-matching form of social exchange represents an exchange in-kind. Each person (by virtue of his or her humanity) deserves a comparable share of resources to other members of a community, but members do not necessarily form long-term bonds or ties. In this form of exchange, there is an emphasis on reciprocity and fairness that is characteristic of Western systems of justice. In this form of ex-change, resources of a similar type are exchanged and primarily for symbolic rather than utilitarian purposes. In such a setting, lian and mianzi are relatively less im-portant because exchanges occur for ritualistic purposes.

These exchanges become increasingly important as a cultural context is imposed on the model of face. In the next chapter, I discuss in detail a number of cultural orientations that influence the display and maintenance of face through the types of ties that emerge in these cultures. For the remainder of this section, I describe such exchanges from a more general perspective.

Individualism-Collectivism

In Figure 7-1, the dominant forms of exchange found in an individualistic culture are market pricing and equality matching, whereas the dominant forms of a collectivistic culture are authority ranking and communal sharing. The reason for this polarization is that the strong focus on individual freedom and achievement stressed in an individ-ualistic culture is best demonstrated in market forms of relationships. In these rela-tionships, people are able to maximize their personal gains through effort and work and enhance their mianzi. For collectivists, the relationship is an important outcome because people identify with their in-group and do not see themselves as autonomous actors. Thus lian becomes critical given the high degree of trust that is placed in one another (e.g., given that gifts cannot be immediately reciprocated, it is essential that in-group members trust that all will contribute fairly to group success and to meeting group responsibilities).

Power Distance

The dominant form of relationship in a high power distance culture is that of author-ity ranking and market pricing relying on mianzi and, to a lesser extent, lian. In this form of exchange, a social hierarchy is maintained to the extent that participants acknowledge and reinforce status differentials among members. For instance, in an organization in a high power distance culture, a CEO's position is reinforced by his or her large office, fancy car, private secretary, company jet, et cetera. These physical manifestations of mianzi emphasize to all members of the company that the CEO is powerful and in charge. Additionally, there is likely to be an important contribution of lian in a high power distance culture inasmuch as charismatic leaders must show significant personal integrity in order to be effective (Conger & Kanungo, 1987; Erez & Earley, 1993). In contrast, an organization in a low power distance culture emphasizes equality and social memberships over personal gain and differentiation. Given that status and material differentials are less significant in this type of society, an effective CEO is someone who garners the personal respect of organizational members for having a strong moral character and vision (which emphasizes lian).

Tight versus Loose

In many respects, the tight versus loose cultural dimension mirrors that of individualism-collectivism. In a tight culture, there is a heightened sense of social conformity and a predominance of rules and norms that guide social behavior. For such social controls to function properly, it is important that people monitor their own actions, even in the absence of social sanctions. A key aspect of a person's propensity to function effectively as a "model citizen" is his or her moral conduct and character; hence lian becomes a focus. In a loose culture, there is an endorsement of individual discretion for action and interpretation of action. So, for instance, the same action (e.g., stealing a loaf of bread) might be viewed as positive (e.g., if the store overcharged the customer on a prior sale) or negative (e.g., if the customer gets a thrill from shoplifting). In such a society, the marketplace, with its general rules for interaction, becomes a guiding definition of fairness. Whatever the marketplace will bear is defined as fair and just. Under such an arrangement, the subtlety and latent nature of lian are unnecessary, and people focus on mianzi in instrumental relationships.

Relationship with Nature

This dimension has three general variants (Kluckhohn & Strodtbeck, 1961). In the first variation, mastery over nature, there is an emphasis on individual achievement and the importance of technology as a means for overcoming the challenges presented by nature (and the supernatural). In this setting, a person's face is determined by personal accomplishments and capability to cope with external demands/constraints. The dominant form of social exchange is market pricing, and action (individual or collective) is seen as a means of harnessing life's challenges. In the second variation, harmony with nature, there is an emphasis on the spiritual and holistic connectedness among facets of the social and physical environments. The emphasis in this type of culture is on lian because it reinforces an endorsement of morality and spiritualism. In other words, lian signals to other cultural members that a person is connected, "in touch," with the subtle forces that interact to influence human circumstance. In Sinha's (in press) description of Indian "psychospiritualism" in management, he suggests that such techniques as yoga and meditation can be useful in helping managers align their morals and character with the demands of the environment in order to be effective in an organization. Although this notion seems quite distant from Western management practices, there is no doubt that a number of American companies have adopted physical health (e.g., lunch-hour fitness programs) and mental health (e.g., biofeedback for stress reduction) programs in order to help their employees become more effective and lower their health risks.

Finally, in the subjugation to nature variant of this cultural dimension the role of lian and mianzi becomes somewhat murky. One possibility is that the dominant form of tie is communal sharing or equality matching, but neither form of face is particularly salient. This would be attributable to a strong view of religious determinism; that is to say, people's outcomes and actions are guided by God and not by purposive behavior. In this circumstance, social exchange and face are observable artifacts resulting from God's divine intervention and guidance rather than from human action. A similar view would be characteristic of people who believe in theological destiny or predetermination. Another possibility is that the important aspect of face operating is that of lian. Under such an assumption, the argument is that an emphasis on lian helps a person fulfill God's purpose for action and that only through engaging in morally righteous acts can a person achieve God's blessing (or the blessings of the gods if someone is polytheistic).

Masculinity/Femininity

In a masculine culture, there is an emphasis on achievement and accomplishment that operates through a market-pricing exchange. The marketplace is ideally suited for such attainments. The result of this cultural orientation is an emphasis on mianzi and the role it plays in reinforcing personal and collective achievements. In a feminine culture, there is an emphasis on nurturing and social interaction; that is to say, relationships are an important end of themselves. The dominant emphasis is on lian in this case. As I discussed earlier, lian becomes a critical aspect of communal sharing because these relationships are built largely on the presumed intentions, and not the proven actions, of people.

Shame versus Guilt

A primary distinction between a shame- versus a guilt-based society is that social controls and the avoidance of external sanctions direct behavior in a shame-based culture whereas internal standards are used for judging actions in a guilt-based society. In a shame-based culture, there is an emphasis on externally imposed standards for evaluation but not in a guilt-based culture. So, for instance, someone who has a physical handicap (e.g., a cleft palate) may be an outcast in a shame-based culture (i.e., the person does not measure up to the society's definition of physical beauty). However, this person is not necessarily an outcast in a guilt-based culture because the handicap is not attributable to personal actions (i.e., the person was born with the feature and did not "earn" it).

The dominant form of exchange in a shame-based culture is authority ranking because evaluations are based on relevant others' views. A person's sense of self is derived from important others and not from internal standards. In this type of culture, lian and mianzi operate together. Lian is key in cementing the connection of an individual to the socially evaluative others, and mianzi reflects the attributes that may be evaluated. In a guilt-based culture, a person's sense of self is derived from internal standards of evaluation. These standards also operate to influence either lian or mianzi.

Summary

One final point worth discussing concerns the dynamic nature of harmony as it functions in various cultural contexts. I mentioned earlier the idea of a dynamic equilibrium in the field of chemistry. In the case of some chemical reactions (e.g., the addition of acetic acid to water), there exist forces that create parallel, opposing reactions that have the net effect of maintaining an equilibrium. However, this equilibrium is not equivalent to a "rest" state as suggested by Newton's first law of thermodynamics. In other words, a dynamic equilibrium implies a constant movement or motion that happens to present no movement or motion because of the nature of corresponding (and opposing) reactions.

My view of harmony is much like that of a dynamic equilibrium. There are forces that operate (generated from an individual's desire for self-definition and evaluation within a social context) to influence the regulation of face. These constant tensions are eloquently illustrated by a quote from La Rochefoucauld's *The Maxims* (as quoted in Blau, 1989:33): "Modesty is due to a fear of incurring the well-merited envy and contempt which pursues those who are intoxicated by good fortune: it is a useless display of strength of mind; and the modesty of those who attain the highest eminence is due to a desire to appear even greater than their position." If one applies the principle discussed in this quote to an understanding of face, then it is possible to see the tensions underlying a dynamic equilibrium in social exchange and harmony. Face regulation reflects the fundamental tensions of wanting a positive self-image balanced with a desire to define oneself in a social context. Such a definition not only requires that a person find out who he or she is relative to others but also requires others to accept this definition and position. The point I have tried to make in this chapter is that this acceptance by others and self is based on various forces enacted through relationships that dictate particular forms of exchange. Thus harmony reflects the dynamic balance of personal distinctiveness and societal endorsement. In the next chapter, I turn my attention to a presentation of the cultural dimensions addressed in this chapter. By examining a more complete representation of these dimensions, it is possible to further understand the nature of face and its manifestations across cultural boundaries.

8

Societal Context

Although my approach up to this point in the book has been focused on a micro-to-macro transition, I am leaving the discussion and description of the organizational context and content aspect of my model for a subsequent chapter in order to provide a context richness for the concepts discussed so far. The constructs of face, social actor, and harmony cannot fully be understood without a more explicit reference to societal context, or what I will refer to as cultural context.

In Chapters 1 and 2, I discussed some fundamental definitions of culture and society that I should bring up again for the sake of clarity. There are important differences between the concepts of society, culture, and social system suggested by Rohner (1984). In his usage, "culture" refers to the shared meanings and characteristic way that a group of people view their world, whereas a society is "the largest unit of a territorially bounded, multigenerational population recruited largely through sexual reproduction, and organized around a common culture and a common social system" (131), and a social system captures "the behavioral interactions of multiple individuals who exist within a culturally organized population" (31). Thus in this chapter I am focusing on those aspects of shared meaning and interpretation characteristic of a given society.

A related topic worthy of redress concerns the nature of culture and how it might best be understood. As I discussed in Chapters 1 and 2, there is significant controversy concerning the nature of cultural meaning and the construct of culture. The perspective that I take in this book is that culture can be captured at the individual level of analysis through people's beliefs, norms, and values and that such an influence is evidenced in their social activities. For instance, if one observes an employee in an Indian company one might see employee actions focused on a spiritual basis of behavior (Sinha, in press). Likewise, the strong emphasis on equity-based rewards predominant in countries such as the United States and Britain reflects their individualistic orientation. Further, I argue that culture is not an intact construct whose meaning is obliterated through segmentation and division, as some authors argue (e.g.,

Geertz, 1973; Martin, 1992); rather, it is a collage of values and beliefs that can be examined in a piecemeal fashion. In this sense, culture is not a construct but is a general category for describing the sharedness of meanings among a given group of people (Rohner, 1984). The importance of culture is not in debating the concept itself but in its capacity for furthering our understanding of social actions in an organizational context (Segall, 1986). However, I agree with the assertions of some scholars (e.g., Brett et al., in press; Lytle et al., 1995; Triandis, 1995), who argue that these dimensions, or elements, of culture are not wholly independent and may interact. Although my discussion will begin with an assumption of independence among these cultural dimensions, I will return to interactivity among the dimensions later in the chapter.

Overview of Cultural Constructs

I have chosen to focus on a limited set of cultural dimensions, namely, individualism-collectivism (Triandis, 1995), power distance (Hofstede, 1980), tight versus loose (Glenn & Glenn, 1980; Witkin et al., 1978), relationship to nature (Kluckhohn & Strodtbeck, 1961), masculinity/femininity (Hofstede, 1980a), and shame versus guilt (Mead, 1934). Certainly, these six dimensions do not encompass all aspects of culture (see Lytle et al., 1995, and Schwartz, 1993, for a listing of many more such dimensions), but I have focused on them because they represent various important aspects of culture that influence social behavior, particularly behavior in an organizational setting.

These dimensions may be thought to influence an individual's behavior in a variety of ways, and it is useful to think of them as operating hierarchically related to an individual in society. The chapter is organized into three primary sections: "Person in Relation to Social Structure," "Person in Relation to Environment," and "Person in Relation to Self." By this I mean that the first three dimensions (individualism-collectivism, power distance, and tight versus loose) define and shape the relationships among people in a culture and the social structure in which they operate. For example, in a high power distance culture, subordinates are not expected (nor do they desire) to question directives provided by their superiors. Likewise, in a tight culture such as Singapore, there is a strong emphasis on adhering to formal rules and practices (as reflected by infamous incidents such as the caning of an American youth guilty of vandalism). These three dimensions of culture, therefore, define the structure of roles in a society, how people relate to one another, and their willingness to subordinate personal interests in favor of other social actors.

The second two dimensions (relationship to nature and masculinity/femininity) focus on the relationship of individuals to objects in their environment. In a culture emphasizing harmony with nature, people work with the constraints of nature rather than attempting to overcome them. For example, Icelanders extensively utilize their natural geothermal resources for energy rather than relying on oil imports as a means of providing clean energy sources. Masculinity/femininity reflects a relatively heterogeneous concept, as I will discuss. In brief, masculine cultures are characterized as emphasizing status and material wealth, whereas feminine cultures emphasize spiritualism and personal harmony. These two dimensions reflect the way that people relate to those aspects of the environment surrounding them as they interact.

The final dimension, shame versus guilt, reflects an attributional and motivational orientation of a person's actions. In a shame-oriented society, people emphasize duty and obligation as a basis for personal actions and attribute others' actions to such impulses. In contrast, a guilt-oriented society is one in which members emphasize personal gain based on an avoidance of engaging in actions that reflect poorly on the person.

I begin my overview by focusing on individualism-collectivism and power distance. I have chosen these dimensions for a number of reasons. First, existing research has provided the most extensive database for these two dimensions in an organizational context. Second, as I discuss in Chapter 7, these two dimensions are useful in mapping cultural effects onto face through the mediating effects of social exchange practices in and across societies. Third, I have provided an extensive discussion of these dimensions in Chapter 7 because it is possible to theoretically describe patterns of interaction between the dimensions ex ante, and such a presentation illustrates an important new direction for cross-cultural management, namely, exploration of interactions among dimensions.

While these six dimensions do not cover all aspects of culture or social behavior, they do represent a spectrum of relevant influences to which others can be added in the future.

Person in Relation to Social Structure

Individualism-Collectivism

Many scholars have used the concepts of individualism and collectivism to describe the relations of people to one another in society. At this point, I will review briefly several prominent perspectives on individualism and collectivism, including those of Parsons and Shils (1951), Kluckhohn and Strodtbeck (1961), Hofstede (1980a, 1984), and Triandis (1995), along with several other commentaries.

The distinction used by Parsons and Shils (1951:80–81) concerning how individuals relate to one another with regard to shared interests is called self-orientation versus collectivity orientation. The essence of their dimension refers to the dilemma of private versus collective gains, that is to say, the disharmony created by the choice of actions that will benefit individual interests (attaining one's goals) over actions that will benefit the collective. According to Parsons and Shils, this dilemma is resolved by an actor who gives priority to either the self- or collective goal or action. The relation of the self-orientation versus collectivity orientation to action at a social system level refers to the role expectations of the actors concerning what actions are permissible for the role incumbent to pursue or give priority to under various settings. A self-orientation suggests that role incumbents are free to pursue private interests regardless of their impact on the interests or values of a given collectivity of which they are members. A collectivity orientation suggests that role incumbents are obliged, as incumbents of particular roles, to take into account the values and interests of the collectivity of which they are members for the given role. The role incumbent is expected to subordinate self-interests to those of the collective should the setting require it.

The defining aspect of Parsons and Shils's discussion of individualism and collectivism is the tendency of an actor to pursue self-interests versus those of his or her collective. Their emphasis on goals and interests constituted a limited role of individualism and collectivism that was later broadened by other authors, although recently Triandis (to be discussed shortly) returned to this more succinct form of the individualism and collectivism construct.

The definition used by Kluckhohn and Strodtbeck (1961) defines the relational aspect of value orientation as individual versus collateral versus lineal. Individualism involves the autonomy over action afforded to the individual. If a culture is individualistic, this suggests that individual goals have primacy over the goals of specific collateral or lineal groups. This does not imply, however, that an individual is free to selfishly pursue personal interests and disregard the interests of society. It means that people have an autonomous responsibility to society through their individual actions and activities. A strong collateral orientation places an emphasis on goals and welfare of the extended group over those of the individual. A person's reference group is typically independent of other groups and so pursuit of goals for the extended group does not usually interfere with other groups, such as the case of the Navajo Indians. The Navajos have numerous autonomous roles and goals; goals of the extended household or clan have priority over all others. Finally, a lineal orientation involves a prioritization of group goals (as with collateral) over time. In other words, continuity of the group and an ordered positional succession are central to lineality. An example of lineality is the British aristocracy, which has been maintained through time by kinship lines and a select system of ascension from the middle class to the aristocracy. Individuals can be members of the aristocracy through their bloodlines or by a very limited and strictly administered succession through the middle class (e.g., obtaining knighthood for special service to the crown). Collaterality and lineality differ in that the latter captures a strict hierarchy of ordered positions, along with movement within the hierarchy, whereas the former merely involves the adherence to commonly held goals or interests of the group.

According to Hofstede (1980a, 1984, 1991), individualism is a collection of values concerning the relation of an individual to his or her collectivity in society. An individualistic society is one in which people think in terms of themselves, or trait terms, and a collectivistic society is one in which an individual is defined with reference to a societal and cultural context (Erez & Earley, 1993:Chapter 4). Individualism and collectivism have moral implications as well. Mao Tse-tung argued that individualism was evil and that the selfishness associated with it would harm the collective. Such a view argues that self-interests are not inconsequential; rather, the success of the collective ensures the well-being of the individual. However, many individualistic countries (e.g., the United States) see their success as based in their self-orientation and its presumed beneficial impact on creativity and initiative.

Individualism and collectivism are related to a number of organizational characteristics as well. Individuals from a collectivistic society call for greater emotional dependence on one another than individuals from individualistic societies, and their organizations are expected to play a stronger role in their lives. For example, in many

Asian cultures an individual's company is expected to provide not only a salary, medical coverage, and other benefits common to the West but also housing, child care, education, and even moral and personal counseling as well as political indoctrination. Hofstede defines individualism and collectivism according to individuals' perceived importance of six work goals; work that is challenging and that gives a personal sense of accomplishment is positively related to it; having training opportunities to improve or learn new skills is negatively related to it; having good physical working conditions is negatively related to it; having freedom to adapt your own approach to your job is positively related to it; having a job that fully uses your skills and abilities on the job is negatively related to it; and having a job that leaves you sufficient time for personal or family life is positively related to it.

Another major effort to define the construct of individualism and collectivism comes from Triandis and his colleagues (e.g., Bontempo et al., 1989; Hui & Triandis, 1985; Triandis et al., 1986; Triandis, 1989a, 1989b, 1995). Triandis argues that individualistic and collectivistic societies vary on a number of relevant dimensions germane to organizations. Collectivistic societies emphasize a number of characteristics including subordination of personal goals to those of the group as a means for attaining individual goals; concern for how one's actions will impact in-group members; a tendency to share resources with in-group members; desirability of interdependence among in-group members; involvement in other in-group members' lives; the perception that in-group values/norms are universally valid and willingness to fight for these values; strong influence of in-group rules on social behavior; view of relationships as nurturing, respectful, and intimate; basing relationships on a principle of equality and altruism rather than on exchange and equity; and the tendency of in-groups to be small and tight-knit as well as quite stable across time.

The first characteristic, subordination of personal goals to those of the group, is posited as the most important in my various empirical studies relying on this construct as a predictor of group interaction and behavior (e.g., Earley, 1989, 1994). In individualistic cultures, people will put their own needs over those of the group. Triandis argues that individualists belong to many groups and flow between them so as to attain personal interests and that they will avoid a particular in-group if it places too many demands on the individual. The collectivist has a stable in-group membership, whereas the individualist belongs to multiple in-groups and has to refresh membership and status in the group constantly. Triandis argues that the number of in-groups to which an individual belongs is a key aspect of individualism and collectivism (Triandis, 1995). Specifically, he argues that individualists form into a multitude of in-groups and stay with these groups until they impose on the individual. At this point, the individualist moves to another group for instrumental gains in order to avoid a restriction on his or her autonomy.

Wagner and Moch (1986) further refined a conceptualization and empirical measure of individualism and collectivism by separating the measure into three categories—beliefs, values, and norms. Their reasoning suggested that the conceptual differences among beliefs (statements held to be true), values (statements that denote evaluations of goodness or evil), and norms (standards for behavior shared by a given group) lead to different assessments of individualism and collectivism focusing on the concept of self- versus group interests. For example, a worker who holds individualistic values and beliefs may behave collectively (e.g., by adhering to production shutdowns imposed by coworkers) depending on his or her work group norms. Based on their conceptualization, Wagner and Moch called for additional theorizing concerning the relevance of individualism and collectivism to organizational behavior theories.

At present, the conceptual work by Triandis (1989b, 1995) appears to be the most extensive discussion focusing on the nature of the in-group and individualism and collectivism. In his recent work, Triandis has extended and developed an interesting two-way analysis of individualism-collectivism using a distinction made by Chen, Meindl, and Hunt (1996) as well as Schwartz (1992) concerning horizontal versus vertical aspects of individualism-collectivism. Triandis (1995) used this distinction as well as his earlier theorizing and proposed four defining attributes of individualism-collectivism, namely, definition of self (independent versus interdependent), structure of goals (individual goals as independent versus compatible with group goals), emphasis on norms versus attitudes (social behavior is most directly related to attitudes versus norms/duty/obligations), and emphasis on rationality versus relatedness (computation of costs and benefits versus prioritization of relationships regardless of costs/benefits). Triandis argues that the underlying aspects of these categories are a cross between a "same" (horizontal) versus a "different" (vertical) self with an interdependent versus independent self. This two-by-two typology provides four forms of individualism-collectivism: horizontal collectivism, vertical collectivism, horizontal individualism, and vertical individualism.

For my purposes, I define individualism and collectivism as a set of shared beliefs and values of a people concerning the relationship of an individual to others in his or her society. It captures emotional and cognitive attachments to particular networks of individuals (Erez & Earley, 1993), and it can be used to understand a person's self-concept. The actions of collectivists reflect pursuit of group goals for both the short and the long term, but for individualists such attachments are of a temporary and instrumental nature. This suggests that individualists may be committed to group goals (just as collectivists are) as long as these goals are parallel and/or complementary to self-interests. The recent work by Triandis is interesting as well because it provides a potential bridge between the constructs of individualism-collectivism and power distance. In some sense, the vertical versus horizontal element to Triandis's typology reflects a role delineation implicit in the concept of power distance, or differentials. For example, the Chinese horizontal and vertical collectivists described by Chen et al. (1996) may reflect an ideological difference based on communism (egalitarian emphasis, or horizontal) versus Confucianism (hierarchical emphasis, or vertical).

As I pointed out in Chapter 7, the distinction provided by the interaction of individualism and power distance is important for understanding several subtle relationships of face. In general, I would expect that lian is most heavily tied to behavior in a collectivistic culture, whereas mianzi is most heavily tied to behavior in an individualistic culture. However, the vertical versus horizontal distinction suggests that the influence of this cultural dimension on face is more complex. The aspect of individualism and collectivism most directly related to face is that of the self versus other distinction that Triandis poses. What this means is that it is most likely that lian aspects of face are stressed in a horizontal form of collectivism in which the "sameness" of people is stressed. If we are all equal, then mianzi should be a less salient aspect of our exchange because it acts primarily to illustrate our differences rather than our similarities. Of course, the opposite would be the case for vertical collectivism. The additional dimension of interdependence would operate as well, but it is most likely to reinforce the vertical versus horizontal distinction. I now turn to a discussion of power distance and differentials.

Power Distance

The next dimension of culture that I will address is that of power distance (Hofstede, 1980a), or the differentials that exist within a society. Hofstede (1980a:99) states: "The power distance between a boss B and a subordinate S in a hierarchy is the difference between the extent to which B can determine the behavior of S and the extent to which S can determine the behavior of B." Further, he argues that power distance is captured by the relative acceptability for such differentials to exist as supported by a social environment and national culture. For example, in low power distance cultures (e.g., Sweden) less emphasis is placed on obedience of children, whereas in high power distance cultures (e.g., Malaysia) parents strongly emphasize obedience of children. Hofstede suggests several interesting implications of power distance for management practices. In a high power distance culture, subordinates are more satisfied and expect a directive style of management from their superiors, whereas in a low power distance culture more participatory practices are expected.

There are a number of antecedents of power distance, including child-rearing patterns, environment, and historical events. A low power distance culture is given rise through a variety of antecedents, including a more severe climate that leads to the need to cope with nature through technological means, an emphasis on education to harness technology and a larger accumulation of national wealth, a wide distribution of such wealth, an emphasis on independence and decentralization of political authority, rapid technological advances, and children coming to question authority in their education. In contrast, a high power distance culture is given rise through a more moderate climate that does not require mastery over nature for survival, less need for technology, lower literacy and educational requirements, less national wealth, more concentration of wealth in the hands of a limited few, dependence of children on parents and elders, and less questioning of authority and teachers. Although such chains are tenuous at best and fictional at worst, technology (to be discussed shortly) plays an important role in the development of power stratification and differentiation in societies.

The consequences of power differentials in organizations are substantial. Hofstede posits that organizations in low power distance cultures are less centralized and flatter and have smaller proportion of supervisory to rank-and-file personnel, smaller wage differentials, low status differentials across ranks, and high qualifications for entry-level positions. In a high power distance culture, there exists greater centralization of authority, tall organization pyramids, a large proportion of supervisory personnel to the overall employee population, large wage differentials and high job status for white-collar jobs, and low qualifications for entry-level positions.

Thus power distance refers to the extent to which members of a culture accept inequality and large differentials between those with power (e.g., superiors) and those with little power (e.g., subordinates). The intellectual origins of Hofstede's use of the term "power distance" are described in his book (1980a:97–102) in great detail. In brief, he relates the concept of power distance to the general tendency of social systems (animal or human) to utilize inequality in relationships. The distribution of power and the concept of inequality are fundamental to human interaction. There are a variety of sources of differential power distribution in a society, such as differences in social status and prestige (of central importance to face), wealth, formal rules and laws, physical or mental attributes, et cetera. These differentials are reflected in a long tradition of studies in sociology, anthropology, and psychology.

Of course, the topic of power differentials in society is the imminent domain of Marx's theory of capitalism (1848) and the plethora of scholarly discussions based on his theory of society and wealth. A central theme of this work is that the nature of production, technology, is a key determinant in the distribution of wealth in a society. Technology, or the means through which raw materials are transformed into products, involves the use of tools, machinery, computers, sociotechnical systems, et cetera. From a Marxian viewpoint, a critical aspect of technology is the impact it has on wealth distribution, as well as its shaping of individuals' values, consciousness, and relationships with others. According to Marx's view (as cited by Braverman, 1974), routinization and technology have the potential to degrade a person's work contribution to that of an "animal" having little control or thought. More recently, Braverman (1974) has argued that routinization has accelerated during this century, and the result has been an increasing alienation of the workforce and inequality between workers and managers. Although the changes present in modern work organizations may not fully support Braverman's analysis, there is evidence to suggest that technological innovations have resulted in the loss of power for employees (Kipnis & Schmidt, 1983) and the redistribution of power within organizations into a technical elite.

Power differentials and the distribution of power have been a central focus for organizational researchers as well. Pfeffer's (1981, 1992) work in this area is a key example of this thinking. According to Pfeffer's approach, power is derived from a variety of sources, such as providing desired resources (e.g., monetary), coping with uncertainty (e.g., the capability to handle and deal with uncertainty in the organizational context), being irreplaceable (e.g., lacking substitutability, or what strategists often refer to as uncertain imitability [Mosakowski, in press]), being central to decision processes (e.g., being a key decision maker who controls decision alternatives or information about these alternatives), and achieving consensus (e.g., a power attribute for the group, or unit, level). The process of power accumulation is most heavily tied to resource control according to Pfeffer's perspective, so that individuals, or groups, with control over key resources will capture the highest levels of control within an organization. How might this perspective prove relevant from a cultural perspective? The key is that in certain societies it is relatively more acceptable for these resources to be concentrated in the hands of particular individuals than to be distributed equally (Pfeffer, 1992). In this sense, power differentials as a cultural value provide the legitimacy through which the actual, unequal distribution of resources may occur. A cultural-level analysis suggests that for some societies such an unequal distribution will not be legitimated, and therefore, we would expect to see little, if any, concentration of resources (and hence power) or vertical differentiation of hierarchy. However, this does not appear to be the case.

In a related vein of research, Tannenbaum et al. (1974) examined the nature of hierarchy in organizations across several countries that differed greatly with regard to their ideological nature, including Austria, Israel, Italy, the United States, and Yugoslavia. They found a wide variety of organizations in these countries, ranging from military organizations to labor unions to private companies, but a general theme appeared to emerge. What they found was that a hierarchy, or a gradient of control, appeared in all of the organizations such that those at the top exercised more control than the shop floor employees. Despite substantial ideological differences (e.g., the former Yugoslavia and Israel's kibbutzim, founded on principles of equality and self-management, contrasted with the United States and Austria, which emphasize individuality and stratification), they found a similar pattern of hierarchical control, although the differences in the kibbutzim sample were attenuated relative to the other samples. Interestingly, there was a significant contrast between the perceived and ideal levels of power sharing reported in several of the countries. For example, in the kibbutzim the ideal level reflected a nearly flat distribution of power (power equality across levels of a managerial board, managers, and workers), whereas the perceived distribution of power reflected a higher level of control for the managerial board or managers relative to the workers. Overall, the Tannenbaum et al. studies of hierarchy reflect the inherent tendency of societies to unequally distribute power among individuals within the society regardless of the ideological stance espoused within the society.

Other organizational researchers have examined the concept of power differentials using Emerson's (1972) power dependence theory. According to Emerson, a basic principle of dependence theory is that the power of party A is based on party B's dependence on A, and vice versa. Additionally, B's level of dependence on A is based on the attractiveness of outcomes A has control over that B may desire. The theory suggests four dimensions of dependence, namely, the availability of alternative partners to A, the importance A places on having a relationship with B, the availability of alternative partners to B, and the importance B places on having a relationship with A.

Lawler and Bacharach (1979) utilize the power dependence framework in studying a wide range of conflict situations. For instance, they have examined subjects' tendencies to use a given tactic for influence and reward expectations based on power differentials. Again, the question is how this stream of research might be relevant for understanding power differentials that may occur in a society. Simply put, their research reaffirms the importance of power differentials in understanding the reactions of Western negotiators and individuals to a conflict setting. Further, Lawler argues that most conflicts have a social structural origin based on interdependent and interrelated positions of the actors or groups involved in the conflict. This suggests that the differentiation witnessed in social evolution (Alexander, 1990) will give rise to the structural dependencies that result in conflict.

Kipnis and Schmidt (1983) have conducted a series of studies of individuals' reactions to power differentials, namely, the utilization of influence tactics in order to deal with the differentials. A basic assumption of this approach is that if individuals lose the ability to control their own behavior, they are subject to manipulation and exploitation by others. The social relations between two or more individuals that have an unequal distribution of power become increasingly distant and impersonal, and these individuals will engage in influence tactics as a means for regaining control.

Further, Kipnis and Schmidt do not view technology as a neutral aspect of transformation; rather, they provide empirical evidence that technology gives rise to hierarchy, which, in turn, removes control from the grasp of employees. The result of this shift is a denigration and exploitation of employees, and their attempt at dealing with such a shift is exemplified by efforts to exert upward influence. This line of reasoning suggests that hierarchy and centralization of power occur differentially in societies depending on their level of technological development, among other factors.

This last point brings up an important aspect in understanding the importance of power differentials to face and a social actor, namely, that a driving force behind the differentials that exist within any given society is attributable, in part, to the nature of technological development and change. The impact of such technology and of the related ways in which people adapt and cope with the conditions of their environment partly determines the acceptability of power differentials in a given society.

It is useful at this point to contrast this form of argument with the one presented by Hofstede in his discussion of power distance. According to Hofstede, low power distance is associated with societies that are technologically advanced based on the general reasoning that such technology gives rise to specialization and the need for sophistication of employees (and all societal members). Such needs for sophistication give rise to extensive education and the active questioning of teachers by their pupils. It is the demand for technological "savvy" that stimulates an active questioning of authority such as we find in the United States. The argument, however, suggests that technological advancement means an increase in routinization of work for employees, and this results in a simplification of work and an increased dependence on key decision makers who control the means of technology. This argument posits that power differentials increase, instead of decreasing, with technological advancements. Such an argument is consistent with the idea of a technological elite in a society.

My own interpretation of these two perspectives is that Hofstede reflects a more long-term perspective and that the technology position fails to incorporate a long-term, dynamic element. More specifically, the technology-as-alienation perspective assumes that people are replaced by technology and are not able to share in the additional responsibilities of planning and enactment surrounding the technology. In addition, this perspective assumes that there is an inherent conflict between technology and individual autonomy, a view that has not been supported by the job enrichment and sociotechnical approaches to production (Katz & Kahn, 1978; Erez & Earley, 1993). From a short-run perspective, the technology view has merit and may reflect balance shifts in power within organizations and society. However, this perspective does not reflect the longer-term influences needed for understanding cultural shifts given that such shifts are long-term.

With regard to face and a social actor, there are a number of important implications of power differentials to social action. According to Mulder's (1977) power distance theory, people with little power will try to gain power while people with significant power will try to maintain their power. It is the exercise of power that gives rise to satisfaction, and this creates a desire to maintain and/or increase power. For the less powerful person, a desire exists to gain power and decrease the distance between him- or herself and the powerful other, and this tendency is enhanced if little difference exists. For a person having greater power, a desire exists to maintain power, and this tendency is enhanced if the distance between him- or herself and the less power-ful other is great. Indeed, Mulder provides empirical evidence for several of these propositions (e.g., Mulder, 1977). What Mulder's analysis ignores, however, is the degree to which these tendencies are manifest by various cultures (Hofstede, 1980a:99). Hofstede posits that the tendency to secure and increase power will differ across cultures because the relative equilibrium point varies by society. In other words, in certain societies (i.e., high power distance) the equilibrium point provides for a large discrepancy between the superior and subordinate but not so in other societies (i.e., low power distance).

What this suggests is that the various social behaviors engaged in by employees (e.g., influence tactics) in organizations to maintain an equilibrium position will be universal in their presence (albeit different in their emic manifestation), but they will vary in the conditions giving rise to their demonstration. The critical "set" point at which certain behaviors will occur varies across societies.

Power differentials are related to face and social action in other ways. In a high power differential society, there is much to lose or gain during social exchanges. In Chapter 3, I described Hu's example of the wealthy Chinese master who had much to lose if he was accused by his servant of not paying the servant his proper due. In a high power distance culture such as precommunist China, face is extremely relevant in reaffirming one's position in a hierarchy. Does this mean that in a low power distance culture face is less relevant? Not at all, for the reasons discussed in Chapter 5. More specifically, in a low power distance culture people are judged to be rela-tively equal to one another, but there is still a desire to differentiate one's power from others. If status, wealth, and position cannot be used to satisfy such a desire, then how can an equilibrium position be determined? It can be determined through an assessment of moral character and goodness. In a low power distance culture, differ-entiation occurs through an assessment of moral character. Even in this type of soci-ety, which presumes to set aside status differentials, there exists a motive to differen-tiate oneself from others (or one's in-group from other groups), which gives rise to some social comparisons.

Thus an analysis of power differentials and distance using face provides an inter-esting supplement to Hofstede's description. I would agree with his argument that societies differ in their acceptance of power inequalities or equilibrium set points. An analysis of these inequalities from a face perspective is interesting because it is possi-ble to propose systematic differences in the types of social behaviors engaged in for dealing with these inequalities. In the case of the low power distance culture, there is an increased emphasis on the lian aspect of face. Actions that reflect on moral character and personal dispositions are likely to be used for balancing and regulating power differentials that may exist or arise. An employee in a low power distance culture such as Sweden reasserts his or her position through moral action and not through the gain of material trappings of position. For the high power distance cul-ture, an emphasis on mianzi is likely to exist. The benefits afforded by hierarchical position (e.g., size of office, view from window, use of executive washroom) are emphasized as a means of furthering power and position relative to others. Pfeffer (1981) refers to a related process of the creation of scarcity as a means of accumulat-ing power. In other words, organizations create scarce resources that are only given to a select few in order to emphasize their relative power over others. Ironically, it is sometimes the mere scarcity of the resource, not its intrinsic value, that gives rise to the importance of the resource. Thus in a high power distance culture, mianzi may be enhanced through organizationally developed structures that preclude all except for a select few from obtaining resources.

Tight versus Loose

The tight versus loose dimension of culture involves the extent to which rules and norms are present and enforced within a given society (Witkin & Berry, 1975). In a tight culture, characterized by many rules governing individuals' actions (Glenn & Glenn, 1980), individuals are expected to conform to existing practices and deviation from those rules is discouraged or condemned. According to Pelto (1968), in loose societies norms are expressed through a wide range of alternative channels; deviant behavior is widely tolerated; values of group organization formality are underdeveloped; and values such as stability, duration, and solidarity are underemphasized. Tight societies are characterized by the opposite situations. For example, Pelto describes Japan and the Israeli kibbutzim as tight societies, whereas Thailand is a loose one.

The most significant work on the concept of tight versus loose has been evidenced by Witkin and Berry and their colleagues (Berry, 1987, 1991; Witkin & Berry, 1975). The dimension of tight versus loose is best understood within the context of their ecological-cultural-behavioral framework, which encompasses multilevel influences on individuals within societies. The model accounts for psychological diversity (individual and group contrasts and similarities) by taking into account two general sources of influence, ecological and sociopolitical context. These general exogenous sources influence the psychological outcomes of cognitive style development through two classes of process variables. The first class of these process variables involves biological and cultural adaptation, which is a macro-level influence. The next class of process variables includes ecological influences, genetic transmission, cultural transmission, and acculturation. Further, the elements of the model are arranged on two levels: a general ecological flow, having its primary effect on ecological influences, biological adaptation, and genetic transmission; and a general sociopolitical context, having its primary effect on cultural adaptation, cultural transmission, and acculturation.

The primary outcome of the model at an individual level is the cognitive style of people within a society. This cultural dimension is particularly interesting because it has a strong, individual-level manifestation that has received much research attention, namely, psychological differentiation (e.g., Witkin & Goodenough, 1977; Witkin, Goodenough, & Oltman, 1979). At an individual level, the tight versus loose dimension is manifest as an individual's capacity to distinguish between an object and its frame or context. Individuals from a loose culture can readily separate object from field, whereas individuals from a tight culture cannot do so. In an organizational context, this suggests that employees from a tight culture are contextually sensitive and use contextual information in order to make sense of particular occurrences. For example, an employee from a tight culture will likely rely on the setting in which job feedback is provided as a way of interpreting the work situation. If the feedback is provided in a public forum, its meaning will be determined, in part, by the reactions of observers to the interaction of an employee with his or her superior.

At the most general level, cognitive styles based on field dependence and independence can be understood as manifesting the differing styles of information seeking that people engage in. When people seek information, field-dependent people look to others for this information just as they look to an external field in perceptual tasks, as evidenced by the various measures used to assess field independence and dependence. (For an excellent review of these measures, I recommend Witkin and Berry's [1975] review of the construct as well as an edited volume by Wapner and Demick [1991] on field dependence and independence.) Field-independent people look to themselves more than external referents. Therefore, there are a number of social behaviors that one might expect to be associated with field dependence and independence. First, people who are field-independent tend to use external referent information less than people who are field-dependent for attitude and judgment change. This is not to say the field-dependent people simply conform under any circumstance. When they need information, they seek it from others and respond accordingly. If information from others is not needed in order to make sense of a given situation, they do not differ in use of external information from people who are field-independent. Second, the degree to which people monitor responses is related to field dependence and independence. Third, people who are field-dependent are better able to recall and process social information and cues than are people who are field-independent, and, finally, field-dependent people are typically judged by others to be more social, gregarious, and interested in people, while field-independent people are often characterized as self-interested, cold, distant, and task-oriented.

Witkin and Berry's model attempts to account for psychological patterns of thinking (e.g., field dependence and independence) in populations by understanding how populations deal with their long-standing ecological situations as well as their more immediate sociopolitical situations. Although the general emphasis of the model is on the ecological and sociopolitical influences on the psychological outcomes, there is a reciprocal influence afforded in the model that captures the attempts of certain societies to harness and manipulate nature (as I discuss further in the section on relationship to nature later in this chapter).

An important implication of this model is that people can actively influence their environment and, hence, the general nature of cognitive styles within their society. How does such an influence come about? Several different approaches can be taken to address this question in the context of culture and society. One approach is through the study of child-rearing practices within a culture. A second approach is to assess post hoc the child-rearing practices associated with cultures differing in their modal cognitive style used. The general studies on child rearing support the conclusion that when there is encouragement within the family for a child to develop an autonomous identity, the child will likely become field-independent. If there is a strong emphasis on obedience to parents and on controlling oneself, then the child becomes field-dependent. In essence, the extent to which a child is encouraged to develop an independent sense of self with discretion for behavior, the greater the degree of field independence.

Ecological and sociocultural factors also play a significant role in shaping field dependence and independence. Much of the research on the influence of ecology on cognitive styles has been conducted with subsistence-level societies, and Berry (in press) suggests that such societies are the best targets for making a direct connection from ecology to cognitive style and culture because there are fewer confounding influences, such as complex economic arrangements and interdependencies. The general influence of ecology on field dependence and independence is that for a sedentary, agricultural society tight control over accumulated food reserves and regulation of interpersonal behavior are important to survival given close group living conditions. However, in a relatively homogeneous but harsh environment, such as the frozen tundra or the desert, those who have high personal autonomy, highly developed restructuring skills, et cetera, are better able to develop the self-reliance needed in the hunter-gatherer groups that form. Complex social organization is not only unnecessary in such harsh environments but also dysfunctional because it distracts from the struggle with nature and the need to be nomadic for gathering food.

With regard to social and cultural influences, there has been a great deal of emphasis on field dependence and independence from the perspective of social conformity and behavior. The relationship of field dependence and independence to the tight versus loose cultural dimension is strong. In tight societies, religious and political powers exert strong control over individual behavior, and obedience is expected. There are many social roles in such a society, and these roles are hierarchically organized in many instances. In loose societies, role diversity is minimized, with only the barest essentials of social organization being present. To the extent that a tight (or loose) emphasis is reflected in child-rearing practices, it is likely that field dependence (or independence) will be observed.

The presumed way in which the tight versus loose dimension impacts cognitive styles in a society operates through more than just child-rearing practices. A key transmission element is the socialization that occurs more broadly. For instance, Barry, Bacon, and Child (1957) demonstrated a general relationship between the ecological and socialization patterns in society. More specifically, they found that ecological conditions were associated with pressures for conformity and obedience. Also, they found that the training of children for responsibility and obedience appears more frequently in agricultural and pastoral societies, whereas training emphasizing achievement, self-reliance, and independence occurs in hunting and gathering societies. As Witkin and Berry (1975:46) suggest, "It is not difficult to see how stress on social conformity may influence development in the direction of limited differentiation. Emphasis on uniform adherence to predetermined external standards during growth is likely to work against achievement of specialization of function in an individualized way, an important attribute of developed differentiation. Continuous reinforced orientation toward external referents also makes difficult achievement of a self differentiated from others."

The general relationship of culture to cognitive style is nicely summarized by Witkin and Berry, who state:

> This review has demonstrated that the concepts derived from differentiation theory can be meaningfully applied across cultures, due largely to the structural nature of differentiation and to its base in a cultural universal-socialization. However, as we have moved across cultural boundaries, the comparative perspective has led us to observe a number of covariates of socialization and a number of other variables which may act independently of it. In particular, the cluster of cultural variables associated with the poles of tight and loose societies has extended our knowledge of the cultural basis of the development of differentiation. Factors such as general pressure toward conformity, the structure of authority, and role diversity and evaluation, all of which may be rooted in demographic and ecological

variation, have been implicated in ways which could not have been forecast from study of the concept within a single culture. (1975:72–73)

Before turning to a further discussion of the relationship of the tight versus loose dimension to face and social functioning, I want to describe a related cultural construct that was proposed and discussed in Hofstede's (1980a) work, namely, uncertainty avoidance. Uncertainty avoidance reflects the emphasis on ritual behavior, rules, and labor mobility within a culture. To some extent, all societies and organizations avoid uncertainty inasmuch as people structure the world around them in order to enhance predictability. Of course, the way in which various societies deal with uncertainty is cultural bound, or emic.

Modern organizational theory emphasizes a number of ways that uncertainty and ambiguity are handled. For instance, Cyert and March (1963:119) argue that organizations handle uncertainty through at least two ways: they rely on decision-making strategies emphasizing immediacy of response (reaction rather than planning), or they rely on a negotiated environment emphasizing standardization, traditions, and contracts in order to avoid the uncertainties of the future. Likewise, Galbraith's information-processing model of organizations (1973) focuses on a number of mechanisms through which organizations buffer themselves from the uncertainty of changing information demands in the environment, such as building up slack resources and increasing information-handling capacities. Hofstede (1980a) argues that organizations cope with uncertainty through their use of technology, rules, and rituals. Technology, for example, provides a short-term predictability concerning production outcomes and procedures. Rules and rituals are employed by organizations in order to create predictability within an organization (Barley, 1990), and they help organizations connect the past to the present and future (Perrow, 1972). For instance, business meetings usually have their own protocols and procedures for conduct, including a ritualized placement of organizational members (seating charts), an initiating event (calling to order), a procedural pattern (who conducts the meeting), a language (business-speak), and even closure (small talk signaling completion of the meeting). These rituals are quickly acquired by new organizational members lest they be sanctioned by more "seasoned" members. Organizations are riddled with various rituals such as memos (and the modern counterpart, e-mail), accounting practices, et cetera. In my teaching experiences in Hong Kong, ever present artifacts reminding us of rituals enacting organizational membership and importance were the pager and mobile phone. So imposing were these devices at the institution I was visiting that the faculty created their own rules for handling potential disturbances (other forms of uncertainty) attributable to these technological leviathans (such as a debate about the wisdom of collecting errant pagers for the professor's personal collection!).

At an individual level, the concept of uncertainty avoidance is somewhat more tenuous from a cultural perspective. Hofstede's measurement of this construct consisted of several items lacking face validity (or, at a minimum, creating substantial confusion concerning their meaning). Hofstede used items to represent his four dimensions that sometimes appear idiosyncratic and post hoc. In some cases, the restricted items used by Hofstede may lead the researcher to wonder what they mean. For uncertainty avoidance, one item Hofstede relied on is an individual's propensity to leave his or her job within a several-year period. It is not clear whether turnover intentions actually measure uncertainty avoidance or some other construct such as organizational commitment, employment mobility patterns, et cetera. Another item Hofstede used was stress experienced by the employee at work, and the final item was the belief that company rules should be adhered to regardless of the consequences. It is perhaps the odd collection of these items that led to Hofstede's subsequent finding that uncertainty avoidance was not a fully etic construct as he originally thought. More specifically, Hofstede and Bond (1988) published an addendum to the original four dimensions suggesting that uncertainty avoidance might best be replaced by Confucian dynamism in Asian cultures. Although individuals from Confucian-based cultures can be measured on uncertainty avoidance, the construct is not a potent one for these cultures. Likewise, it is not at all clear that the countries characterized by Hofstede through his empirical observations are face-valid. At the extreme, a country such as Singapore was rated as the lowest of his sample in uncertainty avoidance, even though people would consistently agree that Singaporean society is extremely tight and rule-bound. (In defense of Hofstede's scheme, the differences may be attributable to temporal shifts, given that his data were collected nearly 25 years ago. Although cultural orientations are long-lasting and enduring, the technological changes toward modernization experienced by Singapore in the last two decades may have moved them toward a more current emphasis on a "tight" culture.)

High uncertainty avoidance is found in countries that report high levels of stress, such as Japan and Belgium, and low uncertainty avoidance is reported in countries such as the United States and Great Britain. Possible antecedents of uncertainty avoidance may include factors such as invasion from neighbors or soil infertility (Triandis, 1995). Uncertainty avoidance tends to be high in societies characterized by a transition toward modernization, religious intolerance and an emphasis on moral absolutes, and a generally aged population. In contrast, low uncertainty avoidance societies generally have tolerant religions, mature and modern industries, and smaller organizations (Hofstede, 1980a:185). At a societal level, the consequences of high uncertainty avoidance include strong nationalism, aggressiveness toward other nations, elaborate legal systems, and low tolerance for citizen protest.

As suggested earlier, from an organization's perspective, the consequences of uncertainty avoidance suggest that managers should be selected because of their seniority and a strong emphasis on loyalty to the firm. In high uncertainty avoidance cultures, managers are unwilling to take risks in their decision making, there is a heavy reliance on rules and standard operating procedures, and employees tend to specialize. In low uncertainty cultures, employees tend to be ambitious, managers have a stronger interpersonal style in their dealings with subordinates, and work activities tend to be somewhat unstructured. High uncertainty avoidance is reflected in a direct style of communication that does not leave much room for ambiguity. Gudykunst et al. (1988) report that uncertainty avoidance explains differences in the use of elaborate versus succinct verbal styles. High uncertainty avoidance results in people having a more elaborate communication style, whereas a succinct style is more prevalent in cultures with low uncertainty avoidance. The use of a direct style is another possible characteristic of high uncertainty avoidance (Erez & Earley, 1993). For example, Israelis have a relatively high uncertainty avoidance (Hofstede, 1980a), which can be used to explain their use of a direct style of communication. Israeli Sabra culture uses the direct style of dugri speech (or "straight talk"), which implies the concern for sincerity in the sense of being true to oneself (Katriel, 1986). Israelis rely on a blunt and direct form of communication, even if such a style involves a direct confrontation with others.

This discussion suggests that uncertainty avoidance is a concept related to the tight versus loose distinction even if its measure is problematic. Tight societies employing extensive rules and expecting strict adherence to them are characteristic of high uncertainty avoidance societies. In countries such as Singapore, the adherence to rules and laws (and the elaborate nature of these laws impinging on nearly every facet of social behavior, including spitting, gum chewing, etc.) is mandated and expected. However, this cultural dimension does not easily lend itself to geographic categorization. For instance, Singapore is a very tight culture, but its regional neighbor Thailand is characterized as a relatively loose culture. Likewise, Sweden is categorized by Hofstede as quite low on uncertainty avoidance even though other researchers characterize it as emphasizing social conformity (tight).

Returning to my discussion of face and social behavior, the implications of the tight versus loose dimension (and the related constructs of field dependence as well as uncertainty avoidance) for face are multifold. Most directly, I would expect a main effect of face related to tight cultures. In general, people from a tight culture are more context/people-sensitive, and so the practices of face regulation are of critical importance. People in a tight culture attend to their personal position and relationships to others more than do people in a loose culture. Second, people in a tight culture have less latitude concerning what constitutes acceptable behavior, and the consequences of deviant behavior are heavily sanctioned.

Third, people in a tight culture place greater emphasis on moral character and lian because this type of behavior and its potential violation affect the very core of social action. The implication of such actions is viewed as derisive and anarchic by one's superiors. The seemingly harsh reactions of the Chinese to the protests in Tiananmen Square reflect a society concerned with the moral character implied by counterrevolutionary activities. The importance of lian in a tight culture is attributable to the implication of these examples, namely, that the very fabric of society may unravel if moral character is in doubt. In a loose culture, a relative emphasis is placed on mianzi because this form of face helps to establish self-importance and personal recognition of accomplishment. The trappings of Trump Tower reinforce Trump's personal accomplishments and successes as a formal monument to himself.

Finally, the nature of information sensitivity reflected in tight versus loose cultures (context/interpersonal awareness) reflects a main effect on lian versus mianzi. People from a tight culture are keenly aware of others' actions and what these actions reflect concerning a person's basic character. Violations of social practices suggest that one has rejected the importance of one's culture or "bu yao lian" (does not want face). People from a loose culture are not so keenly aware of one another, and thus the more externalized manifestations of face are noticed (e.g., type of car, size of office, quality of clothing). It is through such actions that people regulate face in tight and loose cultures, and more important, this regulation is a basis for social exchange and interaction within organizations. People signal their worthiness for organizational membership by regulating face through these various mechanisms across cultures.

In the next two subsections, I turn to dimensions of culture that capture the relationship of people to facets of their environment as well as to social roles and behavior. More specifically, I discuss Kluckhohn and Strodtbeck's (1961) value orientation of relationship to nature, followed by Hofstede's construct of masculinity/femininity.

Person in Relation to Environment

Relationship to Nature

This next dimension that I will discuss is a difficult one in many respects. On the one hand, there is very little written about Kluckhohn and Strodtbeck's (1961:13) value orientation of "Man-Nature," or what I refer to as relationship to nature, in the psychology and anthropology literatures as a specific cultural dimension. On the other hand, there is a voluminous amount of information on the general focus of this dimension in philosophical, religious, and environmental sources. Perhaps to elaborate on this dilemma, it is appropriate to return to Kluckhohn and Strodtbeck's purpose in writing their classic work on value orientations.

The focus of Kluckhohn and Strodtbeck's work was to develop a general classification scheme for the universal problems facing all peoples. As they noted, they assumed that "there is a limited number of common human problems for which all peoples at all times must find some solution. . . . While there is variability in solutions of all the problems, it is neither limitless nor random but is definitely variable within a range of possible solutions. . . . All alternatives of all solutions are present in all societies at all times but are differentially preferred" (10, emphasis in original). By value orientation, Kluckhohn and Strodtbeck meant a patterned set of principles derived from people's evaluative processes (cognitive, affective, and directive) that give order and direction to people's actions and thoughts. Kluckhohn and Strodtbeck distinguish value orientations from the psychologist's concept of value by emphasizing the importance of patterning and the basis on "common human" problems (4–5). In addition, Kluckhohn and Strodtbeck refer to a rank ordering of these value orientations in which the variations within each have characteristic patterns within each culture. For instance, the Spanish-Americans they studied[1] placed a general emphasis on subjugation to nature, mastery, and harmony. Thus a dominant style tends to be ever present, but this does not mean that the secondary or tertiary styles are nonexistent. Subjugation was relatively comparable to mastery in dealing with livestock and other economic issues for the community.

Based on these assumptions, Kluckhohn and Strodtbeck set out to define the general domain of universal human problems. They identified five fundamental problems faced by all people: human nature, relationship to nature, time orientation, activity orientation, and relational orientation. (They note that a sixth problem, conception of space, was insufficiently developed at the time to warrant inclusion in their analyses.) I would add that I have not ignored their other value orientations entirely. For example, human nature is related to my discussion of shame- or guilt-societies (see the next section of this chapter), and relational orientation is a predecessor of individualism and collectivism.

Relationship to nature refers to a general orientation of people to the contextual and spiritual nature of their environment. Three variations of this cultural dimension are mastery over nature, harmony with nature, and subjugation to nature. These variations differ in a number of distinctive ways. Mastery over nature is the first-order (dominant) position for most Anglo-Americans. This position assumes that natural forces are something that can be overcome and harnessed by people and that these forces can be used for various purposes. Bridges over raging rivers, mountains with tunnels drilled through them, the infamous "Chunnel" (the England–France channel tunnel), Hong Kong and the Netherlands' active land reclamation programs, and Israel's irrigation of the desert all constitute examples of a mastery-over-nature orientation. In general, cultures whose primary emphasis is on the utilization of technology as a coping strategy for life's uncertainties are likely to have a mastery orientation. Technological advances are characteristic of people's attempt to adapt nature to their own needs and preferences.

The orientation of a harmony-with-nature culture is quite different. In this setting, there is little or no separation of people, nature, and the supernatural. In a harmony-with-nature culture, people are a natural extension of nature and the supernatural, and a general emphasis on wholeness is exhibited.[2] Sinha (in press) describes an interesting facet of Indian management philosophy, namely, a psychospiritual orientation. In this approach, many Indian managers believe that in order to be completely effective, a manager must get in touch with a general "pure mind" through such methods as yoga or meditation. I note, however, that some aspects of this psychospiritualism border on the next variation that I will discuss, that of subjugation to nature.

A subjugation-to-nature culture believes that the forces of nature (or the supernatural) are inevitable, and therefore a person should not bother to attempt to change the course of events. Kluckhohn and Strodtbeck use the example of their sample of Spanish-Americans, who believed strongly that their shepherding activities were largely controlled by God and the Virgin Mary. As the researchers observed, "In Spanish-American attitudes toward illness and death one finds the same fatalism. 'If it is the Lord's will that I die, I shall die' is the way they express it, and many a Spanish-American has been known to refuse the services of a doctor because of the attitude" (1961:13). This view is consistent with other cultures as well. For example, some Middle Eastern peoples are fatalistic in their view of life, proclaiming, "Allah ahkbah" (God's will) during stressful or difficult situations. Another illustration of this view is presented in Chakraborty's (1993) discussion of Indian spiritualism in management. His argument is that work pressure is God's way of testing personal devotion toward work and that if individuals within a company subscribe to the view that the inner forces (within a person) are more important than the system surrounding an individual, then an organization will be effective.

In assessing this value orientation, Kluckhohn and Strodtbeck used survey items that are illustrative of these positions. For example, for assessing respondents' views of tending their fields, they asked:

> There were three men who had fields with crops (were farmers). The three men had quite different ways of planting and taking care of crops.
>
> C. One man put in his crops, worked hard, and also set himself to living in right and proper ways. He felt that it is the way a man works and tries to keep himself in harmony with the forces of nature that has the most effect on conditions and the way crops turn out.
>
> A. One man put in his crops. Afterwards he worked on them sufficiently but did not do more than was necessary to keep them going along. He felt that it mainly depended

on weather conditions how they would turn out, and that nothing extra that people do could change things much.

B. One man put in his crops and then worked on them a lot of time and made use of all the new scientific ideas he could find out about. He felt that by doing this he would in most years prevent many of the effects of bad conditions.

Which of these ways do you believe is usually best?

Which of the other two ways do you believe is better?

Which of the three ways would most other persons in _____ think is best? (196:85)

This item illustrates the three variations in value orientation of the relationship to nature with regard to an economic activity such as farming, and Kluckhohn and Strodtbeck applied it to other economic and social activities in their assessments.

The relationship to nature orientation is useful in understanding face and related actions. In the case of mastery, there should be a strong emphasis on mianzi because people are viewed as controllers of their own destiny. Through personal and group actions, people can influence their gains and losses and, hence, mianzi. An emphasis on lian is less critical because it is possible to master face (one's social standing) through proper accumulation and interaction in social settings. For example, an employee who works long hours, plays the right sport (the one the boss plays), wears the right clothes, et cetera, is able to succeed in a company and quickly rise through the hierarchy. Although the employee may be engaging in these activities for inner (spiritual or intrinsic) reasons, it is as likely that the actions are enacted for instrumental reasons. In this sense, face is an image to be mastered and manipulated through one's actions.

In contrast, an emphasis on harmony is associated more strongly with lian and the merits of moral character. In order to lead a successful life, a person must deal with others and nature in a fashion that reflects the connectedness among these various elements. Poor moral character (loss of lian) reflects a disruption of the spiritualism needed to experience life from a holistic perspective. In such a culture, an emphasis is placed on lian as a means of ensuring the proper coordination among various systems and groups. An emphasis is placed by employees on the importance of what they are doing (e.g., the products they produce) as well as on how they are doing it. For example, Tom's of Maine produces all-natural products that are environmentally sound. The management philosophy for product development at Tom's of Maine is that its products must reflect their relationship to nature (e.g., through the use of organic ingredients and biodegradable, recyclable containers) as well as their customers' values and needs. Face reflects a willingness to maintain moral standards that reflect a concern for the environment as well as fellow employees.

Finally, the orientation of subjugation to nature is more problematic. It is possible to argue that if one truly believes that fate and action are predestined or the will of God (external forces), why should one worry about lian or mianzi? In other words, the argument reduces to the idea that whatever happens will happen regardless of one's actions or desires. However, it seems more reasonable (and consistent) to suggest that people from a subjugation-to-nature culture will emphasize lian, not mianzi. In other words, people do not struggle against destiny in order to accumulate status or possessions (mianzi) but struggle to lead morally righteous lives (according to a particular theological or philosophical orientation). Kluckhohn and Strodtbeck described the approach to work of the Spanish-Americans in their sample in this fashion. They suggested that the Spanish-Americans are sometimes seen by Anglos as lazy or uninvolved. However, Kluckhohn and Strodtbeck suggest that their acceptance of and choice not to try to overcome work challenges reflect subjugation and not personal predispositions toward laziness. In the next section, I will discuss another aspect of culture concerning how people interact with their contextual world, namely, the dimension of masculinity/femininity proposed by Hofstede (1980a).

Masculinity/Femininity

The masculinity/femininity dimension involves the differentiation of societies on the basis of activity and gender (Hofstede, 1980a). At the outset, at least one disclaimer should be relayed, namely, that Hofstede (1994, personal conversation) recognizes that this labeling has an unfortunate and unintended connotation concerning sex roles. It was not Hofstede's intention to capture or imply gender-based stereotypes using this dimension. However, his 1980 classic muddies this assertion inasmuch as he uses gender as a categorization scheme, including a discussion of work goals most important to men versus women, and he rescaled his index of valued work goals because the respondents were primarily men (278). Despite this, the dimension of masculinity/femininity is presented in my work as a cultural dimension not tied to specific genders; rather, it reflects a number of orientations that may exist within a society.

The concept of masculinity/femininity refers to

> the dominant sex role pattern in the vast majority of both traditional and modern societies as described in the early part of this chapter: that of male assertiveness and female nurturance. It is by no means necessary that men always actually behave more "masculine" than women and women more "feminine" than men, as Bem's experiments have shown; statistically, however, men as a rule will be more on the "masculine" side and women more on the "feminine." . . . The fact that the social-ego difference appears on a worldwide ecological level means that it must be associated with a fundamental dilemma of mankind. This dilemma is the relative strength of nurturance interests (relation with manager, cooperation, atmosphere) versus assertiveness interests (earnings, advancement): of interests which in nearly all traditional and modern societies are traditionally more "feminine" versus those that are traditionally more "masculine." (Hofstede, 1980a:277)

Although this cultural dimension is not intended to be confused with sex roles, it does have its origins (based on Hofstede's own analysis) in gender differences. More specifically, Hofstede argues that sex roles in society are an important reflection of cultural orientation but not that fundamental differences exist (in the sense that they are absolute and attached to biological condition). To this point, he posits that the only true and absolute difference between the genders is childbearing versus childbegetting and that any other differences can only be thought of in statistical and distributional terms. Further, much of what we observe in these distributional terms (e.g., that men emphasize achievement more than women do in their work activities) must be couched within a given cultural context (e.g., that men from culture X emphasize achievement more than women from culture X do in their work activities).

Despite this general assertion, there appear to be general and systematic differences among the genders that give rise to sex role and gender effects attributable to the basic reproductive responsibilities of men versus women. For example, Mead (1967) argued that the typical dominant orientation toward achievement of men (relative to women) is attributable to the reproductive burden placed on women. The very fact that women give birth provides them a very special status of an "irreversible achievement" for which men do not have an equivalent. Therefore, the purpose of a great deal of activity in society is to provide men with some achievements of this irreversible nature. Mead reported three distinctive gender patterns in New Guinea societies. Among the Arapesh, both men and women conform closely to what is stereotyped as "feminine" behavior in the West. Both men and women are passive, peaceful, and deferential, and both nurture others, especially young children. The Mundugumor socialize both sexes to be aggressive, independent, and competitive. Mothers are not especially nurturing, and babies are weaned at a very young age. The Tchambuli reflect gender roles the opposite of what we expect in the West; namely, women are the aggressors and men are more submissive and attempt to make themselves attractive to women. In other cultures, such as several Native American groups, more than two gender roles are enacted (Garbarino, 1976).

In the research of Witkin, Berry, and their associates concerning psychological differentiation (discussed earlier in this chapter), cross-cultural evidence for gender-based differences in cognitive style and perception appears. For example, Berry (1976) conducted an extensive series of field tests among the construct of field dependence and independence among samples from 21 different communities across Africa, Australia, Europe, and North America, and he reports systematic differences in differentiation as a function of gender. In general, males tend to be more differentiated (field-independent) than females. This makes sense if we compare this concept to the self versus other orientation I described earlier. Men, who tend to be more field-independent, are focused on internal frames of reference and value ego gratification and achievement. Women, who tend to be more field-dependent, are focused on external frames of reference and value social relationships and interpersonal interaction. I would emphasize that these are statistical generalizations subject to many other eco-cultural factors (Berry, 1976).

Meadian role theory stresses the impact of social influences on the generation of gender differences in many instances (Boudreau, et al., 1986). Children develop a gender identity based on various categorizations derived from social, verbal, and environmental cues (Bandura, 1986), and their identities are shaped and focused through listening and observing. Although there are potential biological bases for gender differences, such influences are matched (and exceeded) by specific socialization processes that shape identity (Boudreau et al., 1986). Socially endorsed meanings are communicated through structures such as institutions, which serve to perpetuate culture-based gender roles. Schools, courts, and organizations all contribute to the cultivation and perpetuation of gender-based roles (Wood, 1994).

Even though there appear to be systematic differences in the cultural concepts of masculinity and femininity, some scholars question whether it is useful to continue utilizing such a view for empirical purposes. For instance, Gullestad (1993) suggests that although the universality of the axiom that men subordinate women appears to be justifiable at an abstract level, such an assumption is misguided for empirical work because it leads researchers toward the wrong questions. In her study of the construction and decoration of Norwegian homes, she argues that for younger couples there has been a trend for the wife to have much more control over the content and style of the house. For instance, one participant in Gullestad's study commented that each month she buys an ornament for the apartment as a way of reminding herself that she is a solid wage earner. This is not the case for the husband, who often seems somewhat uncomfortable in his own house. To some extent, Gullestad argues, the language reflects the dominance of wives over husbands in their homes, such as children referring to their homes as "my mother's house" and the practice of a husband "returning home to mother" in the case of divorce. The point is that if one sets aside the general assumption that women are subordinate to men, then very different types of questions may be asked reflecting different social structures than were otherwise assumed to exist.

From a psychological perspective, a great deal of research has been conducted on sex roles by Bem and her colleagues (Bem, 1974, 1975; Bem et al., 1976). As part of her research program, Bem developed a sex role inventory, to which subjects respond by judging which of a number of adjectives best represent themselves. Based on an analysis of these data, Bem categorized individuals into one of four types: masculine (e.g., aggressive, ambitious), feminine (e.g., affectionate, understanding), androgynous (e.g., having aspects of both characteristics), and undifferentiated (e.g., having neither aspects strongly salient).

Most of my discussion up to this point has focused on the individual-level manifestations of gender differences and sex roles. However, there are a number of specific implications of Hofstede's construct at a cultural level. For instance, a masculine culture emphasizes differences between genders, whereas in a feminine culture gender differentiation is minimal. The centrality of work in a person's life is greater in a masculine than in a feminine culture, and the general quality of life is emphasized over work more in a feminine culture. In masculine cultures, people prefer salary over reduced working hours and emphasize achievement in the work context. Feminine cultures are characterized by individuals who "work to live" rather than "live to work" (Hofstede, 1980). The emphasis is nicely illustrated by Whyte (1969:31, taken from Hofstede, 1980a:285), who quotes American businessman Charles Kettering:

> I often tell my people that I don't want any fellow who has a job working for me: What I want is a fellow whom a job has. I want the job to get the fellow and not the fellow to get the job. And I want that job to get hold of this young man so hard that no matter where he is the job has got him for keeps. I want that job to have him in its clutches when he goes to bed at night, and in the morning I want that same job to be sitting on the foot of his bed telling him it's time to get up and go to work. And when a job gets a fellow that way, he's sure to amount to something.

This strong and clear emphasis on the centrality of a job to a person's psyche and identity is characteristic of a masculine culture. In a feminine culture, there is much less emphasis on a job per se, and work is seen as an important means of achieving more central and important outcomes such as a successful family, personal or collective interests, et cetera.

A number of societal norms are associated with masculinity/femininity. In a more masculine culture, there is an emphasis on norms such as money and objects (accumulation), performance and growth, "living to work," an achievement ideal, independence and decisiveness, and excelling and trying to be the best at something; things that are big and fast are admired, sex roles are clearly differentiated, with men being more assertive and women more caring, and male domination occurs in various settings. In a more feminine culture, there is an emphasis on norms such as a people orientation, quality of life and environment, "working to live," a service ideal, interdependence and intuition, and leveling (not trying to be better than others); things that are small and slow are admired, sex roles are less differentiated and more fluid, androgyny is an ideal, and sex roles are not associated with differential levels of power (Hofstede, 1980a:294).

The origins and consequences of masculinity/femininity are multifaceted. The ecological basis for the cultural dimension appears unclear according to Hofstede's analysis, and his conclusion is that tradition and history likely account for most of the differences in gender and sex roles that are observed. The origins include such factors as a harsh environment in which cooperation between men and women is needed for survival (feminine culture), historical events such as men being nearly eliminated by war and being replaced by women for function (feminine culture), or uncontrolled family size leading women to retain child development responsibilities (masculine culture). The consequences of masculinity for organizations and society include rewards in the form of wealth and status for the successful achiever, large-scale enterprises and projects, higher job stress, centrality of work to life, and more industrial conflict. The opposite holds true for feminine cultures.

In his analysis of this dimension for organizations, Hofstede stresses the relevance of masculinity/femininity for organizations primarily in terms of industrial strife, conflict, high growth, work stress, achievement, and aggression. That is to say, masculine cultures are essentially fast-paced and aggressive and emphasize growth and development over stability and harmony. For my analysis of face and social behavior it is important to consider the potential impact of masculinity/femininity on the nature of face. I would argue that in a masculine culture people emphasize achievement, and their inward focus leads them to stress the visible signs of achievement as a means of reinforcing their accomplishments. The significance of accumulating wealth is that it symbolizes success. As one consultant/lecturer on negotiation practices commented, "It's not the money; it's the money," meaning that he measured his success by the size of his consulting fee and not the actual wealth. This suggests that mianzi will play a central role in a masculine culture because it focuses on the trappings of success that are easily referenced and demonstrated to the strong achiever. Aggression, competition, et cetera, are not systematic traits; rather, they are the modes of action that are needed in order for someone to accumulate status and position.

In contrast, people from a feminine culture are concerned with proper social functioning and interaction among people. A nurturing and caring perspective focusing on people and their well-being is threatened if individuals place personal gain over interpersonal harmony and functioning. This suggests that the moral character of people is of central concern because such a focus helps to determine the potential of an individual to contribute to interpersonal welfare and reflects a person's likely "balance point." By a "balance point" I mean that crucial point in a feminine culture where people know each other's moral perspective and thus can fully understand their true needs and wants. It reflects a desire to understand another person in a fundamental and personal way that is not attainable through a cursory examination of a person's wealth or position (i.e., getting to know the person and not just his or her role).

This discussion posits, then, that people from a masculine culture will see accumulation and status as a dominant force in their interactions, which means that mianzi will be critical. In contrast, people from a feminine culture see inner character as a dominant force because it is through such an assessment that they can determine another person's true needs and wants. Without such an assessment, people from a feminine culture do not feel they can completely understand another person.

Person in Relation to Self

Shame versus Guilt

In this section, I address an aspect of culture that focuses on an internal characteristic of a social actor, namely, a shame versus guilt orientation. This construct has received a great deal of attention from both anthropologists and psychologists, and I will examine it using these two styles. In their most basic forms, shame and guilt are related but are not the same concept. Shame refers to a situation in which a person has failed to fulfill personal or community ideals for behavior and personal states, whereas guilt reflects a situation in which a person transgresses the moral imperatives of a society (Lazarus & Lazarus, 1994). For example, we might say that a person who has a physical deformity (e.g., a hunchback) experiences shame, but we would not necessarily conclude that this unfortunate person feels guilty about his or her handicap. However, if someone steals from his or her employer but is not caught doing so, that employee may well experience guilt but not shame. Thus a critical dimension of these complex emotions is the degree of publicness implicit in the experience. Shame is a socially focused and oriented experience, and guilt is a personal one. Using this general distinction, it becomes clear how this cultural dimension relates to the concepts of face and social action.

The origins of shame versus guilt from an anthropological perspective can be traced to a number of scholars, including Benedict (1946), Levy (1973), Lynd (1958), Piers and Singer (1971), and Resaldo (1984), to name a few. In fact, the distinction of shame versus guilt is one of the very few distinctions in anthropology that has stood the test of time for its universality. This may be attributable to the fundamental and bridging nature of the construct; shame is essentially a socially based experience, whereas guilt is an individually based experience, and such a distinction maps nicely onto distinctions of societies based on community versus self. An early analysis of the contrast between shame and guilt was evidenced in Benedict's (1946) analysis of Japanese society, as well as work by Campbell (1964) with Greeks and Pitt-Rivers (1954) with Spanish peasants.

The mechanism through which feelings of guilt or shame are produced centers upon the family and community in most cultures. In a society in which a child is trained by a large number of socializing agents, such as an extended family or tight community, a general shame orientation is produced. A group member is afraid of the withdrawal of the love of others (Eberhard, 1967), of being suddenly out of synchronization with his or her environment, or of not living up to the trust that he or she has for him- or herself. In many community-based cultures, the most important thing for people is to avoid shame in the views of others. They have internalized the norms of their group and important socializing agents, and much of their actions are based on avoidance principles (avoiding doing things that will bring on shame).

Guilt is a different type of experience. Guilt reflects "wrongdoing," an actual and real violation of moral standards for personal conduct, and it is typically coupled with experiences of remorse and guilt. The societal member avoids engaging in behavior that will put him or her in a position of violating his or her own code of ethics or standards for behavior. While the more "primitive" and developing types of cultures, with their emphasis on family and the social community, focus on shame, more industrially advanced and progressive communities focus on individual responsibility for action and a moral order driven by guilt.

However, this contrast is not necessarily a simple and clean one, as might be assumed based on my discussion up to this point. For instance, Rosaldo (1984) describes a number of his interpretations of the Ilongots (a tribe of headhunters) concerning the concept of shame and its separation from a Western concept of guilt. He suggests:

> The difficulty with "guilt and shame" is that it sorts just "us" from "them," asking how "they" achieve adherence to their norms and rules in lieu of mechanisms we use to an equivalent sort of end. What is not recognized is the possibility that the very problem— how society controls an inner self—may well be limited to those social forms in which a hierarchy of unequal power, privilege, and control in fact creates a world in which the individual *experiences* constraint.
>
> . . . Thus, Ilongot "shame" is not a constant socializer of inherently asocial souls, but an emotion felt when "sameness" and sociality are undermined by confrontations that involve such things as inequality and strangeness.
>
> . . . My point, in short, is that the error of the classic "guilt and shame" account is that it tends to universalize our culture's view of a desiring inner self without realizing that such selves—and so, the things they feel—are, in important ways, social creations. (148–149)

This point is made by others as well. For instance, Eberhard (1967) describes some of the research conducted on the Burmese by Hitson (1959). He argues that the Burmese, who are described as a shame-based culture, also know the concept and experience of guilt. Likewise, people labeling the Japanese culture as shame-based note that the Japanese also are capable of feeling guilt as a result of personal actions (Rosaldo, 1984). In Western culture, people certainly experience guilt readily and for a multitude of reasons, ranging from broken New Year's resolutions to having taken the last soda in the refrigerator to not having walked the dogs on a given evening. Do Westerners experience shame as well? Certainly there seems to be evidence of this sort in many circumstances, such as having a physical deformity or public embarrassment. Thus it appears that the distinction of shame versus guilt is much like that of competition versus cooperation, namely, both impulses exist in all societies and it is the relative balance that determines the fingerprint for a given culture (Mead, 1967). Drawing on an organizational example, imagine an employee who has set an ambitious work goal for his or her marketing team but through several personal mistakes that he or she could have corrected has caused the team to grossly underachieve its goal. The results of this failure are public teasing by other teams and a formal warning from the company's hierarchy. In this case, the employee experiences both guilt and shame. On the one hand, he or she feels guilty about having let down the team members through inaction or mistakes. By not trying to correct several mistakes that might have been corrected, the employee has violated his or her moral imperative to make an adequate contribution to the team's progress. On the other hand, he or she experiences a sense of shame as a result of the ridicule and teasing from the other teams in the division. The important question becomes one of understanding and predicting which of these forces will contribute most directly (and heavily) to the manager's actions in the future. In a Western context, it is likely that the manager's concern over having violated a moral imperative (not trying to overcome his or her own mistakes) will explain subsequent actions.

The relationship of shame versus guilt to face is not entirely direct. The most direct relationship is that shame-based cultures focus their attention on the lian aspect of face similar to a culture stressing community over individual (e.g., a collectivistic or field-dependent community). Likewise, it is hypothesized that the relationship of mianzi to individuals' actions would be strongest for a guilt-based culture. The general reasoning is that the experience of shame is most likely to occur in a society that is collectivistic or field-dependent, whereas the experience of guilt is most likely to occur in a society that is individualistic or field-independent. In this case, my argument is that the type of face operating is a product of a general orientation toward shame or guilt based on other important cultural values that dominate a given society.

In previous sections of this chapter, I have posed the various cultural dimensions as independent influences on face, but I would argue that these various dimensions interact with one another. For example, in Triandis's vertical collectivism it may be guilt that is operating and thereby influencing a mianzi aspect of face. It is the combination of vertical differentiation and self-orientation that leads an individual to pursue mianzi. In contrast, I would expect that a vertical differentiation and collective orientation would emphasize lian over mianzi, or the duty to maintain the power structure in a company over individual gain. These relationships become even more complex if we consider the different forms of lian and mianzi, as well as the subtleties among forms of shame and guilt that exist in various cultures. Thus the basic nature of shame versus guilt is tied to the other types of values that seem to dominate in a given culture.

In the final section of the chapter, I provide a general integration of these six dimensions of culture in conjunction with face. As I stated at the beginning of this chapter, I chose these six dimensions because they are interrelated to some extent and can be woven together to provide a more complete picture of face in a cultural context.

Collage View of Face and Culture

In my model, I have focused on six dimensions of culture in the analysis of face and social behavior. These dimensions are not intended to be all-encompassing, such as Hofstede's (1980a, 1991) famous typology or Schwartz's (1993) categorization. Nor are these the only dimensions that are likely to be relevant to a further understanding of face in a social context. For example, I have not dealt with the cultural dimension of high versus low context (Hall, 1959), which is related to the level of implied connections among relationships in a given society (e.g., in a high-context culture, relationships among ideas, people, constructs, etc., are highly interdependent and content-specific, whereas in a low-context culture they are less so). It is easy to imagine a connection between context sensitivity and face-related activities. My focus has been on choosing those dimensions that I believe are most directly related to face and that represent different types of cultural influences on people.

My choice of these six dimensions was intended to present a collage, with the overall "picture" of cultural influence to be relatively comprehensive. The relationship of these cultural features to the individual and to face is complex and interdependent. The metaphor I would draw is that of a fish in a saltwater "reef"–style fish tank (meaning a system dependent on a natural ecosystem simulated in a confined space but through which impurities [e.g., fish waste products] are processed using natural biological and chemical processes inherent to a coral reef in nature). In this type of aquarium, an overall significance of the system is not fully captured by individual components of the system. The basic principle underlying the aquatic system is that a great deal of "live" (biologically and biochemically) rock is used to break down the ammonia waste products of the tank's inhabitants through various cycles (e.g., nitrogen, phosphorous, carbon). In this type of system, however, each component of the system can be understood as a legitimate subsystem, and each of these subsystems can be directly impacted through intervention.

In applying my reef tank metaphor to an analysis of culture and its dimensions, I would suggest that these various dimensions interact and must be thought of in systemic terms, but that individual subsystems can be analyzed and understood. For example, if the ecological and cultural environments shift (à la Berry, 1976), this impacts not only psychological differentiation (and its cultural surrogate of tight versus loose) but also related systems such as individualism-collectivism. However, not all subsystems are necessarily influenced in such an example. It is conceivable that such a shift might not impact shame versus guilt or masculinity/femininity.

An additional characteristic of my metaphor is that some of the influences are external to the tank inhabitant, some are internal, and some represent an environment-inhabitant interaction. These cultural dimensions can be classified as "external," "internal," or "person-context." By external, I mean that this aspect of culture influences a person's face and behavior through a primarily structural means. In the case of power distance and individualism-collectivism, these cultural dimensions have their most direct influence on how people relate to one another in structural terms. People in a high power distance culture anticipate and legitimate influence in a downward direction, whereas people in a low power distance culture do not legitimate such an influence. People in a collectivistic culture relate to in-group members as an extension of self and are willing to forego personal goals in favor of group goals, whereas people in an individualistic culture relate to others as independent entities. This distinction, of course, becomes more complex in considering Triandis's (1995) proposed typology of individualism and collectivism. In this example, the relationship of people to one another as self or extensions of the group captures Triandis's notion of "sameness." Degree of interdependence (goal) reflects the characteristic of horizontal versus vertical orientation. Regardless, both characteristics reflect the structural nature of the individual versus the group as a meaningful unit within a society.

The most direct interaction is that of individualism and collectivism with power distance. Indeed, it may be that Triandis's (1995) two-by-two typology is largely a reflection of this interaction and not a fundamental distinction for individualism and collectivism. A key question concerns the nature of the "sameness" aspect to his typology relative to power distance. As I discussed earlier, the sameness component reflects differentiation, which is a fundamental force underlying power distance. It is possible that societies encourage the explicit recognition of differences among people purely for informational purposes, but it seems much more likely that the reason people differentiate themselves from particular others is for the purpose of establishing power differences, class, status, caste, et cetera. What I would argue is that people differentiate between self and other for the purpose of establishing some form of pecking order, which is why organizational members cling to titles, large offices, expense accounts, et cetera. These various distinguishing features enable people to establish a hierarchy, and such a hierarchy is quickly evidenced as people enter and leave an existing setting (such as the scramble for the office of someone of a high rank who leaves the company). Although the desire for such a stratification may not be extreme, Tannenbaum et al.'s (1974) findings concerning hierarchy as a universal feature of organizations suggest that all people seek some degree of "difference" between themselves and others. In a collectivistic culture, this identification is largely based on in-group versus out-group distinctions. Thus the power differentials we observe in cultures are related to the nature of individualism and collectivism to some extent. Although power distance and individualism and collectivism reflect the external or structural aspects of culture, relationship to nature and masculinity/femininity reflect a different form of influence. I refer to these dimensions as person-context because they reflect the relationship of an individual to the environmental and social context. (Please note that I am focusing on a particular aspect of masculinity/femininity, namely, the relationship of people to objects and position as a reflection of social status.) In the case of relationship to nature, Kluckhohn and Strodtbeck (1961) posed three potential relationships: mastery, harmony, and subjugation. People from a mastery-over-nature culture actively seek to dominate and adapt nature (e.g., building covered swimming pools for winter swimming), people from a harmony-with-nature culture seek to work with the constraints imposed by nature (e.g., building desert houses into the side of a hill in order to utilize the earth's natural cooling potential), and people from a subjugation-to-nature culture allow nature's (and theological) constraints to dictate their actions (e.g., Christian Scientists rejecting modern medicine in favor of prayer). In these various examples, the key to understanding the impact of culture on face depends on how a cultural member relates to nature (and the cultural system). For example, in a mastery-over-nature culture, face is likely to be viewed as a outcome that is manipulable through people's actions.

In the case of masculinity/femininity, there is an increased emphasis on overt signs of status and position in masculine cultures. Not so for feminine cultures, in which an emphasis is placed on inner character and relationships with others. In a feminine culture, individuals focus on how their actions reflect on lian, not mianzi. Using my person-in-context reef tank metaphor, this dimension would capture the relationship of the fish to the reef itself. For instance, some fish are incompatible with a reef setting because they are destructive to the reef itself. This would suggest that the "masculine" inhabitant is one that stakes out its territory and demonstrates to other inhabitants its dominance in this territory through signaling behavior (Delbeek & Sprung, 1994).

The final aspect of this metaphor is the nature of the tank inhabitant's inner biological processing. Saltwater fish are highly subject to osmotic influence and expend a great deal of energy maintaining water equilibrium. A key aspect of healthy fish in a tank is their natural equilibrium for water exchange. The cultural dimension of shame versus guilt is analogous to the inner balance achieved by the saltwater inhabitants. In a guilt-oriented society there is an emphasis on people's actions as judged by their own moral standards, whereas in a shame-oriented society there is an emphasis on conformity to social standards external to individuals. It is this distinction that creates an interesting paradox of influence on face.

In the section on shame versus guilt societies, I argued that there is an indirect effect of this dimension on face through related cultural dimensions such as individualism and collectivism as well as the tight versus loose dimension. Using this argument, shame (characteristic of collectivistic and tight cultures) would be most directly related to lian and guilt (characteristic of individualistic and loose cultures) most directly related to mianzi. However, I would expect an additional complication in this case, namely, that shame reflects an external aspect of social behavior (adherence to social norms, necessarily a social and public act more in line with mianzi) and guilt reflects an internal aspect of social behavior (personal judgments of right and wrong, not necessarily a social and public act and thereby consistent with lian). In this sense, guilt versus shame may have multiple and competing influences on face and face-related behavior.

Just as the reef metaphor implies, these cultural dimensions have interactive as well as independent influences on face. Several examples have been presented so far, such as the expectation that people from a collectivistic culture are likely to be from a tight culture and that these two dimensions jointly influence the focus of a culture on shame over guilt. I think that the relationship of these three cultural dimensions is particularly interesting because it is possible to argue that a shame versus guilt orientation is a result of the other cultural orientations. In other words, guilt and shame become very important regulatory influences on individuals who operate in any social system, and they are likely the products of such effects. In a tight culture, there is an emphasis on rules and practices for regulating various aspects of social behavior. It is critical that such a culture operates on a principle of shame in order for the social context to be properly regulated. Of course, it is possible that in a tight culture socialization experienced by children inculcates the norms of society as the values of the individuals. If this is the case, then it is possible that guilt would be the fundamental orientation of cultural members. However, it is unlikely that every cultural member will learn every norm for behavior (Rohner, 1984), so there needs to be some more general regulatory feature within the society. In this case, I would expect that the critical regulatory influence is that of normative imposition and sanctioned behavior. For such a regulatory process to operate properly, it requires that cultural members respond to such sanctions and avoid normative infractions (e.g., a shame-oriented society).

Lian is generally emphasized and reinforced by cultures high on collectivism, low on power distance, tight, oriented toward harmony with nature or subjugation, feminine, and shame-focused. In contrast, mianzi is generally emphasized by cultures high on power distance, loose, oriented toward mastery over nature, masculine, and guilt-focused. Interestingly, the collage for lian appears to most directly apply to developing nations, such as Malaysia or Singapore, rather than to developed ones. More to the point, this general description is probably more consistent with Durkheim's (1933) communal society than it is with a technologically advanced one. Does this imply that only undeveloped or developing nations emphasize lian over mianzi? Not at all. The collage does not necessarily imply that all dimensions operate comparably or equally (Brett et al., in press; Smith & Bond, 1994).

In some cultures, an emphasis on power structure may swamp other cultural dimensions such as shame or relationship to nature. Sinha (in press) describes the role of telling the truth in Indian management. He suggests that Indians generally endorse telling the truth except in cases where the action would lead to the injury of another person. If the truth is undesirable or adverse, it may be withheld. An exception is if the truth holder is subordinate to an individual whom the truth will impact. If the superior might be harmed if the truth is not told, then the subordinate is obligated to tell the superior. In this example, a general rule for social etiquette is overridden by a rule associated with a power structure in a company.

Likewise, some cultural dimensions may take precedence over others depending on the context. For example, Sinha (in press) suggests that many Indian companies that are related to multinational corporations have management practices and governance systems quite consistent with those of their Western counterparts. In smaller, more local companies, there is a more direct reflection of basic Indian management values, including spiritualism and a family orientation. As India becomes increasingly dominated by Western and Japanese MNCs, we may observe an increasingly homogeneous work environment that reflects Western culture to a larger extent than it reflects Indian culture.

Finally, as I mentioned earlier, several of the dimensions act to reinforce one another. For instance, an individualistic culture is reinforced by a loose culture because the weak adherence to specific norms and rules provides ample opportunity for people to "do their own thing," or act individualistically (Triandis, 1995). A shame-oriented culture is reinforced by a high power distance emphasis because the shame orientation enables the proper regulation of social behavior in the presence of powerful others. The relationship of these reinforcing mechanisms works to strengthen the relative emphasis on lian versus mianzi in social interactions. Thus the relationships among these can be complementary or interactive.

Summary

In this chapter, I have examined a number of facets of culture that are relevant to face and associated social actions. The importance of these dimensions of culture is that they provide a general context in which social behaviors and face regulation occur. The specific aspects of behavior engaged in, however, remain more closely tied to the specific context in which an employee operates. Triandis et al. (1993) and Erez and Earley (1993) argue that culture can, to some limited extent, be cognitively activated (e.g., via priming techniques) through contextual intervention. Put simply, it may be possible to influence people to behave individualistically or collectivistically through social contextual manipulations. This argument is consistent with some of the recent work conducted by O'Reilly, Chatman, and their colleagues (e.g., O'Reilly & Chatman, 1994) at the organizational level. Essentially, they suggest that an organizational context imposed on employees shapes perceptions and that these perceptions in turn, influence the organization.

The conceptualization of culture in relation to face is best thought of in terms of Granovetter's (1985) idea of embeddedness. As such, cultural dimensions provide an important contextual feature that shapes general predispositions of employees to respond to the environment in systematic ways. In certain societies these cultural effects are mutually reinforcing, whereas in other societies they are independent or interactive. Through a careful analysis of these cultural characteristics, it is possible to more fully understand the nature of face in an organizational context. It is to this point that I now turn, namely, face and social action within an organizational context.

Notes

1. There is a somewhat common incorrect discussion of Kluckhohn and Strodtbeck in the organizations literature by people who describe cultural dimensions. In particular, people seem to mislabel Kluckhohn and Strodtbeck's studies as cross-national or broadly cross-cultural analysis of cultural values. In fact, Kluckhohn and Strodtbeck conducted their studies among five communities within a 25-mile radius (two Native American villages [Zuni and Navajo]; a Spanish-American community they labeled "Atrisco"; a Mormon village; and a farming village consisting of Texan and Oklahoman homesteaders they labeled as Rimrock and Homestead, respectively). Although these five communities differ markedly in their cultural orientations (as Kluckhohn and Strodtbeck illustrate), this study was not a cross-national analysis of cultural values. It does illustrate, however, that interesting cross-cultural work can be conducted within a given nation-state—a lesson to be learned by some scholars who think that national variation is necessary for understanding the significance and relevance of culture to organizations.

2. Interestingly, the harmony-with-nature perspective emphasizes the interdependence of people and nature consistent with many organizational views espoused today. For example, Katz and Kahn's (1978) open-system view of organizations posits such strong interrelations among various subsystems within organizations. Likewise, living systems theory and control theory (Carver & Scheier, 1981; Klein, 1989; Powers, 1973) reflect an interdependence among various systems within an organization.

9

Organizational Context and Content

The functioning of face and its regulation cannot be divorced from the organizational context in which it occurs. That is, the type of organization a person works and functions in, norms and socialized rules for proper conduct, scripts for action, and rituals and ceremonies governing expectations and behavior all contribute to the display of face and individuals' attempts to secure it. The spouse of a friend who worked for a southwestern-based electronics company once described the process of getting "laid off." Typically, a sales employee being laid off would come back from lunch to the large, open office area and see a security guard standing beside the salesperson's desk. No advance notice of the layoff or firing was given. Next, the ill-fated employee would face the difficult task of collecting his or her belongings as the guard looked on to ensure that no company materials or secrets were being packed. Finally, the employee was ceremoniously stripped of a security/name badge, office keys, and company passes and escorted out of the building. It was said that this procedure was necessary in order to protect important company records and sales files. Of course, this separation ritual instilled a strong sense of discomfort with company-espoused values such as commitment to the employee, cooperation, et cetera. Other organizations in the same business find rather different ways of implementing such employment terminations despite the need for security.

In this chapter, I discuss the nature of organizational context and structure on the display and enactment of face. An argument is presented concerning the dynamic interplay of structure and self-concept, and a number of contextual aspects within organizations are described as a function of face and its regulation. It is emphasized, however, that this chapter is not the central focus of this book, and my intention is to briefly describe the backdrop of organizational context and content as they relate to face. In doing so, I will draw most directly from work on institutional theory (DiMaggio & Powell, 1983; Powell & DiMaggio, 1991; Meyer & Rowan, 1977; Scott & Meyer, 1994) as well as social action theory (Giddens, 1984; Parsons & Shils, 1951). It is beyond my scope and focus to address the vast literature on institutional theory (see Powell & DiMaggio, 1991; Scott & Meyer, 1994; Zucker, 1987; as well as Ghoshal & Westney, 1993, from an international perspective [chapters 1–3 in particular]).

More specifically, I begin by discussing the general framework through which face is influenced (and influences) organizational dynamics based on an institutional analysis. This includes a very brief overview of political and economic influences as well as the impact of organizational fields on the institutional practices that shape face and related behaviors. Next, I describe the impact of organization-specific context and structure on face, including such features as technology, communication, governance structures, and interorganizational dependencies. Finally, I show the relationship of face and its regulation to these facets of an organization as both cause and consequence.

General Issues of Institutions Theory

Institutions and an institutional analysis are very important in understanding the role of face dynamics in an organization. The study of institutions has long been a focus of sociologists, economists, and political scientists, and there has been an explosion of research on the topic during the last twenty years. In its simplest form, institutional theory applied to organizations can be thought of as the study of functioning through an analysis of persistent rules and procedures underlying action. Organizations are viewed as dependent on a wide environment that is the product of rational and nonrational impulses and "less as a coherent rational superactor (e.g., a tightly integrated state or a highly coordinated invisible hand) than as an evolving set of rationalized patterns, models, or cultural schemes. . . . These may be built into the public polity, in the laws, or into modernized society through professional and scientific analyses or the models set by exemplary organizations" (Scott & Meyer, 1994:33).

Scott and Meyer (1994) present a useful overview of a prototypical institutional model consisting of our basic elements. First, the origins of environmental rationalization reflect macrosociological influences on the nature of organizing. Second, these origins give rise to particular dimensions of a rationalized environment such that rules or ideologies describing or prescribing given organizational practices create consistent changes in and across organizations. Third, these general rules and ideologies give rise to the specific mechanisms that shape organizational functioning. That is, organizations develop and perpetuate policies and rules, ideas and beliefs, and myths and rituals in the organizational identities taken on. Finally, the specific nature of a given organization with its peculiar identity and activity patterns exists as a product of institutional forces. The identity, structures, and activity patterns of an organization are the result of institutionalized patterns derived from a rationalized environment.

A useful illustration of this model is presented in work by Orru, Biggart, and Hamilton (1991), who explore the significance of institutional theory in describing the dynamics of competition and organization in East Asia. Specifically, Orru et al. examine the emergence of institutional forms in Japan, South Korea, and Taiwan both within each country as well as across countries. In Japan, they describe two general forms of organizational structure, namely, the intermarket group (e.g., Mitsubishi) and the independent group (e.g., Nissan). An intermarket group has four general characteristics that set it apart from the independent group. First, groups are structured around a horizontal web of large firms. Second, all of these groups have their own banking, insurance, and trading firms that guide their financial and market concerns. Third, each intermarket group has its own "Presidents' Club" (369), consisting of the heads of leading companies within the group, that meets on a monthly basis. Finally, each Presidents' Club–member firm maintains its own corresponding keiretsu, or vertically aligned subsidiary firms. In contrast, the independent groups reflect the more traditional perspective of a keiretsu in which the vertically aligned firms maintain numerous contacts with subcontractors within a single industrial sector. Orru et al. present evidence for the isomorphism of these group arrangements throughout various sectors of the Japanese industrial economy.

The arrangement and structure of the industrial sector of South Korea are in contrast with that of the intermarket or independent groups of Japan. Korean organizations are connected in groupings referred to as chaebol (also see Steers, Shin, & Ungson, 1989). Most chaebol are owned and controlled by a single family and are organized through a central holding company. Chaebol bear some resemblance to both of the Japanese intermarket and independent groups, yet they do not share most of the critical features of either form of Japanese organizational context. For example, Japanese intermarket groups reflect both vertical and horizontal differentiation, whereas chaebol generally reflect a more narrow scope, and their resources are distributed unevenly across these differentiated functions. Second, chaebol do not rely on the consistent relationships of subcontractors as do the keiretsu of Japan. Instead, they often buy or start new firms to care for their own production needs, and they utilize their ties to Japan for many of their supply needs. This tendency to internalize production within a given chaebol is reflected in their size; chaebol account for a very large size of the South Korean economic activity, and they are large in comparison with even Japanese intermarket groups. South Korean business groups reflect a centralized and integrated approach to economic activities, whereas Japanese groups reflect "genuine associations of firms, some more tightly bound to the group than others" (Orru et al., 1991:376).

In contrast with Japan and South Korea, Taiwan reflects a very different form of organizational governance and structure in its associations. Like the chaebol of South Korea, Taiwanese firms are generally based on family associations. However, unlike their Japanese or Korean counterparts, these groups are quite small and do not account for a majority of the industrial sector of Taiwan. Many of the large companies in Taiwan remain single-unit operations and do not belong to any business group. Those existing business groups within Taiwan are often small and contain relatively few members.

From a strict technical-competence perspective (in which structure and form follow an efficient process of production), it is not altogether clear why the Japanese, Korean, and Taiwanese institutional arrangements evolved into these various forms. However, within each country organizations develop along relatively similar lines. Homogeneity of structures within countries but variance across countries suggests that institutional forces are operating on organizations according to the unique cultural and economic circumstances reflected in each of the countries.

According to a traditional perspective, institutionalism (à la Selznick, 1957) includes a number of key features. For example, in traditional institutional theory a high degree of emphasis is placed on the importance of norms and values in shaping individuals' behavior and actions in an organization. According to this perspective, organizational actors are influenced by the basic nature of the norms and values endorsed within a given context, and through a socialization process these norms and values are instilled in an employee. Other key aspects of Selznick's formulation include the central role of conflict of interest as an impetus for the development of strategic alliances, heavy emphasis on creating a committed employee, and the importance of vested interests in predicting the basis of inertia. A heavy reliance was placed on the analysis of group conflict and strategy as a means of achieving collective interests through a political process.

In contrast to this traditional view, a "new institutionalism" has evolved in the literature (Powell & DiMaggio, 1991). According to Powell and DiMaggio (1991:12–14), the new institutionalism differs from the traditional approach in a number of critical ways. First, in traditional institutionalism, the rational interests and purpose of an organization were viewed as perverted through political and conflict influences arising from individual actors' interests. That is, organizations created informal structures based on powerful cliques and coalitions that formed. These structures were thought to detract from the efficient functioning of the organization. In contrast, the new institutionalism views these emergent informal structures as the heart of formal structure. Interorganizational influences diffuse certain departments and operating procedures throughout a given organization through processes of isomorphism. Isomorphism can occur by means of a number of mechanisms, including coercive (conformity based on cultural and external influence), mimetic (conformity as a function of environmental uncertainty), and normative (conformity based on professionalization) mechanisms.

Another important difference between traditional and newer institutional theories is based on the role of cognition and affect in shaping organizational members' actions. In the traditional view, organizational members are influenced by the dominant norms and values espoused within a given organization, and these norms and values are instilled through socialization processes. The product of socialization is the experience of commitment to an organization. In the new institutionalism, a moral frame approach to influence is minimized, and much of what constitutes organizational behavior is based on nonconscious actions guided by schema and scripts. This approach borrows heavily from the psychological approaches typical of researchers like Schank and Abelson (1977) and Wyer and Srull (1980). According to this perspective, people's actions are viewed as a product of automatic routines and scripts that have developed as a function of learning and experience. (I would note, however, that Powell and DiMaggio [1991:15] overstate the difference between a normative/commitment model and a strong cognitive framework. To begin, norms and values shape behavior as a function of experience and socialization leading to scripted behavior [Schank & Abelson, 1977]. Also, the purely cognitive emphasis placed on new institutionalism does not adequately capture current thinking in psychology concerning the interdependence of cognition and affect. That is to say, the adoption of particular schema and scripts over others is guided by the normative and value-based cues provided in a given organizational [and cultural] environment. In this sense, normative and cognitive models have much in common through affective bounds.)

Another difference between the old and new forms of institutionalism is that the old form relies heavily on local environments as a basis for structure and form. In contrast, the new institutionalism reflects an emphasis on nonlocal environments such as organizational fields tied to industries, professions, or national societies. Environments are subtle in their influence on organizations in that they penetrate them by shaping actors' perceptions and worldviews. Ironically, many new institutionalists downplay the centrality of individual actors in shaping an organizational setting despite this embeddedness argument (for a nice exception, see Scott, 1994).

One of the most important differences and evolutions of institutional theory from the perspective of face and social interaction can be traced to the operation of action in an organizational context. In the traditional view, individual action is largely based on the norms and values instilled in an organizational member as reflected in his or her commitment (Selznick, 1957). This idea reflected the Parsonian (Parsons & Shils, 1951) view of behavior as a function of value orientations, cathectics, and the cognitive realm. That is, Parsons argued that action might be thought of as the result of an object gratification process. Individuals act so as to receive gratifications reflecting the dominant norms and values in their social reality. The integration of values within a given collective occurs as an emerging role set based on the prevailing cultural patterns sanctioned within a given society. Culture is composed of three elements—cognitive, cathectic, and evaluative—that serve as a basis for object gratification and attraction. People in a given context shape their behavior so as to satisfy the demands of this cultural context. Behavior is a rational process of gratification pursuit.

An important evolution of this thinking was evidenced in the work of Garfinkel (1967), who argued that social order is not derived directly from some shared patterns of evaluation and social roles, as others argued (e.g., Parsons & Shils, 1951). Rather, Garfinkel suggested that social roles and people's actions are a product of complex symbolic processes encountered through daily mundane experiences. In order for people to make sense of their social world, they employ tacit models of conversation and interaction through their everyday experiences. People enter into conversations with an openness and willingness to overlook the faux pas committed by others. Rules and norms for social interaction operate, and people are motivated to support and endorse these expectations, as long as clear violations are avoided or treated apologetically if they occur. Garfinkel (1967) argued that most of the rules governing social actions are implicit and subtle, and so we only become aware of them if they are breached during the course of social interaction. This view is consistent with the Goffman perspective on face and self-presentation, and I would suggest that this is often the case. However, I will argue that for particular cultural contexts, the rules and practices of face-related behavior are not always so subtle and unconscious. To the contrary, in some societies such face-related behaviors are explicit and clearly understood by the social actors involved in a given interaction. A very important point emerging from Garfinkel's adaptation of Parsons's approach is that norms are not the pervasive and direct influencers of action. Rather, norms guide cognitive systems and rules of procedures that people use in their interactions, and they are often nonconscious to a person.

Giddens (1984) points out the importance of routine in maintaining social structure and reflects this in his concept of structuration. Structuration refers to the continual reproduction of social structure by social members as they interact in daily activities. He suggests that people act to control diffuse anxiety by developing and maintaining routines as they interact socially. There is a reliance on scripted behavior in order to reduce this anxiety. This general view is consistent with my more extensive discussion of Goffman's work in an earlier chapter, inasmuch as social order is based on the enactment of these subtle, ritualized forms of interaction. Collins (1988) furthers this idea as he describes the nature of social structure. He suggests that social structure is best thought of as a series of interaction sequences that are based on a scripted style. People invest cultural resources and emotional energies in interactions that support a given hierarchy as a function of cultural and emotional resources.

As can be seen from this description, institutional theory (as it is presently depicted) characterizes social interaction and behavior as a product of institutional norms and rules evolving from various influences. Forces of various types create an impetus for demands and patterns of action in organizations that may or may not reflect true efficiencies in an economic sense. Further, these patterns (rules) influence the behavior of organizational members as they interact with one another. It is for this reason that I have focused my discussion so heavily on institutional theory. It reflects a set of mechanisms through which people's actions are guided and shaped in order to regulate face. More important, institutional theory can be used to describe the influence of cultural context and social exchange practices (harmony) on face regulation. What is important from the ritual game of exchange in any given society is the sense of affirmation that partners derive from one another after successful encounters. These encounters reinforce our sense of self and clarify our position in a social hierarchy.

An institutional approach provides a basis for linking cultural context to intraorganizational functioning. Although I have described throughout this book the importance of face and its regulation in an organization, it has been unclear how face regulation occurs in a given organizational context. That is, Goffman and other face researchers describe rather generic principles of face regulation that sweep across organizational boundaries. However, as I will describe shortly, many of these behavioral patterns are unique to particular organizations, some are shared among interacting (isomorphic) organizations, and some are generic across organizations within a given culture. In this sense, the neo-institutionalist emphasis on symbolism and ritual captures important patterns of face regulation. More important, it provides us with a linking mechanism for connecting face regulation—*in a particular manifestation*—to cultural context and social exchange. Without this more fine-grained linking device, my discussion would not provide for differences in face regulation across various organizations, and I would suggest that this would represent a major shortcoming for the model.

Institutional Practices and Face

The impact of institutional effects on face can be mapped from two general directions, namely, those occurring within a given organizational environment as well as those impacted from outside the organization. I leave a discussion of the latter topic to a subsequent part of this chapter (on interorganizational dependencies and face), and I now turn to an application of an institutionalist perspective to understanding face and harmony.

In essence, the rules for social interaction, expectations for behavior, and face regulation are best thought of as rituals, ceremonies, et cetera, emergent from institutional forces. Although there has been a clear increase in interest expressed by institutionalists concerning the significance of individual-level actions in organizations (Powell & DiMaggio, 1991:13; Scott, 1994:57), most attention has been to reject the additive role of individual actors in favor of a faceless, collective behavior (Meyer & Rowan, 1977). The potential contribution of individual actors to the institutional practices observed in organizations cannot be overemphasized in my estimation. Although I agree with the general view that actors do not rationally enact all aspects of their world or have additive and collective influences on their social context, it seems premature to dismiss the importance of the individual in shaping an organizational context. That is, the legitimization of particular practices within organizations is tied to the perceptions of individual actors within those organizations.

This synthesis view of the micro- and macrosociological influences within institutional theory is best represented in recent work by Richard Scott (1994:57), who poses a three-part model of institutions. In his layered model, institutions are the interactive product of three general components: meaning systems and social system patterns, symbolic elements including constitutive and normative rules, and regulatory practices that enforce these practices. Institutions, then, reflect these three general elements. Additionally, Scott poses that these institutional elements are influenced by and influence two other levels of the organization: governance structures and actors. Although the connection of institutional elements to governance structures seems clear and direct based on the extensive literature, the potential role of individual actors is very relevant to my discussion of face.

The importance of an individual actor to the nature of institutions is one of cause as well as effect. The case of actor as effect is the most straightforward in terms of face. That is, institutional influences on an organizational member occur through a number of mechanisms, including socialization, identity formation, and sanctions, according to Scott. Socialization reflects the most direct means through which organizational members are taught the "practices" and "rules" of an institution. As I described in more detail in Chapter 6 concerning the social actor, socialization provides a powerful means for indoctrinating an employee. Identity formation is at the very heart of this book, and it reflects the importance of an organization as a factor in shaping a person's self-concept (Erez & Earley, 1993). Finally, sanctions shape the actions taken by employees and help us understand the actions taken over a period of time.

In describing the reciprocal effects of individual actors on emergent institutions, Scott argues that through interpretation and innovation institutional practices are shaped. These impact employees, in turn, through socialization, identity formation, and sanctions. What seems somewhat overlooked in his description is what motivates this cycle from both directions. I argue that it is face regulation. In other words, people shape their environment, as well as allow it to shape them, in order to regulate face. (Of course, there are a multitude of additional influences that are beyond the scope of this book [e.g., learning effects, self-efficacy motives].)

A critical aspect of Scott's view is that through enactment, an institutional context is shaped and reshaped. In describing this notion he draws on Giddens's (1984) discussion of structuration as well as Geertz's (1973) description of culture and meaning systems. The point Scott makes is that through daily actions and activities the context in which behavior is embedded and interpreted is changed. In this sense, people's desire to regulate face according to organization-specific and culture-general rules and practices reinforces and changes the organization context itself. In extending the metaphor of the fish not realizing that it is submersed in water, it is important to note that the fish changes the ecosystem of the water by its presence. It is both the cause and the effect of its own ecosystem. Applying this idea specifically to face and its regulation, it is clear that the motives to maintain lian and promote mianzi lead actors to engage in particular actions and create new rituals and ceremonies (institutionalized practices) consistent with these images. Thus the manager wanting to demonstrate mianzi does not passively await affirmation from his or her subordinates. The manager actively engages in impression management (e.g., works long hours and weekends) to shape opinion. More important, these actions have positive consequences (presumably) that become institutionalized as others come to expect to work long hours in order to maintain mianzi. In this manner, individual actions give rise to collective practices and rituals. A useful linkage can be discovered by tracing existing institutionalized practices back to particular employee actions as motivated by face regulation.

I do not argue, however, that employees are fully rational in their behavioral choices, and many of the specific behaviors engaged in for face regulation are scripted and schema-based. Returning to the example of the late-working manager, there is no doubt that in American culture such action is a potential source of mianzi in all but the most demanding work organizations. In contrast, Japanese managers experience such long hours as the norm for work and are suspect (they lose mianzi and perhaps lian if the behavior is chronic) if they do not put in 12–14 hour workdays, including semiobligatory evenings out with their work team. In both the United States and Japan there is an expectation that a person should work hard and dedicate him- or herself to work, but the enactment of such a general value differs, as might be expected. Employees who endorse a general value of hard work in their company are making rational choices in this context. The specific actions taken to enact and actualize these choices are often scripted or ritualistic.

Although an institutional perspective posits that much of what goes on in an organization is best thought of as a murky and nonconscious set of symbolic rituals and ceremonies (see Oliver, 1991, for a nice elaboration of actors' choices in an institutional context), there are clear and predictable patterns related to face and organization structure as well. In the next section of this chapter, I will describe a number of contextual aspects of organizations as they relate to face. More specifically, I discuss the nature of technology, communication and governance, and interorganizational dependence as they relate to face.

Organizational Content

Technology

I begin my discussion of organizational content with the topic of technology because it has important face validity as well as centrality to the evolving nature of work organizations. No topic seems to be more critical than that of how technology and information systems influence organizational members' self-perceptions and interpersonal behaviors (Erez & Earley, 1993).

The relationships among employees have changed dramatically as a function of information systems and technology, as has the very nature of organizations themselves. In one of the earlier models of how technology potentially impacts organizational functioning, Galbraith (1973) proposed an information-processing perspective of organizations. In this model, Galbraith argued that the capacity of an organization to buffer itself from the throes of uncertainty was a key organizing principle. Organizations would introduce excess inventories, create information-buffering systems, et cetera, as a means of handling potential vagaries of the environment. From a historical perspective, Woodward's classification scheme of technology types represented one of the first major linkages of technology to organization form. She posited three general forms of technology (unit, mass, and process) and found that distinct relationships between these technology classifications and the subsequent structure of the firms exist and that the effectiveness of the organizations was related to a general level of fit between technology and governance/organizational structure. That is, the degree of vertical differentiation increases with the technical complexity of the work performed. From an effectiveness point of view, the most effective firms within a given category adopted a structure appropriate to that technology. For example, unit and process production methods are most effective when matched with an organic structure, whereas mass production is most effective when matched with a mechanistic structure.

This emphasis on technology and governance structure and organization was extended in work conducted by Perrow (1972) in his classification of technology and production. He argued that two core dimensions of technology, task variability and problem analyzability, were critical for understanding appropriate organization form related to function. In a related vein, Thompson argued for a three-part classification of technology using his distinction among long-linked, mediating, and intensive technologies. In the long-linked form, activities are characterized by a fixed sequence of repetitive steps much like that of an assembly-line process. The mediating technology reflects a linkage between clients on the input and output sides of an organization. Banks, retail stores, and post offices are common examples of a mediating form. Finally, intensive technology represents a customized response to a diverse set of environmental demands. The exact form of an organization depends on the specific problems confronted by different organizations, such as research and development units, universities, consulting firms, et cetera. As with Galbraith's argument, Thompson suggested that the key to understanding organizational content and structure was not to focus on the direct linkage of technology to structure. Rather, he suggested that organizations arrange themselves to protect their technology from ambiguity in the environment. Specific technologies determine the selection of response strategies for coping with environmental uncertainty. So, for example, long-linked technology-based organizations might vertically differentiate themselves in order to ensure a steady flow of inputs needed for production.

The significance of technology to face can be thought of as operating in two general directions—upward as reflecting societal norms of exchange and downward as reflecting in a systematic way how people interact with one another. In the case of the upward path, I mean that organization form and functioning are shaped, to a degree, by the nature of how an organization produces its products. This influence of technology on organization form is by no means unilateral as most modern organization theorists would argue, but it is also not inconsequential. I would contend that in its simplest form the technology adopted by organizations reflects both efficiencies as well as institutionalized practices. That is, form follows function and efficiency to a large extent, but it also follows cultural practice. A rather extreme and entirely unsuccessful example of form following cultural practice is evidenced by Mao's Great Leap Forward, in which local Chinese communities were encouraged to develop local energy supplies. The ideological argument was for smallness and self-sufficiency in semiautonomous worker collectives. Rather than centralize energy production and capitalize on potential economies of scale, the ruling Communist Party endorsed the localization of energy by calling for a massive redeployment of resources to create an army of power plants—one for each collective. In this example, technology dictated form (within the worker collectives) as a function of political and cultural ideology.

The downward influence of culture and society on technology is evidenced by a number of modern social movements as well. For example, the search for low-polluting forms of production has stimulated the creation of groups within companies whose purpose is to make such discoveries. The field of corporate social responsibility reflects a general emphasis in many industrialized countries on reducing excessive consumption of natural resources. In this sense, technology becomes an outcome driven by forces existing within and beyond an organization itself.

Although most of the work described by technology-focused organization theorists has attempted to describe the potential impact of production and service provision on functioning within an organization, only recently has attention been refocused on the nature of how specific technologies may influence interpersonal behavior. Much of this work has come out of the field of management and information systems (MIS) as well as information technology, and it includes work by scholars like DeSanctis, Vogel, and Davis on the MIS side and Argote, Goodman, and the Carnegie School on the organizations side.

A great deal of the microtechnology research as it relates to organizational behavior comes from people studying the impact of computer-mediated communication and feedback (e.g., Kiesler, Siegel, & McGuire, 1984) on behavior. Much of the work on computer-mediated interactions has suggested that the buffering provided by an electronic system can have potentially devastating effects if it is used to protect people from the normal social etiquette demanded in discourse. However, electronic communications can provide useful opportunities if it creates a work environment that provides for enhanced sharing of information and ideas. What seems to have received less attention (although I note that this is quickly changing with work by social constructionists) is the proactive role that people take in shaping the technology around them to suit their needs for self-definition and face. A simple but symbolic example of this is the syntax that has developed on the Internet to convey personal information and affective state during e-mail exchange. A smile or laugh, for example, is denoted with a ":)" as a means of conveying affect during "conversations." More important, a syntax conveying relative status and physical characteristics has developed as well, including gender, age, ethnicity, et cetera. These are important signals that are conveyed as a function of face demands. What remains relatively unexplored are the potential difficulties confronted in the use of electronic messaging when parties desire face-related information but are unable to receive such information. Even the very use of technology may symbolize a loss of face for employees in certain cultures. For example, the Office of Technology Assessment issued a report, *The Electronic Supervisor: New Technology, New Tensions* (OTA-CIT-33, Washington, DC: U.S. Government Printing Office, 1987), suggesting that technology monitoring may create animosity and mistrust in employees. From a face perspective, indirect monitoring of employees may signal that they are not considered trustworthy and, therefore, lack lian. Such monitoring may take away from mianzi as well if employees equate such monitoring with "baby-sitting."

How are macro- and microtechnological issues related to face and harmony? I believe that these linkages are best thought of as reciprocally determined, with technology and organization form evolving and adapting based on cultural as well as interpersonal demands. From a cultural perspective, technology represents a means of enacting general themes in a society. For example, in a tight culture there is a high demand for conformity to social practices and custom. Technology may be employed within an organization to monitor adherence to such social practices. An emphasis on social control and regulation is created through a reliance on technology as a means of enforcement. Just as important, in a tight culture a willingness to accept such monitoring is likely to exist (even if it is not perceived as a desirable state of affairs).

From a microorganizational perspective, the forces surrounding face will likely shape the nature and acceptance of technology in the workplace. As suggested earlier, the emergence of computer-based monitoring has met with a great deal of resistance in a culture such as the United States. What is perhaps the most surprising is that this form of monitoring is often used in the United States, despite its strong endorsement of privacy and individual rights. Despite this strong norm in society, electronic monitoring occurs in the workplace as a common occurrence. Much of the resistance to monitoring can be traced to an American worker's "right" to privacy and its implication about status and position. Mianzi demands that an American's right to privacy be upheld. Interestingly, one of the ways to reaffirm mianzi in this instance is to provide an employee with direct control over the monitoring itself (Northcraft & Earley, 1989). What this achieves is a personal sense of control and importance in an otherwise faceless system.

This general discussion suggests that technology is related to face by influencing a person's mianzi. Although excessive, uncontrolled monitoring may cause an employee to lose mianzi, indirect monitoring may send a very different signal. An executive who is so critical to a company that he or she needs to have a beeper or cellular phone (or both) is clearly someone who has mianzi. A hotel in Bangkok, Thailand, that is famous for accommodating exclusive business travelers offers an "executive package" including a cellular phone during the hotel stay. Anyone walking down the streets of Hong Kong quickly realizes the status associated with a cellular phone, and some people purchase "mock" phones just to join the technological elite. In this sense, individuals may create technologies that reaffirm mianzi. A counter to such a privilege occurs for the technologically displaced—that is, people whose positions are taken by technological interventions such as robotics.

As I described, a potential downside of technology for face is related to its implications for lian as well as mianzi. Electronic monitoring and information systems signal to a person that he or she is not trusted and therefore lacks lian. Excessive monitoring is associated with increases in formal grievances against management, worker absenteeism and turnover, and low employee morale. In a very real sense, technology of this type may send a very strong signal to employees that they lack lian. Further, the depersonalization associated with the heavy use of technology sends a potential signal to employees that they are not valued by their organizations, which reduces mianzi. A more indirect influence of electronic monitoring on face is that many of the opportunities to regulate face in a social context are removed in an electronic/technology driven work context. Working at home provides an information-poor environment for assessing and establishing face.

In summary, technology is related to face through two general mechanisms. First, it reflects the larger concerns and impulses of a given society. Technology is a socially constructed phenomenon and not simply a move toward efficiency. Second, technology and its use in an organization signal various aspects of face to an employee. Excessive monitoring may convey a lack of lian and a loss of mianzi. However, the trappings of technology may signal high status and mianzi as well. In the next section, I turn my discussion to the potential relationship of communication and governance to face in an organization.

Face, Communication, and Governance

At first glance the topics of communication and governance might seem quite independent of one another, but I will focus on communication as a process through which particular governance structures influence face and its regulation. Communication is dealt with as a process flow from organizational structures to actors and back again. It is through such flows that institutions "create order and attempt to reduce uncertainty in exchange" (North, 1989:238). In other words, in this section I treat communication (in whatever form it may take) as a mechanism through which institutional practices impact face regulation and discuss how specific governance structures impact individuals in their organizations.

Governance structures are the ways in which individuals within an organization regulate their activities and organize work (Galbraith, 1973). The nature of governance is a central focus of Williamson's (1985) work on transaction costs theory, in which he distinguishes between market and hierarchical forms of governance. Ouchi (1980) distinguishes among three general forms of governance and organization: markets, hierarchies, and clans. The nature of governance arrangements can be viewed as imposed or constructed, depending on one's view of the proactivity of an organizational member. If one assumes that organizational members are largely reactive to the rules imposed on them by society at large (e.g., North, 1991), then governance structure reflects the themes dominant in society. In a limited sense, these structures are assumed to reflect some degree of economic efficiency and utility (Williamson, 1985), although a number of sociological institutionalists (e.g., DiMaggio & Powell, 1983) argue that these governance arrangements arise from a top-down process.

An important point that Scott (1994:73) makes in his discussion of the top-down versus bottom-up construction of governance structures is that both approaches are likely to be operating to be at any given time. That is, efficiency and rational choice guide the adoption of an appropriate governance form (market versus hierarchy) at the same time that organizational fields infuse particular forms in any given organization. When governance forms are viewed in this fashion, it is not surprising that there is relatively high uniformity of governance structures within particular organizational fields and that organizations are slow to adapt despite the seeming irrationality of not doing so. For example, a number of financial disasters for investment and financial institutions have occurred during the last several years. The most famous example of this is likely the Barings Bank debacle, involving the rogue trading behavior of Singaporean trader Nick Leeson. Despite the notoriety and infamy of this case, over a year later Sumitomo Bank faced an estimated $1.8 billion loss attributable to a single rogue trader as well. If a strong efficiency argument is to be made concerning the origins of governance structures and practices in an organization, then it is necessary to explain how such potentially destructive arrangements are allowed to exist. A strong bottom-up approach to governance does not seem to fully capture this type of perpetuation of poor management practice. However, a restrictive top-down approach, as suggested by many sociologists, seems inadequate as well. The sheer variety of specific governance forms observed across cultures (e.g., Orru et al., 1991) suggests that form is developed by cultural orientations of individuals.

The significance of a given governance structure on face regulation lies in the relative emphasis on particular exchange mechanisms. In the chapter on harmony, it was stressed that harmony captures the regulation of face through social exchange processes. Organizational governance structures reinforce certain exchanges over others and make available certain exchanges and not others. For example, in a strongly hierarchical and bureaucratic structure a relative emphasis on mianzi is created. The reason for this emphasis is twofold: first, salience of mianzi reinforces the existence of a hierarchical form of governance; and second, a hierarchical form provides for differentiation among people based on relative status. In a highly differentiated (vertically) organization many trappings of status and position exist. These symbols exist because the organization is differentiated, and they support such differentiation. Through socialization and reward/sanction mechanisms, differences in mianzi become salient and desired. Thus, within any given organization, governance structures reinforce and are reinforced by face regulation. (An important question, then, is why certain governance structures arise under certain, but not all, circumstances. This is clearly beyond the scope of this or any other single book, but the top-down and bottom-up influences described by Scott [1994] are a useful starting point.)

My argument, then, is that the governance structure existing in an organization conveys a number of important facets of information for face regulation. First, it conveys the acceptable rules governing interpersonal behavior in an organization. It determines the outcomes to be emphasized, as well as how to pursue them. Second, the salience of mianzi and/or lian is conveyed by the governance structure. Hierarchical forms signal an importance of status and prestige; clans signal the importance of both mianzi and lian. Third, governance structures reflect the emphases and desires of organizational members. Members socially construct their environment and govern themselves so as to provide opportunities to pursue face based on more general cultural impulses.

As I have described in this section, the governance structure and the relative importance of certain patterns of behavior over others are partly a product of the organizational field in which a company is embedded. In the following section, the potential impact of organizations on one another is discussed using an institutional perspective. The significance of adopting the practices of similar organizations through isomorphic influences is presented and described in relation to expectations underlying face and social exchange.

Interorganizational Effects on Face

This final section focuses on the general context of an organization and what this implies about face regulation. As I described earlier, sociologists generally have taken the approach that institutional models are infused throughout an organizational field. In addition, I draw on recent work by Ghoshal and Bartlett (1990) and Westney (1993) concerning the role of networks and institutions in influencing the functioning of multinational corporations.

From an institutionalist perspective, the forces existing within an organization that perpetuate and shape existing rules and practices represent an incomplete picture of the forces acting on individuals. The external environment represents an additional, critical source of isomorphic impulses, and this metaorganizational level is often referred to as the organizational field (DiMaggio & Powell, 1983) or societal sector (Scott & Meyer, 1983). According to Powell and DiMaggio's (1991:64) usage, an organizational field involves

> organizations that, in the aggregate, constitute a recognized area of institutional life: key suppliers, resource and product consumers, regulatory agencies, and other organizations that produce similar service or products. The virtue of this unit of analysis is that it directs our attention not simply to competing firms, as does the population approach of Hannan and Freeman (1977), or to networks of organizations that actually interact, as does the interorganizational network approach of Laumann, Galaskiewicz, and Marsden (1978), but to the totality of relevant actors. In doing this, the field idea comprehends the importance of both *connectedness* . . . and *structural equivalence*. (emphasis in original)

Further, Powell and DiMaggio argue that the structure and inclusion of firms within a given organizational field are determined empirically based on the observed institutional definitions. The "structuration," or evolved definition, consists of four parts: frequent interactions among parties in the field, emergence of interorganizational structures and coalitions, increase in information load of organizations within a field, and a mutual awareness among organizational participants concerning who is included in the field itself. Powell and DiMaggio cite an early study by Tolbert and Zucker (1983) concerning the adoption of civil service reforms in the United States as a useful illustration of these organizational fields and their influence on field members. It is through a homogenization that uniformity of practices permeates firms within a given organizational field based on various isomorphic forces. (As described earlier, these forces are threefold for DiMaggio and Powell [1983] but other typologies exist, such as Scott's [1994] seven-category basis.)

An extremely useful application and extension of these ideas are presented in a volume edited by Ghoshal and Westney, *Organization Theory and the Multinational Corporation* (1993). The importance of organizational fields in an international context is not as clear as one might expect. Westney (1993:Chapter 3) raises a number of useful challenges to institutional theory that arise in considering a multinational corporation (MNC). First, organizational membership in a given field is considered to be relatively exclusive. That is, a field is defined by the organizations making up some grouping. MNCs represent a threat to this idea because they straddle various fields (both within as well as between countries). This threat is not a new one, and institutionalists have recognized this limitation for quite some time. However, it is a threat that must be addressed in dealing with MNCs. From the MNC perspective, the emerging matrix form of MNCs (with loose interdependencies among subsidiaries across countries) suggests that competing isomorphic influences will be experienced. An American firm operating in Thailand staffed with locals and U.S. expatriates, as well as third-country nationals, experiences management "pulls" from a variety of sources. Compounding this with the differential adaptability of management styles as a function of national culture, such as a high power distance or being tight, suggests that the relative contribution of host, parent, and third-country influences will vary across countries/cultures. In a relatively "loose" culture such as Thailand, the American expatriates and third-country nationals may have a relatively strong influence on the adoption of specific practices within the Thai subsidiary. In contrast, a tight, high power distance culture such as Myanmar may represent a significant host-country influence over parent- and third-country influences. This argument suggests that the "straddling fields" described by Westney (1993) are extremely complex and difficult to understand *ex ante*. Organizational fields, particularly those constituents who are included versus those who are excluded, are sensitive to cultural context as well as business practice.

The determination of which firms are included in a given organizational field and how these fields overlap is likely to be influenced by cultural context through several means. First, the concept of who might be a "member" will vary according to cultural norms within a society. In the case of Taiwanese businesses (Orru et al., 1991), membership in a field is likely to be defined according to tight-knit, family lines. In Japanese intermarket groups, membership is much more widely defined and held. Second, the boundaries delineating "infield" and "outfield" are likely to be malleable and culturally influenced. In relatively loose cultures group memberships are fluid and dynamic, whereas in relatively tight cultures they are inflexible and static. There is no reason not to predict a similar influence and definition as a function of cultural characteristics. Third, the permanence or longevity of an organizational field is tied to cultural context as well, with countries emphasizing slow growth, stability, and inertia likely to have similar characteristics for organizational fields. Fourth, the relative impact of one member on another in such a field is dependent on the general social structure in a country. In the case of Thailand, a high power distance culture, firms with the largest amount of mianzi will dominate the institutional practices of the field. In a low power distance culture, it is more difficult to predict the origins of institutional practices. The relative importance of "market leaders" within a field varies as a function of power distance and other facets of social structure. Finally, the efficiency of interorganizational networks will vary according to cultural context as well. This suggests that the effectiveness of communicating (and institutionalizing) practices across firms will vary by the quality of network connections. Westney (1993:60–61) describes the potential competing isomorphic pulls experienced by a manager within an MNC. My argument is that the strength of such "pulls" will vary as a function of the network and social structure in which a firm is embedded. In some instances, the pull will be quite minimal because mianzi dictates that a unitary and particular source of innovation and practice be followed over others. Of course, there are culturally based forces acting on the composition and functioning of organizational fields and there are economic, technical, et cetera, forces acting as well.

The influence of these interorganizational relationships on face and its contribution to understanding these relationships are substantial. From a "top-down" perspective, organizational fields reflect the general norms and rules of the environment in which they exist. That is, metafields (general social structure) shape the form and function of organizational fields, and these, in turn, shape institutional practices within a given organization. Such influence does not operate simply through an ideological indoctrination of norms and values (e.g., "This is how we Thais do x"); rather, it occurs through indirect and discreet means, such as the structuring of industries, the regulation of business functioning through political rules and laws, et cetera. Cultural influence through values and norms simply represents one of numerous macrosociological influences on organizational fields and, hence, on organizations and their members. This influence can be mapped from the metafield to the employee level through a hypothetical example. Take, for instance, a high power distance culture stressing hierarchy and guidance from senior leaders. In this case, the institutional rules evolving within a given organizational field will follow the guidance provided by the old, established organizational leaders. In an intermarket group from Japan, this may reflect actions of a senior firm in the group or the desires of specific leaders from the "Presidents' Club." In American companies, such an influence can be witnessed through the network dynamics of senior executives of overlapping corporate boards. In a high power distance context, the practices within an organizational field will reflect the practices and actions of dominant field members, and these practices become the institutionalized practices for individual field members. Once institutionalized within a given firm, the practices reflect the "valued" ways of doing things in a company, and adherence to them enhances face (and violations may threaten it). In this way, an eventual downward effect of norms and practices becomes institutionalized.

The degree of congruity across levels (society to organizational field to organization to employee) varies as a function of general societal conditions such as tightness and power distance, as well as the specific personalities of key agents within the chain. These agents can be particular individuals as well as organizations. In a market-oriented society, organizations likely represent the dominant source of isomorphism within any given organizational field because other member firms mimic the successful firms. This is likely to occur for high power distance cultures as well but not simply for economic reasons. The dominant firms (economically) are generally the ones that are placed at the apex of some hierarchy.

From a "bottom-up" perspective, as I described based on Scott's (1994) model, desires to maintain and regulate face reinforce the nature of institutionalized practices. Face in this sense does not involve any organizational member but reflects the dominant members of an organization. The strategic decision makers and power brokers in a given organization reinforce the dominant practices within an organizational field, and, thereby, the practices utilized by other field members, so as to maintain face vis-à-vis other key members within the organizational field. This explanation is consistent with empirical work by network researchers (e.g., Davis, 1991; Krackhardt & Porter, 1987) who found that overlapping corporate advisory boards can be used to map the adoption of managerial practices such as reactions to takeover threats. Although a network perspective can describe how such perpetuation of practices occurs (e.g., corporate board members share information about what their company is doing), and institutions theory can describe what happens (e.g., practices become adopted as a result of mimetic isomorphic effects), neither perspective provides a compelling ex ante explanation concerning why this effect occurs. (I note that the existing mechanisms described by Scott and others offer useful explanations of isomorphism from an organizational perspective, but they do not provide useful ways of making predictions concerning differential adoptions among firms within the same field.) From a face perspective, these adoptions occur as a way of reaffirming one's position within the hierarchy of a given field. (Anecdotally, I have observed that Chinese managers who have been exposed to Western business practices through executive education are often more capitalistic than the capitalists. Although this may reflect a belief by the managers that they are going to be more effective as a result of this indoctrination, it also reflects a desire of managers coming from a hierarchical society to assert their legitimacy [face] in a given social circle of fellow managers.) Establishment of mianzi occurs as individuals who represent their firms exchange perspectives. It is the "legitimacy" DiMaggio and Powell (1983) describe that reflects the desire of firms within a field to maintain "face" at an organization level.

Summary

In this chapter I have focused on the importance of macroorganizational influences on face regulation. Drawing from institutional theory, I argued that the specific ways that organizational members regulate face, as well as the form(s) of face salient to them, are influenced by the institutional environment. This influence, however, is not simply a top-down perspective. Individual actors create an organizational context according to principles of efficiency and self-definition. These enacted contexts give rise to unique governance structures that, in turn, reinforce and shape individual actors' behaviors.

The nature of the organization environment reflects the dominant trends in society as well as individual organizational fields. This multipart influence is important in understanding face because the social exchange factors described earlier are not deterministic. In a given culture, no single form of exchange can be expected to operate at all times. In fact, any society will be characterized by multiple exchange settings reflected in various institutions within the society. That is to say, a single exchange form (e.g., communal sharing) may be dominant, ceteris paribus, but an individual's face is regulated in a particular institutional context (e.g., work organization) at any given time. Despite the general tendency of organizations within a given field to exercise similar institutional practices as a result of isomorphic impulses, a plethora of face-related actions may be observed in a given organization across and within individuals.

The importance of organizational context and content is in communicating general expectations concerning face as well as socializing the rules to regulate it. These rules of the game (North, 1991) reflect macrosociological, economic, and political forces as well as those rules socially constructed by individuals themselves.

In the next chapter, I turn to an integration of the various forces influencing face and its regulation. My purpose is to provide a number of general connections among these components in order to illustrate how face might be used as a broad explanatory variable in future organizational research. The connections made among these components of my overarching model are preliminary and suggestive and, of course, subject to appropriate discussion and debate.

10

Resulting Patterns and Consequences

Throughout the remainder of this book, I will attempt to integrate through a series of examples and applications the face and behavior framework that I propose. Allof the pieces that I have discussed—face, social actor, harmony, societal context, and organizational context and structure—are interdependent, and a full understanding of the model I propose requires a multilevel analysis of these constructs. Although I have attempted to provide an integration of these constructs as I presented them, there is an obvious utility in applying them in several specific contexts in order to better illustrate the functioning of the model. In this chapter, I present the model in the context of four very different cultural and societal contexts, namely, the Czech Republic, India, Sweden, and the United States.

I have chosen to apply the model in these various countries for a number of reasons. First, the cultural values that are dominant in each of these countries differ in a number of important ways. For instance, India is characterized by its vertical collectivism and high power distance (Sinha, 1990, in press), whereas Sweden is characterized by its horizontal individualism (Triandis, 1995). The United States places a strong emphasis on mastery over nature and guilt, whereas the Czech Republic represents an emergence from subjugation to nature and shame toward mastery over nature and shame. Before I begin this discussion, I should make clear that I am dealing with a number of generalizations that are attempts at characterizing entire nations. In the case of India, these characterizations capture the dominant values of over 1 billion people representing the world's largest democracy. What this suggests is that any single representation will inevitably involve some sociotyping as well as stereotyping and an implied shielding of my discussion from the actual variations that are found from region to region, province to province, state to state, city to city, and even organization to organization. This reliance on generalizations, of course, is at the center of the concern of Geertz (1973), among others, about the consistency view of cultures. That is to say, a consistency view presumes that culture is some coherent and knowable entity that is shared, more often than not, by a given group of people.

At least one other conceptual position would posit that such a view is folly (e.g., the fragmentation view described by Martin, 1992), but I return to my original position stated in Chapter 2 that such folly is my premise. In other words, I will readily admit that these generalizations will fail to capture the variability that is witnessed among groups and individuals within a country, but I reassert that the between-country variability exceeds the within-country variability with regard to these generalizations. As a result, it is appropriate to discuss various countries in terms of these generalizations if the intent is to support comparisons among countries.

Finally, I would add that the individual is the final stopping point of my model, and thus what is critical is how the various contextual influences are interpreted by particular individuals. My emphasis is on people as individuals or social actors and my country-level descriptions that follow are guides, and not final categorizations, for individuals within a given country. In other words, I will refer to the "typical" or "average" person from a given country with the caveat that I always ultimately reference a particular individual who holds particular values and ideas within a particular setting. Thus if one attempts to use these country characterizations for predicting the behavior of people in general, then the results are likely to be useful. However, if the purpose is to understand and predict the behavior of any single individual within a country, then these descriptions will inevitably fall short. It is for this reason that I have maintained throughout the book that an individual is the final stopping point for a model of face and behavior.

With these qualifications in mind, I turn my discussion to four country-level examples of face in an organizational context. For ease of reference, I provide a summary of these various characterizations in Table 10-1.

The Czech Republic

The Czech Republic is a rapidly emerging capitalist system with a strong tradition of socialism and communism. Formerly part of Czechoslovakia, it was part of the general alliance of communist countries created by the former Soviet Union. In 1989, Czechoslovakia underwent the "Velvet Revolution," after which the country split into two semiautonomous republics, the Czech Republic and Slovakia, and created separate legislatures (Machann, 1991; McGregor, 1991). While the pace of capitalist reform in the Czech Republic has been quite rapid, management practices and organizational and societal culture reflect a strong orientation toward group identification and collectivism (McGregor, 1991). Although a number of Czech state-owned companies have been fully or partly privatized, evidence suggests that such reforms are still being met with some degree of skepticism. For instance, a strike in the fall of 1994 of over 8,000 workers from the Skoda automobile plant (one of the single largest state-owned companies in the republic) reflected a growing concern among employees that the reforms may be taking place at the cost of economic sovereignty. In this instance, Skoda employees were expressing concern over the privatization of Skoda in an alliance with Volkswagen. Research conducted by Holda and Cermakova (1980) demonstrates that the movement toward capitalism has not supplanted the generally collective orientation of employees and managers. What must be stressed, however, is that the collective orientation in the Czech Republic does not refer to an endorse-

Table 10-1. Relationship of Societal Context to Face in an Organization

Country	IC	PD	TL	RN	MF	SG	Lian	Mianzi	Example Behavior
Czech Republic	C	low	T	M, S	M	G	high	mod. to low	Managers emphasize that they are part of the workers by attending common social functions. Status differentials are available but not used to any strong degree.
India	C	high	T	H, S	F	S	high	high	Managers emphasize that they are deserving of rank and status through their caste and professional training and schooling. Violation of social norms leads to ostracization.
Sweden	IC	low	T	H	F	S	high	mod. to low	Managers emphasize the importance of being a morally conscious person who must help employees realize their potential.
United States	I	mod.	L	M	M	G	low	high	Managers emphasize their position through material and status differentials such as office size, titles, and company benefits.

Note: IC: Individualism/collectivism; I = individualistic, C = collectivistic, IC = horizontal collectivist
   PD: Power distance
   TL: Tight (T) versus loose (L)
   RN: Relationship to nature; M = mastery, H = harmony, S = subjugation
   MF: Masculinity/femininity; M = masculine, F = feminine
   SG: Shame versus guilt; S = shame, G = guilt

ment of communism or socialism; rather, it reflects a team orientation and emphasis on group-based welfare (McGregor, 1991).

Prior to 1989, the dominant management philosophy was one of economic egalitarianism, which suggests that there should be relatively little difference between the salaries and compensation of managers and workers. As a result, the salaries of managers were typically no more than five to six times those of shop floor workers (Nath & Jirasek, 1994). Additionally, a strong emphasis was placed on the general intellectual breadth of every employee's training, resulting in a focus on improving and broadening the skills of employees. However, the exception to this emphasis was reflected in the selection of people to fill high-level positions within companies, because these appointments were made primarily on the basis of a person's status within the Communist Party in addition to merit and potential. As a result, a number of CEOs were selected even though they were not necessarily technically competent to fill their positions. Further, a general informal atmosphere of attempting to maintain one's position developed, even if this required engaging in activities that were ultimately harmful to the state enterprise. Thus CEOs longed for meaningful and important work, but they also had to maintain the proper "political" stance within the party.

The relationship of labor to management was generally harmonious prior to the Velvet Revolution, with a general allegiance sworn to the Communist Party. Although unions were very active at the company and industry levels (including in the negotiation of salary, benefits, etc.), they had little impact at a national level because their activities were largely subsumed under the party. Interestingly, unions owned property inside and outside the Czech Republic. Much of this property was of a resort nature, and it was used by the workers for vacations.

The general tenor of the dominant work and cultural values within the Czech Republic at the time of the revolution was a strong sense of social responsibility (characteristic of many communist countries). Many of the work and life benefits of Czech companies reflected, and still do, a sense that the company takes care of its employees from cradle to grave. For example, many companies provide housing, schooling, medical and dental care, et cetera, for the families of employees (Pearce & Cakrt, 1994; Fogel, 1994). Since the revolution, the general social responsibility claimed by many companies has diminished, but it has not been eliminated by any means. A strong view still prevails that companies have a responsibility to care for their employees even if doing so is detrimental to the companies.

In an assessment of cultural values, Holda and Cermakova found that a sample of university students endorsed a number of values, including living in a happy family, helping those close to oneself, having good friendships, and living and working in peace. These dominant values reflect a general collective orientation of group loyalty and team action but a rejection of a traditional emphasis on political involvement (with the value of being politically active ranked lowest by four separate Czech groups: first- and fourth-year university students, Prague youths, and Ceske Budejovice citizens). Some preliminary evidence, however, suggests that this team orientation may be changing as well for senior-level management. A recent poll conducted by Eschenbach on behalf of the management consulting group of Roland, Berger, and Partner (as reported in *European Business Solutions,* 1994) demonstrated that a sample of 20 senior managers from the Czech Republic endorsed individualistic work values (for themselves) more strongly than did similar samples from Slovakia and Austria. Unfortunately, details of the samples, measures, and sampling procedures are not available, so it is unclear whether this shift represents an actual shift in attitudes or simply methods limitations.

In terms of the six cultural orientations that I presented in Chapter 8, there are several strongly emphasized values. First, the shift of the Czech Republic from a socialist to a market economy has resulted in a de-emphasis on the state as the ultimate source of nurturance for the country, but there still exists a general belief that the system must ultimately care for all employees. In addition, organizations and the government continue to emphasize that people are equal in merit and status and that attempts at differentiating workers from management must not go too far. Thus the Czech Republic is best characterized as being horizontally collectivistic, having a relatively small power distance, despite the nature of economic reforms. This assertion is supported by recent evidence that Earley et al. (1996) have produced, which shows that the level of collectivism in a sample of Czech managers is relatively high (averaging a level quite close to that found in the People's Republic of China and exceeding that found in Israel). It is also supported by the election of Václav Havel, a playwright and poet known for his rejection and satire of obedience to the communist hierarchy, as president of the newly independent country in 1990.

With regard to masculinity/femininity, Nath and Jirasek (1994) argue that traditional Czech society is masculine and male-focused. Despite the emphasis on egalitarianism in Czech society, men maintain a dominant position over women in most of the top management positions in companies. The importance of work, however, reflects a general de-emphasis on the importance of work as anything except a general contribution to society—that is to say, a necessary aspect of societal membership. Likewise, the emphasis in society has shifted from work as a guaranteed but relatively inconsequential aspect of life (with the exception of high-level managers and officials, who often spent a great deal of time trying to maintain their positions) under socialism to one of great concern and interest in the newly emerging market economy (Pearce & Cakrt, 1994). In terms of tightness versus looseness and shame versus guilt, Czech society is best described as a shame society emphasizing the sanctions used in a tight culture. During many years of communism and socialism, social control operated through public enforcement of behavior conducted according to party expectations and rules. By violating these rules, one risked rejection by the party and those who endorsed it.

Finally, I have left the dimension of relationship to nature to the last because it is an interesting case for discussion. A general view of the Czech Republic might suggest that it has a mastery-over-nature orientation, with such evidence as rapid economic growth, joint ventures, the revolution itself, et cetera. However, an interesting case analysis is presented by Pearce and Cakrt (1994) concerning Ferox Manufactured Products, the fictitious name of a large gas and chemical company that underwent significant changes as a result of market reforms. In their discussion of individuals within Ferox, it is clear that many of the traditional values held by employees reflect a general suspicion of things reflecting the party. However, a strong carryover influence is the expectation that the party or company will take care of employees' needs in life. Further, a general feeling lingers that the actions of individuals may have little impact on outcomes because of the potential corruption of the system and high-level individuals acting within the system. As a result, the past orientation under socialism bred a sense of futility of individual action. In this case, there appears to be some general subjugation orientation but the subjugation is to the corrupt systems, not nature. Other scholars discussing socialist systems have expressed similar employee perceptions. Thus I would argue that there remains a general passivity and subjugation orientation among many Czech employees.

With these cultural and organizational contexts as a backdrop, the question becomes how face might operate and influence employee activities. In general, the significance of face in the Czech Republic is twofold. With regard to lian, there is an emphasis on employee and managerial integrity for actions and intent. Particularly with the shift toward a market economy and the multiple promises of reform and a move away from the corruption represented by the appointment of party officials to key positions within companies, there has been an increasing revalidation and belief in the nature of managerial expertise in companies. In the past, lian was an important facet of general social life, as well as family life, but it held less meaning from an employee's perspective of high-level officials within a company. The dominant view was that a person could trust his or her work colleagues and supervisor, but the top-level managers were likely to work on behalf of their own friends and to appease the party. The result of this past record has been the general suspicion and replacement of many high-level company officials (Pearce & Cakrt, 1994)—a trend in many of the developing market economies in central and eastern Europe. The strongest role of lian was placed in the tight worker groups on shop floors and, to a somewhat lesser degree, in the labor unions at large. Currently there is an emphasis on lian as a substitute for formal contracting in organizations, and it is only through lian that social relationships can be maintained and trusted. At least one reason for this is described by Pearce (1993) in her discussion of reforms in Hungary. Pearce suggests that there has been an emergence of the importance of interpersonal trust and social networks as a substitute for formal contracts because such contracts often are subject to the whims of somewhat arbitrary political forces. In a similar vein, Czech managers face a great deal of uncertainty in their economic context (e.g., tax laws change and are implemented but are not formally written down), and so their relationships with others, and dependence on these relationships, enable work to be completed.

Lian plays an additional role in terms of social life. Many benefits are still afforded to Czech citizens as ascribed characteristics, such as housing and medical care. Although some of these benefits are now threatened by market reforms, there has been a strong emphasis on interpersonal relationships and family and less emphasis on accumulation. Lian remains an important facet of work life because work is still seen as something one does rather than something one lives to do. In this sense, the Czech Republic remains somewhat feminine in its orientation.

In the past, most of what employees needed to live was provided by the state, and so obvious differentials in mianzi through material possessions were minimal. Further, the strong emphasis on interpersonal egalitarianism reduced the desire of people to distinguish themselves from one another through symbols of status or power, with the exception of individuals involved in the Communist Party. As a result, there is still a relatively low emphasis on mianzi in Czech society. With regard to status and power, there is a general suspicion of people wanting power and a general rejection by the young generation of desire to pursue political agendas in the future. Clearly, much of this avoidance reflects a rejection of the traditional communist system. As with many economies moving from socialism to capitalism, there has been a relatively recent discovery of consumerism and consumption. There is an increasing emphasis on material consumption (e.g., the purchasing of stereos, televisions, clothing), but it typically reflects an accumulation of goods that are useful for one's family and in-group. Thus mianzi plays an increasing role inasmuch as it reflects the successes of one's family and in-group. However, there is not a strong emphasis on personal status and power relative to others at work, and there remains a strong sense of egalitarianism, so mianzi is not as strongly emphasized as lian.

With regard to various work behaviors, the remaining emphasis on lian and modest orientation toward mianzi are evidenced in a number of ways. For instance, managers continue to emphasize growth and development through training courses and executive education (e.g., the Czechoslovak Management Center was founded on such a premise), but these courses are often attended by a wide range of managers and staff from the same company at the same time. A general business course that I conducted in 1994 just outside Prague was attended by a group of employees of one company ranging from the CEO to assistant managers and specialists (e.g., staff accountants). These employees came from a company with over 5,000 employees, so the differential from top to bottom of the organization was quite large. Despite this, the CEO could not be easily distinguished from his subordinates in terms of style of dress, demeanor, reactions of others to his opinions, et cetera. In fact, it was only after the training course that I even learned that this participant was the company's CEO. Of course, my inexperience with Czech culture might account for my observations (or lack of them), but a Czech professor indicated that this anonymity of higher level employees is often the case in large, state-owned enterprises. Thus the emphasis placed on lian and social belongingness is very important. Another reason for this emphasis on lian in light of the recent reforms is that lian represents a move away from the corrupt systems of the past. Managers emphasize to their employees (and vice versa) that they are in their positions for legitimate reasons and that their intention is to provide for the success and welfare of the enterprise.

India

India represents a society of over 1 billion people speaking over 50 different languages within its political borders. Tremendous diversity exists within India, and its history is immense. The nature of work and organizations in India can be traced largely to a number of historical influences.

First, traditional Indian culture advocated that there are opposing forces in life concerning work and leisure (Sinha, 1990). Work and its related outcomes are not the purpose of man's existence; rather, work is best thought of as a manifestation of one's duty in society. Duty refers to those social and moral obligations that a person incurs toward relatives, friends, and even strangers. People work to discharge these duties, and they detach themselves from the outcomes of work because such an attachment calls into question one's intention in performing the duties. In this sense, duty refers to the fulfillment of obligations to others and does not imply personal attainments. Maintaining relationships and functioning within one's caste (occupational cluster) supported the general economic system within a traditional Indian village, and the hierarchy within family or caste determined the relative allocation of work responsibilities to people. So, for instance, the Brahmins engaged in intellectual, religious, and spiritual pursuits while the Rajputs protected the community against potential attackers. Commerce and trade were managed by the Vaishyas, and the lower castes were subservient to all of the higher level castes. A general philosophy was instilled that manual work was inferior to intellectual pursuits and suitable only for the lower castes (Sinha, 1990:27).

The second influence on Indian work was introduced through the British occupation of India. The British introduced a general scheme of public administration and bureaucracy to India. The premier example of such influence was evidenced in the East India Company, which relied on Indian civil servants, military, and businesspeople alike. The dominant view of the British was that the Indians were only partly human, and British managers were instructed to maintain a strict separation from their Indian subordinates. This is captured in a quote from Myers (1960), who cites the report of a British manager: "Ten years ago when I was first coming to India, an old India hand got me aside and told me, 'Now just forget about these ideas of leadership you have been learning here in Britain. Out there if the workers do not follow instructions, belt them. That will bring them around' " (169, cited in Sinha, 1990:27). This colonial legacy brought a model of bureaucracy to India that was generally distrusted by the locals, and so there was a strong emphasis on centralization, authority, and high power differentials and status. Interestingly, it is likely that such interventions were successful because they were not at all inconsistent with the existing nature of life in the Indian village, with its various divisions of labor and status differentials.

In more recent times, the emergence and emphasis on industrialization and development witnessed during the last 30 years provides yet another influence. With industrialization there has been a great emphasis on technology transfer (Khandwalla, 1987). However, this transfer has not resulted in a strong shift to Western values and culture in the workplace, for a number of reasons. For instance, the emphasis on economic goals has often been set aside for social reasons as companies are established. The strong emphasis in Indian society on social welfare and providing for employee needs has necessitated such an action. Also, many new ventures produced goods that were not economically viable from a purely market viewpoint but that were needed by people in particular regions. This development versus economic perspective has dominated the creation of industries within India, and it is reflected in a very large preponderance of public over private firms. As a result, many companies are run by government officials, who bring with them a strong emphasis on bureaucratization and standardization.

The general social values held onto by people reflect a general spiritualism based on traditional religious and philosophical views (Chakraborty, 1993; Sinha, in press). These dominant values are based on five general factors: hierarchy, embeddedness in a social network, personal over contractual relationships, harmony and tolerance, and duty and obligations to others (Sinha, 1990). According to Sinha (in press), Indians arrange relationships, objects, people, roles, et cetera, in vertical hierarchies such as the caste system. Without question, this strong emphasis on hierarchy reflects the very high power distance found in India and leads to a high sensitivity toward others' status and position. Personal success is not attributed to one's attributes or work; rather, it is attributed to one's superior, "whose blessing and guidance can help a manager advance in his career and [whose] displeasure can destroy it" (Sinha, in press:7).

This interdependence of action is reflected in the very strong emphasis on collectivism in India, and people are best understood in terms of their relationships with others and their position in society rather than as unique individuals (Marriot, 1977). For example, a person's name reflects family lineage and even place of birth. There is a strong emphasis on contribution to the in-group, cooperation, making sacrifices, and "affective reciprocity" (caring for and being cared for by others without asking; Sinha, in press). The downside to this groupism is a bias against "out-group." At the extreme, attitudes of one group toward another are characterized by distrust, hostility, conflicts, et cetera. At more modest levels, these differences reflect interesting trends in political agendas. In a recent election, several of the lower level castes gained increasing political power in an apparent attempt to secure employment for fellow caste members (*Economist,* April 8–14, 1995, 36). People vote along caste lines in order to secure the position of their general social collective.

Indian society is characterized by a strong sense of duty and obligation. A number of rigid expectations govern people's behavior in the discharge of these duties, and in this sense Indian society is tight. However, the maintenance of a superior's position overrides the particulars of one's actions such that this maintenance may necessitate the tolerance and protection of the superior's actions—even if these actions are inefficient or corrupt (Sinha, in press). This general sense of obligation is relevant to an understanding of the femininity of India society. As I described earlier, work is not an end but a means through which duties are discharged. Obligations are an important aspect in understanding work activities. Likewise, Indian society is based on shame, with the motivational impetus arising from the proper respect for hierarchically superior others and fulfilling one's obligations. Membership in lower castes was a traditional reason for experiencing shame, although this no longer appears to be the case to such a strong extent.

With regard to relationship to nature, India is best characterized as a combination of harmony and subjugation. To the extent that one's position in a particular group or caste is fixed from birth, this suggests subjugation to nature. Additionally, the religious underpinnings of Muslim society reflect a theological determinism as well. There is also a strong emphasis on harmony with nature, and Chakraborty (1993) suggests that only through a spiritual approach may a manager achieve his or her full potential. Chakraborty represents management as a type of personal journey in which the inner self is brought into alignment with the forces of nature. He suggests that the subjective circumstances of an employee are more important than the system surrounding the employee and that if various employees are able to collectively align themselves spiritually the result will be an effective organization.

The most direct link of face to Indian employees is through lian and moral character. This linkage is clearly reflected in several themes. First, the centrality of duty and obligations is consistent with the impact of lian-regulated behavior. There cannot be an immediate reciprocity for exchange in the discharge of duties (Sinha, 1990:26) if they are to be meaningful. As a result, one must have faith in the integrity of others' actions and intentions. This system is held together by lian, and any signaling that group members are unwilling to discharge their duties threatens the very existence of the in-group. Second, an emphasis on lian is consistent with a societal emphasis on a need-based approach to social exchange. In other words, if people receive according to need, and not personal or group action, then mianzi becomes much less meaningful. What is most important is that a person fulfills his or her duties to others. Finally, an emphasis on lian reflects the high degree of spiritualism found in many Indian organizations and is consistent with Chakraborty's prescriptions for an effective company.

This discussion of lian is not intended to suggest that mianzi is unimportant. Indian society represents an interesting combination of forces that have been underemphasized thus far in my presentation. Up until this point, most of my examples have polarized lian and mianzi with an implicit idea that one is traded off for the other. Indian society represents a different combination—lian and mianzi (a particular form) are both important and salient. In a need-based exchange society, why would mianzi become an important facet of organizational life? Earlier in this book I described the example of an Indian colleague who said that in his birthplace there was a general belief that personal gain (material possession) must come at the expense of spiritual strength. This suggests that a trade-off exists between mianzi and lian.

Mianzi as a collection of material possessions is not important in Indian culture (relatively speaking), but mianzi as status and position within a social network is of great significance. The whole caste system and emphasis on hierarchy within India reflects mianzi, and much of a person's position relative to others is determined by caste, occupation, schooling, et cetera.

Mianzi as a signaling device for a person's position in a social system is very important in Indian society and organizations. This signaling, however, is not important for personal reasons alone; rather, it provides an anchor for related others in a person's network. For instance, if an employee is slighted by someone concerning his or her status, this slight affects the employee's network, including coworkers, superiors, et cetera, as well as family members and friends. Mianzi becomes an important opportunity for asserting personal and network status and importance in an organization. The importance of status and position in maintaining a hierarchy is reflected in Sinha's (1990:34–35) point: "Hence peer group relationships induce anxiety till the peers are ranked on some real or imaginary dimension and thereby the relationship of manifest equality is transformed into some kind of hierarchy. Even friends are compared and ranked in terms of superior on some dimensions and inferior on others."

Sweden

Sweden is a country of over 9 million people and it is one of the oldest constitutional monarchies in Europe, dating back to the eleventh century. It is a relatively homogeneous country with a number of distinguishing characteristics, such as a highly educated workforce, advanced technology, an extensive service industry, a high standard of living, and an extensive transportation and communication system. The Social Democratic Party is the largest party represented in the Swedish parliament, and since 1982 the Social Democrats have had a central influence on the government. The political administration at the local level is exercised by municipalities, the assemblies of which are elected on the same day as the general elections take place.

Only about 5 percent of the population are not citizens, and of these people over one-half are from the other Nordic countries. The state church is Protestant-Lutheran, accounting for roughly 90 percent of the population, but religion does not play a predominant role in business and leisure activities. Most notable about the Swedes is an adherence to an egalitarian view of life, with the distribution of incomes being quite flat. The government provides for many aspects of a person's life, including housing (in some cases), medical and dental care, et cetera. A very strong emphasis on social welfare throughout Sweden is reflected in nonwork opportunities (e.g., vacations, family leave for both parents) as well as work programs (e.g., training, job design).

The significance of Swedish values and lifestyle to work and employees is obvious in a number of ways. For instance, there is a generally positive work climate between labor unions and management, and a number of laws are in place that reduce the potential for the escalation of labor-management disputes by channeling disagreements to higher authorities for solution. There is a strong sense that employees take an active role in the governance of their organizations, as reflected by worker participation programs and legislative decrees requiring companies to notify employees in advance of any impending organizational changes (e.g., mergers, redesign). Related to this is the Swedish system of workers' councils, legislated councils of codetermination in which employees participate formally with managers in making critical decisions for their organizations. In companies with more than 100 employees, worker representatives may be appointed to the organization's board of directors. Employee training programs are extensive as well, and organizations and the government are jointly responsible for job retraining of workers should organizational changes necessitate job changes (Maccoby, 1991:3).

Swedish industrial success is based on a number of traditional influences, such as disciplined work, high ethical standards, and a strong sense of fairness as well as a desire for developing and maintaining innovative organizations. An interesting value underlying the sense of fairness and egalitarianism found in Sweden is captured by the term "lagom," meaning "just right." The origin of the term is said to be attributable to the times of the Vikings, when a horn was filled with wine and all of the villagers (arranged in a circle) would drink from it. The idea was that each person would drink just enough so that by the time the horn had made the rounds it was empty (Maccoby, 1991). The value of lagom permeates many aspects of Swedish life, and it reflects a collective tolerance and value of restraint. It also emphasizes the value of solidarity among people and helps minimize rivalries.

Within Sweden, there is a strong emphasis on a social contract such that work is a critical part of everyone's life and thus is guaranteed as a basic aspect of societal membership. However, this "iron rice bowl" should not be confused with a Western idea that work is life; rather, it is believed that the general social welfare of a society is guaranteed if everyone is put to productive and useful work. Work, then, provides a number of benefits for all people, including an attachment to society, a personal sense of purpose and belonging, and a contribution to the general welfare. Swedish wages are kept high, and employment is ensured as a way to stimulate economic growth through domestic demand for goods and services. (It is also interesting to note that exports constitute a rather large part of Swedish wealth, accounting for over 35 percent of the total.)

Swedish culture is best characterized as one of constraint and conformity, with an emphasis on individual contributions to society. At a very early age, Swedish children are cautioned to think before they speak or act, lest their actions reflect poorly on them and their family. Traditional views of status and rank are reflected in the general tendency of managers to come from "business" families (there are notable exceptions, such as SAS's Jan Carlzon, whose father was a chauffeur.) This suggests that there is likely to be an accumulation of power within the hands of particular groups, but this is not the case because of a general distrust of people seeking an active role as leaders (business or political). Further, members of the younger generation in Sweden have a general contempt for power differentials and are quick to reject work or conditions they find undesirable, regardless of "duty" (Maccoby, 1991).

The general values found within Swedish society are reflected in a number of famous industrial examples, such as Volvo's experience in designing sociotechnical systems for automobile manufacturing. In a plant located in Uddevalla, the emphasis on teams and interdependence, autonomy, and self-management is reflected. In this plant, car builders are organized into teams of eight to ten employees who have no traditional supervision and are provided with complete discretion concerning how to produce a given automobile and work collectively.

The most obvious aspect of Swedish society is a general collective orientation with little power distance. Triandis and Bhawuk (in press) characterize Swedish society as one of horizontal individualists, but this description is somewhat at odds with the descriptions of Swedish workers by other researchers (e.g., Jonsson, 1991; Maccoby, 1991). In this instance, it appears that there is a strong emphasis on interdependence within Swedish society best characterized as horizontal collectivism with some moderation on the interdependence–independence continuum described by Triandis and Bhawuk. I characterize this hybrid form in Table 10-1 as "IC," meaning that there are aspects of both individualism and collectivism, although I disagree with Triandis and Bhawuk's classification. Swedish society is clearly characterized by a relatively low power distance, reflected in a number of ways, including the rejection of business and political leaders, low income disparities, worker councils and codetermination, and a strong social welfare emphasis. Related to this is the strong emphasis on social conformity and moderation (lagom), suggesting that Swedish society is "tight."

The seeming emphasis on work (e.g., guaranteed employment) suggests a very masculine culture, quite contrary to Hofstede's (1980a) and others' assertions, but this is an inaccurate categorization. The apparent emphasis on work is quite feminine in the sense that work is an extension of life and thus must be adapted and changed in order that it be a meaningful life experience. The active ecology and naturalist movement within Sweden demonstrates a strong orientation toward relationship to nature, which is also reflected by many manufacturing companies (e.g., Volvo, Ericsson Telecom) that emphasize environmental concerns. Finally, Sweden is best characterized as a shame-based culture in which people act according to rules for conforming and not interfering with the personal liberties of others. (It is this last point that provides support for Triandis and Bhawuk's conclusion that Sweden consists of horizontal individualists.)

Sweden represents an interesting culture for a discussion of face. As I argued in Chapter 1, face is not only an "Asian" concern, and Swedish society strongly reinforces this theme. The dominant form of face in Swedish society is that of lian, or moral character. The system of moderation, avoidance of interfering with others' rights, and desire to provide the "best" living conditions in the world for its citizens all reflect a general concern for the morality of how people deal with one another. The term "human dignity" as a basis for industrial organization is often applied to a description of organizations in Sweden (Maccoby, 1991). The critical point is that the various aspects of Swedish life (cultural values, organizational forms, worker representation, production methods, etc.) emphasize the importance of people as interdependent humans who have personal merit and worth. Thus lian is a critical aspect of interpersonal interaction because it reinforces a person's merit in living within such a society. The social contract that provides a good lifestyle to all people binds them to being responsible to that society as well. Jonsson (1991:118) quotes a Swedish worker as saying, "We can no longer say 'this is my job and when I am finished I can rest.' Now we are all responsible for the product, and we must help each other."

Of course, the importance of lian to industrial life can be thought of from another vantage point, namely, that lian permeates the nature of organizations and their structures. Employee and corporate governance systems reflect this notion of responsibility and dignity, and the entire program of the sociotechnical systems implemented in Sweden is consistent with lian. Sweden, then, represents an interesting example in which face is both cause and consequence of various organizational and industrial structures/systems.

What role, then, does mianzi play in the Swedish system? In general, mianzi is a secondary concern, and overt accumulations and status differentials are discounted as inappropriate and morally suspect. People who actively seek power in politics are viewed with suspicion, and managers who focus their efforts on personal gain are shunned as morally corrupt. However, this does not mean that mianzi is unrecognized or unimportant. For instance, Hedlund (1991) points to a largely overlooked aspect of Swedish organizations, namely, the importance of a technical background for managers. He points to the late Marcus Wallenburg, who insisted on using the title of Tekn.Dr. (Doctor of Technology), which he was awarded from the Royal Institute of Technology in Stockholm. This may be somewhat of a carryover from the German-inspired educational system, in which expertise is highly respected. Thus mianzi plays a role in differentiating people through their expertise and knowledge and signals status within a generally egalitarian society.

The United States

In describing the mix of the United States, Maccoby (1991) comments:

> These differences arise partly because U.S. culture is so varied. The United States is more a continent than a country. The dominant values in midwestern states and the Pacific Northwest with large Scandinavian communities are not so different from those of Scandinavia. Latin American culture plays a large role in Florida and the Southwest and merges into the freedom-loving wide-open Western world. California mixes futuristic experimentation with Asian high-tech industry and Latin American spicing. The large Eastern cities are confusing mixtures of dynamic growth, old money and new wealth, black ghettos, and ethnic groups from eastern and southern Europe. The deep South has a culture of its own with traditional rural values and where, surprising to Europeans, there is more successful cooperation between blacks and whites than in any other part of America. (4)

This comment represents the difficulty of trying to describe accurately "American life" and society. In many respects, the fragmented and incoherent social structures within the United States defy coherent description. As I pointed out in Chapter 5, Kluckhohn and Strodtbeck's (1961) analysis of value orientations, yielding fundamental differences in value orientations for a number of communities, was undertaken within a 25-mile-radius circle in New Mexico! In one sense, this is the same difficulty faced in describing any large nation using concepts of society, culture, and sharedness. Earlier I characterized India using general terms and descriptors, and this was no less difficult a task than describing U.S. culture. However, a number of characteristics and facets of U.S. society suggest dominant (or, at the minimum, majority) influences. (I would note that although India has five times the population of the United States, there is an advantage in describing Indian "culture" inasmuch as there is a dominant influence of a tight culture—that is to say, general social conformity and a common ancestry for the general population. In the United States, neither of these conditions are satisfied.)

The United States is a highly individualistic culture in which the focus is on individual accomplishment and self-interest (Erez & Earley, 1993; Hofstede, 1980a, 1991; McGregor, 1991). For instance, Americans are guided by a strong work ethic emphasizing individual achievement and reward as well as a strong individual goal orientation (Hofstede, 1980a; Locke & Latham, 1990; Triandis, 1995). Ample evidence suggests that Americans are generally individualistic (e.g., Hofstede, 1991), and the newly emerging emphasis on teams and teamwork (Hackman, 1990) is useful as long as it does not interfere with personal autonomy. This emphasis on personal autonomy and discretion is reflected to a large degree by the cultural "looseness" of U.S. society. There exists a tolerance for peculiarity (one but needs to visit my hometown of Los Angeles to bear witness to such eccentricities) and unique activities on the part of people, and diversity is embraced rather than shunned.

U.S. society is characterized by a moderate power distance according to previous work by Hofstede (1980a, b). Although someone might quibble about the specific level of power distance, there seems to be a moderate level at which leadership is of strong interest to people, status is often signaled, and socioeconomic status is diverse and wide-ranging, but equality is stressed in various social institutions, including the judicial and political systems. There is a general willingness of employees to regard their superiors' views as important and significant, but there is a lack of willingness to follow directives without question.

In the United States, there is a strong tendency toward a mastery-over-nature orientation, with technology used as a basis for solving organizational problems (clearly, the Deming "craze" supports such a view) as well as life problems, whereas some other countries question the extensive use of technological means to extend life (e.g., life support systems). The importance of technology as a solution for organizational demands is reflected in a quote from a manager at General Electric (Howard, 1986:27): "In the not too distant future . . . an engineer will sit down at a design computer terminal, take the basic customer information, and just punch the numbers in. Then, the computer will automatically generate all the design, drafting, planning, and machining data and all the capacity planning information necessary to effectively load the machines in the shops." Of course, this emphasis on a technological fix has led some to question the dehumanization of work (e.g., Braverman, 1974).

Finally, the United States is a generally masculine culture that is guilt-based in its orientation. The masculinity is reflected by a continuing emphasis on the importance of work, although some of the trends of the 1980s have suggested a shift from a work-dominated to a lifestyle-influenced approach to life. For example, many of the health emphases newly emerging in companies reflect a view that corporate efficiency depends on personal welfare and satisfaction (Howard, 1986). Despite these pressures, other forces push people toward an increased emphasis on work. This is evidenced by the increasing numbers of dual-career couples and single parents who must work increasingly long hours in order to maintain their standard of living. The guilt orientation of Americans can be traced back to Christian doctrine with an emphasis on personal worth based on personal standards of goodness.

As I argued earlier in this book, U.S. society is dominated by an emphasis on mianzi. Despite the recent calls for a rediscovery of family values, business ethics, et cetera, an overwhelming influence of mianzi on employee action remains. Mianzi takes its own unique form in the United States relative to other countries, such as India or the Czech Republic. In particular, emphasis is placed on mianzi as it enables people to define themselves uniquely within their social structure. This definition is based on a view of the self as isolated, rather than integrated, from a general social context, but it is a definition that reasserts relative position within a social context. In this sense, Americans have a love-hate relationship with each other. That is to say, mianzi is important for asserting one's personal significance and importance within the context of a social system. For instance, Festinger's (1957, 1964) social comparisons theory reflects such an effect. When placed in a context of being able to observe others' examination scores, students choose referent others who are similar in ability to themselves. The advantage in doing so is that a person can uniquely define his or her accomplishments, but without the self-degradation that might occur should a highly competent other be compared.

Mianzi certainly has a social component to it in the United States contrary to the simplistic view of overt materialism that is often stressed. Within work organizations, people seek out symbols and recognition for personal achievements through such trappings as large offices (a former colleague of mine actually counted ceiling tiles as a measure of success), expense accounts, computers, et cetera. These symbols are significant because they provide affirmation that a person is important relative to others in a social setting. In this sense, the emphasis of Americans is on mianzi through accumulation for social status reasons, in contrast to Indians, who emphasize mianzi through relationships and education for social status.

Despite this emphasis on mianzi, this is not to say that lian is without significance. There has been a resurgence of interest in business schools concerning the topic of business ethics (e.g., Treviño, 1986), although it is not clear that such an interest is attributable to a reemergence of morality in business or another opportunity to discover a competitive edge. For instance, a well-known business school in the United States hired an endowed chair for ethics (as many schools have done) several years ago. Interestingly, the scholar was most highly accomplished in the field of game theory in social psychology and not in business ethics (having never even been on a business school faculty)! I believe this reflects the general trend in American business that lian is viewed as important but primarily because it provides for an instrumental advantage in conducting business. Of course, there are important and notable exceptions such as Tom's of Maine, which was founded on a philosophy of environmental and personal responsibility. However, if one examines the icons of American society, it is easy to observe such figures as Madonna, Mick Jagger, O. J. Simpson, and Bill Gates, and it is much more difficult to take notice of those responsible for social concerns and values. Thus lian is viewed as somewhat important to the extent that it is instrumental in maintaining an edge over one's competitors.

Summary

The focus of this chapter has been the presentation of several "cases" in which the importance of face in employee behavior is illustrated. I have attempted to capture the key aspects of several cultures and demonstrate their relevance for lian and mianzi and to suggest a number of ways the organizational context within each country contributes to this interplay. An important theme in this chapter is that face is best understood within the context of a given culture through an examination of the culture as a multifaceted collage in which various dimensions interact to produce various types of influences on face and an employee's behavior within an organization.

Although these "cases" are generalizations, they illustrate several important points in applying my framework to organizational behavior. First, cultures are a combination of various dominant influences that may complement or conflict with one another. The result is that in a society such as India, both lian and mianzi are stressed and important. However, the specific aspect of mianzi emphasized in India is not the form stressed in the United States. Second, social relationships and structures in a given society influence the type of face emphasized (e.g., the low power distance and egalitarianism of Sweden is associated with an emphasis on lian). Third, organizational behavior is influenced by people's regulation (harmony) of face in their social setting. I stress the phrase "influenced by" because I do not mean to imply that face dictates behavior, just as cultural and organizational variables do not dictate behavior. People engage in various face-related actions as a way of defining their roles vis-à-vis others as well as their social context. Thus an employee who engages in impression management with his or her boss is attempting to establish (or maintain) face balanced with how such actions might impact others' (e.g., coworkers) views.

The conclusion is that face and its regulation in a general context are complex and dependent on "initial conditions." By initial conditions I mean the situational and personal characteristics that influence face and its presentation. In order to provide some additional clarity concerning the importance of face to organizational behavior, I turn my attention to applying face to several important aspects of organizational behavior in the final chapter of this book. It is my hope that this discussion will stimulate a research agenda for scholars interested in this topic from an organizations perspective.

Conclusions and Research Agenda

In this chapter, I apply my framework to several organizational topics. Rather than simply summarize my framework, it seems to be more useful to apply it in several content areas, using organizational examples as a basis for stimulating a research agenda for the future. I have chosen several areas because of their centrality to organizational behavior and face, namely, social exchange and reward allocation, negotiation and conflict management, and impression management and feedback seeking. I would stress, however, that my choice of areas is intended to provide examples of how the model might stimulate research, not to serve as a directive limiting the application domains.

Social Exchange and Reward Allocation

A great deal of research has been focused on the nature of social exchange and reward allocation across cultures. For instance, Tornblom, Jonsson, and Foa (1985) compared the use of three allocation rules (equity, equality, need) in the United States and Sweden. They hypothesized that the egalitarian emphasis characteristic of Sweden would result in a higher priority being placed on an equality exchange rule rather than on need or equity, whereas Americans would most emphasize equity over equality or need. The results of their study supported their hypotheses. Murphy-Berman, Berman, Singh, Pachuri, and Kumar (1984) examined the allocation rules of need, equity, and equality with respect to positive and negative reward allocations (bonus pay versus pay cuts) in the United States and India. As predicted, they found that Indian managers preferred a need rule over equality and equity, whereas Americans preferred equity over the other two. They concluded that their results may reflect that in India people are less responsive to merit pay because societal status is determined largely by affiliation and caste rather than by individual achievement. Bond, Leung, and their colleagues (e.g., Bond et al., 1982; Leung & Bond, 1984) have examined reward allocation preferences in Chinese samples. They found that the Chinese, who are considered to be collectivistic, use an equality rule in allocating rewards to in-group members more than do Americans (who are guided by individualistic values) but that there exists a general endorsement of an equity rule in both American and Chinese samples. More recently, however, Chen (1995) found a reversal of this typical pattern (Chinese preferring equality over equity and Americans preferring equity over equality) in his study of Chinese and American managers. He found that Chinese managers (in the People's Republic of China) were more inclined to use an allocation rule based on equity over equality, with a heavy emphasis on material over social rewards.

With regard to face, social exchange, and group process, a number of hypotheses can be posed. For instance, a heavy emphasis on need and equality rules, characteristic of collectivistic or tight cultures, should be associated with lian rather than mianzi. However, using the representation presented in Figure 7-1, I would argue that only in a communal-sharing context would lian dominate relative to mianzi. In such cultures, need and equality allocations presume that people are equally meritorious, so differential allocations are not appropriate. In an authority-ranking context, lian is important in order for people to establish their legitimacy in the social structure (showing that they are worthy of group membership and, therefore, equally deserving as other group members), but mianzi is very important as well in order to establish relative position within the in-group. However, in a culture emphasizing equity allocations alone, mianzi becomes increasingly important given that it is a unit that can be gained or lost in proportion to an individual's contributions.

Applying this reasoning to the Leung and Bond (1984) versus Chen (1995) findings, it is possible to reconcile, in part, these apparently contradictory findings. In the Leung and Bond (1984) studies, group membership (in-group versus out-group) was shown to play an important moderator role, with the behavior of the Chinese subjects to out-group members more equity-based than that of their American counterparts. It was only among Chinese subjects who were dealing with in-group members and were perceived as being high-input allocators (allocators who put in their own fair share of effort) that the heavy use of an equality rule emerged. Otherwise, an equity rule was endorsed by the Hong Kong Chinese, subjects. (Note: It is important to remember that the Leung and Bond subjects were Hong Kong Chinese, whereas the Chen subjects were mainland Chinese. Based on my experiences with both cultures, I would interpret this as being consistent with a combination of authority-ranking and market-pricing exchanges inasmuch as lian is demonstrated through a general contribution to in-group welfare, and mianzi is given in accordance to individual contribution. Group membership, however, guarantees some general level of allocation based on equality norms.) A careful examination of the Chen (1995) role-play (in which a subject is asked to assume the position of the head of a 1,000-employee company) suggests that his participants may not have perceived their "employees" as both in-group and providing high input. Collectivists who do not contribute their fair share (in-group but low-input allocators in the Leung and Bond studies) lose lian, and their subsequent group interactions become increasingly instrumental and focused on mianzi. This discussion suggests that collectivists who have lost lian will be treated as an out-group, with an increasing reliance on mianzi and instrumental exchange.

Negotiation and Conflict Management

A great deal of research has been conducted on the topic of international negotiation (e.g., Fisher, 1980; Graham, 1985; Graham et al., 1988; Harnett & Cummings, 1980; Kumar, 1994; Ting-Toomey, 1988; Wilson, 1992). While even a brief review of this literature is beyond the scope of this book, I would like to build on the work of Ting-Toomey (1988) in discussing the role of face in negotiations and conflict management. For Ting-Toomey (1988), an important aspect of face and conflict arises from the context (Hall, 1959) of a given culture. In a high-context culture, people understand a message's meaning based on its context (how and where something is said often outweighs what is actually said). In such a culture, face represents much more than just self-presentation—it often captures a sense of family and honor. In a low-context culture, communication is more literal, with an emphasis on the message itself (Hall, 1959). Thus face becomes a transient signal during a specific interaction (Triandis & Albert, 1987; Erez & Earley, 1993; Ting-Toomey, 1988:228).

This approach to social interaction converges with face in a number of ways. In a high-context culture, an emphasis is placed on a lian form of face for several reasons. First, in such a culture there is a heightened sensitivity to others and their sense of self. This sensitivity is similar to Wilson's (1993) moral concept of sympathy, and the loss of lian is the loss of morality. Second, high-context cultures often reflect strong social networks and ties. People avoid face-threatening acts not only for the target person's sake but also to avoid offending those individuals with whom the target has a strong connection. As suggested earlier, poor job performance reviews for a Chinese worker reflect poorly on the worker's family as well as on him- or herself. Face-threatening acts threaten both the target and key nodes of expressive relations, including close friends, family, et cetera. In a negotiation context, this suggests that represented constituencies will vary in relevance to social exchanges based on long-term, in-group connections (high context) versus short-term individualistic ones (low context). This means that in countries such as Singapore or South Korea, an emphasis is placed on signaling the character of one's negotiating group and avoiding actions that threaten the negotiating partner and therefore potentially dishonor the negotiating group.

A low-context culture typically uses market-pricing or equality-matching principles. Communication, norms of behavior, styles of exchange, et cetera, are adhered to for the purpose of exchanging resources in a predictable fashion. People's actions are taken literally, and they act in such a way as to maintain a cordial interaction. Successful interactions rely on clear exchange rules with a goal of personal gain. A low-context culture relies on mianzi because it does not require subtle interpretations of morality or values for a negotiated exchange. A low-context culture focuses directly on mianzi, with an emphasis on enhancing someone else's status through compliments and ingratiating tactics. For example, the politeness of Americans may be instrumental because group memberships are variable and one can never predict who will be a "friend" in the future (Triandis, 1994).

Several implications of this discussion for research on negotiation and conflict can be illustrated with an organizational example. For instance, Americans have been criticized for their abrupt negotiation style with their Japanese counterparts (e.g., Graham & Sano, 1984). One reason for this apparent style conflict is that two different types of face processes are operating. To the Japanese, coming from an authority-ranking setting, both lian and mianzi are central concepts. To the American, coming from a mix of market-pricing and equality-matching exchanges, face is viewed as transient and limited to the specifics of the discussion setting. The more "long-term" approach emphasized by Japanese negotiators (Kumar, 1994) reflects an emphasis on establishing moral character and trust in the relationships. This conflict is not simply a differing set of expectations about a relationship (or a stronger emphasis on "face" by the Japanese). The difference reflects a relative emphasis on lian versus mianzi. For the Japanese, the critical issue is assuring that the negotiating partner has honor and integrity and is meritorious for inclusion in the in-group (i.e., is a legitimate negotiating partner). Questions of mianzi are important but derived in a straightforward fashion from the social structure in which people interact. That is to say, ambiguity exists during the early phase of a negotiation as the foreign partner's intentions and integrity are explored. Once lian is established, the Japanese negotiators view the exchange of resources (mianzi as well as organizationally relevant outcomes) as obvious based on participants' position in a social hierarchy. This is in sharp contrast to the Americans, who view the preliminaries (lian) as somewhat less consequential (as one American negotiator said, "I don't have to marry them, just deal with them") but are concerned about mianzi. In American business, mianzi is desired, but the social mechanisms found in Japan for guiding allocation are absent. As a result, actions that might be beneficial for gaining mianzi are more likely to be enacted by Americans because no rules and norms exist governing who receives what allocations/resources. The moderate emphasis placed on mianzi by Americans and the strong emphasis of the Japanese have the potential to generate conflict in other ways. For instance, in a short-term joint venture, a Japanese partner might be asked to assume a subservient status temporarily, after which both partners will profit. However, this arrangement will cause the Japanese partner to lose mianzi, and so the partner is likely to resist such a relationship. To the American, a laissez-faire attitude is taken given that the outcome is increased profits for both partners. Thus the potential for conflict arises not because one culture is concerned with face and the other is not but because the two cultures are focused on different aspects of face in their negotiations.

Impression Management and Feedback Seeking

Perhaps the most relevant literature to a discussion of face across cultures is that of impression management and feedback seeking. A great deal of this literature is predicated on the assumption that individuals seek to maintain a positive self-image (Goffman, 1959) and that many actions of an individual are directed toward this outcome. Impression management recently has been the focus of organizations literature, including work at the macro level by Ginzel, Kramer, and Sutton (1993) and work on self-regulation (Tsui & Ashford, 1994). There are at least six reasons why people manage impressions (Tedeschi & Riess, 1981): role enactment as symbolic discourse, avoiding blame and taking credit, self-esteem maintenance, strategic self-presentations, power and social influence, and creating connotative impressions (e.g., evaluation of potency). Role enactment involves the impressions made in order to symbolically reinforce one's roles. Avoiding blame and taking credit, as well as self-esteem maintenance, involve a self-regulatory process whereby a person's self-concept is safeguarded through the management of impressions formed by others.

Strategic self-presentations as well as power and social influence bear the most direct relation to a discussion of face. Early work by Jones (1964) on strategic self-presentation suggested people ingratiate themselves through a variety of tactics such as making positive self-statements (e.g., impressing the receiver with the sender's capabilities or status), making positive statements about the other person (e.g., flattery or social approval), conforming to the receiver's opinion, and doing a favor for the receiver. Ingratiation is highly related to mianzi, although there is some overlap with lian as well. For instance, ingratiation tactics such as flattery and doing someone a favor are ways of enhancing face for others by increasing their mianzi. Making positive self-statements may be relevant to both mianzi and lian depending on the nature of the information conveyed. If self-statements signal power and status, this strengthens mianzi. Statements concerning a person's moral standards and values are most relevant to conveying critical information concerning lian. The ingratiation tactic of conforming to the receiver's opinion suggests an alignment of basic values with those of the receiver and, therefore, the idea that one's moral character is consistent with the valued other's character.

What face has to offer over a traditional view of ingratiation tactics for impression management is that the content and frequency of particular tactics being used are related to the form of face most prominent in a given culture. For instance, it would be hypothesized that Americans (with a strong mianzi focus) would engage in ingratiation tactics consisting primarily of flattery and doing others favors, whereas the Chinese (with a strong lian focus) would be oriented toward conformity with others' opinions and providing self-statements of personal values and beliefs.

The relationship of face to power and influence operates through mianzi. Status, prestige, and accumulated wealth are all means by which individuals acquire and maintain their power. For a strongly mianzi-focused culture, the acquisition of power and status becomes the center of much activity. In a lian-focused culture, the relative emphasis on character and values makes the emphasis on prestige and status less relevant, with self-worth being judged by personal actions rather than by personal accumulations. Even in a culture focused on lian, however, the accumulation of power and status is important. For instance, Chinese culture is strongly oriented toward lian, but it has long been viewed as a society quite concerned with power, status, and political maneuvering (Li, 1978). How can these positions be reconciled? Perhaps by noting that in a mianzi-focused culture what is sought after is often quite different than in a lian-focused culture and that the base of power reflects these differences. Not only does a focus on face lead to different predictions concerning what types of power bases are used, but also similar categories of power (e.g., reward power) may operate quite differently across cultures emphasizing lian or mianzi.

A Final Organizational Example

As a final illustration, I draw upon an organizational example based on a personal conversation with former Ford Motor Company CEO Donald Peterson.[1] During Peterson's time at the helm of Ford, he introduced a number of organizational interventions aimed at changing the organizational culture of Ford. One such intervention was aimed at changing the bureaucratic and hierarchical nature of Ford to a more participative and team-based approach to management. After extensive planning and development, Ford implemented a multistep intervention including a number of managerial programs for decentralizing decision making and control at Ford in order to stimulate corporatewide participation and employee empowerment. The results, according to Peterson, were reasonably strong in the United States but not at all effective in Ford of Europe and Ford of Asia. After Ford of Europe explored the potential problems with the program implementation, it was discovered that some "cultural" differences were in operation.

The most obvious explanation of this failure to transfer the managerial successes of Ford from the United States to Ford of Europe is simply that the techniques used, participation and empowerment, are inappropriate or unsuitable for European culture. As a point of discussion, I focus on the implementation of innovations in Ford operations in Germany. German society is based largely on market-pricing and authority-ranking forms of exchange (i.e., high power distance and moderately collectivistic). The managerial interventions used are consistent with the moderate collective orientation found in Germany. This suggests that the problem was not the transfer of the techniques themselves, and evidence from Ford interviews with management suggest that this was not the source of the problems. A second, obvious possibility is that the German managers resented and resisted being told "what to do." In other words, resistance occurred because management resented being told in an authoritarian fashion what program to adopt. However, this hypothesis is rejected given the strong power distance found in German society.

A less obvious but more compelling interpretation is generated by using face. In this case, what the German managers resisted was neither the specific managerial techniques nor the idea that these techniques were imposed "from above." What they resisted was that "from above" was really "from Detroit," and they viewed the legitimate authoritarian structure as Ford of Europe and not Ford of Detroit. As a result, they lost mianzi after being assigned managerial directives from a "higher level" but an illegitimate source. Had these interventions been introduced by Ford of Europe, a hierarchically legitimate authoritarian structure, resistance to the changes would have been overcome. By receiving the directives from Ford of Europe, the German managers would maintain face.

This anecdote illustrates the potential of face to aid our understanding of cross-cultural management interventions. Without such constructs, the first and second hypotheses posed above would have been accepted even though they did not capture the true work dynamic.

Summary

The purpose of this book has been to provide a current understanding of the concept of face and to illustrate its usefulness in organizational research across cultures. Two fundamental forms of face were discussed, lian and mianzi, based on the existing literature. In addition, the importance of social exchange was posited as an important way to understand the types of face most active in a given cultural and organizational context. It was posed that multiple aspects, or dimensions, of culture are the most relevant to a presentation of face, namely, individualism-collectivism, power distance, tight versus loose, relationship to nature, masculinity/femininity, and shame versus guilt.

My model of face posits that individuals vary on two general aspects of self-presentation, namely, an emphasis on values and moral character (lian) and an accumulation of status and prestige (mianzi). In the case of lian, this is a fundamental birthright and a characteristic that may be maintained or lost but generally not gained. A fall from grace is difficult to overcome. With regard to mianzi, this is a social currency that can be gained or lost with each and every social interaction. In some societies, mianzi is thought of as a symbolic indicator of status relative to others, such as a university degree, social standing, caste, et cetera. For others, mianzi refers to the physical and monetary characteristics that set people apart from one another, such as office size, salary, et cetera.

Social exchange is governed by a number of different forms: authority ranking, communal sharing, equality matching, and market pricing. It is through these forms of exchange that we can better understand the way cultural values and orientations influence the relative emphasis placed on forms of face in a society. For instance, in a tight culture (strongly rule-based) there is a stronger emphasis on lian than on mianzi because moral character is a more central concern for maintaining the standards of society.

Finally, the general form of this model has been applied to a number of societies and a number of organizational topics in order to provide some new understanding of existing findings and approaches. What seems particularly promising with a model focused on face is that it provides us with new ways to look at existing research, and the model I present has ample room for expansion and adaptation (e.g., focusing on new aspects of culture, delineating specific subcategories of lian and mianzi). Perhaps the most important feature of this model is that face reflects a universal concept of self rather than a universal dimension of culture or organizational form. This has the potential for helping researchers avoid overgeneralizations and the low predictability that has inherently limited international and intercultural organizational behavior research. While it is useful to understand the social strata from which people come, it is essential to understand how and why they act as unique individuals within an international and organizational context.

Note

1. I would like to thank Donald Peterson for his helpful description of this organizational example based on his presentation during a seminar at the Graduate School of Management, University of California, Irvine. My depiction of the Ford example is not intended to represent precise facts of the case but is used for purposes of illustration alone.

References

Abrams, Dominic, & Michael A. Hogg
1990   *Social identity theory: Constructive and critical advances.* New York: Springer-Verlag.

Alexander, J. C.
1990   *Culture and society: Contemporary debates.* New York: Cambridge University Press.

Allport, G. W., P. E. Vernon, & G. Lindzey
1960   *A study of values.* Boston: Houghton Mifflin.

Asch, S.
1951   "Effects of group pressure upon the modification and distortion of judgment." In H. Guetzkow (Ed.), *Groups, leadership, and men,* 177–190. Pittsburgh: Carnegie Press.

Ashford, S. J., & G. B. Northcraft
1992   "Conveying more (or less) than we realize: The role of impression-management in feedback seeking." *Organizational Behavior and Human Decision Processes,* 53:310–334.

Ashford, S., & Anne S. Tsui
1991   "Self-regulation for managerial effectiveness: The role of active feedback seeking." *Academy of Management Journal,* 34:251–280.

Bacharach, S. B., & E. J. Lawler
1980   *Power and politics in organization.* San Francisco: Jossey-Bass.

Bandura, A.
1986   *Social foundations of thoughts and action: A social cognitive theory.* Englewood Cliffs, NJ: Prentice Hall.

Bandura, A.
1969   *Principles of behavior modification.* New York: Holt Rinehart and Winston.

Barker, R. G., & P. V. Gump
1964   *Big school, small school: High school size and student behavior.* Stanford, CA: Stanford University Press.

Barley, S. R.
1990   "The alignment of technology and structure through roles and networks." *Administrative Science Quarterly,* 33:24–60.

Baron, James N., & Karen S. Cook
1992   "Process and outcome: Perspectives on the distribution of rewards in organizations."
Administrative Science Quarterly, 37:191–197.

Barry, H., III, M. K. Bacon, & J. L. Child
1957   "A cross-cultural survey of some sex differences in socialization." *Journal of Abnormal Psychology,* 55:327–332.

Baum, Joel A. C., & Jitendra V. Singh
1994   "Organizational niches and the dynamics of organizational founding." *Organization Science,* 5:483–501.

Bazerman, Max H., George F. Loewenstein, & Sally B. White
1992   "Reversals of preference in allocation decisions: Judging an alternative versus choosing among alternatives." *Administrative Science Quarterly,* 37:220–240.

Bem, S. L.
1975   "Sex role adaptability: One consequence of psychological androgyny." *Journal of Personality and Social Psychology,* 31:634–643.

Bem, S. L.
1974   "The measurement of psychological androgyny." *Journal of Clinical and Consulting Psychology,* 42:155–162.

Bem, S. L., W. Martyna, & C. Watson
1976   "Sex typing and androgyny: Further explorations of the expressive domain." *Journal of Personality and Social Psychology,* 34:1016–1023.

Benedict, Ruth
1946   *The chrysanthemum and the sword.* Boston: Houghton Mifflin.

Benedict, Ruth
1934   *Patterns of culture.* Boston: Houghton Mifflin.

Berry, J. W.
1976   *Human ecology and cognitive style.* Beverly Hills, CA: Sage/Halsted.

Black, Stuart, & Mark Mendenhall
1990   "Cross-cultural training effectiveness: A review and a theoretical framework for future research." *Academy of Management Review,* 15:113–136.

Black, Stuart, Mark Mendenhall, & Gary Oddou
1991   "Toward a comprehensive model of international adjustment: An integration of multiple theoretical perspectives." *Academy of Management Review,* 16:291–317.

Blanchard, F. A., R. H. Weigel, & S. W. Cook
1975   "The effect of relative competence of group members upon interpersonal attraction in cooperating interracial groups." *Journal of Personality and Social Psychology,* 32:519–530.

Blau, Peter M.
1989   *Exchange and power in social life.* Brunswick, NJ: Transaction Publishers.

Blau, Peter M.
1955   *The dynamics of bureaucracy.* Chicago: University of Chicago Press.

Blau, P. M., & R. A. Schoenherr
1971   *The structure of organizations.* New York: Basic Books.

Bond, Michael H. (Ed.)
1988a   *The cross-cultural challenge to social psychology.* Newbury Park, CA: Sage.

Bond, Michael H.
1988b   "Invitation to a wedding: Chinese values and global economic growth." In P. Sinha & H. Kao (Eds.), *Social values and development*, 197–209. New Delhi: Sage.

Bond, Michael H., & T. S. Cheung
1983   "The spontaneous self-concept of college students in Hong Kong, Japan, and the United States." *Journal of Cross-Cultural Psychology*, 14:153–171.

Bond, Michael H., & P. W. H. Lee
1981   "Face-saving in Chinese culture: A discussion and experimental study of Hong Kong students." In A. Y. C. King & R. P. L. Lee (Eds.), *Social life and development in Hong Kong*, 288–305. Hong Kong: Chinese University Press.

Bond, Michael H., Kwok Leung, & K. C. Wan
1982   "How does cultural collectivism operate?: The impact of task and maintenance contributions on reward allocation." *Journal of Cross-Cultural Psychology*, 13:186–200.

Bond, Michael H., & Chung Kwok Venus
1991   "Resistance to group or personal insults in an ingroup or outgroup context." *International Journal of Psychology*, 26:83–94.

Bontempo, R., S. A. Lobel, & H. C. Triandis
1989   "Compliance and value internalization among Brazilian and U.S. students." Unpublished manuscript.

Boudreau, Frances, Roger Sennott, & Michele Wilson
1986   *Sex roles and social patterns*. New York: Praeger.

Boyacigiller, N., & N. J. Adler
1991   "The parochial dinosaur: Organizational science in a global context." *Academy of Management Review*, 16:262–290.

Braverman, H.
1974   *Labor and monopoly capital: The degradation of work in the twentieth century*. New York: Monthly Labor Press.

Braverman, Phillip H.
1976   "Managing change." *Datamation*, 22:111–113.

Breckler, S. J., & A. G. Greenwald
1986   "Motivational facets of the self." In R. M. Sorrentino & E. T. Higgins (Eds.), *Handbook of motivation and cognition: Foundations of social behavior*, 145–164. New York: Guilford.

Brett, Jeanne M., Catherine H. Tinsley, Maddy Janssens, Zoe I. Barsness, & Anne L. Lytle
In Press   "New approaches to the study of culture I/O psychology." In P. C. Earley & M. Erez (Eds.), *New perspectives on international/organizational psychology*. San Francisco: Jossey-Bass.

Brockner, Joel, Steven Grover, Michael O'Malley, Thomas Reed, et al.
1993   "Threat of future layoffs, self-esteem, and survivors' reactions: Evidence from the laboratory and the field." *Strategic Management Journal*, 14:153–166.

Brown, B. R.
1968   "The effects of need to maintain face in interpersonal bargaining." *Journal of Experimental Social Psychology*, 4:107–122.

Brown, B. R., & H. Garland
1976   "Constituency communication, concession-making, and face-saving in a bilateral monopoly bargaining situation." Unpublished manuscript, Rutgers University.

Brown, Paula, & Stewart Levinson
1978 "Universals in language use." In E. N. Goody (Ed.), *Questions and politeness*, 56–289. Cambridge: Cambridge University Press.

Campbell, J.
1964 *Honour, family, and patronage*. Oxford: Clarendon Press.

Cantor, N., & J. F. Kihlstrom
1987 *Personality and social intelligence*. Englewood Cliffs, NJ: Prentice Hall.

Carver, Charles S., & Martin F. Scheier
1990 "Origins and functions of positive and negative effect: A control-process view." *Psychological Review*, 97:19–35.

Carver, Charles S., & Martin F. Scheier
1981 *Attention and self-regulation: A control theory approach to human behavior*. New York: Springer-Verlag.

Chakraborty, S. K.
1993 *Managerial transformation by values: A corporate pilgrimage*. New Delhi: Sage.

Chang, Hui-Ching, & G. Richard Holt
1994 "A Chinese perspective on face as inter-relational concern." In Stella Ting-Toomey (Ed.), *The Challenge of Facework: Cross-cultural and interpersonal issues*, 95–132. Albany: State University of New York Press.

Chen, Chao C.
1995 "New trends in reward allocation preferences: A Sino-U.S. comparison." *Academy of Management Journal*, 38:408–428.

Chen, Chao, James Meindl, & James Hunt
1996 "Tradition and change: Cultural adaptation in China." Unpublished manuscript.

Clegg, S. R.
1981 "Organization and control." *Administrative Science Quarterly*, 26:545–562.

Clegg, S. R.
1977 "Power, organizational theory, Marx, and critique." In S. Clegg & D. Dunkerley (Eds.), *Critical issues in organizations*, 21–40. London: Routledge and Kegan Paul.

Coch, L., & J. R. P. French
1948 "Overcoming resistance to change." *Human Relations*, 1:512–532.

Collins, R.
1988 "The micro contribution to macro sociology." *Sociological Theory*, 6:242–253.

Conger, J. A., & R. Kanungo
1987 "Toward a behavioral theory of charismatic leadership in organizational settings." *Academy of Management Review*, 12:637–647.

Cook, Karen S.
1987 *Social exchange theory*. Beverly Hills, CA: Sage.

Cook, K. S., & Mary R. Gillmore
1984 "Power, dependence and coalitions." In E. Lawler (Ed.), *Advances in group processes*, 1:27–58. Greenwich, CT: JAI Press.

Coser, L. A., C. Kadushin, & W. W. Powell
1982 *Books: The culture and commerce of publishing*. New York: Basic Books.

Cushman, P.
1990 "Why the self is empty: Toward a historically situated psychology." *American Psychologist*, 45:599–611.

Cyert, R. M., & J. G. March
1963 *A behavioral theory of the firm.* Englewood Cliffs, NJ: Prentice Hall.

D'Andrade, R.
1984 "Cultural meaning systems." In R. A. Shweder & R. A. Levine (Eds.), *Culture theory: Essays on mind, self, and emotion,* 65–129. Cambridge: Cambridge University Press.

Davis, Gerald F.
1991 "Agents without principles?: The spread of the poison pill through the intercorporate network." *Administrative Science Quarterly,* 36:583–613.

Delbeek, J. C., & J. Sprung
1994 *The reef aquarium: A comprehensive guide to the identification and care of tropical marine invertibrates.* Coconut Grove, FL: Ricordea Publications.

Deutsch, Morton
1975 "Equity, equality and need: What determines which value will be used as the basis of distributive justice." *Journal of Social Issues,* 31:137–149.

Deutsch, Morton
1973 *The resolution of conflict: Constructive and destructive processes.* New Haven, CT: Yale University Press.

Deutsch, Morton
1961 "The face of bargaining." *Operations Research,* 9:886–897.

DiMaggio, P. J., & W. W. Powell
1983 "The iron cage revisited: Institutional isomorphism and collective rationality in organizational fields." *American Sociological Review,* 48:147–160.

Donnenwerth, G. V., & U. G. Foa
1974 "Effects of resource class on retaliation to injustice in interpersonal exchange." *Journal of Personality and Social Psychology,* 29:785–793.

Durkheim, Emile
1933 *The division of labor in society.* G. Simpson, trans. New York: Free Press.

Earley, P. Christopher
1994 "The individual and collective self: An assessment of self efficacy and training across cultures." *Administrative Science Quarterly,* 39:89–117.

Earley, P. Christopher
1993 "East meets West meets Mideast: Further explorations of collectivistic and individualistic work groups." *Academy of Management Journal,* 36:319–348.

Earley, P. Christopher
1989 "Social loafing and collectivism: A comparison of United States and the People's Republic of China." *Administrative Science Quarterly,* 34:565–581.

Earley, P. Christopher, Cris Gibson, & Chao Chen
1996 "How did I do versus how did we do?: Cultural contrasts of performance feedback utilization and self-efficacy." Working paper, University of California, Irvine.

Earley, P. Christopher, & E. Allan Lind
1987 "Procedural justice and participation in task selection: Control-mediated effects of voice in procedural and task decisions." *Journal of Personality and Social Psychology,* 52:1148–1160.

Earley, P. Christopher, & T. R. Lituchy
1991 "Delineating goal and efficacy effects: A test of three models." *Journal of Applied Psychology,* 76:81–98.

Earley, P. Christopher, & Elaine Mosakowski
1995 "Experimental international management research." In B. J. Punnett & O. Shenkar (Eds.), *Handbook of international management research*, 83–114. London: Blackwell.

Earley, P. Christopher, & Harbir Singh
1995 "International and intercultural management research: What's next?" *Academy of Management Journal*, 38:327–340.

Eberhard, Wolfran
1967 *Guilt and sin in traditional China.* Berkeley: University of California Press.

Edelmann, R. J.
1990 *The psychology of embarrassment.* Chichester: John Wiley.

Edelmann, R. J., & S. E. Hampson
1979 "Changes in non-verbal behavior during embarrassment." *British Journal of Social and Clinical Psychology*, 18:385–390.

Eden, Dov
1984 "Self-fulfilling prophecy as a management tool: Harnessing Pygmalion." *Academy of Management Review*, 9:64–73.

Eden, Dov, & Gad Ravid
1982 "Pygmalion versus self-expectancy: Effects of instructor- and self-expectancy on trainee performance." *Organizational Behavior and Human Performance*, 30:351–364.

Eisenstadt, Jeanne W.
1970 "Interpersonal orientation, coping style, and two dimensions of sociometric choice." *Human Relations*, 23:515–531.

Eisenstadt, S. N.
1954 "Studies in reference group behavior: 1. Reference norms and the social structure." *Human Relations*, 7:191–216.

Ekeh, P. P.
1974 *Social exchange theory: The two traditions.* Cambridge, MA: Harvard University Press.

Emerson, Richard M.
1972 "Exchange theory, parts I and II." In J. Berger, M. Zelditch, & B. Anderson (Eds.), *Sociological theories in progress*, 2:38–87. Boston: Houghton Mifflin.

Emerson, Richard M.
1962 "Power-dependence relations." *American Sociological Review*, 27:31–41.

Emler, Nicholas, & Nicholas Hopkins
1990 "Reputation, social identity, and the self." In Dominic Abrams & Michael A. Hogg (Eds.), *Social identity theory: Constructive and critical advances*, 113–130. New York: Springer-Verlag.

Epstein, S.
1973 "The self-concept revisited, or a theory of a theory." *American Psychologist*, 28:408–416.

Erez, Miriam, & P. Christopher Earley
1993 *Culture, self-identity, and work.* New York: Oxford University Press.

Etzioni, Amitai
1973 *Genetic fix: The next technological revolution.* New York: Free Press.

Etzioni, Amitai
1968 *The active society.* New York: Free Press.

Farh, J. L., G. H. Dobbins, & B. S. Cheng
1991 "Cultural relativity in action: A comparison of self-ratings made by Chinese and U.S. workers." *Personnel Psychology,* 44:129–147.

Farh, J. L., P. C. Earley, & S. C. Lin
In Press "Impetus for action: A cultural analysis of justice and organizational citizenship behavior in Chinese society." *Administrative Science Quarterly.*

Farh, J. L., P. M. Podsakoff, & D. W. Organ
1990 "Accounting for organizational citizenship behavior: Leader fairness and task scope versus satisfaction." *Journal of Management,* 16:705–721.

Festinger, Leon
1964 *Conflict, decision, and dissonance.* Stanford, CA: Stanford University Press.

Festinger, Leon
1957 *A theory of cognitive dissonance.* Evanston, IL: Row, Peterson.

Festinger, Leon
1954 "A theory of social comparison processes." *Human Relations,* 7:117–140.

Fisher, G.
1980 *International negotiations: A cross cultural perspective.* Chicago: Intercultural Press.

Fiske, Alan P.
1991 *Structures of social life: The four elementary forms of human relations: communal sharing, authority ranking, equality matching, market pricing.* New York: Free Press.

Foa, Edna B., & Uriel G. Foa
1976 "Resource theory of social exchange." In J. W. Thibaut, T. T. Spence, & R. C. Carson (Eds.), *Contemporary topics in social psychology.* Morristown: General Learning.

Foa, Uriel G., John Converse Jr., Kjell Y. Tornblom, & Edna B. Foa
1993 *Resource theory: Explorations and applications.* San Diego: Academic Press.

Foa, Uriel G., & Edna B. Foa
1974 *Societal structures of the mind.* Springfield, IL: Charles C. Thomas.

Foa, Uriel G., H. Glaubman, M. Garner, Kjell Y. Tornblom, & L. N. Salcedo
1987 "Interrelation of social resources: Evidence of pancultural invariance." *Journal of Cross-Cultural Psychology,* 18:221–233.

Fogel, D. S., & Suzanne Etcheverry.
1994 "Reforming the enonomies of central and eastern Europe." In D. S. Fogel (Ed.), *Managing in emerging market economies,* 3–33. Boulder, CO: Westview Press.

Frank, J. D.
1973 *Persuasion and healing: A comparative study of psychotherapy,* rev. ed. Baltimore, MD: Johns Hopkins University Press.

Freeman, J.
1982 "Organizational life cycles and natural selection processes." *Research in Organizational Behavior,* 4:1–32.

French, J. R. P., & B. Raven
1959 "The bases of social power." In D. Cartwright (Ed.), *Studies in social power,* 150–167. Ann Arbor: Institute for Social Research, University of Michigan.

Freud, S.
1930 *Civilization and its discontents.* Joan Riviere, trans. New York: Cope and H. Smith.

Gabrenya, William K., Jr.
1988 "Social science and social psychology: The cross-cultural link." In Michael H. Bond (Ed.), *The cross-cultural challenge to social psychology,* 48–66. Newbury Park, CA: Sage.

Galaskiewicz, Joseph, & Stanley Wasserman
1989 "Mimetic processes within an interorganizational field: An empirical test." *Administrative Science Quarterly,* 34:454–479.

Galbraith, Jeffrey
1973 *Designing complex organizations.* Menlo Park, CA: Addison-Wesley.

Garbarino, M.
1976 *Native American heritage.* Boston: Little, Brown.

Garfinkel, H.
1967 *Studies in ethnomethodology.* Englewood Cliffs, NJ: Prentice Hall.

Gecas, V.
1982 "The self concept." *Annual Review of Psychology,* 8:1–33.

Geertz, Clifford
1973 *The interpretation of cultures.* New York: Basic Books.

Gersick, Connie J. G.
1988 "Time and transition in work teams: Toward a new model of group development." *Academy of Management Journal,* 31:9–41.

Gersick, C. J. G., & J. R. Hackman
1990 "Habitual routines in task-performing groups." *Organizational Behavior and Human Decision Processes,* 47:65–97.

Ghoshal, S., & C. B. Bartlett
1990 "The multinational corporation as an interorganizational network." *Academy of Management Review,* 15:603–625.

Ghoshal, S., & E. Westney
1993 *Organization theory and the multinational corporation.* New York: St. Martin's Press.

Gibson, Cristina
1995 "The determinants and consequences of group-efficacy in work organizations in U.S., Hong Kong, and Indonesia." Ph.D. dissertation, University of California, Irvine.

Giddens, Anthony
1989 *The structure of social action.* Cambridge: Cambridge University Press.

Giddens, Anthony
1984 *The constitution of society.* Cambridge: Polity.

Gillmore, Mary R.
1983 "Structural determinants of coalition formation: Sources of solidarity." Ph. D. dissertation, University of Washington, Seattle.

Ginzel, L. E., R. M. Kramer, & R. I. Sutton
1993 "Organizational impression management as a reciprocal influence process: The neglected role of the organizational audience." In L. L. Cummings & B. M. Staw (Eds.), *Research in organizational behavior,* 15:227–266. Greenwich, CT: JAI Press.

Girvetz, H. K.
1973 *Beyond right and wrong: A study in moral theory.* New York: Free Press.

Gleick, James
1987   *Chaos: Making a new science.* New York: Viking.

Glenn, E. S., & C. G. Glenn
1981   *Man and mankind: Conflicts and communications between cultures.* Norwood: Ablex.

Goffman, Erving
1974   *Frame analysis: An essay on the organization of experience.* New York: Harper and Row.

Goffman, Erving
1967   *Interaction ritual: Essays in face-to-face behavior.* Chicago: Aldine.

Goffman, Erving
1959   *The presentation of self in everyday life.* Garden City, NY: Doubleday.

Graen, G. B.
1976   "Role-making processes within complex organizations." In M. D. Dunnette (Ed.), *Handbook of industrial and organizational psychology,* 1103–1181. Chicago: Rand McNally.

Graham, John. L.
1985   "The influence of culture on the process of business negotiations: An exploratory study." *Journal of International Business Studies,* 16:79–94.

Graham, John L., D. K. Kim, C. Y. Lin, & M. Robinson
1988   "Buyer-seller negotiations around the Pacific Rim: Differences in fundamental exchange processes." *Journal of Consumer Research,* 14:48–54.

Graham, John L., & Yoshihiro Sano
1984   *Smart bargaining: Doing business with the Japanese.* Cambridge: Ballinger.

Granovetter, M.
1985   "Economic action and social structure: The problem of embeddedness." *American Journal of Sociology,* 91:481–510.

Greenberg, J.
1982   "Self-image versus impression management in adherence to distributive justice standards: The influence of self-awareness and self-consciousness." *Journal of Personality and Social Psychology,* 44:5–19.

Greenberg, Jerald, & Robert Folger
1983   "Procedural justice, participation, and the fair process effect in groups and organizations." In P. Paulus (Ed.), *Basic group processes,* 235–256. New York: Springer-Verlag.

Gudykunst, W. B., S. Ting-Toomey, & E. Chua
1988   *Culture and interpersonal communication.* Beverly Hills, CA: Sage.

Gullestad, Siri E.
1993   "A contribution to the psychoanalytic concept of autonomy." *Scandinavian Psychoanalytic Review,* 16:22–34.

Hackman, J. R.
1990   "Introduction." In J. R. Hackman (Ed.), *Groups that work (and those that don't),* 1–18. San Francisco: Jossey-Bass.

Hackman, J. R., & G. R. Oldham
1980   *Work redesign.* Reading, MA: Addison-Wesley.

Hahn, F. H.
1984   *Equilibrium and macroeconomics.* Oxford: Blackwell.

Haire, M., E. E. Ghiselli, & L. W. Porter
1966. *Managerial thinking: An international study.* New York: Wiley.

Hall, Edward T.
1959 *The silent language.* New York: Anchor Press.

Hannan, M., & J. Freeman
1977 "The population ecology of organizations." *American Journal of Sociology,* 82:929–940.

Harkins, S. G., & R. E. Petty
1983 "Social context effects in persuasion." In P. B. Paulus (Ed.), *Basic group processes,* 147–178. New York: Springer-Verlag.

Harnett, David L., & Larry L. Cummings
1980 *Bargaining behavior: An international study.* Houston: Dame Publishers.

Hedlund, G.
1991 "Managing international business: A Swedish model." In M. Maccoby (Ed.), *Sweden at the edge,* 201–220. Philadelphia: University of Pennsylvania Press.

Herskovits, M. J.
1955 *Cultural anthropology.* New York: Knopf.

Herzberg, Frederick
1966 *Work and the nature of man.* Cleveland, OH: World Publishing Company.

Hick, John
1967 "Christianity." In Paul Edwards (Ed.), *The encyclopedia of philosophy,* 2:104–109. New York: Macmillan.

Hinkle, Steve, & Rupert J. Brown
1990 "Intergroup comparisons and social identity: Some links and lacunae." In Dominic Abrams & Michael A. Hogg (Eds.), *Social identity theory: Constructive and critical advances,* 48–70. New York: Springer-Verlag.

Hitson, Hazel M.
1959 *Family patterns and paranoidal personality structure in Boston and Burma.* Cambridge, MA: Radcliff College.

Ho, David Yau-Fai
1976 "On the concept of face." *American Journal of Sociology,* 81:867–884.

Ho, E. K. F.
1994 "Validating the five-factor model of personality." B. A. thesis, Chinese University of Hong Kong.

Hoelter, J. W.
1985 "The structure of self-conception: Conceptualization and measurement." *Journal of Personality and Social Psychology,* 49:1392–1407.

Hofstede, Geert
1991 *Culture and organizations: Software of the mind.* London: McGraw-Hill.

Hofstede, Geert
1984 "The cultural relativity of the quality of life concept." *Academy of Management Review,* 9:389–398.

Hofstede, Geert
1983 "The cultural relativity of organizational practices and theories." *Journal of International Business Studies,* 14:75–89.

Hofstede, Geert
1980a *Culture's consequences: International differences in work related values.* Newbury Park, CA: Sage.

Hofstede, Geert
1980b "Motivation, leadership, and organization: Do American theories apply abroad?" *Organizational Dynamics* (Summer): 42–63.

Hofstede, Geert, & Michael H. Bond
1988 "The Confucius connection: From cultural roots to economic growth." *Organizational Dynamics* (Spring): 4–21.

Holda, D., & Z. Cermakova
1980 "Sociological research into value orientation." *Sociologicky Casopis,* 16:90–101.

Holland, J.
1973 *Making vocational choices: A theory of careers.* Englewood Cliffs, NJ: Prentice Hall.

Homans, George C.
1961 *Social behavior: Its elementary forms.* New York: Harcourt Brace and World.

Homans, George C.
1958 "Social behavior as exchange." *American Journal of Sociology,* 63:597–606.

House, Robert J., & Denise Rousseau
1990 "On the bifurcation of OB or if it ain't meso it ain't OB." Working paper, the Wharton School, University of Pennsylvania.

Howard, R.
1986 *Brave new workplace.* New York: Penguin Books.

Hu, Hsien C.
1944 "The Chinese concepts of 'Face.' " *American Anthropologist,* 46 (January–March): 45–64.

Hui, C. C.
1984 Individualism-collectivism: Theory, measurement, and its relation to reward allocation." Ph. D. dissertation, University of Illinois, Champaign.

Hui, C. H., & Harry C. Triandis
1985 "Measurement in cross-cultural psychology." *Journal of Cross-Cultural Psychology,* 16:131–152.

Huston, Ted L., Gilbert Geis, & Richard Wright
1976 "The angry Samaritans." *Psychology Today* (June): 61–85.

Hwang, Kwang-kuo
1987 "Face and favor: The Chinese power game." *American Journal of Sociology,* 92 (4):944–974.

Jackson, Susan E., et al.
1992 *Diversity in the workplace: Human resources initiatives.* New York: Guilford.

Jahoda, Gustav
1988 "J'Accuse." In Michael H. Bond (Ed.), *The cross-cultural challenge to social psychology,* 86–95. Newbury Park, CA: Sage.

Jahoda, Gustav
1984 "Do we need a concept of culture?" *Journal of Cross-Cultural Psychology,* 15(2):139–152.

Jahoda, Gustav
1980   "Theoretical and systematic approaches in cross-cultural psychology." In H. C. Triandis & W. W. Lanbert (Eds.), *Handbook of cross-cultural psychology,* 1:69–142. Boston: Allyn and Bacon.

James, L. R., S. A. Mulaik, & J. M. Brett
1982   *Causal analysis: Assumptions, models, and data.* Beverly Hills, CA: Sage.

Jones, Edward E.
1964   *A social psychological analysis.* New York: Appleton.

Jones, Edward E., & T. S. Pittman
1980   "Toward a general theory of strategic self-presentation." In J. Suls (Ed.), *Psychological perspectives on the self,* 1:231–262. Hillsdale, NJ: Erlbaum.

Jonsson, B.
1991   "Production philosophy at Volvo." In M. Maccoby (Ed.), *Sweden at the edge,* 123–149. Philadelphia: University of Pennsylvania Press.

Kahreman, D., & A. Tversky
1984   "Choices, values, and frames." *American Psychologist,* 39:341–350.

Kanfer, F. H.
1980   "Self-management methods." In F. H. Kanfer & A. P. Goldstein (Eds.), *Helping people change,* 2nd ed., 334–389. New York: Pergamon Press.

Kanfer, Ruth, & P. L. Ackerman
1989   "Motivation and cognitive abilities: An integrative/aptitude-treatment interaction approach to skill acquisition." *Journal of Applied Psychology,* 74:657–690.

Kanter, R. M.
1989   *When giants learn to dance.* New York: Simon and Schuster.

Kanter, R. M.
1972   *Commitment and community.* Cambridge, MA: Harvard University Press.

Katriel, T.
1986   *Talking straight: Dugri speech in Israeli Sabra culture.* Cambridge: Cambridge University Press.

Katz, D., & R. L. Kahn
1978   *The social psychology of organizations,* 2nd ed. New York: Wiley.

Kelley, H. H., & J. W. Thibaut
1978   *Interpersonal relations: A theory of Interdependence.* New York: Wiley.

Kerr, N.
1983   "Motivation losses in small groups: A social dilemma analysis." *Journal of Personality and Social Psychology,* 45:819–828.

Khandwalla, P. A.
1987   *Organizational behaviour research in India: A review.* Ahmedabad, India: Indian Institute of Management.

Kiesler, Sara, Jane Siegel, & Timothy McGuire
1984   "Social psychological aspects of computer-mediated communication." *American Psychologist,* 39:1123–1134.

Kihlstrom, J. F., & N. Cantor
1984   "Mental representations of the self." In L. Berkowitz (Ed.), *Advances in experimental social psychology,* 17:2–48. New York: Academic Press.

Kihlstrom, J. F., N. Cantor, J. S. Albright, B. R. Chew, S. B. Klein, & P. M. Niedenthal
1988 "Information processing and the study of the self." In L. Berkowitz (Ed.), *Advances in experimental social psychology,* 21:145–178. New York: Academic Press.

King, Y. C.
1989 "Mien, 'shame,' and the analysis of Chinese behavior." In K. S. Yang (Ed.), *The psychology of the Chinese.* Taipei: Kui-Kuan Books. (In Chinese.)

Kipnis, David & Stuart Schmidt
1983 "An influence perspective on bargaining." In M. Bozerman & R. Lewick (Eds.), *Negotiating in organizations,* 303–319. Beverly Hills, CA: Sage.

Klein, Howard J.
1989 "An integrated control theory model of work motivation." *Academy of Management Review,* 14:150–172.

Klein, Katherine, Fred Dansereau, & Rosalie Hall
1994 "Level issues in theory development, data collection, and analysis." *Academy of Management Review,* 19:195–229.

Kluckhohn, Florence, & Frederick Strodtbeck
1961 *Variations in value orientation.* Westport, CT: Greenwood Press.

Kohlberg, L.
1969 "Stage and sequence: The cognitive developmental approach to socialization." In
D. A. Goslin (Ed.), *Handbook of socialization theory and research,* 347–480. Chicago: Rand McNally.

Krackhardt, David, & Lyman W. Porter
1986 "The snowball effect: Turnover embedded in communication networks." *Journal of Applied Psychology,* 71:50–55.

Kramer, Roderick
1991 "Intergroup relations and organizational dilemmas: The role of categorization processes." In L. L. Cummings & B. M. Staw (Eds.), *Research in organizational behavior,* 13:191–228. Greenwich, CT: JAI Press.

Kraut, A. I., & S. Ronen
1975 "Validity of job facet importance: A multinational, multicriteria study." *Journal of Applied Psychology,* 60:671–677.

Kumar, Rajesh
1994 "Communication conflict in intercultural negotiations: The case of American and Japanese business negotiations." Working paper, Pennsylvania State University.

Kunda, Z.
1987 "Motivated inference: Self-serving generation and evaluation of causal theories." *Journal of Personality and Social Psychology,* 53:636–647.

Lachman, R.
1983 "Modernity change of core and periphery values of factory workers." *Human Relations,* 36:563–580.

Lane, H. W., & J. J. DiStephano
1992 "The impact of culture on management." In *International management behavior,* 2nd ed., 17–58. Boston: PWS Kent Publishing.

Latane, G., K. D. Williams, & S. Harkins
1979 "Many hands make light the work: The causes and consequences of social loafing." *Journal of Personality and Social Psychology,* 32:822–832.

Lawler, E. J., & S. B. Bacharach
1979   "Power dependence in individual bargaining: The expected utility of influence." *Industrial and Labor Relations Review,* 32:196–204.

Lawman, Edward, Joseph Galaskiewicz, & Peter Marsden
1978   "Community structure as organizational linkage." *Annual Review of Sociology,* 4:455–484.

Lazarus, Richard S., & Bernice N. Lazarus
1994   *Passion and reason: Making sense of our emotions.* New York: Oxford University Press.

Leung, Kwok, & Michael Bond
1989   "On the empirical identification of dimensions for cross-cultural comparison." *Journal of Cross-Cultural Psychology,* 20:133–151.

Leung, Kwok, & Michael Bond
1984   "The impact of cultural collectivism on reward allocation." *Journal of Personality and Social Psychology,* 47:793–804.

Leung, Kwok, Michael Bond, & S. Schwartz
1990   "The role of expectancies and values in predicting justice behaviors in two cultures." Paper presented at the International Congress of Applied Psychology, Kyoto, Japan.

Leung, Kwok, & H. Park
1986   "Effects of interactional goal on choice of allocation rule: A cross-national study." *Organizational Behavior and Human Decision Processes,* 37:111–120.

Levi-Strauss, C.
1969   *The elementary structures of kinship,* rev. ed. Boston: Beacon.

Levy, R.
1973   *The Tahitians.* Chicago: University of Chicago Press.

Lewin, K.
1951   *Field theory and social science.* New York: Harper.

Li, Dun J.
1978   *The ageless Chinese: A history,* 3rd ed. New York: Charles Scribner's Sons.

Li, Dun J.
1975   *The civilization of China.* New York: Scribner.

Lim, Tae-Seop
1994   "Facework and interpersonal relationships." In Stella Ting-Toomey (Ed.), *The challenge of facework: Cross-cultural and interpersonal issues,* 209–229. Albany: State University of New York Press.

Lin, Yu-tang
1939   *My country and my people.* New York: Reynal and Hitchcock.

Lind, E. Allan, & Tom R. Tyler
1988   *The social psychology of procedural justice.* New York: Plenum.

Liska, Allan E.
1992   *Social threat and social control.* Albany: State University of New York Press.

Loasby, Brian J.
1991   *Equilibrium and evolution.* New York: Manchester University Press.

Locke, E. A., & P. G. Latham
1990   *A theory of goal setting and task performance.* Englewood Cliffs, NJ: Prentice Hall.

Lord, R. G., & M. C. Kernan
1990   "M&A demographics of the decade: The top 100 deals of the decade." *Mergers & Acquisitions,* 25:107–112.

Lord, R. G., & M. C. Kernan
1987   "Scripts as determinants of purposeful behavior in organizations." *Academy of Management Review,* 12:265–277.

Lynd, H.
1958   *On shame and the search for identity.* New York: Harcourt Brace.

Lytle, A., J. M. Brett, Z. I. Barsness, C. H. Tinsley, & M. Janssens
1995   "A paradigm for confirmatory cross-cultural research in organizational behavior." In B. M. Staw & L. L. Cummings (Eds.), *Research in organizational behavior,* 17:167–214. Greenwich, Ct: JAI Press.

Maccoby, M. (Ed.)
1991   *Sweden at the edge.* Philadelphia: University of Pennsylvania Press.

Machann, C.
1991   "The 'ethnic situation' in Czechoslovakia after the revolution of November 1989." *Journal of Ethnic Studies,* 18:135–141.

Maehr, M. L., & L. A. Braskamp
1986   *The motivation factor: A theory of personal investment.* Lexington, MA: Lexington Books.

Markus, Hazel, & S. Kitayama
1991   "Culture and the self: Implications for cognition, emotion, and motivation." *Psychological Review,* 98:224–253.

Markus, Hazel, & Ziva Kunda
1986   "Stability and malleability of the self-concept." *Journal of Personality and Social Psychology,* 51:858–866.

Markus, Hazel, & E. Wurf
1987   "The dynamic self-concept: A social psychological perspective." *Annual Review of Psychology,* 38:299–337.

Marriot, M.
1977   "Changing identities in South Asia." In K. A. David (Ed.), *The new wind: Changing identities in South Asia,* 120–152. Chicago: Aldine.

Marsella, Anthony J.
1994   "The measurement of emotional reactions to work: Conceptual, methodological, and research issues." *Work and Stress,* 8:153–176.

Marsh, H.
1986   "Global self-esteem: Its relation to specific facets of self-concept and their importance." *Journal of Personality and Social Psychology,* 51:1224–1236.

Martin, Joanne
1992   *Cultures in organizations: Three perspectives.* New York: Oxford University Press.

McCrae, R. R., & P. T. Costa, Jr.
1987   "Validation of the five-factor model of personality across instruments and observers." *Journal of Personality and Social Psychology,* 52:81–90.

McCrae, R. R., & P. T. Costa, Jr.
1985   "Updating Norman's 'adequate taxonomy': Intelligence and personality dimensions in natural language and in questionnaires." *Journal of Personality and Social Psychology,* 49:710–721.

McGregor, J. P.
1991 "Value structures in a developed socialist system: The case of Czechoslovakia." *Comparative Politics,* 23:181–200.

McKelvey, Bill
1982 *Organizational systematics: Taxonomy, evolution, classification.* Berkeley: University of California Press.

Mead, George H.
1934 *Mind, self, and society.* Chicago: University of Chicago Press.

Mead, M.
1928 *Coming of age in Samoa.* New York: Morrow Paperback Editions.

Mead, M.
1967 *Cooperation and competition among primitive people.* Boston: Beacon.

Meindl, J. R., R. G. Hunt, & W. Lee
1989 "Individualism-collectivism and work values: Data from the United States, China, Taiwan, Korea, and Hong Kong." *Research in Personnel and Human Resources Management,* suppl. 1:59–77.

Merton, R. K.
1968 *Social theory and social structure.* New York: Free Press.

Messick, D. M.
1988 "On the limitations of cross-cultural research in social psychology." In M. H. Bond (Ed.), *The cross-cultural challenge to social psychology,* 41–47. Newbury Park, CA: Sage.

Messick, D. M., & D. M. Mackie
1989 "Intergroup relations." *Annual Review of Psychology,* 40:45–81.

Meyer, J., & B. Rowan
1977 "Institutional organizations: Formal structures as myth and ceremony." *American Journal of Sociology,* 83:340–363.

Miller, D.
1990 *The Icarus paradox.* New York: Harper-Collins.

Mischel, W.
1973 "Toward a cognitive social learning reconceptualization of personality." *Psychological Review,* 80(4):252–283.

Misumi, J.
1984 "Decision-making in Japanese groups and organizations." In B. Wilpert & A. Sorge (Eds.), *International perspectives on organizational democracy,* 92–123. New York: Wiley.

Morris, C. W.
1956 *Varieties of human value.* Chicago: University of Chicago Press.

Morrison, E. W., & R. J. Bies
1991 "Impression management in the feedback seeking process: A literature review and research agenda." *Academy of Management Review,* 16:522–541.

Mosakowski, Elaine
In Press "Strategy making under causal ambiguity." *Organization Science.*

Mulder, Mauk
1977 *The daily power game.* Leiden: Martinus Nijhoff Social Sciences Division.

Murdock, G. P.
1957 "World ethnographic sample." *American Anthropologist,* 59:664–687.

Murdock, G. P.
1945 "The common denominator of cultures." In R. Linton (Ed.), *The science of man in the world of crisis,* 123–142. New York: Columbia University Press.

Murphy-Berman, V., J. Berman, P. Singh, A. Pachuri, & P. Kumar
1984 "Factors affecting allocation to needy and meritorious recipients: A cross-cultural comparison." *Journal of Personality and Social Psychology,* 46:1267–1272.

Myers, C. A.
1960 *Industrial relations in India.* Bombay: Asia Publishing.

Nath, R., & J. Jirasek
1994 "Transformation management in Czechoslovakia." In D. S. Fogel (Ed.), *Managing in emerging market economies,* 69–84. Boulder, CO: Westview Press.

Neale, Margaret A., & Max H. Bazerman
1991 *Cognition and rationality in negotiation.* New York: Free Press.

Nelson, R. R., & S. G. Winter
1982 *An evolutionary theory of economic change.* Cambridge, MA: Harvard University Press.

Newman, W. H.
1992 *Birth of a successful joint venture.* Lanham: University Press.

Ng, S. H.
1982 "Power and intergroup discrimination." In H. Tajfel (Ed.), *Social identity and intergroup relations,* 83–117. Cambridge, MA: Cambridge University Press.

Norman, W. T.
1963 "Toward an adequate taxonomy of personality attributes: Replicated factor structure in peer nomination personality ratings." *Journal of Abnormal and Social Psychology,* 66:574–583.

North, D. C.
1990 *Institutions, institutional change, and economic performance.* Cambridge: Press Syndicate of the University of Cambridge.

North, D. C.
1989 "Institutional change and economic history." *Journal of Institutional and Theoretical Economics,* 145:230–237.

Northcraft, Greg, & Susan Ashford
1990 "The preservation of self in everyday life: The effects of performance expectations and feedback context on feedback inquiry." *Organizational Behavior and Human Decision Processes,* 47:42–64.

Northcraft, Greg, & P. Christopher Earley
1989 "Technology, credibility, and feedback use." *Organizational Behavior and Human Decision Processes,* 44:83–96.

Oakes, P. J., & J. C. Turner
1980 "Social categorisation and intergroup bias: Does minimal intergroup discrimination make social identify more positive?" *European Journal of Social Psychology,* 10:259–301.

Oliver, Christine
1991 "Strategic responses to institutional processes." *Academy of Management Review,* 16:145–179.

Olson, M.
1965 *The logic of collective action.* Cambridge, MA: Harvard University Press.

O'Reilly, C., & J. Chatman
1994 "Working smarter and harder: A longitudinal study of managerial success." *Administrative Science Quarterly,* 39:603–627.

Organ, D. W.
1987 *Organizational citizenship behavior: The good soldier syndrome.* Lexingon, MA: Lexington Books.

Orru, M., N. W. Biggart, & G. G. Hamilton
1991 "Organizational isomorphism in East Asia." In W. W. Powell & P. J. DiMaggio (Eds.), *The new institutionalism in organizational analysis,* 361–389. Chicago: University of Chicago Press.

Osgood, C. E.
1974 "Probing subjective cultures, parts 1 and 2." *Journal of Communication,* 24:21–34, 82–100.

Ostroff, Cheri
1993 "Comparing correlations based on individual-level and aggregated data." *Journal of Applied Psychology,* 78:569–582.

Ouchi, William G.
1980 "Markets, bureaucracies, and clans." *Administrative Science Quarterly,* 25:129–141.

Parsons, Talcott
1977 *The evolution of societies.* Englewood Cliffs, NJ: Prentice Hall.

Parsons, Talcott, & Edward A. Shils
1951 *Toward a general theory of action.* Cambridge, MA: Harvard University Press.

Pearce, Jone
1993 "Toward an organizational behavior of contract laborers: Their psychological involvement and effects on employee coworkers." *Academy of Management Journal,* 36:1082–1096.

Pearce, Jone, & M. Cakrt
1994 "Ferox Manufactured Products and Air Products and Chemicals: A joint venture." In D. S. Fogel (Ed.), *Managing in emerging market economies,* 85–102. Boulder, CO: Westview Press.

Pelto, J. J.
1968 "The difference between 'tight' and 'loose' societies." *Transaction,* April, 37–40.

Pelto, P. J.
1966 *The nature of anthropology.* Columbus, OH: Merrill Books.

Penman, R.
1994 "Facework in communication: Conceptual and moral challenges." In Stella Ting-Toomey (Ed.), *The challenge of facework: Cross-cultural and interpersonal issues,* 15–45. Albany: State University of New York Press.

Perrow, Charles
1972 *Complex organizations: A critical essay.* Glenview, IL: Scott, Foresman.

Pfeffer, J.
1992 *Managing with power: Politics and influence in organizations.* Boston: Harvard Business School Press.

Pfeffer, J.
1981 *Power in organizations.* Boston: Pitman.

Pfeffer, J., & G. R. Salancik
1978 *The external control of organizations.* New York: Harper and Row.

Piers, Gerhart, & Milton B. Singer
1971 *Shame and guilt: A psychoanalytic and cultural study.* New York: W. W. Norton.

Pitt-Rivers, J.
1954 *The People of the Sierra.* New York: Criterion Books.

Piven, F. F., & R. A. Cloward
1971 *Regulating the poor: The functions of public welfare.* New York: Pantheon.

Powell, W. W., & P. J. DiMaggio
1991 *The new institutionalism in organizational analysis.* Chicago: University of Chicago Press.

Powers, W. T.
1973 *Behavior: The control of perception.* Chicago: Aldine.

Pugh, D. S., & R. Payne.
1976 *Organizational behavior in its context: The Aston programme III.* Farnborough, Hants: Saxon House.

Pye, Lucien
1982 *Negotiating with the Chinese.* Santa Monica, CA: Rand Corporation.

Rawls, John
1971 *A theory of justice.* Cambridge, MA: Harvard University Press.

Redding, S. Gordon, & Michael Ng
1982 "The role of 'Face' in the organizational perceptions of Chinese managers." *Organization Studies,* 3(3):201–219.

Resaldo, Renata
1989 *Culture and truth.* Boston: Beacon.

Richardson, Kenneth D., & Robert B. Cialdini
1981 "Basking and blasting: Tactics of indirect self-presentation." In James T. Tedeschi (Ed.), *Impression management theory and social psychology research,* 41–53. New York: Academic Press.

Robbins, R. H.
1973 "Identity, culture, and behavior." In J. Honigmann (Ed.), *Handbook of social and cultural anthropology,* 1199–1222. Chicago: Rand McNally.

Rogers, T. P., N. A. Kuiper, & W. S. Kirker
1977 "Self-reference and encoding of personal information." *Journal of Personality and Social Psychology,* 35:677–688.

Rohner, R. P.
1984 "Toward a conception of culture for cross-cultural psychology." *Journal of Cross-Cultural Psychology,* 15(2):111–138.

Rohner, R. P., & M. Chaki-Sircar
1988 *Women and children in a Bengali village.* Hanover, NH: University Press of New England.

Rokeach, M.
1973 *The nature of human values.* New York: Free Press.

Ronen, S.
1986 *Comparative and multinational management.* New York: Wiley.

Ronen, S.
1982 "Clustering countries on attitudinal dimensions: A review and synthesis." Paper presented at the 20th International Congress of Applied Psychology, Edinburgh, United Kingdom.

Ronen, S.
1978   "Personal values: A basis for work motivational set and work attitude." *Organizational Behavior and Human Performance,* 21:80–107.

Ronen, S., & O. Shenkar
1985   "Clustering countries on attitudinal dimensions: A review and synthesis." *Academy of Management Review,* 10:435–454.

Rosaldo, M. Z.
1984   "Toward an anthropology of self and feeling." In R. A. Shweder & R. A. Levine (Eds.), *Culture theory: Essays on mind, self, and emotion,* 137–157. New York: Cambridge University Press.

Rosener, Judy B.
1990   "Ways women lead." *Harvard Business Review,* 68:119–125.

Rousseau, Denise M.
1985   "Issues of level in organizational research: Multi-level and cross-level perspectives." *Research in Organizational Behavior,* 7:1–37.

Sampson, Edward E.
1989   "The challenge of social change for psychology: Globalization and psychology's theory of the person." *American Psychologist,* 44:914–921.

Sampson, Edward E.
1981   "Cognitive psychology as idealogy." *American Psychologist,* 36:730–743.

Sampson, Edward E.
1977   "Psychology and the American ideal." *Journal of Personality and Social Psychology,* 35:767–782.

Sandel, M. J.
1982   *Liberalism and the limits of justice.* Cambridge: Cambridge University Press.

Sarnoff, Irving
1966   *Society with tears,* 1st ed. New York: Citadel Press.

Schank, Roger, & Robert Abelson
1977   *Scripts, plans, goals, and understanding.* Hillsdale, NJ: Erlbaum.

Schein, E. H.
1985   *Organizational culture and leadership.* San Francisco: Jossey-Bass.

Schlenkar, B. R.
1982   "Translating actions into attitudes: An identity analytic approach to the explanation of social conduct." In L. Berkowitz (Ed.), *Advances in experimental social psychology,* 15:243–277. New York: Academic Press.

Schlenkar, B. R.
1980   *Impression management: The self-concept, social identity, and interpersonal relations.* Monterey, CA: Brooks/Cole.

Schneider, B.
1990   *Organization climate and culture.* San Francisco: Jossey-Bass.

Schneider, B.
1987   "The people make the place." *Personnel Psychology,* 40:437–453.

Schwartz, Shalom H.
1993   "Cultural dimensions of values: Toward an understanding of national differences." Unpublished paper.

Schwartz, Shalom H.
1992 "The universal content and structures of values: Theoretical advances and empirical tests in 20 countries." In M. P. Zanna (Ed.), *Advances in experimental social psychology,* 25:1–65. New York: Academic Press.

Schwartz, Shalom H., & W. Bilsky
1987 "Toward a universal psychological structure of human values." *Journal of Personality and Social Psychology,* 53:550–562.

Scott, W. R., & J. W. Meyer
1994 *Institutional environments and organizations: Structural complexity and individualism.* Thousand Oaks, CA: Sage.

Scott, W. R., & J. W. Meyer
1983 "The organization of societal sectors." In J. W. Meyer & W. R. Scott (eds.), *Organizational environments: Ritual and rationality,* 129–154. Beverly Hills, CA: Sage.

Segall, M. H.
1986 "Culture and behavior: Psychology in global perspective." *Annual Review of Psychology,* vol. 37, 153–162.

Segall, M. H.
1984 "More than we need to know about culture, but are afraid not to ask." *Journal of Cross-Cultural Psychology,* 15(2):153–162.

Selznick, Phillip
1957 *Leadership in administration: A sociological interpretation.* New York: Harper and Row.

Sherman, S. J., C. M. Judd, & B. Park
1989 "Social cognition." *Annual Review of Psychology,* 40:281–326.

Shweder, R. A., & R. A. Levine (Eds.)
1984 *Culture theory: Essays on mind, self and emotion.* Cambridge: Cambridge University Press.

Sinha, Jai B. P.
In Press "A cultural perspective on organizational behavior in India." In P. C. Earley & M. Erez (Eds.), *New perspectives on international/organizational psychology.* San Francisco: Jossey-Bass.

Sinha, Jai B. P.
1990 *Work culture in the Indian context.* New Delhi: Sage.

Skinner, B. F.
1953 *Science and human behavior.* New York: Macmillan.

Smart, Ninian
1967 "Buddhism." In Paul Edwards (Ed.), *The encyclopedia of philosophy,* 1:416–420. New York: Macmillan.

Smith, Adam
1759/1976 *The theory of moral sentiments.* D. D. Raphael & A. L. Macfie (Eds.). Oxford: Clarendon Press.

Smith, M. Brewster
1991 *Values, self, and society: Toward a humanist social psychology.* New Brunswick, NJ: Transaction Publishers.

Soon, Ang, Larry L. Cummings, Detmar Straub, & P. Christopher Earley
1993 "The effects of information technology and the perceived mood of the feedback giver on feedback seeking." *ISR: A Journal of the Institute of Management Sciences,* 4:240–261.

Staw, Barry, & Robert Sutton
1992   "Macro organizational psychology." In J. K. Murnighan (Ed.), *Social psychology in organizations: Advances in theory and research*, 350–384. Englewood Cliffs, NJ: Prentice Hall.

Steers, R. M., Yoo Keun Shin, & Gerardo Ungson
1989   *The chaebol: Korea's new industrial might.* New York: Harper and Row.

Stover, Leon E.
1962   " 'Face' and verbal analogues of interaction in Chinese culture: A theory of formalized social behavior based upon participant-observation of an upper-class Chinese household, together with a biographical study of the primary information." Ph.D. dissertation, Columbia University.

Stryker, Sheldon
1980   *Symbolic interactionism: A social structural version.* Menlo Park, CA: Benjamin/Cummings.

Tajfel, Henri
1982   "Social psychology of intergroup relations." *Annual Review of Psychology,* 33:1–39.

Tajfel, Henri
1978   *Differentiation between social groups: Studies in the social psychology of intergroup relations.* London: Academic Press.

Tajfel, Henri
1972   "Experiments in a vacuum." In J. Israel and H. Tajfel (Eds.), *The context of social psychology: A critical assessment,* 69–119. London: Academic Press.

Tajfel, Henri, C. Flament, M. G. Billig, & R. F. Bundy.
1971   "Social categorization and intergroup behavior." *European Journal of Social Psychology,* 1:149–177.

Tajfel, Henri, & J. C. Turner
1986   "The social identity theory of intergroup behaviour." In S. Worchel and W. G. Austin (Eds.), *Psychology of intergroup relations,* 7–24. Chicago: Nelson-Hall.

Tannenbaum, A. S., B. Kavcic, B. Rosner, M. Vianello, & G. Weiser
1974   *Hierarchy in organizations.* San Francisco: Jossey-Bass.

Tedeschi, James T.
1981   *Impression management theory and social psychology research.* New York: Academic Press.

Tedeschi, James T., & Marc Riess
1981   "Identities, the phenomenal self, and laboratory research." In James T. Tedeschi (Ed.), *Impression management theory and social psychology research,* 3–22. New York: Academic Press.

Thibaut, John W., & Howard H. Kelley
1959   *The social psychology of groups.* New York: Wiley.

Thibaut, John W., & Laurens Walker
1975   *Procedural justice: A psychological analysis.* Hillsdale, NJ: Erlbaum.

Ting-Toomey, Stella
1988   "Intercultural conflict styles: A face negotiation theory." In Y. Kim & W. Gudykunst (Eds.), *Theories in intercultural communication,* 213–235. Newbury Park, CA: Sage.

Ting-Toomey, Stella (Ed.)
1994   *The challenge of facework: Cross-cultural and interpersonal issues.* Albany: State University of New York Press.

Ting-Toomey, Stella, & B. Cocroft
1994 "Face and facework: Theoretical and research issues." In Stella Ting-Toomey (Ed.), *The challenge of facework: Cross-cultural and interpersonal issues,* 307–340. Albany: State University of New York Press.

Ting-Toomey, Stella, Ge Gao, Paula Trubinsky, Zhizhong Yang, Hak Soo Kim, Sung-Ling Lin, & Tsukasa Nishida
1991 "Culture, face maintenance, and styles of handling interpersonal conflict: A study in five cultures." *International Journal of Conflict Management,* 2(4):275–296.

Tjosvold, Dean
1983 "Social face in conflict: A critique." *International Journal of Group Tensions,* 13:49–64.

Tjosvold, Dean
1974 "Threat as a low-power person's strategy in bargaining: Social face and tangible outcomes." *International Journal of Group Tensions,* 4:494–510.

Tjosvold, Dean
1973 "The use of threat by low-power persons in bargaining." Ph.D. dissertation, University of Minnesota.

Tjosvold, Dean, & Ted L. Huston
1978 "Social face and resistance to compromise in bargaining." *Journal of Social Psychology,* 104:57–68.

Tolbert, Pamela, & Lynne Zucker
1983 "Institutional sources of change in the formal structure of organizations: The diffusion of civil service reform, 1880–1935." *Administrative Science Quarterly,* 28:22–39.

Tornblom, K. Y., D. Jonsson, & U. G. Foa
1985 "Nationality resource class and preferences among three allocation rules: Sweden vs. USA." *International Journal of Intercultural Relations,* 9:51–77.

Torr, Christopher
1988 *Equilibrium expectations and information: A study of the general theory and modern classical economics.* Boulder, CO: Westview Press.

Tosi, Henry
1992 *The environment/organization/person contingency model: A meso approach to the study of organizations.* Greenwich, CT: JAI Press.

Trafimow, D., Harry C. Triandis, & S. G. Goto
1991 "Some tests of the distinction between the private self and the collective self." *Journal of Personality and Social Psychology,* 60:649–655.

Treviño, Linda Klibe
1986 "Ethical decision-making in organizations." *Academy of Management Review,* 11:601–617.

Triandis, Harry C.
1995 *Individualism and collectivism.* Boulder, CO: Westview Press.

Triandis, Harry C.
1994 "Culture: Theoretical and methodological issues." In H. C. Triandis, M. D. Dunnette, & L. Hough (Eds.), *Handbook of industrial and organizational psychology,* 2nd ed. Palo Alto: Consulting Psychologists Press.

Triandis, Harry C.
1989a "Cross-cultural studies of individualism and collectivism." In J. Berman (Ed.), *Nebraska symposium on motivation,* 41–133. Lincoln: University of Nebraska Press.

Triandis, Harry C.
1989b   "A strategy for cross cultural research in social psychology." In Joseph P. Forgas & J. Michael Innes (Eds.), *Recent advances in social psychology,* 491–499. Amsterdam: Elsevier North-Holland.

Triandis, Harry C.
1972   *The analysis of subjective culture.* New York: Wiley.

Triandis, Harry C., & R. D. Albert
1987   "Cross-cultural perspectives." In F. M. Jablin, L. L. Putman, K. H. Roberts, & L. W. Porter (Eds.), *Handbook of organizational communication: An interdisciplinary perspective,* 264–95. Beverly Hills, CA: Sage.

Triandis, Harry C., & Dharm P. S. Bhawuk
In Press   "Culture theory and the meaning of relatedness." In P. C. Earley and M. Erez (Eds.), *New perspectives on international/organizational psychology.* San Francisco: Jossey-Bass.

Triandis, H. C., R. Bontempo, H. Betancourt, M. Bond, K. Leung, A. Brenes, J. Georgas, H. C. Hui, G. Narim, J. B. P. Singha, J. Verma, J. Spangenberg, H. Tonzard, & G. de Montmollin
1986   "The measurement of etic aspects of individualism and collectivism across cultures." *Australian Journal of Psychology,* 38:257–267.

Triandis, Harry C., R. Bontempo, M. J. Vilareal, A. Masaaki, & N. Lucca
1988   "Individualism and collectivism: Cross-cultural perspectives on self-ingroup relatonships." *Journal of Personality and Social Psychology,* 54:328–338.

Triandis, Harry C., C. McCusker, H. Betancourt, S. Iwao, K. Leung, J. M. Salazar, B. Setiadi, J. P. B. Sinha, H. Taizard, & Z. Zaleski
1993   "An emic-etic analysis of individualism-collectivism." *Journal of Cross-Cultural Psychology,* 24:366–383.

Tsui, Anne S., & S. Ashford
1991   "Reactions to demographic diversity: Similarity-attraction or self-regulation." *Academy of Management Best Paper Proceedings,* 240–244.

Tupes, E. C., & R. E. Christal
1961   "Recurrent personality factors based on trait ratings." In *USAF ASD Technical Report* (No. 61-97).

Turner, J. C.
1987   *Rediscovering the social group.* Oxford: Blackwell.

Turner, J. C.
1985   "Social categorization and the self-concept: A social-cognitive theory of group behavior." In E. J. Lawler (Ed.), *Advances in group processes: Theory and research,* 2:77–122. Greenwich, CT: JAI Press.

Turner, J. C., Edna B. Foa, & Uriel G. Foa
1971   "Interpersonal reinforcers: Classification, inter-relationship, and some differential properties." *Journal of Personality and Social Psychology,* 19:168–180.

Turner, J. C., M. A. Hogg, P. J. Oakes, S. D. Reicher, & M. Wetherell
1987   *Rediscovering the social group: A self-categorization theory.* Oxford: Blackwell.

Vanbeselaere, N.
1987   "The effects of dichotomous and crossed social categorization upon intergroup discrimination." *European Journal of Social Psychology,* 17:143–156.

Van Maanen, J., & E. H. Schein
1977   "Toward a theory of organizational socialization." In B. M. Staw (Ed.), *Research in organizational behavior,* 1:209–264. Greenwich, CT: JAI Press.

Varian, H. R.
1993   *Intermediate microeconomics,* 3rd ed. New York: W. W. Norton.

Von Mises, L.
1949   *Human action: A treatise on economics.* New Haven, CT: Yale University Press.

Vroom, Victor
1964   *Work and motivation.* New York: Wiley.

Wagner, John A., III, & Michael K. Moch
1986   "Individualism-collectivism: Concept and measure." *Group and Organization Studies,* 11:280–304.

Wapner, Seymour, & Jack Demick
1991   *Field dependence-independence: Cognitive style across the life span.* Hillsdale, NJ: Erlbaum.

Weber, M.
1904–1906/1958   *The Protestant ethic and the spirit of capitalism.* Talcott Parsons, trans. New York: Charles Scribner's Sons.

Weber, M.
1947   *The theory of social and economic organizations.* Talcott Parsons, trans. New York: Free Press.

Weick, Karl E.
1985   "Sources of order in underorganized systems: Themes in recent organizational theory." In Y. Lincoln (Ed.), *Organizational theory and inquiry: The paradigm revolution,* 106–136. Beverly Hills, CA: Sage.

Weick, Karl E.
1969   *The social psychology of organizing.* Reading, MA: Addison-Wesley.

Weldon, E., & G. M. Gargano
1985   "Cognitive loafing: The effects of accountability and shared responsibility on cognitive effort." *Personality and Social Psychology Bulletin,* 14:159–171.

Westney, D. Eleanor
1993   "Cross-Pacific internationalization of R&D by U.S. and Japanese firms." *R & D Management,* 23:171–181.

Whitely, W., & G. W. England
1980   "Variability in common dimensions of managerial values due to value orientation and country differences." *Personnel Psychology,* 33:77–89.

Wholey, D. R., & J. Brittain
1989   "Characterizing environmental variation." *Academy of Management Journal,* 32:867–882.

Whyte, W. F.
1969   *Organizational behavior: Theory and application.* Homewood, IL: Dorsey Press.

Williamson, Oliver E.
1985   *The economic institutions of capitalism: Firms, markets, relational contracting.* New York: Free Press.

Williamson, Oliver E.
1981   "The modern corporation: Origin, evolution, attributes." *Journal of Economic Literature* 19:1537–1568.

Williamson, Oliver E.
1975   *Markets and hierarchies.* New York: Free Press.

Wilpert, B.
1984   "Participation in organizations: Evidence from international comparative research." *International Social Sciences Journal,* 36:355–366.

Wilson, James Q.
1993   *The moral sense.* New York: Free Press.

Wilson, Steven R.
1992   "Face and facework in negotiations." In L. L. Putnam & M. E. Roloff (Eds.), *Communication and negotiation,* 176–205. London: Sage.

Witkin, Herman A., & John W. Berry
1975   "Psychological differentiation in cross-cultural perspective." *Journal of Cross-Cultural Psychology,* 6(1):4–87.

Witkin, Herman A., & Donald R. Goodenough
1977   "Field dependence and interpersonal behavior." *Psychological Bulletin,* 84(4):661–689.

Witkin, Herman A., Donald R. Goodenough, & Philip K. Oltman
1979   "Psychological differentiation: Current status." *Journal of Personality and Social Psychology,* 37:1127–1145.

Wood, Julia T.
1994   *Gendered lives: Communication, gender, and culture.* Belmont, CA: Wadsworth.

Wyer, R. S., Jr., & T. K. Srull
1980   "The processing of social stimulus information: A conceptual integration." In R. Hastie, T. M. Ostrom, E. B. Ebbesen, R. S. Wyer Jr., D. L. Hamilton, & D. E. Carlson (Eds.), *Person Memory: The cognitive basis of social perception,* 227–300. Hillsdale, NJ: Erlbaum.

Yan, Hairong
1995   "The concept of 'face' in Chinese proverbs and phrases." *Proverbium.* Berkeley: California Folklore Society.

Yang, M.
1945   *A Chinese village.* New York: Columbia University Press.

Zajonc, Robert B., & Hazel Markus
1982   "Affective and cognitive factors in preferences." *Journal of Consumer Research,* 9:123–131.

Zucker, Lynne
1987   "Institutional theories of organization." *Annual Review of Sociology,* 13:443–464.

Index

Face, Harmony, and Social Structure continues author P. Christopher Earley's investigations of the differences among people within organizations in different cultures. The concept of "face," as set forth by Earley, is a reflection of the individual's struggle for self-definition and understanding, of which a key component is a positioning of self relative to others in a social setting. Face is at the heart of social behavior and provides a consistent linking mechanism to understand behavior across cultures.

Earley uses this concept of face as a basis for examination of cross-cultural organizational behavior from an individual's personal perspective. In this work, he develops a mid-range theory of individual behavior, self-concept, and interpersonal process in an effort to explain cultural differences in organizational settings. He sets up a cross-level model, and then attempts to provide a single coherent force—"face"—as an engine driving the entire system that can be used to integrate various social and organizational mechanisms in predicting people's behavior. This understanding of how and why people behave certain ways is a critical tool for studying the impact of individual behavior on the functioning of organizations.

Earley's work represents a new theory of self-presentation and face within a cross-cultural context, integrating a cross-level approach ranging from the individual to the organization and to the societal levels of discussion. *Face, Harmony, and Social Structure* is a truly interdisciplinary work that brings elements of psychology, sociology, and anthropology to organizational studies. It will be illuminating reading for professionals and scholars of management and organizational behavior, as well as to academics in cross-cultural psychology and anthropology.

tries See the World Eyy....... . `
sity Press 1997).